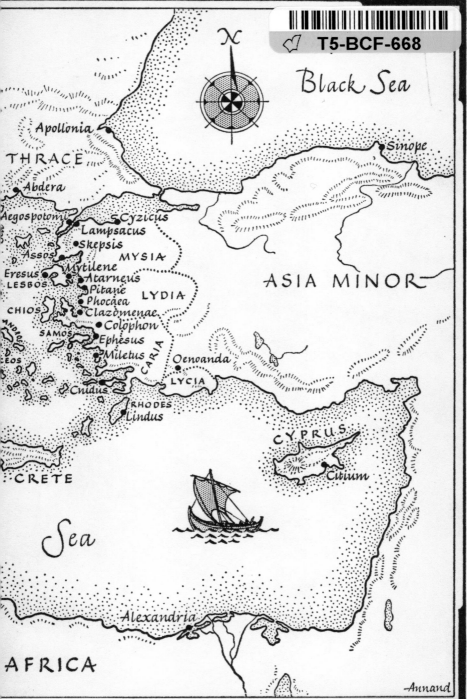

Black Sea

Apollonia

THRACE

Sinope

Abdera

Aegospotomi

Cyzicus

Lampsacus

Skepsis

Assos

MYSIA

ASIA MINOR

Mytilene

Eresus

Atarneus

LESBOS

Pitane

LYDIA

Phocaea

CHIOS

Clazomenae

Colophon

SAMOS

Ephesus

ANDROS

Miletus

TEOS

CARIA

Oenoanda

Cnidus

LYCIA

RHODES

Lindus

CYPRUS

Citium

CRETE

Sea

Alexandria

AFRICA

Annand

A HISTORY OF
ANCIENT WESTERN
PHILOSOPHY

IMPRIMI POTEST: Arthur J. Ryan, C.Ss.R.

NIHIL OBSTAT: John M. Kelly, C.S.B.

IMPRIMATUR: ✠ James Cardinal McGuigan
Archiep. Torontin.

Toronto, die 23 Julii, 1959

A HISTORY OF ANCIENT WESTERN PHILOSOPHY

Joseph Owens, C.Ss.R.

PONTIFICAL INSTITUTE OF MEDIAEVAL STUDIES, TORONTO

NEW YORK

APPLETON · CENTURY · CROFTS, INC.

Preface

The following text is meant for use in undergraduate work. It is intended especially for circles in which a working grasp of Platonic and Aristotelian philosophy is considered paramount. Plato and Aristotle, however, develop their doctrines closely against the whole background of preceding Greek thought. To understand them in their own setting, an extensive and at times intensive knowledge of Presocratic teachings is required, as well as some acquaintance with the activities of the Lesser Socratics and of Isocrates. In consequence, the treatment of later movements in ancient western philosophy has had to be cursory, even though for several centuries in antiquity the Epicureans and the Stoics exercised more widespread influence than did the Academy or the Peripatos.

A principle that has become increasingly evident in the last few decades is the necessity of viewing content in close relation to form in the interpretation of the Greek philosophers. The content of their thought cannot safely be separated from the form in which it was originally expressed by the ancient thinkers themselves. For this reason, as far as is possible and practical, the words of the philosophers in short quotations are made the regular means for illustrating their thought. The original phrasing as a rule projects their teaching with an appeal and an exactitude that no paraphrase could hope to equal. It serves to respect the personality and individual trends of each thinker, and gives valuable protection against the deep-rooted tendency to look upon all ancient philosophies as cut of the same cloth and as merely more or less

successful attempts to do the same work. It helps to minimize
the delightfully facile procedure of grouping individual thinkers
according to the various "isms," such as monism or materialism
or hedonism. Living philosophies tend rather to cut across those
systematic classifications. Keeping the thought in close association with the form of expression guards against distortions of this
nature. Also, the words of the philosophers themselves remain
more deeply engraved in the memory, and are the best means of
retaining one's grasp of the different philosophies in their proper
perspectives. Gradual acquaintance from the very beginning of
the philosophy course with short citations, moreover, should lead
the student to longer selections given in anthologies. In the case
of the more enterprising learner it should serve as an introduction
to the writings of the philosophers themselves, in particular to
those of Plato and Aristotle.

Under philosophy or love of wisdom there was included in the
ancient writers much that today is placed outside its bounds. All
the branches of mathematics, for instance, were regarded as part
of philosophy, as well as rhetoric and literary criticism (poetics)
and all the sciences that investigate the natural phenomena. Today these form studies different from what is regarded as philosophy proper. The treatment of their early stages is best left to
their own departments. Whole sections of what the ancient writings presented as philosophy, like rhetoric, poetics, the measurements and movements of the heavenly bodies, and the details of
the natural phenomena may accordingly be omitted in a modern
survey of their philosophical teachings. In this way the historical
study is kept focused upon the sciences that today are grouped
together under the general title of philosophy—logic, philosophy
of nature, metaphysics, philosophy of knowledge or epistemology,
ethics, and political philosophy. Details from other spheres need
be mentioned only when they are helpful towards understanding
the genesis and progress of these sciences. In a word, "philosophy" for the purposes of this study is kept within the conventional
restriction that, outside the conferring of the doctorate in other
subjects under the formula "Ph.D.," is regularly given the term
today.

The history of ancient western philosophy has by no means
been handed down to posterity in the form of a complete picture.

It has to be reconstructed slowly and laboriously from comparatively scanty sources that too often leave wide scope for controversy and doubt. The nature of these sources has to be kept in mind. From the last decades of the fourth century B.C. the Greeks showed considerable interest in writing the history of their own philosophies and the lives of their outstanding thinkers. They tended to group their philosophers in dynastic "successions," as they pictured certain men inaugurating trends of thought and others carrying on the work in a sort of genealogical succession. They thrived on collections and summaries of the various philosophical teachings, as well as on anecdotes and personal touches meant to give a living portrait of the men who stood high in their intellectual traditions. Of all such general biographical and historical undertakings only one has survived. It is the work of Diogenes Laertius, written probably in the first half of the third century A.D.,[1] and known under the title of *Lives and Opinions of Eminent Philosophers*.

This work was quite evidently intended for the non-philosophical Greek public. It appeals to the intellectual curiosity and vanity of Hellenistic culture, making a special point, for instance, of stressing who was the first to coin a traditional saying or term. It has to a considerable extent the character of a scrapbook, abounding in biographical information and stories and doctrinal summaries culled, not necessarily at first hand, from the whole preceding literature on the subject. It testifies to wide enough reading but to little critical discernment, and even when it does attempt a critical judgment it is for the most part sadly lacking in profundity. However, it gives fairly regularly the sources from which its information was taken. With this knowledge and with the texts and fragments and other general information available, it can to a certain measure be controlled and accordingly used as the over-all source for the reconstruction of the history of Greek philosophy. Of its author, nothing is known except what can be gathered from the work itself.

The more strictly doctrinal accounts begin with the surveys that Aristotle in various parts of his treatises makes of the work of his predecessors. As a rule, however, the Stagirite presents

[1] See Richard Hope, *The Book of Diogenes Laertius*, Its Spirit and Its Method (New York: Columbia University Press, 1930), pp. 5-9.

their teachings quite narrowly from the viewpoint in which he himself was interested at the moment. In those particular Aristotelian settings Theophrastus, his successor, drew up the opinions of the natural philosophers and in this way inaugurated the long line of Greek doxographers. These were men who continued to publicize in summary form, after the model of Theophrastus, the teachings of the Greek philosophers on nature. Of the original doxography, the *Physical Opinions* of Theophrastus, only fragments survive, taken from much later doxographers and commentators. Further, extended accounts of the Skeptical philosophies and their targets have been preserved in the works of Sextus Empiricus, a writer of the late second century A.D. Lives of Pythagoras, Plato, Aristotle, Plotinus and Proclus by Neoplatonic authors have survived. Of the works of the philosophers themselves, only those of Plato and Plotinus have been handed down in what seems to be their entirety. A large portion of the Aristotelian school treatises are extant. Of all the other more ancient philosophers, except for a few short treatises and letters, only fragments collected from later writers survive.

Such in the main are the comparatively scanty sources in which the history of Greek philosophy has been handed down to our times. From these any reconstruction, naturally, is bound to be quite inconclusive and continually debatable in detail. Even where the material is abundant, as with Plato and Aristotle, it has afforded ground for widely varying interpretations. If for these two philosophers there were available only such meager fragments as are extant for so many other Greek philosophers, one can readily imagine how far from what is now known any reconstruction of their thought would be. Try, for instance, to figure out a reconstruction of Plato's doctrine of Ideas based upon the account of Diogenes Laertius (III, 10-15)! One can therefore realize the caution that is necessary in reconstructing more ancient doctrines from the fragments and reports handed down. The safest procedure is to keep as closely as possible to the wording of the fragments. The texts themselves remain immortal, while interpretations of them change. Construction, however, there has to be; but it should be kept to the minimum. The student, moreover, should be made continually aware of what is construction and what is evidence. It is hardly fair even to an undergraduate to present him with a ready-made and rigid picture of the history of ancient western philosophy when the sources are so tenuous. He should be saved the difficult and time wasting effort of having to rid himself in graduate work of a host of misconceptions unwittingly acquired in his undergraduate days. Even in his introductory studies, accordingly, he should be kept alive to the nature of the sources upon which the historical constructions are based. He will not then expect the story of ancient philosophy to run as smoothly as a novel.

In spite of all these considerations regarding the unsatisfactory extent of the sources, however, enough remains to serve abundantly the practical purposes of the study as an introduction to philosophical thinking. In fact, from this viewpoint, the problem for purposes of a usable text is to select the most suitable materials, since all cannot be brought within compass of a single volume. In watching through those remnants the themes of western philosophy as they were progressively given their definite form, in reliving the problems and solutions as they actually arose, the student has as it were an experimental and laboratory introduction to European thought, with all its advantages over an introduction through dry and detached formulations that have been uprooted from their natural, lifegiving soil. For this practical and pedagogical use the sources are quite sufficient. They ensure for Greek philosophy a place in the curriculum as the soundest available introduction to any general study of philosophy within the framework of western culture.

The more thoroughly the work of the ancient thinkers becomes understood, the better is it able to serve this purpose of providing an apt introduction to sound philosophical thinking habits. The continued and at times startling progress of research in topics of ancient philosophy during the last few decades has entailed unceasing revision of currently accepted views. This alone is sufficient to provide excuse for a new text on the subject, in spite of the many excellent manuals that have appeared in recent times.

The "Selected Readings and References" at the end of the chapters are meant to indicate in each case a few bibliographical items, in English where possible, that should be sufficient to open up to the reader the field of scholarly work in the particular topics. In these works may be found the detailed information and the further bibliographical indications that are necessary for term papers and seminar work. Bibliographies covering the field up to about the end of the first quarter of the present century may be found in Karl Praechter's *Die Philosophie des Altertums,* which is the first volume of Ueberweg's *Grundriss.* For works appearing from 1934 on, the "Antiquité Grecque et Romaine" section of the *Répertoire Bibliographique de la Philosophie* should be consulted. It is published every three months by L'Institut Supérieur de Philosophie, Louvain, Belgium. The immediately following list gives instances of works that are of more or less general scope in the field of ancient western philosophy. In the ensuing text, chronological and biobibliographical information is offered, to be drawn upon as the instructor sees fit in presenting the different philosophies in their respective historical settings.

SELECTED READINGS
AND REFERENCES

Diogenes Laertius, *Lives of Eminent Philosophers,* with an English translation by R.D. Hicks, 2 v. (London [W. Heinemann] & New York; G.P. Putnam's Sons, 1925), in The Loeb Classical Library.

Doxographi Graeci, ed. Hermann Diels (Berlin: Reimer, 1879).

Apollodors Chronik, Eine Sammlung der Fragmente von Felix Jacoby (Berlin: Weidmann, 1902), in *Philologische Untersuchungen,* XVI.

Karl Praechter, *Die Philosophie des Altertums* 12th ed. (Berlin: Mittler, 1926), in Friedrich Ueberweg's *Grundriss der Geschichte der Philosophie,* v. I. There is an English translation of the 4th edition by G.S. Morris, *History of Philosophy* (New York: Charles Scribner's Sons, 1872-1874), v. I.

Eduard Zeller, *Die Philosophie der Griechen* (7th ed., ed. W. Nestle, I,1, Leipzig: Reisland, 1923. I,2, 6th ed., 1920. II-III, 5th ed., 1922-1923). There is an English translation of the fourth edition of the First Part, by Sarah F. Alleyne, 2 v. (London: Longmans, Green & Co., 1881), and an Italian translation, with additional notes to take account of later research, of the First Part as far as the Pythagoreans by R. Mondolfo, 2 v. (Florence "La Nuova Italia," 1932-1938).

Charles M. Bakewell, *Source Book in Ancient Philosophy* (New York: Charles Scribner's Sons, 1907).

Thomas Vernor Smith, *Philosophers Speak for Themselves,* Guides and
    Readings for Greek, Roman, and Early Christian Philosophy
    (Chicago: University of Chicago Press, 1934).
Arthur Hilary Armstrong, *An Introduction to Ancient Philosophy*
    (London: Methuen, 1947).

ACKNOWLEDGMENTS

As far as feasible, the short passages illustrating the teachings of
the various ancient philosophers are quoted according to standard
translations, with the hope of leading the student to further use of
these works. Grateful acknowledgment is made to the publishers of
these translations—to the Oxford University Press, Inc., for permission
to make the citations from Aristotle according to the masterly Oxford
translation, *The Works of Aristotle Translated into English* (general
editor, W.D. Ross, Oxford, 1908-1952), and to make those from Epicurus according to Cyril Bailey's *Epicurus The Extant Remains* (Oxford, 1926); to the Clarendon Press for permission to quote from the
long established Jowett translation of Plato, *The Dialogues of Plato*
(Oxford, 1871); to Basil Blackwell, Publisher and to the Harvard
University Press, for permission to quote a number of the early fragments according to the translation of Kathleen Freeman in her truly
helpful *Ancilla to the Pre-Socratic Philosophers* (Oxford, 1948); likewise to the Harvard University Press for permission to cite Diogenes
Laertius according to the R.D. Hicks translation of *Lives of Eminent
Philosophers* (London, & Cambridge Mass., 1925) in the Loeb Classical Library, and similarly to quote some other authors as noted from
that invaluable collection of Greek and Latin classics; and to the Cambridge University Press for permission to quote some of the Heraclitus
fragments according to the translations in G.S. Kirk's monumental study
Heraclitus The Cosmic Fragments (Cambridge, Eng., 1954), with permission likewise of the Macmillan Company of Canada Limited. Permission of Edward Arnold (Publishers) Ltd. and Harper & Brothers
to reprint, in Chapter I, n. 15, a passage from F.M. Cornford's *From
Religion to Philosophy* (London, 1912), is also gratefully acknowledged. My thanks are further due to my colleagues in the department
of Philosophy in the University of Toronto, and to Professors J.R.
O'Donnell and J. Sheridan of the Classics department, for help in
consultation on a number of difficult points; and to various libraries in
Canada and the United States for the courteously granted use of their
facilities.

J.O.

Table of Contents

PART II

THE DEVELOPMENTS OF GREEK PHILOSOPHY

PART III

THE FLOWERING OF GREEK PHILOSOPHY

AND THUS IT WAS FROM THE GREEKS
THAT PHILOSOPHY TOOK ITS RISE:
ITS VERY NAME REFUSES TO BE
TRANSLATED INTO FOREIGN SPEECH.

Diogenes Laertius, I,4; tr. R. D. Hicks.

ABBREVIATIONS

AGP—*Archiv für Geschichte der Philosophie.*

AJP—*American Journal of Philology.*

CQ—*Classical Quarterly.*

CR—*Classical Review.*

Class. Phil.—*Classical Philology.*

DK—Diels-Kranz, *Die Fragmente der Vorsokratiker* (5th ed., Berlin, 1934-1937).

D.L.—Diogenes Laertius, *Lives and Opinions of Eminent Philosophers.*

EGP—J. Burnet, *Early Greek Philosophy* (4th ed., London, 1930).

JHS—*Journal of Hellenic Studies.*

JP—*Journal of Philology.*

Philol.—*Philologus.*

Rh. Mus.—*Rheinisches Museum für Philologie.*

SVF—*Stoicorum Veterum Fragmenta,* ed. H. v. Arnim (Leipzig, 1903-1924).

Wien. Stud.—*Wiener Studien.*

Part One

THE ORIGINS OF GREEK
PHILOSOPHY

[CHAPTER 1]

The Beginnings of Natural Philosophy

THE IONIANS

GREEK PHILOSOPHY was born in the Ionian city-states that dotted the western coast of Asia Minor and adjacent islands. These city-states, according to general Hellenic tradition, had been founded by Greeks from the mainland, perhaps to some extent forced away under pressure of the Dorian invasion. The Greeks, however, were not able to penetrate beyond a coastal strip that varied in depth from twenty to thirty miles. They were held back by the Lydians and the Carians, whose kingdoms lay just beyond the the coastal strip, and who in turn felt the pressure of the giant Mede and Persian realms behind them.

In accordance with this situation, the Ionians sought their livelihood in seafaring and commerce as well as in the produce of their rugged though fertile land. They grew keenly interested in the stars by which they guided their ships and in pertinent meteorological data for both sailing and agriculture. They were quick in making use of geometrical and astronomical knowledge gathered from the Chaldeans and Egyptians. But they pushed their inquiries to a level not attained by these more ancient peoples. In so doing they gave rise to a new type of thinking that from their time on has been called philosophy.

Such is the over-all picture of the awakening and development of Ionian intellectual interests as given in the surviving testimonia. Such, in partcular, is the oldest explicit historical account de-

3

scribing the origins of Western philosophical thought. Aristotle
of Stagira, writing in the last half of the fourth century B.C., summed up as follows the progressive stages traversed by the early
Greek thinkers: ". . . they wondered originally at the obvious
difficulties, then advanced little by little and stated difficulties
about the greater matters, e.g. about the phenomena of the moon
and those of the sun and of the stars, and about the genesis of
the universe."[1] The Stagirite, naturally, had at his disposal information that is not available today. He is careful and critical in
recording facts, even though he may make his interpretation of
the facts from a very narrow angle of his interest at the moment.
In this particular passage of the *Metaphysics,* he is trying to show
that men both in his day and in previous times pursued philosophy
in order to escape ignorance, since aside from any utilitarian
purpose people have a natural desire to know the causes of things.
Wonder, accordingly, is the true beginning of philosophy.
Actually, the motives of the earliest Greek thinkers seem to have
been sufficiently utilitarian in character. But be that as it may,
the surviving fragments of the Presocratics fully confirm the
fact that interest in matters like the phenomena of the sun and
the moon and the stars ended in the inquiry about the genesis of
the whole universe. When, as Aristotle (*Metaph.*, A 1,981b27-29)
points out in this connection, inquiries concerning the "why" of
happenings are pushed to the ultimate causes of things, and so
arrive at causes about which one cannot ask a further "why," then
one is already in the domain of wisdom or philosophy.

Philosophy, meaning love of wisdom, became therefore the
name given to the inquiry into the first principles and causes of
things. It is the endeavor to understand all things in the light of
what is basic and ultimate from the standpoint of human reason.
The first of the Greeks to bring the inquiries to the point at which
they reached this plane was, in Aristotle's account, Thales of
Miletus. At any rate, with either Thales or his pupil Anaximander

[1] *Metaph.*, A 2,982b13-17; Oxford tr. Except where circumstances require
reference in a more complete form, Greek works will be cited according to
the abbreviated titles given in H. G. Liddel and Robert Scott, *A Greek-
English Lexicon* (Oxford: University Press, 1940), I, xvi-xxxviii. On wonder
as the only beginning of philosophy, see Plato, *Tht.*, 155D.

the Greek biographers[2] began the history of the men whom they called their philosophers. The wonder evoked by prehistoric traditions and the thoughts expressed by numerous poets and lawgivers undoubtedly paved the way. Contacts with other peoples stimulated and helped Ionian thinking. But whatever preparatory role such activities may have played, and whatever indirect influence Egyptian, Iranian, or even Indian currents of thought may have exercised, no one has yet been able to trace the origins of Greek philosophy proper to any source other than the Greeks themselves. It is among the Ionians that the beginnings of Western philosophy in the genuine sense are to be found.

The work of the early Greek philosophers has been interpreted in various ways by modern historians. It has been regarded as a pursuit of physical science in a quite positivistic mentality (Burnet), or as a rational transcription of mythological traditions (Cornford), or as an intellectual seeking of the divine (Jaeger). The last interpretation need not be at variance with Aristotle's account; for the permanent ground of changeable things was what fourth-century Greek thinkers looked upon as the divine, and in the permanent were the first principles and causes to be sought. Nor can there be any doubt about the strong mythological background against which the Ionians did their thinking; but whether that background directed their thought to the philosophical plane is quite a different problem. Similarly, practical motives were incontestably present in their efforts, as was also an eagerness for positive knowledge; but again, whether practical and empirical interests were the determining feature of their philosophical activity is a further and different question. These modern interpretations may be kept in mind as the story of Greek philosophy unfolds, to see just how far they are substantiated and how far they are set aside by the actual data.

[2] Cf. Diogenes Laertius, Lives, I,13; 21. Modern historians likewise begin their histories of Greek philosophy proper with one or the other of these two Milesians. Hermann Diels, in the first four editions of his Fragmente der Vorsokratiker (1903, 1906, 1912, 1922) began with Thales. In the fifth (1934-1937) and subsequent editions, edited by Walther Kranz, an opening section is devoted, according to the express wishes of Diels himself, to teachers or writers, who, though not properly philosophers, nevertheless prepared the way for the beginnings of genuine philosophical thought.

THALES OF MILETUS *(FL.* 585 B.C.)

Chronology. According to the Greek historian Herodotus,[3] himself from Asia Minor and writing about a century and a half later, Thales of Miletus predicted the eclipse that ended a five-years' war between the Lydians and the Medes. Historical and astronomical evidence dates this eclipse May 28, 585 B.C. There is no reason for questioning the information that Thales' name was connected in popular tradition with the eclipse. This suffices to indicate that he was well-known and active in that year. The fashion of the Greek chronologists in dating a remote philosopher was to take an outstanding event in his life as the means of fixing his *floruit* or prime, which they conventionally placed at the age of about forty years. Since Greek tradition indicated that Thales lived to old age, another forty years could be added to his life span. According to this highly artificial method one would expect to find the dating 625-545 B.C. for his life. Actually, the fifty-eighth Olympiad (548-545 B.C.) was the time given for his death. But it seems that the first year of the thirty-fifth Olympiad (640-639 B.C.) was the date set for his birth by Apollodorus of Athens, a second-century B.C. chronicler, according to the traditional text of Diogenes Laertius (I,37), though the year 625 may have been meant. The different ages—either seventy-eight or ninety years—given to Thales in the biographical tradition indicate, however, an awareness of some confusion regarding the dates assigned him. All that one can say with sufficient evidence is that he was already in the public eye around the year 585 B.C.

Life. No other details of Thales' life are known with certainty. Miletus, situated on the ancient gulf of Latmos, had long been prospering and had taken the lead among the Ionian city-states.[4] The accounts and stories preserved by Diogenes Laertius represent Thales as belonging to a distinguished Milesian family, engaging first in political life and then in the study of nature, and as having received no formal instruction apart from visiting Egypt and consorting with the priests there. He is included in all the lists of the Seven Sages of Greece, and is said to have been the first who was so designated.

The accounts[5] in general portray Thales as a man keenly interested

---

[3] *Hist.,* I,74. Herodotus critically enough accepts this story while rejecting another (I,75) about Thales. These passages may be found in Diels-Kranz, 11A 5;6.

[4] For information here and elsewhere on the Greek city-states, see Kathleen Freeman, *Greek City-States* (London: Macdonald, 1950).

[5] These accounts and stories, with detailed references to sources in Diels, may be found neatly assembled in K. Freeman's *The Pre-Socratic Philosophers, A Companion to Diels* (Oxford, 1946), pp. 49-55. The same holds respectively for the accounts concerning the other Presocratics.

in all the practical questions of his day: statesmanship for the political safety of the Ionian cities, astronomy for the assistance of shipping, meteorological knowledge for the furtherance of agriculture. The stories, with one notorious exception, represent him as a man of great practical wisdom. But that exception is perhaps the best known of all. While gazing at the stars he fell into a pit and was told by a servant girl that because he was so eager to know what was in the sky he could not see what was there at his feet. This story is related by Plato[6] as hearsay and as a jest applying to all philosophers. It has the earmarks of a joke thought up during the Periclean age when the Sophists were looked down upon by men of practical affairs. On the other hand, the story that Thales made a small fortune by cornering all the olive-presses during the year in which his knowledge showed him in advance that there would be a great harvest of olives, sounds, as related in Aristotle,[7] like a counter-story invented by the opposite side. Here, as elsewhere with the early philosophers, the traditional stories have little reliability from the standpoint of historical exactitude. They give rather the picture of the philosopher that grew up in the popular mind of later ages. They require discerning criticism to bring to light, where possible, any original facts that may lie behind them.

PHILOSOPHICAL TEACHINGS

Water the Origin of Things. Whether Thales wrote anything was not known definitely in antiquity. At least nothing survived. The earliest source for his doctrines is Aristotle. The Stagirite, speaking of the philosophers who explained all things by material principles only, recorded: "Thales, the founder of this type of philosophy, says the principle is water (for which reason he declared that the earth rests on water), getting the notion perhaps from seeing that the nutriment of all things is moist, and that heat itself is generated from the moist and kept alive by it . . . , and from the fact that the seeds of all things have a moist nature, and that water is the origin of the nature of moist things."[8] Aris-

[6] *Tht.*, 174A. The same story in slightly different form is reported in D.L., I,34. DK, 11A 9; 1(34).

[7] *Pol.*, I II,1259a6-19 (DK, 11A 10). The numerous legends about Heraclitus, for instance, illustrate the growth of popular stories to portray the mentality of a philosopher.

For a survey of the archaelogical evidence concerning early Ionian civilization, see G. M. A. Hanfmann, "Ionia, Leader or Follower?" *Harvard Studies in Classical Philology,* LXI (1953), 1-37.

[8] *Metaph.*, A 3,983b20-27; Oxford tr. *Cf. Cael.*, II 13,294a28-b6. (DK, 11A 12;14).

totle seems to be reporting an orally transmitted saying of Thales: "The earth rests on water." The saying is understood, however, not merely as a reflexion occasioned by the sight of the vast expanses of sea surrounding the land, but as presupposing that everything in the universe is ultimately derived from water. For Aristotle, in his own terminology, this meant that with Thales water was the "first principle" of cosmic development. Why did Thales think in this way? Aristotle was curious to know, but apparently had nothing definite to guide him. He offers his own conjectures of the reasons that *perhaps* led Thales to this conception. Nourishment, heat, and living organisms are observed to come from moist things, and water is the origin of the moist.

Vital Character of the Universe. For Aristotle, then, Thales' notion of cosmic development was that of a living process, in which water is the origin of the seeds, the nutriment, and the vital heat. It identifies motion with life, and so finds the principle of all motion, including inorganic activity, in soul: "Thales, too, to judge from what is recorded about him, seems to have held soul to be a motive force, since he said that the magnet has a soul in it because it moves the iron."[9] Accordingly, wherever there is motion—and for Aristotle himself, speaking metaphorically, motion extends as a sort of life throughout all natural things[10]—there will have to be soul: "Certain thinkers say that soul is intermingled in the whole universe, and it is perhaps for that reason that Thales came to the opinion that all things are full of gods."[11]

Does this last statement mean that for Thales not only a *vital* element but also a *divine* principle permeated all things? Aristotle does suggest this, but only as a conjecture. The Stagirite is trying, in his own philosophical background, to connect a reported saying of Thales, "All things are full of gods," with the doctrine of the omnipresence of soul. The original saying of Thales, however, may well have been a religious utterance having no connection at all with any definite cosmic teaching.[12]

Observational Starting-Point. Such are the meager data that

---

[9] *De An.*, I 2,405a19-21; Oxford tr. (DK, 11A 22).
[10] *Ph.*, VIII 1,250b14-15. For Aristotle, natural motion is not necessarily vital motion.
[11] *De An.*, I 5,411a7-8; Oxford tr. (DK, 11A 22).
[12] On this view see Étienne Gilson, *God and Philosophy* (New Haven: Yale University Press, 1941), pp. 1-14.

have been handed down by Aristotle. Later accounts do not sub-
stantially add to them. One is tempted to systematize them and
say that for Thales[water was both animated and divine and in
this way was able to function as the first principle of all things.
Such efforts have been made from antiquity on. But the sources are
obviously much too vague to warrant any such reconstruction.
They indicate, however, that Thales based his conclusions on the
observation of natural phenomena, and possibly, if he argued
from the activity of amber[13] as well as the magnet, on some ex-
perimentation. They do not exclude, though, preoccupation with
a search for the divine.

Are there on the other hand any indications of a mythological
origin for Thales' teachings? Aristotle, in the first passage quoted
above, continues: "Some think that even the ancients who lived
long before the present generation, and first framed accounts of
the gods, had a similar view of nature; for they made Ocean
and Tethys the parents of creation, and described the oath of the
gods as being by water, to which they give the name of Styx; for
what is oldest is most honourable, and the most honourable thing
is that by which one swears. It may perhaps be uncertain whether
this opinion about nature is primitive and ancient, but Thales at
any rate is said to have declared himself thus about the first
cause."[14] Aristotle is well aware of the reputed mythological origin for this philosophical conception of nature. It had been pub-
licized, whether humorously or seriously, by Plato.[15] But the

[13] D.L., I,24, quoting Hippias of Elis, a Sophist of the second half of the
fifth century B.C.; DK, 11A 1(24).

[14] *Metaph.*, A 3,983b27-984a3; Oxford tr. (DK, 11A 12).

[15] *Cra.*, 402BC; *Tht.*, 152E and 180CD. *Cf.* Achilles' report on Pherecydes
in DK, 7B 1a. In this connection it is well to note the general conception of
philosophy that lies behind F. M. Cornford's interpretation of the evidence:
"Almost all philosophic arguments are invented afterwards, to recommend,
or defend from attack, conclusions which the philosopher was from the
outset bent upon believing, before he could think of any arguments at all.
That is why philosophical reasonings are so bad, so artificial, and so uncon-
vincing. To mistake them for the causes which led to a belief in the conclusion, is generally to fall into a naive error. The charm of the early Greek
philosophers lies in the fact that, to a large extent, they did not trouble to
invent bad arguments at all, but simply stated their beliefs dogmatically."
From Religion to Philosophy (London, 1912), p. 138.

For more recent studies of the relation of mythology to Greek philosophical notions, see Henri and Henriette A. Frankfort et al., *The Intellectual
Adventures of Ancient Man* (Chicago: University of Chicago Press, 1946),

Stagirite is skeptical about its truth. He seems merely to suggest it as a background against which the doctrine might have been rendered easily acceptable to the age. As a philosophy of nature, however, he does not trace further back than Thales the teaching that water is the first principle of the universe. Any more definite evidence is lacking.

The conclusion indicated by these data is that today one can arrive merely at the conception of Thales' natural philosophy as it was recast in Aristotle's mind; and Aristotle in these passages about Thales speaks cautiously and as though he were dependent on a vague oral tradition. There was enough, however, for the Stagirite to see in Thales the beginning of the type of thinking that starts from observation of the natural phenomena and seeks to trace them back to their ultimate material source. It was in his eyes the beginning of natural philosophy. On that point, and that point alone, can Thales be given a position in the history of philosophical thought. Aristotle is trustworthy enough in recording facts, and in this case he does not seem to press them too far. He is interpreting them only from his own point of view, and, as will be seen later in the case of Heraclitus, he possibly may not be conveying the correct emphasis that the recorded doctrines had in their original setting. But he leaves little doubt that in Thales he himself found the oldest traceable source of the way of thinking that continued through the Milesians and developed into the natural philosophies of the Greeks.

There is no need to credit Thales with coining any technical philosophical vocabulary. It may well be that his investigations and his sayings rather struck off a chance spark that began truly philosophical inquiry. The sources do not allow any decisive answer to the question. There was, in fact, the other Greek tradition that commenced the history of philosophy with Anaximander, Thales' pupil. Moreover, the notion of the origin of all things from water was fairly common in the mythological traditions of

esp. pp. 373-387 (=Before Philosophy, in Penguin Books); Gertrude Rachel Levy, The Gate of Horn (London: Faber, 1948), esp. pp. 300-312; W.K.C. Guthrie, The Greeks and Their Gods (London: Methuen, 1950), esp. pp. 131-144; E.R. Dodds, The Greeks and the Irrational (Berkeley and Los Angeles, 1951), pp. 179 ff.; Kirk-Raven, The Presocratic Philosophers, pp. 8-72.

the Greeks and the peoples with whom they came in contact. It
is reasonable to suppose, nevertheless, particularly when one considers the manner in which Aristotle[16] speaks, that Thales must
have presented this doctrine in some special way that at least
allowed it to become the prototype of truly philosophical inquiries
into the origin of the universe.

Similarly, the notion that the whole universe is animated and
that the cosmic processes somehow parallel the vital activity of
which men are conscious in their own living, seems to have a long
background in prehistory[17] and need occasion no surprise in
Thales. The Ionians, in fact, never experienced any difficulty in
looking upon organisms as things derived from inorganic matter.
In this setting and in view of Aristotle's account, there can be no
question of trying to bring Thales' doctrine into line with modern
scientific theories of abiogenesis that consider sea water the best
medium for the formation of organic matter. Rather, the water
itself was already, for Thales, impregnated with life. It was something vital in itself, and not just a medium for the formation of the
original living things. All matter, whether organic or inorganic,
would be living matter, according to the general lines of Thales'
reported teaching.

Finally, there is no indication that Thales was at all concerned
with ascribing to water any formal character of simplicity in a
philosophical sense, such as the later notion of a "first principle"
might require. Nor can one infer that he gave it any abstractive
status under the guise of "the moist." Rather, as far as can be

[16] For instance, Aristotle (*Metaph.*, A 3,984a3-5; DK, 38A 7) refuses to
discuss the doctrine as presented by Hippon of Samos because of the super-
ficiality of his intelligence. Uvo Hölscher, "Anaximander und die Anfänge
der Philosophie," *Hermes*, LXXXI (1953), 387, however, argues that
Thales could not have based his teaching in this regard on any Greek
tradition.

[17] "At all events we may infer that somewhere back in human prehistory
there was a primaeval stage in which the cosmos was regarded as vaguely
alive and as more or less similar to man's body, or consciousness, or mind,
or thought, or word, or right action." G. P. Conger, "Did India Influence
Early Greek Philosophies?" *Philosophy East and West*, II (1952), 108.
". . . the Greeks sought to extrapolate man into the expanse of the cosmos
and regarded the cosmos as a living organism. . . . The conception of the
world as a living body was present in all periods of Greek science." S. Sambursky, *The Physical World of the Greeks*, tr. Merton Dagut (London:
Routledge & Kegan Paul, 1956), p. 40. See also W. K. C. Guthrie, *In the
Beginning* (London: Methuen, 1957), pp. 61-62.

gathered from Aristotle's cautious description, [Thales seemed intent only on finding a primitive vital stuff or matrix from which the universe as men know it could grow. Yet he proceeded in a way that actually did open up a properly philosophical inquiry into the nature of the ultimate matter from which all sensible things are derived. This was enough to ensure for him the place that he has traditionally held at the beginning of Greek philosophy. But he himself, in his view of water as the origin of all things, appears merely to have envisaged as it were a plasm from which the visible world could develop. In that light his reported statements make sufficient sense.

ANAXIMANDER OF MILETUS (CA. 610-546 B.C.)

Chronology.   Anaximander was known in Greek tradition as the countryman, pupil, associate, and successor of Thales. This should locate him in the immediately following generation. Apollodorus, in the second century B.C., appears to have read something in a summary of Anaximander's doctrines indicating that his age was sixty-four at the time of the fall of Sardis (546 B.C.), and that he died shortly afterwards. The date of his birth is likewise transmitted by Hippolytus, a Christian ecclesiastic of the early third century A.D., as the third year of the forty-second Olympiad (610-609 B.C.). This information tallies sufficiently in placing Anaximander in the generation after Thales, whether the chronological schema was worked out as usual on artificial grounds (e.g., Freeman) or whether it was in this case based upon something more definite (Burnet).

Writings.   Anaximander is represented in general by Greek tradition as continuing the type of natural investigation inaugurated by Thales. In this sense he was viewed as following Thales in a sort of dynastic succession. His written teachings on the cosmic processes, at least in part or in a summary, seem to have been read by Aristotle and by Theophrastus, the Stagirite's immediate successor. No reliable titles of any of his writings, however, have survived; and most likely, according to the custom of the time, no titles were used by Anaximander himself. Only one continuous sentence, quoted in indirect discourse, and a few other words are extant from these writings. The accounts of his doctrines come from Peripatetic (i.e., the school founded by Aristotle) sources and have been handed down in Peripatetic language. One very late (fourth-century A.D.) report, probably reflecting the attitude not of Ionia but of fifth-century B.C. Athens, states that he was the first known Greek who dared produce a written treatise on nature.

PHILOSOPHICAL TEACHINGS

The Unlimited. The one surviving sentence, quoted by Theophrastus, reads: ". . . the first principle of existing things is *the unlimited; . . .* but into those from which the existing things have their coming to be, do they also pass away, *according to necessity; for they give justice and make amends to one another for their injustice, according to the ordering of time.*"[18] The term "the unlimited" is attributed to Anaximander unanimously by Greek tradition.[19] The words from "according to necessity" on bear the stamp of his times. The rest is quite regular Peripatetic language, and need not go back further than Theophrastus. Whether the technical terms "first principle," "existing things," "coming to be," and "pass away" belonged to the original text of Anaximander is open to argument.[20]

According to the Peripatetic interpretation of this sentence, Anaximander is finding as the first principle of all things an unnamed something that he called "the unlimited," instead of water as in Thales. He was led to this conclusion by observing the changes of the four elements into one another, and explaining these changes by an eternal motion that separated out from an original mixture the opposites hot and cold, moist and dry, and

---

[18] *Fr.* 1, found in Simplicius, *Phys.*, 24.14-20; *cf.* 150.20-25. Simplicius, a commentator on Aristotle in the sixth century A.D., took it from the *Physical Opinions* of Theophrastus.

The fragments of the Presocratics will be cited according to the numbering in Diels-Kranz (DK). English translation of these fragments may be found in K. Freeman's *Ancilla to the Pre-Socratic Philosophers* (Oxford, 1948).

[19] Whether the text of Simplicius just quoted (*supra,* n. 18) states expressly that Anaximander was the first to use the term "unlimited" of the first principle, is a matter of dispute. G. S. Kirk, *CQ*, XLIX (1955), 23, argues for the affirmative. W. W. Jaeger, *The Theology of the Early Greek Philosophers* (Oxford, 1947), pp. 25-29, interprets it as meaning that Anaximander was the first to use the term "first principle."

On the contemporary background that would lead Anaximander to conceive the unlimited as a "mixture," see B. Wiśniewski, *Rev. des Études Grecques*, LXX (1957), 51-52. *Cf. infra*, n. 26.

[20] *Cf.* Jaeger, *Theology*, pp. 18 ff.; G. S. Kirk, *CQ*, XLIX (1955), 32; Burnet, *EGP*, p. 52, n. 6.

so on. The primordial mixture contained within itself all the known elements and was identified in character with no one of them (DK, 12A 9; 9a).

In the actual words of Anaximander, the process by which things come to be and pass away was described in the metaphor of a court scene in the marketplace of an Ionian city-state. Time, the judge, evens out the tensions arising among things from their respective encroachments upon one another.—This seems to reflect the notion that the predominance of darkness at night is succeeded by that of light during the day, the reign of cold in winter by that of heat in summer, wet weather by dry, life by death, composition by dissolution, and so on, all according to the necessitating process of time. The original source of all these changes, the unlimited, was further described by Anaximander as "eternal and ageless" (*Fr.* 2), "deathless and indestructible" (*Fr.* 3), and, possibly, as something that "encompasses all and steers all things."[21] The unlimited, consequently, can never become exhausted and is never diminished by the things that proceed from it. The notion expressed by the term "unlimited" was, accordingly, that of *quantitatively inexhaustible*. As steering or governing all things, the unlimited itself quite evidently appeared to the Peripatetics as somehow exercising the ordering function metaphorically attributed to time in Anaximander's own phrasing.

Indeterminate Nature of Primal Stock. Very little more can be gathered from the fragments themselves, even with the help of Peripatetic tradition. This tradition had no doubt that Anaximander first introduced "the unlimited" as a philosophical term, and that he meant it in the quantitative sense of an inexhaustible reservoir for cosmic development: "He was the first to posit it as unlimited, so that he could make use of it unstintedly for the generation of things."[22] The later Greeks, however, did not regard the notion of the unlimited as the distinguishing feature of Anaximander's doctrine. Rather, they used the term in general to describe the original plasm in all the Milesians. They looked upon water for Thales, and air for Anaximenes, as likewise unlimited in

[21] Aristotle, *Ph.*, III 4,203b11-14; DK, 12A 15. See W. W. Jaeger,*Paideia*, tr. Gilbert Highet (New York, Oxford, 1939-1944), I, 157; *Theology*, pp. 29-30.

[22] Simplicius, *In Cael.*, 615.15-16; DK, 12A 17. *Cf.* Aëtius, I, 3,3 (*Dox. Graec.*, p. 277.13-15; DK, 12A 14).

serving as the primal stock of cosmic generation.[23] In Anaximander the inexhaustible character of the original stuff was specially emphasized, as the epithets "eternal" and "ageless" seem to imply; but with him as with the other Milesians it appeared to the Peripatetics as a quantitative attribute of some basic natural body. In Anaximander they located this primitive body as a nature intermediate between water and air, or fire and air, or water and fire. The intermediate rather than the unlimited character of the primal matrix they regarded as the characteristic feature in his doctrine. His original stock was "an indeterminate something" (*aoriston ti*)[24] in the sense of exhibiting none of the qualifications of the things issuing from it. Because of this contrast of "indeterminate" and "unlimited" in the traditional interpretation of Anaximander, it is very unlikely that the term "the unlimited" implied for him the notion of qualitative indeterminateness. It seems to have designated only the inexhaustible feature of the qualitatively indeterminate body.

Why did Anaximander change from a definitely characterized source like that of Thales to an indeterminate one? The reason given by Aristotle, speaking in general of the natural philosophers who made the first principle something different from any of the determined bodies, was that the other elements might not be destroyed by it. An unlimited determined body would render its opposite impossible—air, for instance, being cold, would if unlimited destroy the opposite characteristic in fire, heat.[25] Apparently, in Anaximander's language, this would mean that a thing's injustice could not be restrained if it had an inexhaustible capacity for paying retribution! That is quite apparently an interpretation made in the light of Aristotle's own doctrine, but no other has been handed down in Greek tradition.

The Opposites. According to the Peripatetic accounts, all the opposites—hot and cold, moist and dry, and so on—were for Anaximander already *contained within* the primordial matrix. They had merely to be "separated out" by the eternal motion that gives rise to the world process. The unlimited therefore was

---

[23] See Aristotle, *Ph.*, III 4,203a16-18; Simplicius, *In Ph.*, 458.23-26 (DK, 11A 13); *In Cael.*, 615.18-20. In regard to Thales, *cf.* D.L., I,36 (DK, 11A 1).

[24] Simplicius, *In Cael.*, 615.14. *Cf. In Ph.*, 458.35-459.4.

[25] Aristotle, *Ph.*, III 5,204b22-29. *Cf.* Simplicius, *In Ph.*, p. 480.1-4.

a mixture in which no one of the opposites predominated, and so no one of them could characterize it in any definite quality. It underwent no genuine alteration (i.e., qualitative change) itself as the opposites issued from its inexhaustible reservoir. There need be little doubt that Aristotle saw grounds in the text of Anaximander for interpreting the unlimited as a mixture comparable to the original mixtures of the later philosophers Anaxagoras and Empedocles, but what the grounds were cannot now be determined satisfactorily. Nor can one discover just how much of the more explicit Anaxagorean doctrine Aristotle and his school were reading back into the second of the Milesian thinkers, when they made these interpretations of his teaching.

This doctrine, apparently, does not leave any room for a real change of one thing into another. When the things make reparation to *one another,* they merely return the excess of each opposite into the anonymity of the original stock, according to the eternal motion, which is merely local, not qualitative, change. As the eternal motion is not ascribed to any external cause, it would have to be considered as intrinsic to the primal body. That is, the primordial mixture of all the opposites is regarded as something living, as a sort of original plasm from which the universe grows after the manner of a living thing.[26]

---

[26] ". . . Anaximander believed that in this living matrix the nascent world developed either like an egg or like an embryo in the womb." W. K. C. Guthrie, *CQ,* L (1956), 42. The original plasm ". . . was its own mover, in other words it was alive." *Ibid.,* p. 44. See also H. C. Baldry, *CQ,* XXVI (1932),29-30. On the embryological analogy of the "separating off," see Baldry, pp. 27, n. 8; 29. These and other biological forms of expression reported for Anaximander (DK, 12A 10) militate against any view that he represents a break with the tradition of imagining the universe as a living being, e.g.: ". . . there is nothing in any of the doctrines of Anaximander which remotely suggests any of the teachings attributed to Thales." G. B. Burch, *Review of Metaphysics,* III (1949), 140, n. 5. That tradition has been regarded as ". . . the animism that it was Anaximander's chief glory to have banished from his philosophy." W. I. Matson, *Review of Metaphysics,* VI (1953), 395. The extant testimonia, however, do not allow interpretation in the modern sense of organic evolution; see Burnet, *EGP,* pp. 70-71; Cornford, *Principium Sapientiae,* pp. 170-171; W. K. C. Guthrie, *In the Beginning,* pp. 32-33; J. H. Loenen, *Mnemosyne,* ser. 4, VII (1954), 215-232. To explain Anaximander's teaching in the sense of organic evolution, E. Schrödinger, *Nature and the Greeks* (Cambridge, Eng., 1954), p. 66, has to suggest that the testimonia were distorted through ignorance.
On the Peripatetic equating of Anaximander's primal body with the mixtures of Anaxagoras and Empedocles, see Aristotle, *Metaph.* Λ 2,1069b-

Cosmogony. Later Greek tradition has handed down a number of statements regarding the details of the cosmic processes in Anaximander. What was first separated off was described as growing like a living organism. Worlds unlimited in number issued from the primal matrix. The earth is round like a pillar, hanging free in the center (and so not floating on anything, as in Thales). Its top surface is the inhabited part. Living things issued from what is moist. These organisms had at first to be protected from a dry environment. Men were originally generated within a certain type of fish (the *galeus*, a species of shark). They were kept inside the fish until they attained sufficient development to look after themselves. This, of course, is quite a different conception from modern theories of organic evolution. It seems to have been based upon the observation of the way in which a viviparous Aegean fish protected and nursed its young.

With Anaximander there begins to appear a certain consciousness of the problems involved in positing an ultimate material source for the cosmic processes and in accounting for the observable changes of one thing into another. The implication of the formal elements required in the change from one opposite to another, the problem of how an indeterminate principle could give rise to determinate things, the necessity of an order regulating cosmic changes, the impossibility of allowing to the first principle the character of any of the things that proceed from it—all these were read into his doctrines by the Peripatetics. But how aware Anaximander himself was of these technical problems, and how far he coined a technical vocabulary to cope with them, can hardly be determined now. He seems quite evidently to have continued the Milesian tradition of finding the origin of the universe in a primitive vital stuff, and of projecting its development after the manner of the organic life that men see around them and experience within themselves. But he did stress the *order* of that living process as well as the *inexhaustible* feature of its primary

---

20-22 (DK, 59A 61); *Ph.,* I 4,187a20-23 (DK, 12A 9); Simplicius, *In Ph.,* 24.21-25; 154.14-16 (DK, 12A 9; 9a). The only ground suggested by the testimonia for the interpretation in the sense of a mixture, is the notion "separating off," which with Anaximander seems to have been a biological analogy.

source and the *eternal* character of its intrinsic motion. These tenets continued to play an important role in subsequent Greek philosophy.

Anaximander's reasons for making the primordial body indeterminate in character, however, could not have been cogent enough to make any strong impression on his own immediate times. His "successor," Anaximenes, while maintaining the inexhaustible nature of the original stock and the general Milesian development of the universe after the manner of a living body, proceeded like Thales to locate the matrix of cosmic growth in a definitely characterized body. Nor is there enough evidence available to determine just how much emphasis Anaximander himself placed upon the doctrine of the unlimited. His notion of the origin of man, as well as the Peripatetic interpretations of his general teachings, quite definitely points to observation as the starting point of his thinking. The mythological language that he used was looked upon by the Peripatetics as a poetic way of expression. Whether he himself characterized the unlimited as "the divine," or whether this view was a fourth-century interpretation based merely on the epithets "eternal," "deathless," and "indestructible," which to the fourth-century mind implied divinity, is a question that is open to debate.

ANAXIMENES OF MILETUS (*FL.* 528/525 B.C.?)

Chronology. Greek tradition describes Anaximenes as a Milesian and the pupil, associate, and successor of Anaximander. This should place him in the generation immediately after Anaximander, and so locate his main activity in the last half of the sixth century B.C. Information regarding his exact dates is scanty and confused. There is some indication that his *floruit* was placed in the sixty-third Olympiad (528-525 B.C.) by Apollodorus and his death about 498 B.C.[27] The usually accepted chronology, however, places his death, not his *floruit*, in the sixty-third Olympiad. At any rate, his death most likely occurred before the fall of Miletus in 494 B.C., since there is no report of his being in exile. Nothing is known about his life.

Writings. Diogenes Laertius reports that Anaximenes wrote simply

[27] See G. B. Kerferd, *Museum Helveticum*, XI (1954), 117-121. Kerferd, however, suggests 528-525 B.C. for Anaximenes' birth. On the text of D.L., II, 3, see *ibid.*, p. 117.

and unaffectedly. This seems to be meant in contrast to the poetic prose
of Anaximander. Only one sentence has survived.

PHILOSOPHICAL TEACHINGS

Air the Primal Source. The extant sentence reads: "As our
soul, being air, keeps us together, so do breath and air encompass
the whole cosmos" (*Fr. 2*). The term "encompass" is the same
word that seems to have been used already by Anaximander to
describe the function of the primordial matrix. This indicates that
air for Anaximenes is playing the role of the original plasm of
the cosmos. As air controls human life, so does it control the ordered universe. But from his explanation of cosmic development
only one word has survived—"loosened" or "slack" (*Fr. 1*), describing a rarefying process.

Condensation and Rarefaction. As seen through Peripatetic
tradition, Anaximenes agreed with his predecessor in teaching that
the first material principle is one and unlimited, but differed from
him in holding that it is not indeterminate but is a determined
body, air. Through a process of rarefaction and condensation it
becomes the different things in the universe. When it is rarefied,
fire arises; when condensed, wind, cloud, water, earth, stones,
with the other things proceeding from these. As with Anaximander, the process takes place through an eternal motion of the original body. This would mean, against the general Milesian background, that the motion was regarded as intrinsic to the primal
matrix, giving the entire cosmic development the character of a
vital process.

Particular Doctrines. Detailed teachings of Anaximenes reported by Greek tradition are that the earth is flat, like a table,
and is borne upon air. This seems to parallel Thales' doctrine
that the earth rests on water. As the vast expanse of water seemed
to surround the land, so now the unlimited extent of air is considered to be encompassing both the water and the earth. Further,
the air of itself is invisible; it becomes visible through "the cold
and the hot and the wet and the moving."[28] The cosmos keeps

[28] Hippolytus, *Ref.*, I,7,2; DK, 13A 7. "Air" had a wide sense: "The air of
Anaximenes and of many subsequent thinkers is undistinguishable from
vapour, wind, or breath; and the transition from breath to spirit, i.e. soul,
is well known." Sambursky, *The Physical World of the Greeks*, p. 9.

continually changing according to different periods of time (DK, 13A 11). In common with Anaximander and Anaxagoras, Anaximenes is cited as stating that the nature of soul is "air-like" (DK, 12A 29). He understands "soul" (DK, 13A 23; B 2) not merely in the vague Homeric sense of "life," but as something of a considerably more definite nature.[29]

Why did Anaximenes return to a definitely characterized body for his primal stock of cosmic development? Why was he not swayed by his predecessor's reasoning that the original source of things had to be a nature that was identified with none of them? The answer has not been handed down by Greek tradition. From what is known of his general doctrine, it looks as though Anaximenes, like Anaximander, was grappling with the problem of accounting for the observable changes of one thing into another, and sought their explanation in the phenomena of condensation and rarefaction. These processes seem to have been viewed by him in a basically quantitative, and not qualitative, manner. Such a view would obviously lead not to a mixture from which things could be separated out, but to a definite nature capable of expansion and contraction. Air would fill this role. Its function in sustaining human life, along with its apparently unlimited expanse surrounding the water as well as the earth, would point to it as the matrix that originates and supports the life of the cosmos. However, there is not enough evidence to affirm with anything like certainty that such was the course of his reasoning. His efforts continue quite clearly, though, in the general Milesian direction of explaining the development of the universe after the fashion of a vital process, and give even stronger indications than those of his predecessors of being based definitely upon observation of the changes in the sensible world. He comes to closer grips with the problem of change. In the one sentence remaining from his treatise, the technical term "cosmos" in the sense of the ordered universe is found used.

The destruction of Miletus by the Persians under Darius in 494 B.C. ended its prominence as the center of philosophical endeavors. Its tradition, however, was carried to the mainland of

---

[29] See Jaeger, *Theology*, p. 208, n. 63.

Greece and was continued at Athens by Anaxagoras of Clazomenae.

OTHER EARLY VIEWS

Fire. Thales had looked upon the earth as floating on the vast surrounding water, and apparently as deriving its growth and sustinence from that primordial water. Anaximenes had regarded the whole cosmos as borne about upon the air, and as being sustained and controlled by that surrounding air just as a man is kept alive by his soul. The Greek conceptions of the universe, however, had been consolidating in the notion of a region of fire (*aither*) as the place of the heavenly bodies, outside and beyond the realm of air.[30] One would expect, accordingly, to find thinkers who would go beyond the air and see in fire the primal stuff from which the universe developed. Hippasus of Metapontum, in southern Italy, is reported by Aristotle (*Metaph.*, A 3,984a7; DK, 18A 7) to have taught that the first principle of the universe was fire. Hippasus had been a Pythagorean. The earliest Pythagorean conception may have located in light or fire the positive constituent of the universe, and a later pattern placed the primal fire at the center. But there is no guarantee that Hippasus was thinking in either of these ways, as he was not considered an orthodox Pythagorean. No details, in fact, are known of the way in which he conceived fire as the origin of the cosmos, and his views are impossible to reconstruct. Coupled with his name in ascribing the primal role to fire in the Aristotelian report is Heraclitus of Ephesus. Parmenides of Elea also saw in fire the positive constituent of the cosmos. In both Heraclitus and Parmenides, however, the type of treatment is very different from that of the Milesians. Their views, consequently, have to be considered against a different background and from their own special standpoints.

Earth. The general pattern according to which the Milesian teachings developed would seem to exclude earth, found only in the central region of the universe, from exercising the function

---

[30] See Otto Gilbert, *Die Meteorologischen Theorien des Griechischen Altertums* (Leipzig: Teubner, 1907), pp. 17-33, esp. p. 31. *Cf.* W. K. C. Guthrie, *In the Beginning*, pp. 50-52; *CQ*, L (1956), 40-41.

of the primal matrix. It is not surprising, then, to find Aristotle's
express testimony that no philosopher in tracing the development
of the cosmos from a single element gave that role to earth.[31] The
reason given by the Stagirite is that to a philosopher earth on
account of its coarse texture would not appear simple enough to
function as the unique primary element. Even though this reason
may be entirely an interpretation of Aristotle's own, and need not
at all reflect any concern in the early thinkers with a requirement
of simplicity in the primordial stock, there does not seem to be
any reason for questioning his factual statement that no philosophical doctrine making earth primary was to be found in the
history of Greek thought. However, Aristotle notes that in the
poetry of Hesiod as well as in popular conceptions earth had been
regarded as the most primal of bodies. In view of such considerations, it is the statement of Xenophanes in this regard to be considered a philosophical teaching or merely a poetic and popular
reflection? The fragment reads: "For all things are from earth,
and to earth do all things finally return" (*Fr. 27*). On account of
the place given Xenophanes in the traditional history of Greek
philosophy, the claims that his surviving fragments express philosophical doctrine call for some examination.

XENOPHANES OF COLOPHON (570-478 + ? B.C.)

Chronology. In another extant fragment, Xenophanes declared
that he had wandered up and down the land of Greece for sixty-seven
years, and that at the time of his exile he was already twenty-five years
old (*Fr. 8*). Colophon, an inland city of Ionia about fifteen miles
north of Ephesus, was taken by the Medes and Persians in 545 B.C. If
Xenophanes had to leave Ionia at this time, he would have been born
about 570 B.C., and would die in extreme old age not too long after
478 B.C. Other testimonia likewise indicate that he lived well on into
the first quarter of the fifth century, dying a very old man. The traditional chronology placed his *floruit* in the sixtieth Olympiad (540-537
B.C.), apparently because of his reputed connection with the colony
of Elea, founded about 540 B.C.

Writings. The extant fragments of Xenophanes are all in verse.

[31] *Metaph.*, A 8,989a5-12. For the doxographical interpretations, see DK,
21A 36. On the mythological background, see Guthrie, *In the Beginning*,
pp. 21-28.

Elegiacs and regular hexameters, they apparently formed part of compositions meant for public recitation. They indicate the work of a professional rhapsodist who made his living by reciting in his travels from town to town his own poems instead of the Homeric epics recited by the traditional rhapsodists. While acknowledging that Homer was the educator of all Greece, he took mordant issue with the anthropomorphic and shameful conceptions of the Homeric gods (DK, 21B 10-16). He also complained that athletes received greater emoluments for their performances that he did for his, though his craft was far more valuable for the public welfare. He was credited with having written epics on the foundation of Colophon and of Elea, but no fragments of them have survived. There is nothing unlikely about his having composed either of these, but if he did write the one on Elea it need not imply any continued residence in that colony or any part in the type of philosophy to which it subsequently gave its name.

REPUTED PHILOSOPHICAL TEACHINGS

Cosmological. Later Greek doxographers (DK, 21A 36) did in fact interpret Xenophanes' statement that all things come from earth as meaning that earth is a primal nature or first principle of everything in the fashion of the Milesian cosmologies. But Xenophanes also wrote in similar vein: "All things that come into being and grow are earth and water" (*Fr.* 29; tr. Freeman), and "For we all were born of earth and water" (*Fr.* 33). These utterances seem more like a poet's reflections on the transitory character of earthly things or his expression of folklore traditions, even though they may well have been thought out against the general background of Milesian cosmological notions. They read like the words of a poet that later on were given an original philosophical implication. Aristotle and Theophrastus, however, did not discover any such cosmological doctrine in his verses.

Theological. Xenophanes wrote: "There is one god, among gods and men the greatest, not at all like mortals in body and mind "(*Fr.* 23; tr. Freeman). This is hardly the utterance of one who today could be called a monotheist. It praises a god who is the greatest among a plurality of gods, a sort of a *primus inter pares*. As it stands, it need be nothing more than the rhapsodist's hymn to a Zeus purged of Homeric anthropomorphism; Zeus was indeed the greatest among the Olympian gods. Again, Xenophanes proclaimed: "He sees as a whole, thinks as a whole, and hears as a whole" (*Fr.* 24; tr. Freeman). In the background of Xenophanes' attack on the anthropomorphic conceptions of the gods, can one see in this any more than the assertion that a god does not depend upon separate organs like eyes, ears, and brain for his knowledge? Similarly, a god does not require the toil of bodily members to accomplish his purpose, but only his mere thought: "But without toil he sets everything in motion, by the thought of his mind" (*Fr.* 25; tr. Freeman). The Homeric Zeus had but to nod his head, and what he wanted would be accomplished. Xenophanes is emphasizing that the god's mere thought suffices. Unlike Xenophanes himself, this type of god need not complain about having to wander up and down the land of Greece until he is ninety-two years old: "And he always remains in the same place, not moving at all, nor is it fitting for him to change his position at different times" (*Fr.* 26; tr. Freeman).

These are the only fragments into which a positive philosophical conception of god may be read. Considering the general background of their author, one is hardly justified in making them express later philosophical meanings that may indeed be found in Aristotle's doctrine, but which Aristotle himself did not think of seeing in such assertions of Xenophanes. Aristotle (*Rh.,* II 23,1399b6-8; DK, 21A 12), in fact, takes for granted Xenophanes' belief in a plurality of immortal gods.

Epistemological.   Finally, there are fragments that have been interpreted in the philosophical sense of a mild type of skepticism. Xenophanes stated: "And no man then has seen the truth nor will there ever be any who knows about the gods and all the things that I mention. For if he should succeed in the highest degree in saying something completely correct, nevertheless he himself does not know it; and 'seeming' is wrought upon all things" (*Fr.* 34). This fragment acknowledges the existence of what is certain, but claims that it will never be attained by man, even though a man happens to say it without knowing it for certain. So a man can speak of things only as they seem to him. Xenophanes is evidently disclaiming any absolute norm by which he can judge and prove that what he is saying about the gods and about things in general is true. He is presenting his views, however, as bearing some resemblance to the truth: "Let these things be reputed as similar to what is true" (*Fr.* 35). Do these fragments imply a doctrine of philosophical skepticism? Or are they merely the apology of a poet for his inability to give a full account of his lofty themes? Xenophanes speaks in general as though he had no thought of questioning the existence of what is certain and true,[32] but is insisting on the incapacity of men to attain it fully. This does not give evidence of a deliberately worked out philosophical skepticism, or of any interest in consciously developing such a doctrine. However, along with Parmenides and Zeno of Elea, he was in later times referred to as a patron of skeptical doctrine. His notion of "appearance" as "similar to the true" will undergo considerable development in the course of Greek philosophy.

Xenophanes' fragments, then, hardly exhibit the character of writings meant to express original philosophic thought. They have the earmarks of work produced by an earnest and vigorous rhapsodist, who caught the popular taste of the age with his pungent satire, and who was able, it seems, to ply his trade successfully even in his ninety-second year; but they can hardly claim to express the reflections of a philosopher. They justify in this respect the light way in which Aristotle dismisses the views of their author, saying that Xenophanes "did not make anything very clear, nor does he appear to have attained the nature of either of these causes, but gazing upon the whole heaven he says that the one is god."[33]

[32] Diogenes Laertius, IX,20 (DK, 21A 1), notes as an error the statement of Sotion, a third-century B.C. writer of *Successions,* that Xenophanes was the first to say that all things are incomprehensible. Sextus Empiricus (*Pyrrh.Hyp.*, I,225; cf. *Adv.Math.*, VII,46-52) regarded him as a dogmatist.
[33] *Metaph.*, A 5,986b22-24; cf. *Cael.*, II 13,294a24 (DK, 21A 30;47). Plato (*Sph.*, 242D; DK, 21A 29) speaking in a semijocular way, makes the Stranger from Elea say that the Eleatic tribe, starting with Xenophanes and *even earlier,* assumed the unity of all things. Plato had already (*Tht.*, 180CE; cf. 152E) represented the dramatically opposed school of the Heracliteans as having its origin in the traditional Greek poets, and apparently wished to parallel this origin for the doctrine of Parmenides. But Xenophanes seems to have been the only poet available for the purpose, so Plato contents himself with having the Eleatic Stranger trace the teaching vaguely to Xenophanes and "even earlier." This is the oldest context in which the combination of Xenophanes and Parmenides is found. Aristotle (*Metaph.*, A 5,986b-21-22) records the combination, remarking that Parmenides *is said* to have been the pupil of Xenophanes. Such was the relationship, accordingly, that the doxographical tradition from Theophrastus on took for granted. Parme-

RETROSPECT

The early Ionian cosmologies quite evidently represent sincere philosophical efforts to explain the growth and processes of the visible universe in terms of corporeal natures. Their thinking did not reach the point where incorporeal or supersensible principles would be called upon to explain the corporeal. The corporeal, rather, was taken for granted and regarded as ultimate. Their general conception of cosmic development after the manner of vital processes, moreover, allowed them also to take for granted the motion in the universe. The material that formed the cosmos was looked upon as self-moving or vital, and so no question of an external cause to initiate the motion needed to arise. Greek philosophy, accordingly, began in a framework that rendered such a question superfluous.

The qualitative aspects under which cosmic changes were viewed by the Ionians could hardly help but give prominence to the doctrine of the opposites. The changes from hot to cold, moist to dry, dense to rare, and so on, were apparently the phenomena that sparked the early Milesian thinking. The perceptible qualitative differences resulting from these changes absorbed and retained all the attention. In Anaximander, the explanation of

nides became the second in the "succession" of the Eleatic dynasty in philosophy. The Peripatetic treatise *On Melissus, Xenophanes, and Gorgias* (in Aristotle, 974al ff.) circulated as Xenophanes' teaching a general synopsis of Eleatic doctrine, as this doctrine was understood in later Greek tradition. The evidence available today, however, hardly indicates that there was in historical fact any *special* connection of Xenophanes with Elea, either geographically or philosophically. Diogenes Laertius (IX,20) classes him as a "sporadic" philosopher (i.e. not belonging to any school), while on the other hand listing him (I,15) and treating of him immediately ahead of Parmenides as though Parmenides were his dynastic "successor." On the history of the modern critique of Xenophanes' position in Greek philosophy, see Jaeger, *Theology*, pp. 51-54. Karl Deichgräber, "Xenophanes ΠΕΡΙ ΦΥΣΕΩΣ" *Rh. Mus.*, N.F. LXXXVII (1938), 31, notes how Xenophanes cannot be measured by the same norms as Anaximander or Parmenides. G. B. Kerferd writes: "Was Xenophanes a philosopher or not? is a modern question which has no proper answer when it is applied to an early thinker like Xenophanes." "Review" (of Mario Untersteiner, *Senofane, Testimonianze e Frammenti*), *Gnomon*, XXIX (1957), 131. For the view that Xenophanes has to be regarded as a natural philosopher, however, see A. Lumpe, *Die Philosophie des Xenophanes von Kolophon* (Munich, 1952), pp. 36-43; C. Corbato, *Annali Triestini*, XXII (1952), pp. 205-214.

change as a passage from one opposite to another may have been consciously developed. At any rate, the conception of sensible change as requiring a basic material that passed from one opposite characteristic to the other continued to be a challenging position in Greek philosophy and occasioned much subsequent discussion. But in the meantime, other ways of explaining the sensible universe had been initiated. One was a mathematical explanation, in terms of numbers and quantity. Another was a moral projection, in terms of human conduct. A third was a metaphysical account, in terms of being and not-being. These new ways of thinking posed problems for subsequent cosmologists, and led to modifications and deepening in their teachings. The immediate "successor" of Anaximenes was, according to Greek tradition, Anaxagoras. But his philosophy, though based strongly in the Milesian background, is profoundly influenced by the new mathematical and metaphysical conceptions of the universe, and so belongs to a different era of Greek philosophy.

SELECTED READINGS AND REFERENCES

A. For the Presocratics in General

PRIMARY SOURCES

Hermann Diels, *Die Fragmente der Vorsokratiker*, 5th ed., Walther Kranz (Berlin: Weidmann, 1934-37). The 6th to 8th editions (1951-1956) are reprints, with added *Nachträge* or appendices. An English translation of the fragments that are considered to be the original words of a Presocratic philosopher (given under section B in Diels) is to be had in Kathleen Freeman's *Ancilla to the Pre-Socratic Philosophers* (Oxford: B. Blackwell, 1948). The information contained in the other fragments (given under section A in Diels) is summarized and discussed by Miss Freeman in *The Pre-Socratic Philosophers, A Companion to Diels* (Oxford: B. Blackwell, 1946).
Selections: Milton Charles Nahm, *Selections from Early Greek Philosophy*, 3rd ed. (New York: Appleton-Century-Crofts, 1947).

SECONDARY SOURCES

John Burnet, *Early Greek Philosophy*, 4th ed. (London: A. & C. Black, 1930). Later reprints are of this edition. The first edition was published in 1892.

W. A. Heidel, "Qualitative Change in Pre-Socratic Philosophy," *AGP*, XIX (1906), 333-379.

Francis Macdonald Cornford, *From Religion to Philosophy* (London: E. Arnold & Co., 1912). Reprint, New York: Harper, 1957.

————, *Principium Sapientiae: The Origins of Geek Philosophical Thought* (Cambridge, Eng.: University Press, 1952).

H. C. Baldrey, "Embryological Analogies in Pre-Socratic Cosmogony," *CQ*, XXVI (1932), 27-34.

Harold Cherniss, *Aristotle's Criticism of Presocratic Philosophy* (Baltimore: Johns Hopkins Press, 1935).

————, "The Characteristics and Effects of Presocratic Philosophy," *Journal of the History of Ideas*, XII (1951), 319-345.

Werner Wilhelm Jaeger, *The Theology of the Early Greek Philosophers* (Oxford: Clarendon Press, 1947).

J. B. McDiarmid, "Theophrastus on the Presocratic Causes," *Harvard Studies in Classical Philology*, LXI (1953), 85-156.

Geoffrey Stephen Kirk and John Earle Raven, *The Presocratic Philosophers* (Cambridge, Eng.: University Press, 1957).

B.   FOR THE MILESIANS

ANAXIMANDER

W. A. Heidel, "On Anaximander," *Class. Phil.*, VII (1912), 212-234.

————, "Anaximander's Book, The Earliest Known Geographical Treatise," *Proceedings of the American Academy of Arts and Sciences*, LVI, (1921), 239-288.

F. M. Cornford, "Innumerable Worlds in Presocratic Philosophy," *CQ*, XXVIII (1934), 1-16.

W. Kraus, "Das Wesen des Unendlichen bei Anaximander," *Rh.Mus.*, N.F. XCIII (1950), 364-379.

G. B. Burch, "Anaximander, the First Metaphysician," *Review of Metaphysics*, III (1949), 137-160.

W. I. Matson, "The Naturalism of Anaximander," *Review of Metaphysics*, VI (1953), 387-395.

J. H. Loenen, "Was Anaximander an Evolutionist?" *Mnemosyne*, ser. 4, VII (1954), 215-232.

G. S. Kirk, "Some Problems in Anaximander," *CQ*, XLIX (1955), 21-38.

B. Wiśniewski, "Sur la Signification de l'*Apeiron* d'Anaximandre," *Revue des Études Grecques*, LXX (1957), 47-55.

ANAXIMENES

W. A. Heidel, "The ΔΙΝΗ in Anaximenes and Anaximander," *Class. Phil.*, I (1906), 279-282.

G. B. Kerferd, "The Date of Anaximenes," *Museum Helveticum,* XI (1954), 117-121.

W. K. C. Guthrie, "Anaximenes and TO ΚΡΥΣΤΑΛΛΟΕΙΔΕΣ," *CQ,* L (1956), 40-44.

C. FOR XENOPHANES

H. Fränkel, "Xenophanesstudien," *Hermes,* LX (1925), 174-192.

C. M. Bowra, "Xenophanes, Fragment 1," *Class. Phil.,* XXXIII (1938), 353-367.

W. W. Jaeger, "Xenophanes and the Beginnings of Natural Theology," in *Albert Schweitzer Jubilee Book* (Cambridge, Mass.: Sei-Art Publishers [1945]), 397-424; or, Chap. III in Jaeger's *The Theology of the Early Greek Philosophers* (Oxford: Clarendon Press, 1947), pp. 38-54.

Adolph Lumpe, *Die Philosophie des Xenophanes von Kolophon* (Munich: W. Foth, 1952).

C. Corbato, "Studi Senofanei," *Annali Triestini,* XXII (1952), 179-244.

Mario Untersteiner, *Senofane, Testimonianze e Frammenti* (Florence: La Nuova Italia, 1956).

H. Herter, "Das Symposium des Xenophanes," *Wien.Stud.,* LXIX (1956), 33-48.

[CHAPTER 2]

The Beginnings of the Mathematical Conception of the Universe

PYTHAGORAS OF SAMOS (*FL. CA.* 540/530 B.C.?)

Chronology. The reputation of Pythagoras in the Greek world had already been established by the end of the sixth century, for he is mentioned in a fragment of Xenophanes and in some of Heraclitus.[1] Later testimony states that he went to Italy to escape the tyranny of Polycrates at Samos (*ca.* 540-522 B.C.). Apparently for that reason his *floruit* was placed in the sixtieth (540-537 B.C.) or the sixty-second (532-529 B.C.) Olympiad. This would make him roughly a contemporary of Anaximenes. Diogenes Laertius (VIII, 44) records that most historians said he died at the age of ninety. Seventy-five was the lowest age reported for his life span.

Life and Work. According to the testimonia, Pythagoras first appears as living on the island of Samos, off the Ionian coast just north of Miletus. He was therefore of the same general Ionian culture as the Milesian philosophers. He is reported to have visited Egypt and Persia, learning their mathematics and their mystic lore, though these accounts may be based merely on phases of his teaching. Going to Italy in middle life, he seems to have lived for about twenty years (possibly 529-509 B.C.) at Croton on the southern coast of the Italian peninsula,

---

[1] DK, 21B 7; 22B 40, 81, 129. *Fr.* 129 of Heraclitus may now be accepted as genuine; so O. Gigon, *Untersuchungen zu Heraklit* (Leipzig, 1935), pp. 94, 140, 142; G. S. Kirk, *Heraclitus: The Cosmic Fragments* (Cambridge, Eng., 1954), p. 390.

taking a leading part in its political affairs. He then went to Metapontum on the Gulf of Tarentum and died there, deeply mourned by the people. His house was made into a temple. He does not seem to have left any writings. He had founded at Croton a society that was primarily religious in character and purpose, but which cultivated learning and engaged in marked political activity with rising and falling fortunes. Both men and women were admitted to membership. They were divided into two classes, initiates and learners. There were strict rules of abstinence, based apparently on cult taboos rather than on ethical doctrine, and of silence, and possibly—though this is highly disputable—of secrecy in regard to the Pythagorean doctrines and cult practices. However, the information on the way of living in the society is vague and often conflicting. The society seems to have died out around the middle of the fourth century B.C. On account of his activity in Italy Pythagoras, though an Ionian, is placed by the later Greek writers in a new dynasty of philosophers, which they called the Italian "succession" (D.L., I, 13).

PHILOSOPHICAL TEACHINGS

Transmigration of Souls.   The fragment of Xenophanes records, as hearsay, a story that Pythagoras, when passing a dog that was being beaten, said: "Stop! Cease your beating, because this is really the soul of a man who was my friend: I recognized it as I heard it cry aloud."[2] This indicates that in his own day Pythagoras was reputed to have taught a doctrine of transmigration of souls, understanding "soul" in the sense of something that survived bodily dissolution and continued to live a personal life. It is just possible that some kind of a tripartite division of the soul, as a basis for three different types of life, may go back to Pythagoras, but no trustworthy details on this question are available.

Mathematics.   Greek tradition of the latter half of the fourth century B.C. says that Pythagoras engaged in wonder-working and in mathematics, being the first to carry the study of arithmetic beyond the needs of commerce. This implies interest in mathematics for its own sake, and so a purely theoretical or speculative interest. His esteem for the purely theoretical is illustrated in a story that seems to go back to the fourth century B.C. When

[2] DK, 21B 7; tr. Freeman. That the friend was a man and not just the dog is explicit in the Greek text.

asked who he was, he replied "A philosopher," and explained the notion by comparing life to the Great Games. To these, some went to compete for prizes, others to sell wares, but the most fortunate were there as spectators. The speculative or theoretical (having in Greek the sense of "contemplative") pursuit of truth is the life of the philosopher, and is the highest of all lives. This was considered by the Greeks to be the first use of the term "philosopher" or "lover of wisdom," and it implied in its Pythagorean setting that no man, but only God, is properly said to be wise.

Moral Teachings. The saying "Friends have all things in common" was attributed to Pythagoras, as well as a number of other moral maxims. It is difficult, however, to see any strictly philosophical doctrine underlying these maxims as they are accredited to him. But the general concept of treating virtuous conduct in terms of harmony and mathematical proportions[4] may well have been initiated by Pythagoras himself. It was reported, though, as a strictly mathematical and not a properly ethical treatment of the virtues.

Any closer details about the doctrines of Pythagoras are vague and unreliable. Plato and Aristotle refer to him with surprising reserve, and seem to have had no certain knowledge of his own philosophical teachings, as distinguished from those of his later followers. It is more likely that his transmigration doctrine had a cult background rather than any properly philosophical basis. How far his reported mathematical work carried him cannot be determined, but his later followers used numbers as the means of explaining the cosmos and so developed a conception of the universe based upon mathematical proportions. To what extent that tendency was already actual in Pythagoras himself cannot be definitely established. His wide learning and varied interests are sufficiently attested by the fragments of Heraclitus and Empedocles.[5] The practice of teaching Pythagorean doctrine as the utter-

[3] D. L., VIII, 8; *cf.* I, 12. Pythagoras is also reported (Aetius, II, 1, 1; *Dox. Graec.*, p. 327. 8-10, DK 14, no. 21) to have been the first to call the universe the "cosmos," on account of its order.

[4] This conception of the virtues is attributed to Pythagoras in the Aristotelian *M M*, I 1,1182a11-14 (DK, 58B 4).

[5] DK, 22B 40, 129; 31B 129. No matter how much Pythagoras' own knowledge and intellectual activity may be scaled down by criticism of the extant

ances of Pythagoras himself is indicated by the use of the caption *Ipse dixit* (*Autos epha*), which became proverbial (D.L., VIII, 46).

THE PYTHAGOREANS

Earlier Pythagoreans.   Of the earlier Pythagoreans, no fragments have survived; nor is there any definite information about the teachings contained in the written works attributed to them. Some influences of Pythagorean doctrine may have passed into Greek medical science through the activity of Alcmaeon of Croton, probably early in the fifth century B.C. Alcmaeon is reported (D.L., VIII, 83; DK, 24A 1) to have received instruction from Pythagoras, but whether he himself should be called a Pythagorean is left doubtful by the testimonia. He is said to have maintained a fundamental doctrine of opposites, and to have regarded health as their equal balance in the living organism (*Fr.* 4). He may well have influenced the development of Pythagorean doctrine in this regard, rather than being himself a product of it. There is not sufficient evidence to furnish any certain knowledge of his relation to the Pythagoreans and their activities.

Later Pythagoreans.   The first published account of Pythagorean teachings was attributed to a later disciple, Philolaus of Croton or Tarentum, whose work is placed in the latter half of the fifth century B.C. As early as the middle of the first century B.C. a treatise under his name with the usual title *On Nature*, and purporting to set forth the Pythagorean doctrines, was quoted (D.L., VIII, 85; DK, 44A 1). The authenticity of the extant fragments, however, is not sufficiently established to allow their use as original fifth-century statements of Pythagorean teaching. An associate and pupil of his, Eurytus, a native of one of the Pythagorean centers in southern Italy, is credited by Aristotle (*Metaph.*, N 5,1092b10-13; DK, 45, no. 3) with working out definite numbers for the respective natures of man, horse, and other living things. No writings of Eurytus have survived.

The most prominent Pythagorean in the first half of the fourth century B.C. was Archytas of Tarentum, a pupil of Philolaus and a contemporary and friend of Plato. He was an outstanding general and political leader in the western section of the Greek world, a remark-

---

sources of information, these fragments, as well as the testimony of Herodotus (IV, 95; DK, 14, no. 2), require that at least something be left him to explain his wide reputation and the influence of his name on subsequent Greek thought. The semilegendary atmosphere surrounding him, however, and the lateness of the more extensive testimonia, leave the details of his life and teaching open to question.

able mathematician, and an uncompromising exponent of the notion
that all things have to be explained by mathematics. He maintained
that correct knowledge of all things, both in general and in particular,
is mathematical: "Mathematicians seem to me to have excellent discernment, and it is in no way strange that they should think correctly
concerning the nature of particular existences. For since they have
passed an excellent judgment on the nature of the Whole, they were
bound to have an excellent view of separate things" (*Fr. 1*; tr. Freeman). He was interested in problems concerning the process of learning, and in applying mathematical notions to the guidance of human
conduct (*Fr. 3*). He is reported to have been in the forefront in advancing the Pythagorean science of harmonics and music, and to have
been the first to systematize mechanics by the application of mathematical principles.[6]

The dearth of acceptable fragments from works of the Pythagoreans
themselves leaves the reports of later writers as the necessary source
for a reconstruction of their doctrines. Modern reconstructions (e.g.,
those of Burnet, Cornford, Raven) made on the basis of these accounts
vary quite widely. The safest policy is to remain as close as possible to
the earliest doctrinal accounts, those of the fourth century B.C., even
though they are quite often vague and indecisive on points of detail.

PHILOSOPHICAL TEACHINGS OF THE PYTHAGOREANS

Culture.   The reports in general seem to show that the Pythagoreans were keenly interested and active in the promotion of
education, memory training, health, and moral conduct, as well as
in the advancement of mathematics in general, and astronomy,
harmonics, and mechanics in particular. From a philosophical
viewpoint, however, their primary contribution was their thoroughgoing mathematical conception of the universe.

Mathematical Conception of Things.   Aristotle records: ". . .
the so-called Pythagoreans, who were the first to take up mathematics, not only advanced this study, but also having been
brought up in it they thought that its principles were the principles of all things."[7] This was understood as meaning that real
things were actually numbers: "Again, the Pythagoreans, because
they saw many attributes of numbers belonging to sensible bodies,
supposed real things to be numbers, . . ."[8] Accordingly, the two

---

[6] D.L., VIII, 83 (DK, 47A 1). Regarding music, see DK, 47A 16-19b.
[7] *Metaph.*, A 5,985b23-26; Oxford tr. (DK, 58B 4).
[8] *Metaph.*, N 3,1090a20-23; Oxford tr. *Cf.* A 8,990a21-29 (DK, 58B 22).

basic constituents of the universe, the unlimited and the limit, are mathematical natures, and so, consequently, is everything else in the cosmos: ". . . they thought that finitude and infinity were not attributes of certain other things, e.g. of fire or earth or anything else of this kind, but that infinity itself and unity itself were the substance of the things of which they are predicated. This is why number was the substance of all things."[9] The Pythagorean "unlimited" appeared to Aristotle as something in the realm of the sensible, extending as a sort of space outside the heavens: ". . . the Pythagoreans place the infinite among the objects of sense (they do not regard number as separable from these), and assert that what is outside the heaven is infinite."[10] It is as it were breathed in by the heavens: "The Pythagoreans, too, held that void exists and that it enters the heaven itself, which as it were inhales it, from the infinite air."[11] Mathematically it had the character of evenness, while its opposite, the limited, had that of oddness. Together they constituted the one, and the one was the principle of the other numbers and so of the whole universe: "Evidently, then, these thinkers also consider that number is the principle both as matter for things and as forming both their modifications and their permanent states, and hold that the elements of number are the even and the odd, and that of these the latter is limited, and the former unlimited; and that the One proceeds from both of these (for it is both even and odd), and number from the One; and that the whole heaven, as has been said, is numbers."[12] The construction of the world seems to have been envisioned as a limiting of successive parts of the unlimited

[9] *Metaph.*, A 5,987a15-19; Oxford tr. (DK, 58B 8).

[10] *Ph.*, III 4,203a6-8; Oxford tr. (DK, 58B 28). Later testimonia (DK, 58B 1a; 14; 15) call the Pythagorean unlimited principle the "indefinite dyad." Aristotle (*Metaph.*, A 6,987b25-27), however, implies that in this regard the Pythagoreans themselves had always looked upon it as unitary, and urges that the conception of that principle as a dyad is peculiarly Platonic, so interpreting the dual character seen in its Platonic formulation "the great and the small."

[11] *Ph.*, IV 6,213b22-24 (Oxford tr.); *cf. Fr.* 196, 1513a30-33. DK, 58B 30.

[12] *Metaph.*, A 5,986a15-21; Oxford tr. (DK, 58B 5). The ones or units out of which sensible things were constructed had to be of course spatially extended monads. Aristotle found no explanation in the Pythagoreans of the way in which such spatially extended *units* could be possible: "For they construct the whole universe out of numbers—only not numbers consisting of abstract units; they suppose the units to have spatial magnitude. But how the first I was constructed so as to have magnitude, they seem unable to say" (*Metaph.*, M 6,1080b18-21; Oxford tr. DK, 58B 9).

by the limit, but through the one: ". . . they say plainly that when the one had been constructed, whether out of planes or of surface or of seed or of elements which they cannot express, immediately the nearest part of the unlimited began to be constrained and limited by the limit."[13] The details of the whole process, as can be seen from these lines, remained obscure in Aristotle's sources of information. He had no doubt, however, that all the Pythagorean ones or monads and the numbers and things constituted by them were spatial realities, and that the Pythagoreans recognized no other type of things than the sensible. The heavens not only formed a harmony, but actually made music as they revolved.[14]

Though usually saying that for the Pythagoreans things *are* numbers, Aristotle also refers to them as holding that things *imitate* numbers. It is possible that the Pythagoreans differed among themselves in this regard, or that earlier views proceeded as though number were a property of things, and then gradually developed into the notion that number was the essence of things. However, there is practically no definitive information about the historical development of the Pythagorean doctrines.[15]

The Opposites. The doctrine of the opposites was highly regarded among the Pythagoreans. According to Aristotle,[16] some of them drew up the table of the most important opposites as follows:

1) Limit and unlimited	6) Resting and moving
2) Odd and even	7) Straight and curved
3) One and plurality	8) Light and darkness
4) Right and left	9) Good and bad
5) Male and female	10) Square and oblong

Of these opposites the first pair, the limit and the unlimited, seems to have been considered as basic, and the other pairs as

[13] *Metaph.*, N 3,1091a15-18; Oxford tr. (DK, 58B 26)

[14] *Cael.*, II 9,290b12-291a10 (DK, 58B 35). The music is unnoticed, because men are accustomed to it from birth, and have never experienced any contrasting silence.

[15] A reconstruction of the evolution of Pythagoreanism during the fifth century, in function of alleged Eleatic opposition, is offered by J. E. Raven, *Pythagoreans and Eleatics* (Cambridge, Eng., 1948), pp. 163-164.

[16] *Metaph.*, A 5,986a23-26 (DK, 58B 5), using the terminology of the Oxford tr.

its various aspects or expressions. Accordingly, all in the first column would come under the aspect of the good.[17] The one that is listed as the opposite of plurality is quite apparently different from the one that is the principle of number and of the Pythagorean cosmogony.[18] This latter one is constituted by the union of both the basic opposites, and so can be identified with neither. As a result the Pythagorean doctrine remains fundamentally dualistic, and in that respect differs profoundly from the Milesian philosophies. The conception of the cosmos as something that breathes, the description of its elements as seed, the aspects of male and female in its basic opposites, all indicate, however, that the Pythagoreans agreed with their contemporaries in regarding the whole universe as a living thing, even though they were giving it a mathematical explanation.

Number the Basis of Knowledge. Although every individual argument brought against them can be countered, the weight of scholarly opinion is at present against the authenticity of the fragments attributed to Philolaus.[19] They are regarded by some able critics as post-Aristotelian. As the treatise from which they seem to have been quoted was accepted in the first century B.C., they may still be looked upon as a fairly ancient account of what was understood as Pythagorean doctrine. The opening words of the treatise presented it as an explanation of the harmonious constitution of nature and of the whole universe and of all the things contained within the cosmos, in terms of composition between the unlimited and limiting factors (*Fr.* 1). Number is the only means by which things can be understood: "And in fact all things that can be known have a number; for it is not possible for anything either to be thought or to be known without this"

---

[17] Cf. *E N,* I 6,1096b5-6 (DK, 58B 6); II 6,1106b29-30 (58B 7).

[18] See Raven, *Pythagoreans and Eleatics,* pp. 11-19.

[19] On the case for the authenticity of the Philolaus fragments, see R. Mondolfo, *Rivista di Filologia e d'Istruzione Classica,* LXV (1937), 225-245, or Zeller-Mondolfo, *Filosofia dei Greci* (Florence, 1932-1938), II, 367-382; W. Wiersma, "Die Fragmente des Philolaos und das Sogenannte philolaische Weltsystem," *Mnemosyne,* 3a ser. X (1942), 23-32. For the case against, see I. Bywater, *JP,* I (1868), 21-53; E. Frank, *Plato und die Sogenannten Pythagoreer* (Halle, 1923), pp. 263-335; Raven, *Pythagoreans and Eleatics,* pp. 97-100, or Kirk-Raven, *The Presocratic Philosophers* (Cambridge, Eng., 1957), pp. 308-311.

(*Fr.* 4). Number, accordingly, is the basis of all human knowledge: "For the nature of Number is the cause of recognition, able to give guidance and teaching to every man in what is puzzling and unknown. For none of existing things would be clear to anyone, either in themselves or in their relationship to one another, unless there existed Number and its essence" (*Fr.* 11; tr. Freeman). The cognoscibility of things implies the presence of a basic limiting factor: "For to start with, there will not even be an object of knowledge, if all things are unlimited" (*Fr.* 3). The other basic factor, the unlimited, could apparently be presumed in the general background of preceding Greek thought.

Cosmology. The first of the composites, the unit or the one, is located at the center of the universe: "The first composite, the One, which is in the centre of the Sphere, is called Hearth" (*Fr.* 7; tr. Freeman). According to the testimonia (DK, 44A 13-22), this was explained in sensible terms as meaning that at the center or hearth of the universe is located the original fire. It governs the cosmos. Round it circles a body called the counter-earth.[20] Then come the earth, moon, sun, and five planets, bringing the total number to ten, with the inclusion of the central fire. The decad is the perfect number, because it is the sum of the first four numbers, and so contains the nature of the point ("one"), the line ("two"), the first plane figure ("three"), and the solid ("four"). The universe, accordingly, is explained in terms of harmonies and numerical proportions. The periphery is a region of fire, like the center. All astronomical phenomena repeat themselves cyclically, in Great Years, as distinguished from solar years.

The Soul. The doctrine of metempsychosis is presented as meaning that the body (*sôma*) is as it were a tomb (*sêma*) for the soul: "The ancient theologians and seers also bear witness that because of certain punishments the soul is yoked to the body and buried in it as in a tomb" (*Fr.* 14; tr. Freeman). As the punishment is of divine origin and so is presumed to be just, one may not licitly escape from this custody by suicide (DK, 44B 14).

If genuine, the fragments of Philolaus show a deep interest in the problem of knowledge in fifth-century Pythagoreanism. Such

[20] On the necessity, from a mechanical viewpoint, of the counter-earth in the Pythagorean cosmos, see G. B. Burch, *Osiris*, XI (1954), 286-289.

an interest would have been but a natural consequence of the mathematical conception of the universe, so different from that of ordinary human cognition. The view of knowledge expressed in the fragments seems to have been accepted without need of explanation by Archytas (DK, 47B 1) and to have been presumed by Eurytus (DK, 45, no.3). In the latter half of the fifth century the problem of human knowledge was discussed widely enough in terms of truth and appearance (*doxa*). There should be nothing surprising in its emergence, well before the time of Plato, among the fifth-century Pythagoreans.[21]

Testimonia from later antiquity furnish an abundance of details about Pythagorean doctrines and practices. It is impossible to weave all the information into one coherent fabric of thought. The influence of the Pythagoreans on subsequent Greek philosophy, however, was profound and lasting. They brought to the fore the possibility and even the necessity of providing a quantitative explanation of the cosmos. In doing so they presented a lead and a challenge that thinkers coming after them could not ignore. There can be little doubt, in view of the reports of Aristotle and the fragments attributed to Philolaus, that at least some of them identified the natures of things with the mathematical characteristics exhibited by those things. This would be somewhat after the manner in which a modern physicist, because he can give a quantitative explanation of any sensible phenomenon, may be tempted to think that no other kind of explanation is required. That was the challenge emerging from Pythagorean philosophy. It was met, all too devastatingly, by the overpowering emphasis placed by Aristotle upon the basic role of substantial principles in explaining natural things. Quantity, in the Aristotelian setting, was merely an accident. Its principles, though fully recognized in their own order, could not be expected to provide the ultimate account of natural things. The lead given by the Pythagoreans, however, continued to exert a certain influence throughout the course of Greek thought, though only centuries after the close

[21] D. H. T. Vollenhoven, *Geschiedenis der Wijsbegeerte,* Vol I (Franeker, 1950), p. 465, locates the epistemology of the Philolaus fragments as between Empedocles and Plato.

of antiquity did it blossom into the fullness of its power to explain the natural phenomena.[22]

Pythagorean interest in the virtuous life may be presumed to have stimulated much discussion on the virtues. Details, however, are lacking, except that the Pythagorean treatment of them was mathematical, not ethical. To find the beginnings of a specifically ethical inquiry, that is, in terms of human habituation rather than of rigid mathematical or other theoretical principles, one must look elsewhere. These beginnings are to be found in the scroll of the great Ephesian sage, Heraclitus.

SELECTED READINGS AND REFERENCES

I. Bywater, "On the Fragments Attributed to Philolaus the Pythagorean," *JP*, I (1868), 21-53.

Sir Thomas Heath, *A History of Greek Mathematics* (Oxford: Clarendon Press, 1921), I, 65-117; 141-169.

F. M. Cornford, "Mysticism and Science in the Pythagorean Tradition," *CQ* XVI (1922), 137-150; XVII (1923), 1-12.

R. Mondolfo, "Sui Frammenti di Filolao," *Rivista di Filologia e d'Istruzione Classica*, LXV (1937), 225-245. Also in E. Zeller-R. Mondolfo, *La Filosofia dei Greci* (Florence: "La Nuova Italia," 1932-1938), II, 367-382.

Kurt v. Fritz, *Pythagorean Politics in Southern Italy* (New York: Columbia University Press, 1940).

W. A. Heidel, "The Pythagoreans and Greek Mathematics," *AJP*, LXI (1940), 1-33.

Edwin LeRoy Minar, *Early Pythagorean Politics* (Baltimore: Waverly Press, 1942).

Vincenzo Capparelli, *La Sapienza di Pitagora*, 2 vols. (Padua: Cedam, 1941-1944).

John Earle Raven, *Pythagoreans and Eleatics* (Cambridge, Eng.: University Press, 1948).

G. B. Burch, "The Counter-Earth," *Osiris*, XI (1954), 267-294.

J. S. Morrison, "Pythagoras of Samos," *CQ*, L (1956), 135-156.

[22] "The pioneering work of Pythagoras and his school in this field was continued by Plato and the mathematicians of the Hellenistic era, and finally given a new significance by Galileo, Kepler and mathematical physics from Newton to our own day." S. Sambursky, *The Physical World of the Greeks* (London, 1956), p. 26. "This Pythagorean conception is the starting-point from which our modern mathematization of physical phenomena developed." *Ibid.*, p. 28.

[CHAPTER 3]

The Beginnings of Moral Philosophy

HERACLITUS OF EPHESUS (*FL. CA.* 500 B.C.)

Chronology. Heraclitus refers to Pythagoras, Xenophanes, and the Milesian geographer Hecataeus, in the past tense (*Fr.* 40). This would place him in a period when Pythagoras and Xenophanes had already become well-known, and after the reputation of Hecataeus, who was active in political life during the first decade of the fifth century B.C., had been established. So the *floruit* of Heraclitus cannot be placed much before 500 B.C. Actually, the sixty-ninth Olympiad (504-501 B.C.) is the dating given in traditional Greek chronology. Whether this dating is artificial (i.e., forty years after Xenophanes) or not, there is no special reason for questioning it. Diogenes Laertius records further that Heraclitus died at the age of sixty (IX,1;3. DK, 22A 1).

Life. Except for the very approximate date of his *floruit* and an indication that he belonged to one of the ruling families of Ephesus, a flourishing city on the Ionian coast north of Miletus and opposite the island of Samos, nothing is known with certainty about Heraclitus' life. The many stories handed down about him furnish no further reliable information. Most of them seem to have been invented to illustrate characteristics that emerge clearly enough from the extant fragments of his work. This is especially noticeable in regard to his haughty, extremely aristocratic temperament: "The best men choose one thing rather than all else: everlasting fame rather than things mortal. The majority are satisfied, like well-fed cattle."[1] He speaks as though he were entirely out of sympathy with the prevalent democratic move-

---

[1] *Fr.* 29; tr. Freeman. *Cf. Frs.* 24 and 49.

41

ments, roundly condemning his fellow citizens for expelling "Hermodorus, the most valuable man among them, saying: 'Let us not have
even one valuable man; but if we do, let him go elsewhere and live
among others'" (*Fr.* 121; tr. Freeman). He implies forcefully enough
that democracy is not the only possible kind of government: "To obey
the will of one is also law (*nomos*)" (*Fr.* 33). He also castigates in
bitingly sarcastic phrases the leading figures of the Greek intellectual
world.[2]

Another characteristic seen in his work earned for Heraclitus the
traditional name of the "dark" (*skoteinos, tenebrosus*) philosopher. The
earliest extant explanation of this epithet is found in Cicero,[3] who says
that it was given him because he commented very obscurely on nature.
The pathetic legend of Heraclitus as "the weeping philosopher," who
used to shed tears of sadness whenever he appeared in public, can be
traced back no further than to Sotion, the teacher of Seneca, and seems
to rest quite apparently on a misunderstanding of a technical Peripatetic term used by Theophrastus. Theophrastus remarked that the
broken and unfinished character of Heraclitus' writings on nature was
due to his impulsiveness or restlessness, but the term he used was
later understood in its ordinary sense of "melancholy."[4]

Writings.   Over one hundred fragments have survived from what
the ancients read on the scroll of Heraclitus. These fragments have a
style peculiarly their own, a style that is terse, incisive, and *oracular*,
with a rounded phrasing and a lapidary character that render para-
phrasing or summarizing difficult. It makes frequent and forceful use
of play on words. The style suggests pointedly enough that Heraclitus,
in the manner of his age, was speaking in the role of a prophet who had
a specially inspired truth to manifest to his people. The oracular note
in the fragments is an important consideration for their interpretation.
Here, as elsewhere among the Greek philosophers, literary form cannot
safely be separated from content in probing the meaning of philosophical texts.

The function of an oracle for Heraclitus is sketched plainly enough

---

[2] See *Frs.* 40, 42, 56, 81, 104, 106, and 129. *Cf. Fr.* 70. On the basis of
Fr. 121, K. Reinhardt, *Parmenides und die Geschichte der Griechischen
Philosophie* (Bonn, 1916), p. 157, dates the scroll of Heraclitus as quite
some time after 478 B.C. The indication was also used by Zeller, *Philosophie
der Griechen*, 6th ed. (Leipzig, 1920), I (2), 786.

[3] *De Fin.*, II,5,15. In the third century B.C. the Skeptic satirist Timon of
Phlius had referred to Heraclitus as enigmatic or riddling (D.L., IX,6;
DK, 22A 1).

[4] See G. S. Kirk, *Heraclitus: The Cosmic Fragments* (Cambridge, Eng.,
1954), p. 8; Cora E. Lutz, "Democritus and Heraclitus," *Classical Journal*,
XLIX (1954), 309-314.

in one of his fragments: "The lord whose oracle is at Delphi neither speaks nor conceals, but indicates."[5] The oracular style of the fragments proclaims sufficiently that they express their meaning as a whole, and strive to "indicate" or point out the truth rather than probe or analyze or elucidate it. Such a style is particularly adapted to the moralist or the preacher. It is hardly the manner of expression that would be selected by a man whose purpose was to give a physically scientific account of the cosmic processes.

The scroll of Heraclitus, after the manner of the times, apparently had no original title. Later titles were given it by different editors or commentators. One of these titles characterizes it as a work on nature, others as a guide to moral conduct. The notion that it was meant to be a work on nature quite evidently stems from the doxographical tradition. Aristotle, in seeking traces of his own material cause among his predecessors, mentioned that Thales made the first principle of cosmic generation water, Anaximenes air, and "Heraclitus the Ephesian . . . fire."[6] In this setting the doxographers grouped Heraclitus among the natural philosophers. On the other hand, an ancient grammarian named Diodotus, who wrote a commentary on the scroll, gave it a moral title and declared expressly that it was not a treatise on nature but upon human conduct, and that the physical teachings in it have merely a paradigmatic role.[7]

The ancients regularly cited the work of Heraclitus as though it had the form of a continuous prose composition. It was a *syggramma* or a *logos*. The notion of a continuous path by which the scroll was traversed is apparent in an ancient, probably Stoic, epigram: "Do not be in a hurry to unwind to the centre-stick the roll of Heraclitus the Ephesian; the path is hard indeed to traverse. There is gloom and unrelieved darkness; but if an initiate lead you, it shines more brightly than the shining sun."[8] According to the testimonia, it appeared confused,

[5] *Fr.* 93; tr. Freeman. *Cf. Fr.* 92. Diogenes Laertius (IX,6; DK, 22A 1) mentions that the scroll of Heraclitus was placed in the temple of Artemis.
[6] *Metaph.*, A 3,984a7-8; *cf. Fr.* 90, *infra*, n. 28. DK, 18A 7.
[7] D.L., IX,15; *cf. ibid.*, no. 12. The term used is *politeia*, understood, as the title shows clearly enough, not in the sense of constitution or government, but in its meaning of the daily life of a citizen, or ethical living in general. *Cf.* Polybius, XVIII,43,6; *NT, Eph.*, II,12, *Phil.*, I,27 and III,20; Eusebius, *Eccl.Hist.*, VI,19,7.
[8] D.L., IX,16; tr. Kirk, *Cosmic Fragments*, p. 11. *Cf.* the reported impression of Socrates: "The part I understand is excellent, and so too is, I dare say, the part I do not understand; but it needs a Delian diver to get to the bottom of it." D.L., II,22; tr. Hicks. *Cf. ibid.*, IX,12. On the influence of Heraclitus upon the style of subsequent writers, see Eduard Norden, *Die Antike Kunstprosa* (2nd impression, Leipzig and Berlin, 1909), pp. 18-24.

obscure, and incomplete when read by those looking for physical doctrines; but at times it made itself so clear and illuminating that even the dullest could *easily* understand it and derive from it elevation of soul.[9] These descriptions point to some kind of a unified prose composition, probably rich in pithy apothegms or even including one or more collections of them. Ancient testimony does not support a modern conjecture that Heraclitus merely gave oral expression to a number of catchy and so easily remembered sayings that were collected and written down by admirers only after his death. The two fragments known to have been located at the beginning of the work (*Frs.* 1 & 2), moreover, are in continuous prose. They seem meant to introduce a discourse written in the same way, rather than a haphazard collection of disjointed sayings.

However, in spite of all these indications of a unified discourse, the extant fragments defy all efforts at arranging them in any systematic doctrinal order. One is dependent today on the first two fragments, whose location at the beginning of the scroll is known from ancient testimony, for over-all information about the type of treatise that they were meant to introduce. In them the key notions and the character in general of the discourse have to be sought. These notions may then be followed up through the other fragments that mention them. There seems to be no more satisfactory manner of approaching the texts of Heraclitus today.

PHILOSOPHICAL TEACHINGS

Moral Message. The opening words of the initial fragment have been understood by commentators in widely varying ways. If they are taken in the natural sense that they would have at the time in commencing a scroll, they can refer only to the treatise or discourse or prophetic message (*logos*) that one is about to read: "The following *logos,* ever true, men are found incapable of understanding, both before they hear it and when they once have heard it. For although all things take place in accordance with this *logos,* they seem like people of no experience, when they make experience of such words and deeds as I set forth, distinguishing each according to its nature and declaring how it is. But the rest of men do not know what they are doing after they

---

[9] D.L., IX,7. On Theophrastus' comment, see Jula Kerschensteiner, "Der Bericht des Theophrast über Heraklit," *Hermes,* LXXXIII (1955), 385-411.

have awakened, just as they forget what they do while asleep."[10] What Heraclitus is undertaking to explain, accordingly, is the true nature of "words and deeds." This formula could suggest the epic goal of human conduct, which was to be "a speaker of words and a doer of deeds."[11] All things, Heraclitus proclaims, take place according to the truth that he is propounding, yet men are not able to understand it, even after hearing it announced. The rest of men, those not fortunate enough to hear read to them the message of Heraclitus, are living merely in a dream world, unaware of what they are doing in their waking hours. The fragment quite patently seems meant to introduce a discourse proclaiming how men should act when they are awake, or how conscious human conduct is to be directed.

The Common Wisdom. The second fragment, apparently drawing the consequence of the first, and exploiting a similarity in the Greek word forms, continues: "Therefore one should follow the common; but though the *logos* is common, the many live as though they had a private wisdom."[12] The theme is still how men should conduct their lives. To avoid living in a private and meaningless dream world, they are urged to direct their lives according to the common wisdom set forth in the Heraclitean message, even though they have failed to understand it through their own experience and still do not understand it right away

[10] *Fr.* 1; *cf. Frs.* 34, and 21, 26, 71, 72, 73, 117. (In *Fr.* 72, *logos* is a later addition; *cf.* Kirk, pp. 44, 47). The contemporary use of *logos* for an oracular response may be seen in Pindar, *Pythian Odes,* IV,59. *Logos* in the first fragment has often been interpreted in sense of a cosmic law or reason, a sense that is unknown before Stoic times. The meaning given to *logos* here, however, need not seriously affect the understanding of Heraclitus' doctrine, since the content of the *logos* in either case is the same. The term *logos* is used in several other senses in the fragments (*Frs.* 31, 39, 45, 87, 108, 115), all commonly recognized meanings at the time. It seems very unlikely the Heraclitus intended to give without any explanation at all a new meaning to the term, a meaning that would be strange to the men of his age. See O. Gigon, *Untersuchungen zu Heraklit* (Leipzig, 1935), pp. 1-4.

[11] *Iliad,* IX, 443. See W. W. Jaeger, *Paideia* (tr. Highet), I,6-7. What appears to be a paraphrase in *Fr.* 112 reads: ". . . wisdom is to speak the truth and to act according to nature, paying heed (*thereto*)"; tr. Freeman. Similarly *Fr.* 73: "We must not act and speak like men asleep"; tr. Freeman. The Homeric formula, however, in the wording used by Heraclitus, could have the meaning of word and thought in general; see R. Schottlaender, "Drei Vorsokratische Topoi," *Hermes,* LXII (1927), 444-446.

[12] *Fr.* 2. *Fr.* 89 seems to be a paraphrase. *Cf. Fr.* 17.

when it is proclaimed to them in words. Heraclitus means that the capacity to attain wisdom is common to all,[13] but that the quest is difficult and laborious,[14] and so men have to be goaded on with blows to the proper pastures of their souls.[15] He takes upon himself the task of driving men to the pursuit of moral wisdom by his bitter tongue-lashings.

The Common Unity. The opening fragments, accordingly, introduce a *logos* containing a message of moral wisdom. They focus attention upon the solidarity experienced through living in the common world of men, as opposed to the dreamlike isolation of a life separated from one's surroundings. The message is raised above the status of the private wisdom of anyone, even of Heraclitus: "Having listened, not to me, but to the *logos*, it is wise to agree (*homo*LOG*ein*) that all things are one." (*Fr.* 50). What is this wisdom, which reveals the unity of all things? It is the ability to see the all-pervading unity of common direction in which things are guided: "What is wise is one thing, to understand rightly how all things are steered through all."[16] It is not the detailed learning accumulated by the traditional teachers of Greece: "Much learning does not teach one to have intelligence; for it would have taught Hesiod and Pythagoras, and again, Xenophanes and Hecataeus" (*Fr.* 40; tr. Freeman). Yet it requires extensive research into the multiple facts with which it is concerned: "Men who love wisdom must be inquirers into very many things indeed."[17] It appears, therefore, to be *practical* knowledge.

In true Greek fashion Heraclitus locates the unity of moral life in the common activity of the city-state, in which the individual life of each citizen is merged. But the Ephesian sage finds the roots of this life in a subsoil far deeper than the unity of a city-state. He sees it ultimately based upon the one common direction and governance that wisdom shows running through all things: "Those who are speaking with intelligence must find their strength in what is common to all, as a city-state in its law, and

---

[13] See paraphrases in *Frs.* 113 and 116. *Cf.* also *Fr.* 16.
[14] *Frs.* 22 and 123.
[15] *Fr.* 11. On the interpretations, see Kirk, *Cosmic Fragments*, p. 262.
[16] *Fr.* 41. *Cf. Frs.* 64 and 66.
[17] *Fr.* 35; tr. Freeman. *Cf. Frs.* 47 and 55. If the word "philosophers" or "lovers of wisdom" in *Fr.* 35 is genuine, the fragment is the oldest extant passage in which the term occurs.

much more strongly. For all human laws are nourished by one, the divine. For it prevails as far as it wishes, and is sufficient for all and superabounds."[18] The common wisdom that pervades the universe is in this way characterized as divine, whether or not one cares to personify it in the traditional mythology: "That which alone is wise is one; it is willing and unwilling to be called by the name of Zeus" (*Fr.* 32; tr. Freeman). Just as day and night form the one twenty-four-hour cycle, winter and summer the one year, so the opposites are contained in the all-pervading unity of the common or divine: "God is day night, winter summer, war peace, satiety hunger, and undergoes alteration in the way that (*fire?*) when it is mixed with spices is named according to the scent of each of them."[19]

Unity of Opposites. This unity of direction in the manifold tensions of the universe is difficult for men to see: "They do not apprehend how being at variance it agrees with itself: there is a connexion working in both directions, as in the bow and the lyre" (*Fr.* 51; tr. Kirk). As the coincidence of pulls in opposite directions makes possible both the shooting of the arrow and the playing of the lyre, so in the ordered universe is unity brought about by the required balance of opposite tensions. In the cosmos, however, the all-pervasive connection of tensions is deeply concealed: "The real constitution of things is accustomed to hide itself" (*Fr.* 123; tr. Kirk). Yet it is much more effective, for: "An unapparent connexion is stronger than an apparent" (*Fr.* 54; tr. Kirk). This persistent unity can be maintained amidst the ever-different and continually varying multiplicity of circumstances only by what appears to be continual change of direction, just as to keep expressing the same continuous thought when writing, one's hand has to go up and down, back and forth, and round about: "Of letters [*or* of writers] the way is straight and crooked; it is one and the same."[20] Life, accordingly, should not be allowed to stagnate in the rigid molds fixed by tradition: "(*We must not*

---

[18] *Fr.* 114. *Cf. Frs.* 43 and 44. *Fr.* 114, like *Frs.* 1 and 2, plays on the Greek word for "common."

[19] *Fr.* 67; following tr. Kirk, *Cosmic Fragments*, p. 184. *Cf. Fr.* 57. H. Fränkel, *Tr. Am. Philol. Assn.*, LXIX (1938), 230-244, suggests "oil" instead of "fire" for the missing word.

[20] *Fr.* 59; tr. Kirk, *Cosmic Fragments*, p. 97. In the same context was quoted *Fr.* 60: "The way up and down is one and the same."

act like) children of our parents."[21] Rather, like a mixed drink, one's life must be continually shaken up and down, back and forth, in varying directions, if it is to keep up its unity and balance: "The 'mixed drink' also separates if it is not stirred."[22] Consequently, in restless strife and war lies the abiding condition of unity in an ordered universe: "One must know that war is common and right is strife and that all things are happening by strife and necessity."[23]

Relativity. The things that form the poles in this strife and tension, accordingly, take on what may be directly opposite aspects as they come into different relations with their environment: "Sea is water most pure and most polluted; for fish it is drinkable and life giving; for men, undrinkable and destructive" (*Fr.* 61), and "Donkeys prefer chaff to gold."[24] Even in relation to the same individual, according as he is differently disposed at different times, does the judgment of what is good change: "Disease makes health pleasant and good, hunger satisfaction, weariness rest."[25] Every day brings its differences: "The sun is new each day" (*Fr.* 6; tr. Freeman). For the same individual continuing in the same course of life the proximate circumstances are ceaselessly changing: "Upon those who step into the same rivers different and again different waters flow."[26] In the world in

---

[21] *Fr.* 74; tr. Freeman. Yves Battistini, *Héraclite d'Ephèse* (Paris, 1948), p. 46, adds to the fragment "tradition, terre dénuée"; *cf. ibid.*, p. 21.

[22] *Fr.* 125; tr. Freeman. The term for "stirred" is the usual Greek word for motion. *Cf. Fr.* 84a: "It rests by changing"; tr. Jaeger, *Paideia*, I, 182. *Cf.* also *Fr.* 10 and the context of *Fr.* 65.

[23] *Fr.* 80; tr. Kirk, *Cosmic Fragments,* p. 238. *Cf. Fr.* 53. Heraclitus is said (Aristotle, *E E,* VII 1,1235a25-28) to have rebuked Homer for wishing that strife be removed from the world, for its removal would destroy the world order.

[24] *Fr.* 9; tr. Freeman. *Cf. Frs.* 4, 7, 13(37), and 29.

[25] *Fr.* 111; tr. Freeman. *Cf. Frs.* 48, 56, 57, 58, 79, 124, and the paraphrases in *Frs.* 82 and 83. *Fr.* 23 implies that opposites are required for the cognition of opposites.

[26] *Fr.* 12; tr. Kirk. *Cf. Frs.* 49a and 91. The words "we are and we are not" in *Fr.* 49a seem to be a later gloss; see Kirk, *Cosmic Fragments,* p. 373. On the Bywater *Fr.* 41, see W. G. Rabinowitz and W. I. Matson, "Heraclitus as Cosmologist," *Review of Metaphysics,* X (1956), 251-254. For further discussion of the river fragments, see G. Vlastos, *AJP,* LXXVI (1955), 338-344; G. S. Kirk, *Museum Helveticum,* XIV (1957), 162-163. *Fr.* 12 is restricted to human life by Aimé Patri, "Note sur la Symbolique Héraclitéenne de l'Eau et du Feu," *Revue de Métaphysique et de Morale,* LXIII (1958), 129-134.

which one lives the change from opposite to opposite characteristics is perpetually going on: "Cold things warm themselves,
warm cools, moist dries, parched is made wet" (*Fr. 126*; tr. Kirk).

Regulative Medium. The unremitting process of change,
nevertheless, takes place eternally according to fixed measures:
"This (world-) order did none of gods or men make, but it always
was and is and shall be: an ever-living fire, kindling in measures
and going out in measures."[27] Fire, so mobile in character, is
viewed as the medium of exchange that regulates all the changes,
just as money functions in the market: "All things are an equal
exchange for fire and fire for all things, as goods are for gold and
gold for goods."[28] This is understood in the sense that fire changes
into the other things: "Fire's changes: first sea; and of the sea,
the half is earth, the half lightning-flash" (*Fr. 31*; tr. Kirk). Fire
itself is the governing and regulative force in the universe:
"Thunderbolt"—understood in the sense of fire—"steers all
things."[29] There does not seem to be anything supersensible,
therefore, in Heraclitus' understanding of the cosmic guiding
force.

Affective Basis. The common unity throughout all these
changes is perceived by wisdom. But that power of understanding
is not based upon any merely human way of living and acting,
but upon a higher way that is termed divine: "For human *êthos*
does not have right judgments, but divine (*êthos*) has" (*Fr. 78*).
Moral opposites arise only from the viewpoints that men set up
for themselves, not from the divine: "To god all things are beautiful and good and just, but men have supposed some things to be
unjust, others just."[30] Accordingly, the training and education of
the Greek *paideia* are necessary in order to make proper use of
sensible and traditional knowledge: "The eyes and ears are bad
witnesses for men if they have barbarian souls" (*Fr. 107*; tr. Free-

---

[27] *Fr. 30*; tr. Kirk. *Cf. Fr. 94*. On the testimonia concerning the periodical
world-conflagration, see R. Mondolfo, "Evidence of Plato and Aristotle re-
lating to the *Ekpyrosis* in Heraclitus," *Phronesis*, III (1958), 75-82.

[28] *Fr. 90*; tr. Kirk. Fire, accordingly, does not play the role of a "first principle" of cosmic generation for Heraclitus. Rather, like any point in the
circumference of a circle (*cf. Fr. 103*), it functions always as the common
beginning and end of the particular processes.

[29] *Fr. 64. Cf. Fr. 66*.

[30] *Fr. 102*; tr. Kirk. *Cf. Fr. 67*.

man). A man's character and habituation are therefore the basis of his destiny: "*Êthos* for a man is his guiding genius (*daimon*)" (*Fr.* 119). This implies, then, that the affective basis of wisdom provides the means of seeing all things from the divine viewpoint. It shows why men are so slow at attaining wisdom: "(*Most of what is divine*) escapes recognition through unbelief."[31] Hence arises the need for probing one's own disposition in accordance with the traditional Greek moral precept of self-knowledge, expressed by Heraclitus in the words: "I sought out myself" (*Fr.* 101).

The Soul. The soul is conceived by Heraclitus in a quite material manner, as a sort of nature like fire or air: "A dry (desiccated) soul is the wisest and best" (*Fr.* 118; tr. Freeman). Hence drunkenness is bad, for it is harmful to the dry nature of the soul: "A man, when he gets drunk, is led stumbling along by an immature boy, not knowing where he is going, having his soul wet" (*Fr.* 117; tr. Freeman). The depths of the soul, nevertheless, cannot be fully penetrated: "You would not by your going discover the limits of soul though you traveled over every path, so deep has it a measure."[32] Souls survive after death, at least for a while, and receive their appropriate recompense: "There await men after they are dead things which they do not expect or imagine."[33]

Beneath the mordant phrasing of the Heraclitean fragments lies an astonishingly rich treasure of penetrating moral insight and truly philosophical vision. This wisdom, however, becomes apparent only after prolonged reflection on their contents and sympathetic effort at grasping what they signifiy as a whole. Technical precisions are useless in interpreting them. Any attempts, for instance, to distinguish between what Heraclitus means by "wisdom" and "knowledge" and other such words can only cloud the issue. The fragments just *indicate* vividly, they do not analyze or systematize. Careful study of what the words and imagery used in the fragments meant to the readers of the time is of course

---

[31] *Fr.* 86; tr. Freeman. *Cf. Fr.* 18 and the context of *Fr.* 19. In Pindar, *Nemean Odes*, VIII, 35-36, an *êthos* is something to be prayed for.

[32] *Fr.* 45. *Cf. Fr.* 115.

[33] *Fr.* 27; tr. Freeman. *Cf. Frs.* 25 and 63. See G. S. Kirk, *AJP*, LXX (1949), 387-390.

necessary to guard as far as possible against arbitrary or merely subjective interpretations. But after such preliminary information has been acquired, one can but ponder over the fragments and strive to grasp their meaning globally.

So approached, the fragments reveal a surprisingly keen grasp of the basic problem in moral science. How may a consistent and abiding norm be had in a realm where incessantly changing circumstances always affect the morality of human conduct? Heraclitus saw clearly that the particular opposites were not in themselves the determining factor. Rather, particular things are continually passing over from one aspect to the opposite. What is good at one time or for one individual becomes bad at other times or for other individuals. A persisting balanced tension among opposites in those ever-changing particulars is what has to be attained and preserved. This can be done only by continually adapting the course of one's conduct to the ever-deviating mold of the circumstances. Only in this ever-varying way may consistently virtuous conduct be achieved. The measure or mean remains constant, even though from any particular point of view all that appears is change from one opposite to another. In fact, it is only such unceasing change that makes stability and unity possible in the moral order. Accordingly, wisdom, which attains things from the common or divine viewpoint, does not consist in detailed knowledge of particular things. It is not something merely theoretical or static. It is a dynamic grasp of one's own continually changing relations to and activity in the surrounding common world. Hence emerges the basic role that one's own habituation as well as momentary disposition will play in this practical knowledge.

These fundamental considerations are taken up and developed highly by Plato and Aristotle, though with no traceable dependence on their first and incisive formulation by the early Ionian thinker. With Heraclitus, indeed, the technical terminology for distinguishing practical from theoretical knowledge, and the details of how the mean sets up all the moral virtues, are not as yet developed. But the Ephesian has taken the traditional Greek morality of "Know thyself" and "Nothing in excess" and has explained it with genuine philosophical depth. In so doing he has attempted to establish what the surrounding world has to be like if it serves as the theater in which human conduct understood in this way takes place. It has to be a region of continued and ever-varying change, change that alone enables it to preserve a consistent and enduring pattern, a common that merges with the notion of the divine. This common pattern men should always be experiencing in their daily lives, though as a matter of fact they appear unaware of it and find it hard to understand even after it has been explained and inculcated through the prophetic Heraclitean message. The Milesians had projected upon outside reality the notion of the vital functioning that they experienced within themselves. Heraclitus is projecting rather the moral activity of which he is conscious within himself, and after its pattern he is explaining the processes and constitution of the whole external world. He has, true enough, a doctrine of fire changing into all other things. But rather than looking upon that fire as a primal matrix from which the cosmos grew, Heraclitus is regarding it as the basic medium that allows in an unoriginated universe the ever-deviating type of changes required by his conception of moral conduct.

The Ephesian sage was classed as a "sporadic" philosopher, for he had no recognizable predecessor in his own type of thinking, and left no known disciples. Later in the fifth century there were men who were referred to as Heracliteans or as having Heraclitizing tendencies. Plato remarked that they grew spontaneously of themselves, without learning their doctrines from anyone.[34] They claimed that there is only flux, with no stability whatsoever, not even such as would allow the fixed meanings of words necessary for the use of ordinary language. Their teaching was summed up in the formula "All things are flowing" (*panta rei*).[35] The ones whom Plato had in mind seem to have been fifth-century Sophists like Protagoras and Cratylus. Eclectic and practically-minded teachers of that sort may well have invoked

---

[34] *Tht.* 180BC. On the doctrinal affinities of the "Heracliteans" with Parmenides' conception of the cosmos, see Reinhardt, *Parmenides*, pp. 241-247.

[35] See *Cra.*, 439C. Aristotle (*Metaph.*, Γ 5,1010a12-15; DK, 65, no. 4) describes Cratylus as blaming Heraclitus for saying that you could not step twice into the same river, maintaining himself that you could not step into the *same* river even once. Such a "Heraclitean" realized clearly enough that the doctrine of the Ephesian did not exclude sameness and permanence. Cf. Plato, *Cra.*, 402A; DK, 22A 6.

the patronage of the celebrated Ephesian for some of their doctrines. But the outright denial of stability and the lack of confidence in the fixity of ordinary speech cry out against any genuine descent of such later doctrines from the thought of Heraclitus himself.

Aristotle, against the background of this "universal flux" interpretation, looked upon Heraclitus as denying the first principle of demonstration, namely, that a thing can be and not be in the same respects at the same time. Yet the instance he cites from Heraclitus for such a denial is the statement that the good and the bad are the same,[36] understanding this in the sense that goodness and badness are identical. In the fragments themselves, however, Heraclitus means evidently enough that a particular thing may be good in one set of circumstances and bad in another set. He is in no way denying the stability of the notions themselves. Fixed notions of all the opposites are in fact required by the measured balance of tensions that constitutes the all-pervading unity and persistence of the Hercalitean cosmos. But in view of their own emphasis on the "universal flux" interpretation, there need be little wonder that Plato and Aristotle did not seek to ground expressly their own moral doctrines upon the foundations already established by the great Ephesian sage.

The Stoics saw in the Heraclitean identification of fire and wisdom the outlines of their own doctrine of the cosmic *logos,* and gave that meaning, till then unknown, to the term *logos* in the opening fragments of the scroll. Christians like Saint Justin Martyr and Clement of Alexandria greatly admired Heraclitus for his moral standards, while the third-century ecclesiastic Hippolytus regarded him as a fount of heresy. Modern writers still disagree widely over the worth and the character of his sayings. All this testifies to something perennial about his wisdom, and points to a philosophical depth that assures for Heraclitus one of the foremost positions in the history of Western thought. The fragments that remain from his *logos* or scroll may still be pondered over, not as a historical curiosity nor merely for their influence on the development of other thinkers, but for the intellectual profit to be derived from the intrinsic wealth of their own proper content. They offer a consistent and thought-provoking

[36] *Top.,* VIII 5,159b30-33; *Ph.,* I 2,185b20-25.

interpretation of a common world in which the accepting of birth
and life involves the accepting of death (*Fr.* 20). They are amply
sufficient both in number and in content to establish the position
of their author not as a cosmologist in the Milesian tradition nor
as a metaphysician of universal flux, but as a profound moralist,
in fact as the first moralist[37] in the western world whose teachings
were developed on a genuinely philosophical plane.

SELECTED READINGS AND REFERENCES

Heracliti Ephesii Reliquiae, ed. Ingram Bywater (Oxford: Clarendon
Press, 1877). English tr. by G. T. W. Patrick, *The Fragments of
the Work of Heraclitus of Ephesus on Nature* (Baltimore: N. Murray,
1889).

W. A. Heidel, "On Certain Fragments of the Pre-Socratics," *Proceedings
of the American Academy of Arts and Sciences,* XLVIII (1913),
695-716.

H. Fränkel, "A Thought Pattern in Heraclitus," *AJP,* LIX (1938), 309-
337.

————, "Heraclitus on God and the Phenomenal World," *Transactions
of the American Philological Association,* LXIX (1938), 230- 244.

E. L. Minar, "The Logos of Heraclitus," *Class. Phil.,* XXXIV, (1939),
323-341.

William C. Kirk, *Fire in the Cosmological Speculations of Heraclitus*
(Minneapolis: Burgess Publishing Co., 1940).

W. J. Verdenius, "Notes on the Presocratics," *Mnemosyne,* 3a ser., XIII
1947), 271-284.

Geoffrey Stephen Kirk, "Heraclitus and Death in Battle," *AJP,* LXX
(1949), 384-393.

————, "Natural Change in Heraclitus," *Mind,* N. S. LX (1951), 35-
42.

————, *Heraclitus: The Cosmic Fragments* (Cambridge, Eng.: University
Press, 1954).

————, "Men and Opposites in Heraclitus," *Museum Helveticum,* XIV
(1957), 155-163.

[37] ". . . il *moralista* (forse il primo moralista ellenico . . .)" C. Mazzantini,
Eraclito (Torino, 1945), p. 24. "Heraclitus is the first thinker who not only
wishes to know the truth but also holds that this knowledge will renew
men's lives." W. W. Jaeger, *Theology,* p. 113. ". . . the real motive of
Heraclitus' philosophy: not mere curiosity about nature (although this was
doubtless present too) but the belief that man's very life is indissociably bound
up with his whole surroundings." Kirk-Raven, *The Presocratic Philosophers,*
pp. 204-205.

P. Merlan, "Ambiguity in Heraclitus," *Proceedings of the XIth International Congress of Philosophy* (Amsterdam [North-Holland Publishing Co.] and Louvain: E. Nauwelaerts, 1953), XII, 56-60.

G. Vlastos, "On Heraclitus," *AJP*, LXXVI (1955), 337-368.

J. Owens, "The Interpretation of the Heraclitean Fragments," in *An Étienne Gilson Tribute,* ed. Charles J. O'Neill (Milwaukee: Marquette University Press, 1959), pp. 148-168.

[CHAPTER 4]

The Beginnings of Metaphysics

PARMENIDES OF ELEA (*FL. CA.* 485 B.C.?)

Chronology. On three different occasions in his dialogues Plato[1] refers to a meeting of Parmenides of Elea with Socrates. At the time of the meeting Parmenides is described as an old man of about sixty-five, and Socrates as still very young. There is no other definite testimony about such a visit of Parmenides to Athens. Plato, however, makes the settings of his dialogues quite realistic. There seems to be no reason why among all the early philosophers he should single out Parmenides for a dramatic meeting with Socrates if a *glaring* anachronism could in this case be tolerated. On the other hand, he need not have been prevented from using dramatic liberties[2] to stretch the respective ages of Parmenides and Socrates by a few years each. Socrates, already able to carry on a philosophical conversation with Parmenides, can hardly be considered as much less than sixteen at the time. Allowing him seventy years of age at the time of his execution in 399 B.C., one has to date the dramatic meeting somewhere between 455 and 450 B.C. As Parmenides is represented as being about sixty-five, he would have had his *floruit* twenty-five years earlier, 480-475 B.C. Even conceding Plato the dramatic liberty of making Socrates a few years older and Parmenides a few years younger than they really were at the time, one can hardly push back the *floruit* with this criterion much further than 485 B.C.

That dating, however, is still not early enough to coincide with the chronology handed down by Diogenes Laertius (IX, 23; DK, 28A 1), which places the *floruit* of Parmenides in the sixty-ninth Olympiad

---

[1] *Prm.*, 127A; *Tht.*, 183E; *Sph.*, 217C. DK, 28 A 5.
[2] In the *Menexenus* an anachronism of some seventeen years is permitted. This anachronism is understandable enough in the circumstances of the dialogue; for an explanation, see Pamela M. Huby, "The *Menexenus* Reconsidered," *Phronesis*, II (1957), 110-111.

(504-501 B.C.), the same as for Heraclitus. The colony of Elea had been founded in 540-539 B.C. on the west coast of the Italian peninsula somewhat to the south of the Gulf of Salerno by refugees from Phocaea, the most northern city of Ionia. Apparently the date of its foundation was set by the chronologists as the *floruit* of Xenophanes, who was considered to be the founder of Eleatic philosophy. The *floruit* of the next in "succession," Parmenides, would accordingly be dated forty years after, so around 500 B.C., and that of the third, Zeno, still another forty years later, 460 B.C. Without confirming evidence, this dating seems too highly artificial to be at all acceptable.

Life. A sufficiently reliable Greek tradition states that Parmenides was an associate and follower of a Pythagorean named Ameinias, who introduced him to the life of thought. He was also represented as having taken an active part in the political life of Elea, and as having been one of its principal lawgivers. Belonging to a Phocaean colony, he would naturally have been brought up in a setting of traditional Ionian culture.

Writings. The only writing of Parmenides to which the ancients referred is his poem. In the sixth century A.D., about a thousand years after the Eleatic's time, Simplicius observed that copies of the poem were becoming rare, and accordingly he transcribed long sections of it in his own writings. These and other extant fragments are sufficient to show that the poem was composed as a literary whole, even though it may be looked upon as having three closely connected parts. The first is a sort of apocalyptic introduction now called the Proem. The second, of which an estimated nine-tenths has been preserved, was known in later antiquity as the section on Truth. The third part, of which conversely perhaps less than ten per cent has survived, was named the section on Opinion, that is, on things as they *appear* to men. These three parts are connected in the text in a way that makes them a single unified composition. They should be meant, therefore, to work out successively one continuous theme. All three may be expected to proceed from the same inspiration, and all three should be required for the understanding of Parmenides' message. That is the presumption suggested by the form of the Eleatic's work, and so is the presumption that is to be used in approaching the poem, at least until evidence from the content indicates a different procedure.

Why Parmenides expressed his philosophy in verse instead of the prose regularly used by the Ionians is not stated either in the poem or in the more ancient testimonia. Possible reasons can readily be suggested, but are difficult to establish with any certainty prior to a thorough study of the fragments. The impressiveness of the epic form in conveying an apocalyptic message, for instance, need not have been the compelling reason, since Heraclitus in a similar situation used prose. Even in antiquity it was remarked that the poetic form rendered obscure the presentation of the Eleatic's thought. In the present state of the text, uncertainties and ambiguities in important passages add to the difficulty of understanding it. The poem (*Fr.* 1.24) seems to introduce Parmenides as a youth, and in its general style and enthusiasm and utterly uncompromising spirit it tends to bear out the impression that it is the work of a comparatively young man, say in the middle thirties. This, as well as comparisons made with other Greek poetry, would suggest some time in the first decade of the fifth century as a likely date for its composition.[3] The evidence here, however, can hardly be considered as either definite or conclusive. As far as can be determined, the poem originally did not have any title. Later on it was referred to as *On Nature.*

Whatever the explanation may be for Parmenides' use of verse, the fact remains that his thought was expressed in poetic form. This point of form, in accordance with the general norm that content may not be separated from form in studying a Greek philosopher, can hardly be allowed to pass unnoticed in approaching the Eleatic's philosophy. It may quite reasonably be expected to have a pertinent meaning for the interpretation of his thought.

PHILOSOPHICAL TEACHINGS

A. *The Initiation to Parmenidean Doctrine*

The Road to the Goddess. The introduction or Proem of Parmenides' work follows the general manner of presentation used in Hesiod's *Theogony* (1-108), in which the goddesses appear to Hesiod at the foot of their sacred mountain and communicate to him what is "true" (28) about how the immortal gods came to be. In corresponding fashion Parmenides represents himself as being borne aloft into the presence of an unnamed goddess and inspired by her with knowledge of all things, both of the undaunted, convincing "Truth," and of the "Opinions of

---

[3] On its comparison with other Greek poetry, see C. M. Bowra, "The Proem of Parmenides," *Class. Phil.*, XXXII (1937), 97. W. J. Verdenius, "Notes on the Presocratics," *Mnemosyne*, XIII (1947), 285, arguing against the view that Parmenides was a young man at the time of writing the poem, would take the Greek term *Kouros* at *Fr.* 1.24 in the sense of "disciple" instead of "youth."

mortals," that is, of things as they appear[4] to mortal men. In these latter no true reliability is found, yet about them also Parmenides is to learn from the goddess, in order that he may understand how the world as it appears to men had to be extending in an acceptable way throughout the whole of reality.[5] The way of thinking to which Parmenides is initiated,[6] however, lies outside the pathway trodden by men. The goddess observes, nevertheless, that no sinister Fate is prompting him to travel over the new road, but, on the contrary, sanctioned Right and Justice (*Fr.* 1.26-28), as though a journey on it is something permissible and recommended.

The apocalyptic method of introduction, as well as the poetic symbols and images used in the poem, was in common circulation at the epoch and would readily be understood by the contemporary public. This indicates, accordingly, that there is nothing farfetched or unusual about Parmenides' approach to his subject. The literary form that he employed accords fully with the age in which he wrote.

[4] The meaning of the Greek term *doxai* here is much wider than "opinions." It includes the physical appearances themselves. See F. M. Cornford, "Parmenides' Two Ways," *CQ*, XXVII (1933), 100. In a word, the *doxai* are the world as it is present to men—"die Welt, so wie sie für die Menschen da ist." H. Schwabl, "Sein und Doxa bei Parmenides," *Wien. Stud.*, LXVI (1953), 59. On the text at *Fr.* 1.29, see G. Jameson, *Phronesis,* III (1958), 21-29.

[5] The correct interpretation of *Fr.* 1.31-32 is crucial for understanding the whole poem. On the explanation, see K. Reinhardt, *Parmenides und die Geschichte der Griechischen Philosophie* (Bonn, 1916), pp. 5-10; W.J. Verdenius, *Parmenides* (Groningen, 1942), 49-57; Jean Zafiropulo, *L' École Éléate* (Paris, 1950), 294-297; H. Schwabl, *loc. cit.;* J. Beaufret, *Le Poème de Parménide* (Paris, 1955), pp. 23-32. The emphasis is on the word "acceptable," on account of its position in the phrasing and its play in Greek on the word for "things that appear." The general notion seems to be that Parmenides is also to learn why reality had to appear to him and to other men in the way that it does, even though he now knows that it is whole and immobile. The knowing man "can't help *seeing* change, though he *knows* it isn't real . . ." G. Vlastos, *Tr. Am. Philol. Assn.*, LXXVII (1946), 71, n.38a. The term "real," however, when so denied to the world of appearance, has to be understood in the Eleatic sense of "being."

A mythological background for the contrast of the reliability of truth with the instability of things that appear, may be found in the contrast of the unshaken abode of the gods with the lack of that stability in human affairs, as described in the opening lines of Pindar's sixth Nemean Ode.

[6] On the notion implied here of initiation into the mysteries, see W. W. Jaeger, *Paideia*, I,176-177, and Bowra, *Class. Phil.*, XXXII (1937), 109-110.

Means of Progress. The road along which Parmenides travels is described as "uttering many things" (*Fr.* 1.2), and the mares that draw his chariot as "pondering many things."[7] Justice, the "manifold avenger" (*Fr.* 1.14; reminiscent of Anaximander's doctrine), holds the requiting keys to the ethereal gates. Plurality and change continually appear in the means that bring Parmenides to the furthest heights of his desire. Under the allegorizing of the Proem it would seem that the multiple and changing things of the sensible world are the means that lead him to his new way of thinking. His point of departure, in a word, was, like that of the Ionians, the visible and tangible world around him.

Light. The notion most strongly emphasized in the allegorizing of the Proem, however, is that of light. In his journey Parmenides leaves the dwellings of night and is carried up into the light, guided by sun maidens who toss aside their veils, while the chariot's axle blazes in its sockets. Light is definitely presented as the goal towards which he is traveling, the goal that he is attaining more and more as the journey progresses. When he reaches the end of this journey towards light, the multiplicity of the forces that raised him up has receded into the background, and the single voice of the goddess gives utterance to the apocalyptic message.[8]

B. The Doctrine of Being

The Ways of Inquiry. The goddess begins the instruction of Parmenides by showing him the only ways of inquiry that can be thought of, "the one, that (it) is, and that (for it) not to be is not

---

[7] *Fr.* 1.4. The translations are those of Verdenius, *Parmenides*, pp. 11-12. For a discussion, see A. Francotte, "Les Disertes Juments de Parménide," *Phronesis*, III (1958), 83-94.

[8] On the mythological background of the goddess in this role, see Bowra, *Class. Phil.*, XXXII (1937), 106. "If she is anything, she is the source of light and enlightenment." *Ibid.* The forces that bring Parmenides upwards— the mares, the sun maidens, Right, Justice, the goddess—are all personified in the feminine gender. From what Aristotle and Aetius say (texts in DK, 28A 52-53), Parmenides seems to have associated darkness with the male and light with the female. For the Pythagoreans, on the contrary, male was in the same column as light, and female in the one with darkness. On the meaning of Dike in the poem, see H. Fränkel, "Parmenidesstudien," *Nachrichten v. d. Gesellschaft d. Wissenschaften zu Göttingen* (1930), pp. 158-169.

possible; this is the way of conviction, for it follows truth: the second, that (it) is not, and that (for it) not to be is of necessity, which is a path, I tell you, that is entirely outside the scope of inquiry; for you could neither recognize (that which) is not, for this is not possible, nor could you express it. For that which it is possible to think is the same as that which can be."[9]

The first way of inquiry, then, proceeds according to being. Here, and throughout the poem, Parmenides consistently abstains from expressing a subject that could be. Even when he uses the participial form of the verb, he is still not expressing anything else than "being." He continually speaks as though *that* which is and its *being* are identical. The way of thinking that follows truth he introduces merely as "is." He has to *imply*, of course, a subject that is, but he seems careful to speak in a manner that does not

[9] *Frs.* 2-3. *Fr.* 3 is open grammatically to the translation: "For it is the same thing to think and to be" or "For thinking and being are identical." Undoubtedly knowledge as well as anything else turns out to be identical with being in Parmenides' way of truth, and knowledge in a special way exhibits the same characteristics as being; but in the context at this stage of the reasoning, his point is merely that one cannot think except in terms of being because only what can be can be thought of. Similarily, *Fr.* 8.34 "Knowing and the condition of knowledge are the same, for you will not find knowing without (that which) is," naturally means in the context that without "being" as its object there cannot be any knowing. Yet from the time of Simplicius (*In Ph.*, 87.17; 144.23) the first sentence has been understood repeatedly in the sense that "thinking is the same as the object of thought," after the fashion of an Aristotelian separate substance or of the starting point of an Idealistic system of thought. This translation is somewhat difficult linguistically, since the expression used does not seem as a rule to have carried at the time the notion of finality ("that for the sake of which thought is") that would be required to interpret it as "object of thought"; see Kurt v. Fritz, "ΝΟΥΣ, ΝΟΕΙΝ, and their Derivatives in Pre-Socratic Philosophy (Excluding Anaxagoras). Part I, From the Beginnings to Parmenides," *Class. Phil.*, XL (1945), 238. The translation: "Thinking is the same as the thought that *it is*," though awkward, is possible, and ultimately has the meaning that thought has to be explained in terms of being. See Verdenius, *Parmenides*, pp. 40-42.

The parallelism with the statement "(for it) not to be is of necessity" (*Fr.* 2.5) requires the notion of impossibility expressed in the translation "It is not possible (for it) not to be" (*Fr.* 2.3). If *Fr.* 3 followed in sequence, the same notion of possibility would naturally be carried over and would be expected in the sense: "For that which it is possible to think is the same as that which can be." For a discussion of the controversy, and a defense of the opposite view, see E. D. Phillips, *Philosophical Review*, LXIV (1955), 548-552. "Thinking and being are the same," in the sense that the real world has to be named being, is defended by L. Woodbury, *Harvard Studies in Classical Philology*, LXIII (1958), 156-157.

commit him to any distinction whatsoever between that subject and its being.[10] To convey this nuance in English, one has to place the impersonal subject "it" in parentheses before the different forms of the verb "to be."

What is this subject, though, that Parmenides looks upon as identical with its being? Nowhere in the fragments does he explicitly say what it is. But was there any necessity to explain it? "(What) is," to the ordinary hearer of Parmenides' verses, could hardly be understood as anything else than the world of sense experience, the world that includes one's self and all other men and visible and tangible things, the world that preceding thinkers from Thales on had studied and described. The cosmos apparent to all would obviously be taken as that which is and can be. The continually changing world of Ionian speculation and of common experience, accordingly, is what a man in Parmenides' circumstances of time and place could refer to without further explanation as "(what) is," and expect to be understood by his fellows. He may have drastic interpretations to make about the meaning of "is," but at least his starting point, common to both his hearers and himself, could hardly be anything else than the world in which he and they lived in common, the world of plurality and change from which his journey in the Proem had commenced.

Also, in Parmenides' manner of speaking, being is presented as involving its own intrinsic necessity. "(It) is" is wrapped up with the statement that "(for it) not to be is impossible." Similarly, "(it) is not" implies that "(for it) not to be is of necessity." No explanation or demonstration is as yet offered of the necessity implicit in being and the impossibility that characterizes notbeing. Parmenides speaks as though one is supposed to see vividly this necessity of being as well as its identity with its subject, if one contemplates intently the nature of being. At this stage of the poem one can only note that Parmenides so introduces being, and await the further development of his doctrine to see the full implications of that way of viewing it.

The other way of inquiry, (it) is not, cannot even be entered.

[10] On Parmenides' implied identification of being and subject, see Hermann Fränkel, "Review" (of Willem Jacob Verdenius, *Parmenides: Some Comments on His Poem*), *Class. Phil.*, XLI (1946), 169b. *Cf.* Verdenius, *Parmenides*, p. 32.

It does not come within the range of human achieving to know (that which) is not. For the moment, the reason given is quite pragmatic. Just try to think that (what is) is not. You try, and you find that you cannot. It will not work. You can think only in terms of being. The second way of inquiry, then, in its pure form, turns out to be a way that human thought cannot at all enter. It is not the way, accordingly, in which ordinary men or any men think.

The Way of Mortals. Not only from the way of pure not-being, however, does the goddess bar Parmenides, but also from a mixed way, the way ordinarily followed by men, a way in which not-being is a constituent along with being. She forbids him this way for the same reason that the way of not-being could not be followed, namely that not-being is not.[11] Yet not-being is given by men the same status as being; it is regarded by them as existent, as being, with the result that being and not-being are confused with each other. Proceeding in this way, men know nothing (they are uninitiated). They wander about facing double, perplexed, undiscerning. They are trying to go in both directions at the same time. Parmenides is warned not to let any customary way of thinking or ordinary experience or the unseeing eye and reverberating ear and tongue force him along this way. Rather, he is commanded to judge by reasoning (*logos*) the argument that is being propounded "with much contest."[12] This means clearly enough that one has to go against what the senses show and what tradition has handed down, and judge solely by difficult rational discourse, that is, by the reasoning that is so earnestly and painstakingly developed in the poem.

Signs of Truth. Only one way remains open, then, to Parmenides. It is the way of being. How is it to be recognized? There are a number of signposts on it to give assurance that it is being followed. On the way of truth, (what) is will appear as incapable of any becoming or of any perishing. It will reveal itself as an indivisible whole, something entirely unique. It will be completely

---

[11] *Frs.* 7.1 and 8.15-16. *Fr.* 7.1, however, may have followed *Fr.* 6.2; see Rosamond K. Sprague, "Parmenides: A Suggested Rearrangement of Fragments in the 'Way of Truth,'" *Class. Phil.*, L (1955), 124-126. It is interpreted in an anti-Pythagorean sense, as meaning that a dead person cannot come back to life, by K. Reich, "Parmenides und die Pythagoreer," *Hermes*, LXXXII (1954), 291.

[12] *Fr.* 7.5. On the translation, see Verdenius, *Parmenides*, p. 64.

immobile. It will be fully perfect everywhere and in every way. The goddess proceeds to show how these signs follow from the very nature of being.

Ingenerate, Imperishable. First, being cannot come to be or perish, for it is something complete, motionless, and without end; it neither was nor will be, but is now, as a whole all together. These aspects are closely linked. Why can it have no origin? Would one care to say that it might originate from not-being? But not-being, as has been seen, is inconceivable. One cannot think that way. Moreover, what necessity could make it at any time spring into being, starting from not-being? In not-being there is no such necessity or compelling force that could account for any being. So being must be there in its entirety or it will not be there at all. Nor, on the other hand, will sound reasoning ever admit that from being could anything apart from itself, that is, apart from being, arise.[13] For this reason, namely on account of the absolute completeness necessarily involved in being, it cannot either come into being or perish. Becoming and perishing, therefore, are inadmissible in the way of truth (*Fr.* 8.3-21).

This reasoning is quite clearly based on the view that there is no distinction between being and that which is. It allows no subject that could receive or lose being. Such a subject would be other than being and so in Parmenides' conception would be wholly identified with not-being; and not-being, he has insisted, just cannot be. Accordingly, being could not originate from not-being, for there is no such thing. Conversely, whatever is, is identified with being and so cannot in any way be apart from being; being, therefore, cannot be the origin of being. The *complete* identity of subject and being, consequently, allows no addition or diminution of being in any way whatsoever, and so renders impossible any becoming or perishing.

Indivisible, Continuous, Unique. Furthermore, being is not divisible. The reason is that being is all alike, and nowhere more or less. All is full of being and is continuous, being closing in with being (*Fr.* 8.22-25). —Again, the argument is based upon the re-

---

[13] *Fr.* 8.12, following Reinhardt's (*Parmenides,* pp. 40-42) emendation. So Simplicius (*In Ph.,* 78.25) explains the argument. Such, according to Aristotle (*Ph.,* I 4,187a33) was the background against which Anaxagoras had to reason.

fusal to admit any subject that could have being in different ways or in different degrees. There is just being, in which no distinction nor grading, no qualitative nor quantitative differences can be found. Any distinguishing characteristic, to exercise in reality its function of distinguishing, would have to *be,* and so would entirely coincide with being. (What) is allows no room for any heterogeneity whatsoever. It is described here as a sort of quantitative continuum, yet it is a continuum that is in no way divisible.

In another fragment (*Fr.* 4), which is difficult to place, Parmenides is asked to observe that absent things are firmly present to the mind, because it will not cut off being from being, no matter where in the cosmos. This would mean that mind, in uniting all the things of the visible universe in its conception of being, merely reflects the veritable unity of all things as they coalesce in the one reality.

Motionless. Next, any kind of motion is impossible. Motion involves the beginning of some new situation and the ending of another; but all becoming and all perishing have been ruled out by true conviction. This applies equally to local motion. So being remains always in the same place. Thus being is in no way incomplete or indefinite, for it is not lacking in anything; if it were lacking in anything at all, it would be lacking in everything (*Fr.* 8.26-33).—Again, the operative notion is the thoroughgoing identity of being with that which is. There is no subject apart from being, which could possess just so much being and lack other being. There is just the "is." There is no such thing as a place outside being, consequently, into which it could move. There is no possibility of any space that it might fill, yet does not. It is complete, in the manner of something extended that leaves no room for any further possibility of extension.

Accordingly, "there is not and will not be anything else apart from being" (*Fr.* 8.36-37). Therefore all things that mortals have set up in their beliefs are merely a name for being[14]—construc-

---

[14] Taking the article at *Fr.* 8.38 in the sense of a relative: ". . . which all things are but a name for" (tr. Davidson). *Cf.* Plato, *Tht.,* 180E (ed. Stallbaum). Usually, however, the article here is taken in the sense of "therefore." On the different readings for *Fr.* 8.38, see W. F. Gaymans, *Parmenides* (Assen, 1941), p. 38; Woodbury, pp. 147-154. "The names that mortal men give *must* be given to that-which-is, because there *is* nothing else to which they can refer." Woodbury, p.149.

tions like becoming and perishing, being and not being, change
of position or of color (*Fr.* 8.38-41). —All the changes in the
sensible world, then, are merely artificial designations for the
single all-embracing being. They are all completely identified in
reality with being. Even the expressed contrast between being
and not-being is but an artificial construction; there is really only
being. This would mean that just as the names given by men do
not affect the intrinsic constitution of the things so named, neither
do these artificial constructions placed upon it by the human mind
affect the intrinsic nature of (that which) is.

Perfectly Self-Identical.   Finally, being is from every side complete "like the mass of a well-rounded sphere, equally balanced
from its centre in every direction; . . ."[15] The reason is that being
is limited to the uttermost degree and there is no not-being that
could anywhere prevent it from reaching its limits equally. —Here
perfection and limitation are equated, apparently after the Pythagorean manner, in the sense that definiteness is perfect and indefiniteness is imperfect. Being is everywhere limited to being,
and so is everywhere definitely and perfectly being. (What) is is
completely self-identical. No not-being is allowed in the guise of
subjects other than being, subjects that could possess being in
different degrees and so have the status of *beings* that were not
completely identical with their own being.

[15] *Fr.* 8.43-44; tr. Freeman. Cornford, *CQ*, XXVII (1933), 103-107, interprets Parmenides' being in a mathematical sense. Yet what concerns
Parmenides primarily in the sphere simile is the *bulk* of the sphere. Any
mathematical solid would be obviously divisible, as Plato (*Sph.* 244E)
pointed out, and so could hardly have been meant by Parmenides when he
was emphasizing the indivisibility of being. The sphere is just a comparison;
"It is only a simile; the round shape as such is irrelevant to Parmenides'
thought: he is concerned only with the formal property of all-around
equality." Gregory Vlastos, "Equality and Justice in Early Greek Cosmologies," *Class. Phil.*, XLII (1947), 162b. See also A. H. Coxon, *CQ*, XXVIII
(1934), 140, who remarks that the best commentary on the sphere simile is
Fr. 5: "It is all one where I begin, for I shall come back thither again."
K. Bloch, "Über die Ontologie des Parmenides," *Classica et Mediaevalia*,
XIV (1953), 3-4 and 28, uses *Fr.* 4 to interpret it. A discussion in comparison
with the Pythagorean table of opposites may be found in J. E. Raven,
Pythagoreans and Eleatics, pp. 31-32; *cf.* pp. 39-40. On Parmenides' emphasis
on "wholeness" rather than on unity and on the readings at *Fr.* 8. 5-6, see
Mario Untersteiner, "L'Essere di Parmenide è 'ΟΥΛΟΝ' non 'ΕΝ'," *Riv.
Critica di Storia della Filos.*, X (1955), 5-23. On the doubtful character of
Fr. 5, see G. Jameson, *Phronesis* III (1958), 16-21.

C. The Doctrine of the Cosmos

Mortal Opinions. The goddess then continues: "At this point I stop giving you my reliable account and thought about truth; from here on, learn of things as they appear to mortals, listening to the deceptive construction (*cosmos*) of my words" (*Fr.* 8.50-53). —How reality actually is has been described. That is the stable and trustworthy picture of all that exists. The rest of the poem undertakes to show how the universe appears to men. Parmenides, nevertheless, is still remaining on the road of truth. He has been forbidden by the goddess to enter any other. He is still receiving instruction from her lips, and so is still viewing things from the standpoint of light and truth. The construction or *cosmos* upon which he is now focusing his attention may be thoroughly unstable and deceptive. But he is proceeding in full awareness of that deceptive character, an awareness that can come only from his vantage point on the road of truth.[16] There is no indication that he is in any way leaving that road.

Basic Duality. First, the fundamental error of mortals is pointed out: "They have established (*the custom of*) naming two forms, one of which ought not to be (*mentioned*): that is where they have gone astray."[17] By custom, then, men set up two

[16] Verdenius, *Parmenides*, p. 59, notes that the translation at *Fr.* 8.52 should not read "deceitful," and (p.48) that according to all extant evidence the last section of the poem was interpreted in antiquity as Parmenides' own seriously proposed doctrine. Only with the help of the goddess, remarks H. Schwabl, *Wien. Stud.*, LXVI (1953), 71, does it become possible to know appearance as appearance.

[17] *Fr.* 8.53-54; tr. Freeman. This text, according to the interpretation given it, vitally affects one's understanding of the final section of the poem. Taken at its face value it allows one to see how Parmenides is still following the one and the same road, the road of being, as he gives his explanation of the cosmos; see Hermann Fränkel, "Review"—same as supra, no. 10, *Class. Phil.*, XLI (1946), 170b. The text seems strained when it is made to read "of which it is not right to name (so much as) one," Cornford, *CQ*, XXVII (1933), 109, or, in the diametrically opposite sense, "it is not permitted to name only one of them," Verdenius, *Parmenides*, p. 62; see G. Vlastos, *Tr. Am. Philol. Assn.*, LXXVII (1946), 74. Similar to the latter translation are " 'it is wrong to name one' rather than two," Raven, *Pythagoreans and Eleatics*, p. 39, and "dont aucune n'est permise seule," Zafiropulo, *ad loc.* Not precisely the duality, but rather the introduction of the form not-being, constitutes the erroneous way; for being rather than unity is Parmenides' criterion of truth.

forms for their thinking, whereas they should use only one. What are these forms? The goddess describes how men differentiate them: "They have distinguished them as opposite in form, and have marked them off from another by giving them different signs: on one side flaming fire in the heavens, mild, very light (*in weight*), the same as itself in every direction, and not the same as the other" (*Fr.* 8.55-58; tr. Freeman). The first form, then, is flame or fire or (*Fr.* 9.1) light. It is described as "the same as itself in every direction." This coincides with the description of being, from the viewpoint of perfect self-identity. Like being, moreover, it is emphatically "not the same" as its opposite. It is separated from its contrary just as drastically as being was distinguished from not-being. Its opposite is then described: "But this too is by itself the opposite, unknowing night, dense and heavy in form" (*Fr.* 8.58-59). It is set apart, "by itself the opposite," just as sharply as not-being was from being. Parmenides speaks as though light and darkness were respectively being and not-being. The testimony of Aristotle, moreover, written at a time when the whole poem was in circulation and the third section not limited to the present meager fragments, is explicit on this point: Parmenides identified fire with being and its opposite, earth, with not-being.[18] Since the goddess had implied that one of the two forms is legitimate, she could hardly do otherwise, after the immediately preceding section of the poem, than make it coincide in every way with being. The opposite form, the dense and heavy type, earth or night or darkness, which cannot legitimately even be named, and which is the cause of the mistaken human way of viewing things, answers fully the role given to not-being in constituting the mixed way of mortals.

The Cosmos. Parmenides is to receive from the goddess a proper and complete account of the world-order that is constructed with these two forms, in order that no judgment of mortal men may overreach him (*Fr.* 8.60-61). Correct knowledge of how the world as it appears is constructed, then, will prevent him from falling victim to any of the current illusions about the nature of the universe. As it is constructed by men in their thinking, the cosmos as a whole possesses the two forms in equal volume: "But since all things are named Light and Night, and

[18] *GC*, I 3,318b6-7; *cf. Metaph.*, A 5,986b27-987a2. DK, 68A 42; 28A 24.

names have been given to each class of things according to the power of one or the other (*Light or Night*), everything is full equally of Light and invisible Night, as both are equal, because to neither of them belongs any share (*of the other*)."[19] —Neither of the two forms can ever participate in the other, just as in the preceding section of the poem being could never in any way become not-being, and not-being could never come into being. But men in their thinking combine the two forms in various proportions, and according to the different proportions the different types of things are constituted and the world of plurality and change is constructed. One of the forms, darkness, as Parmenides' reasoning had shown, should never have been set up. But once it is set up in equal status with being, it furnishes a second basic principle and so allows an acceptable explanation of the world as it appears to mortals. Accordingly, Parmenides (*Frs.* 10-18) is able to offer an account of the nature and genesis of the heavens, the sun, the moon, and the stars, as well as of the cosmic forces and of human activity.

Cognition. Human cognition itself is explained through the varying combination of the two basic forms: "For according to the mixture of their much wandering constituents at each time, does thinking occur in men; for the nature of their constitution is for men, all and each, the same as what thinks; for that which is the more is (the) thought."[20] —One's knowledge, then, and so

[19] *Fr.* 9; tr. Freeman. The Kirk-Raven (p. 282) interpretation is that neither shares in nothingness. The translations "nichts ist möglich, *was* unter keinem von beiden steht" (Kranz) and ". . . since there is nothing that does not belong to either" (Verdenius, *Parmenides*, p. 77) eliminate the notion of participation. Yet the meaning seems clearly enough to be that light and darkness, in constituting visible things, remain everywhere *unchanged in themselves* and *so* equal, *because* neither can participate in the other.

On the meaning at *Fr.* 8.61, "that no judgment of mortals should ever overcome you," see A. Patin, "Parmenides in Kampfe gegen Heraklit," *Jahrbücher für Class. Philol.*, Supplbd. XXV (1899), 498-499; on the *daimon* in *Fr.* 12, J. S. Morrison, "Parmenides and Er," *JHS*, LXXV (1955), 60; and on *Fr.* 14, Werner W. Jaeger, "Ein Verkanntes Fragment des Parmenides," *Rh. Mus.*, C (1957), 42-47.

[20] *Fr.* 16. On the interpretation of this difficult passage, see K. Riezler, *Parmenides* (Frankfurt, 1934), pp. 65-71; Verdenius, *Parmenides*, pp. 6-30; Vlastos, *Tr. Am. Philol. Assoc.*, LXXVII (1946), 66-74. On its relation to *Fr.* 4, see Jean Bollack, "Sur Deux Fragments de Parménide (4 et 16)," *Revue des Études Grecques*, LXX (1957), 56-71.

one's conscious identity as an individual, is set up according to the ever-changing proportion of light and darkness that makes one's constitution at any given moment. The average constitution of mortals does not give light any too great predominance. But as the proportion is "much wandering" or continually changing, light is able to predominate more and more in some cases, as for instance in Parmenides when he was being borne aloft from the region of darkness into the region of light. Total predominance of darkness, on the other hand, would mean complete oblivion, the death of the individual.[21]

Light is therefore identified with knowledge as well as with being. The symbolism of the Proem in this way becomes apparent. The multiple, changing cognition of the sensible world is the means by which Parmenides rises. The one genuine form, light, keeps predominating more and more as he sees things increasingly from the viewpoint of light, the viewpoint solely of being. When he reaches the level where light fully predominates, he sees things under the aspect of being only. But that stage, apparently, is reached only in moments of special inspiration and illumination. Ordinarily, even Parmenides will have to view things from the standpoint of the senses, according to the ordinary balance of the combination in his constitution as a mortal man. He will speak of the universe as it appears and as it is accepted by men in general: "In this way, therefore, according to appearance, did these things emerge, and are now, and shall henceforth from now on grow and come to an end; for which men have established a name as a distinguishing sign for each" (*Fr.* 19).

Philosopher of Nature. The poem of Parmenides has undertaken to explain the visible and tangible universe, the universe that the Ionian thinkers before him had endeavored to probe. It shows no interest in any other reality. Parmenides, therefore, correctly appeared to Aristotle[22] and the Greek doxographers as a physicist in the ancient sense, a philosopher of nature. His poem

---

[21] *Cf.* Theophrastus, *De Sensu*, 4; in Diel's *Dox. Graec.*, p. 500 (DK, 28 A 46). On a possible religious background for this doctrine, see Vlastos, *op. cit.*, pp. 72; 75-76.

[22] *Metaph.*, A 3,984b3-4; 5,986b28-34. The general Eleatic dialectic of being, however, is contrasted with the starting point of the physicists at *Ph.*, I 2,184b15 ff.

was quite properly called a work on nature. Its sole purpose was to explain the physical world, the world in which men live. But in investigating that world, Parmenides was struck first and foremost by the consideration that it exists, it is. What led him to focus his thought so keenly in this consideration cannot now be traced, but the poem shows forcefully enough that he centered his whole attention on the aspect of being that was so evident in the world as he saw it. Probing that aspect deeply and earnestly, he saw clearly how real that being was, and he could not look upon it otherwise than as a reality itself. Viewed in that way, it at once began to pulverize everything it touched, and to absorb all things into its own all-embracing and undifferentiated unicity, including the sensible things from which Parmenides' cognition started. In poetic inspiration the Eleatic saw it as the form of light, light that extended throughout space in the great well-rounded sphere of the heavens,[23] yet reached from place to place instantaneously just as in human cognition distant things are as present as close ones, without any discernible motion. Being, knowledge, and light coincided in their characteristics and were looked upon as the same nature.

Since Parmenides had no notion of any kind of reality above the sensible, this could only mean that being and knowledge were a physical reality, a natural form, light. Aristotle is very pointed in his statements that the Eleatic ". . . thought 'that which is' was identical with the sensible world" (*Metaph.*, Γ 5,1010a2-3; DK, 28A 24; Oxford tr.), that what was shown to be one by reason appeared as multiple through sensation (*Metaph.*, A 5,986b32-33; DK, 28A 24), and that because he had no conception of any other kind of being than sensible things he applied to them notions of stability that were true only of the supersensible (*Cael.*, III 1,298b21-24; DK, 28A 25). In the sense that he did not mean to go beyond the *physical* world Parmenides was a physicist (in the Greek sense) rather than a *meta*physician. He conceived the whole of what is as a physical form, and investigated both how it is and how it appears. From this standpoint he could legitimately be viewed by Greek tradition as a philosopher of nature.

Metaphysical Insight. In spite of such a limitation in his point

[23] See J. E. Boodin, "The Vision of Parmenides," *Philos. Rev.*, LII (1943), 588.

of view, however, Parmenides saw vividly and expressed forcefully the implications of what it means for a thing to be, when the aspect of being is viewed as a real and meaningful form. Seen as having a content, it could not leave room for anything else. There was absolutely nothing else that could be. Because it was being, it included everything. Because it was a form, it was finite. Complete and perfect in itself, it allowed no possibility of motion or change. In all this there need be no doubt about the depth and vigor of a truly metaphysical insight, in the sense of treating things from the viewpoint of their being. Though working as a natural philosopher, Parmenides has with astonishing penetration set before the eyes of Western thought the basic metaphysical problem, the problem of being. He has isolated the aspect of being, he has presented it as a form with a content, and has shown what that content embraces. Under this guise, being will remain for the Greeks something that is immediately conceptualized rather than judged; and no matter how much it is later raised to the level of the supersensible, it will in its Parmenidean background retain with them the status of a limited, definite, meaningful form.

Against this background subsequent philosophers will have to struggle in their efforts to allow some genuine being to multiplicity and change. The great Eleatic thinker has sketched the issues so clearly that he can be opposed only by denying all content to being or by finding a way in which not-being or things other than the nature of being somehow are. The former alternative, popular in recent times, was not attempted by the Greeks. They stayed in that regard within the Parmenidean position of the problem, namely that being is meaningful. Against the same background, they did not attempt to locate being outside the realm of formal determination in any existentialist fashion. Remaining within Parmenides' notion of being as a meaningful form, they strove to show in one way or another that his extreme conclusions about plurality and change did not follow in their entirety. Since the Eleatic in this way so definitely isolated the problem of being and gave it the framework in which it was presented to the consideration of subsequent metaphysicians, he may without any hesitation be called the founder of Western metaphysics.

Other Basic Problems. Besides the general problem of being, other fundamental issues in philosophy are outlined in the Eleatic's poem. The five top genera for Plato, Being, Sameness, Otherness, Motion, Rest, are treated in it in those very terms. The Platonic problems of the one and the many, as well as of motion and stability, are set down in it. The difference between Truth and Opinion, stable and unstable cognition, is the problem that will result in Plato's doctrine of the Ideas and their participation by sensible things. Aristotle (*Cael.*, III 1,298b15-24; DK, 28A 25) regards Parmenides as the first to see that there could be no *knowledge* without some absolutely unchanging entity. The difficulties signalized by the Eleatic in requiring stable elements to explain corporeal change will provide a sensitive background for the Aristotelian *Physics*. The three kinds of change most exploited by the Stagirite (substantial, qualitative, local) are distinguished in the poem.

Moreover, Parmenides, though still predominantly intuitional in his procedure, sets out much of his thought in the form of strict reasoning.[24] Before him doctrines were merely stated or set forth in a vivid and striking way. Even in Heraclitus they were just "indicated." But in Parmenides they are reasoned to, at least in considerable measure. However, even though he distinguishes the way of reasoning from the way of appearance, Parmenides is not interested in analyzing the tools of the reasoning processes. He does not treat of concepts, judgments, premises, conclusions, or other thought forms as such. He can hardly, then, be called a logician, no matter how logically he reasoned in actual practice.

Unoriginated Universe. Parmenides' doctrine of the cosmos, as well as his doctrine of being, exercised important influence in the immediately following epoch.[25] But the Greeks of later generations, after the development of metaphysics, centered their interest chiefly on his doctrine of being, with the result that comparatively few of the lines handed down by them come from the final part of the poem. Similarly, the writings of Parmenides' disciples Zeno and Melissus concentrate on what he said about

[24] See K. v. Fritz, *Class. Phil.*, XL (1945), 241a; Verdenius, *Parmenides*, pp. 3-4.

[25] Reinhardt, *Parmenides*, pp. 242-247, argued that the Eleatic doctrine of appearance had greater influence on subsequent Greek thought than the doctrine of being.

being. Accordingly, the sequence of the different sections of the poem has not been properly understood, and the doctrine of the cosmos has been neglected, or explained away as not expressing Parmenides' own views, or as utterly impossible to reconcile with his doctrine of being. Yet those who read the poem in antiquity regarded the last part as expressing his own seriously meant teaching. He explained the multiple and ever changing cosmos with the aid of a second form, darkness (night, earth, cold, ignorance, not-being), that men by custom set up in their cognition. It is given, illegitimately, a status equal to that of light or being. Though always retaining its own nature, darkness is able to combine with light in multiple and ever-varying proportions to make that which is *appear* as men ordinarily see it. With these two forms, then, Parmenides accounts for all the plurality and motion in the sensible universe.

The second form, of course, as absolute nothingness, has no positive effect whatsoever in reality. Purely negative, it is merely the failure of men to know being in its fullness, a failure that can be remedied only as light predominates more and more in human cognition, and finally, in a moment of supreme inspiration, completely overwhelms the darkness. In such a moment a man sees everything solely in the light of being, he lives in the fullness of being and knowledge, he *is* in truth that fullness. When, on the other hand, as the ever-varying change of the proportions in his constitution of the two basic forms runs its course, darkness comes to predominate completely, the individual man as a separate appearance is extinguished. The individual who is born, who grows, who philosophizes, who in his cognition sets up the variegated cosmos, is, like anything else set apart from the unity of the unique being, merely a particular deficiency that *appears* in the one reality.

But the problem still remains: Why should such deficiencies ever even appear? How can the unique, perfect being allow itself to appear in ways other than it is? No answer is to be found in the fragments, nor is there any trace of one having been given by Parmenides. But could he be asked to give one? Was an answer at all necessary, or was the very possibility of the question excluded by the Eleatic's position of the problem? To require a reason why such deficiencies come to appear would be to place them on the level of being and truth. It would destroy the very subject of the query. It is a question that just cannot be asked in the Parmenidean framework. Given the Eleatic's doctrine of being, no rational justification of the cosmos could be attempted, and none was required or even allowed. As a matter of fact, the deficiencies in being do appear, and they can be analyzed into their two basic constituents: being, which is real, and not-being, which is an illegitimate convention. But there is no possibility, and moreover no need, to look for a reason why they should appear at all, or why they appear in the way they do. They just do not follow from reality, and could never be grounded in it. Less than with any previous Greek philosopher do the cosmic processes require for Parmenides an originating cause. But they can and should be studied as they appear, in order that no merely human view should outwit any one who has been initiated into being. In this way the Eleatic's thought rounds out and completes itself as a thoroughgoing account of reality, both how it is and how it appears to men.

Parmenides' Inspiration. An attentive and sympathetic reading of the fragments amply suffices to show that Parmenides is urged on by something more than a detached and dry sequence of propositions about being. Is a mystical experience of reality necessary, then, to account for the earnestness and depths of his conviction about the unicity and immobility of being, in the face of sense cognition? Was some incommunicable vision the source of his unshakeable and uncompromising attachment to his extraordinary views? There is no evidence that anyone who read the poem in antiquity thought so. Nor do there seem to be implied in the fragments any doctrinal tenets that cannot be explained in terms of communicable knowledge. Parmenides speaks as though endeavoring to express plainly what should be evident to all who seriously try to think, rather than attempting to transcribe in rational terms the results of an incommunicable experience. What else, then, may explain his intransigence and his enthusiasm? Is a poetic inspiration at the thought of light penetrating instantaneously and without motion throughout the vast expanses of the universe, making distant things present to sight, exhibiting upon further contemplation the perfection and so the unicity implied in the aspect of being as well as in the activity of knowledge—is all that sufficient to account for the fervor and clarity of the Eleatic's message? Was his vision so overwhelmed by the sheer splendor of being's formal manifestations that he was blinded to its ambiguities? If such were the case, the reason why Parmenides wrote in verse becomes obvious. He considered himself a poet, and used the poet's medium of expression. At least, form and content go together in this interpretation of Parmenides' work.[26] It shows, too, why there can be no substitute for reading his thought in its native poetic cast.

But no matter what may have been the source of the Eleatic's ardor and the explanation of his profound intellectual acumen, his philosophy gave beyond doubt a new direction to the development of Greek thought. His doctrine of being has for the most part been isolated by historians from its original setting and been interpreted in widely differing ways, and has even been disparaged as a monotone or as a sediment remaining from the dissolution of preceding philosophies. Nevertheless subsequent thinkers had to take account of it and justify their own procedures in the face of its reasoning. No matter what interpretations have been given it, its influence continues in philosophical circles right through to the present day. Its vividness, depth, and earnestness, as well as its unabated influence, mark its author as one of the truly great philosophic geniuses in the history of Western thought. There is in fact little exaggeration in saying that without a sufficient grasp of the way in which the problem of being was originally placed by Parmenides, the subsequent long-drawn-out controversies upon the subject become impossible to understand.

No way has yet been found of establishing any satisfactory relation between the poem of Parmenides and the scroll of Heraclitus. Chronologically, they could well have been written at the same time, in utter independence of each other. Cases have been made out on both sides to show that the one was criticizing the other, but neither side can adduce sufficient evidence to justify its

[26] On the case for requiring a mystical vision, see Verdenius, *Mnemosyne,* 4a ser. II (1949), 126-128, who rejects (pp. 118-119) a merely poetic vision. For a discussion of Parmenides' poetic art, see M. Untersteiner, *Parmenide* (Turin, 1925), pp. 175-180. On the possibility that Parmenides was reacting against eastern thought currents in developing his doctrine of being, see G. P. Conger, *Philosophy East and West,* II (1952), 122-123.

claims. If Heraclitus had been attacking Parmenides, would he not surely have mentioned him scathingly by name, just as he mentions other figures of the Greek intellectual world? If on the other hand Parmenides had meant his doctrine to be an attack on Heraclitus, would he not have been much more specific in citing the catchy Heraclitean phrases?[27] Besides, what motive would either have had for a thoroughgoing attack upon the other? Both the Parmenidean and the Heraclitean philosophies, though from radically different viewpoints, advance the unity of all things, the incessant change going on from moment to moment in the cosmos, and the basic role of fire in the constitution of reality as well as its identification with wisdom and truth. Everything looks rather as though the poem and the scroll were produced about the same time at opposite extremities of the Greek world without any influence of either one upon the other.[28] The technique of presenting their doctrines as diametrically opposed does not appear until Plato sets them up dramatically as the extreme opposites in the realm of philosophical thought. The fragments of the Eleatics who come after Parmenides show no consciousness of special opposition to Heraclitus, nor any tendency to regard his doctrine as the furthest removed from their own dialectic; and at least Melissus of Samos can hardly be presumed

[27] Even the term *palintropos*, "reversing," as used by Parmenides (*Fr.* 6.9), does not seem to have anything to do with the notion of that word as used by Heraclitus (DK, 22B 51); see Verdenius, *Parmenides*, pp. 77-78. On *palintropos* as the original term in the Heraclitean fragment, see Walther Kranz, "ΠΑΛΙΝΤΡΟΠΟΣ 'ΑΡΜΟΝΙΗ," *Rh. Mus.*, CI (1958), 250-254. For a defense of the ancient alternative *palintonos*, "working in both directions" see G. S. Kirk, *The Cosmic Fragments*, pp. 210-218, and Kirk-Raven, *The Presocratic Philosophers*, pp. 193-194.
However, on the view that Heraclitus and Parmenides are not to be regarded as independent of each other, see Reinhardt, *Parmenides*, pp. 208-221.
[28] The chronological order of the poem and the scroll is, of course, impossible to determine. The scroll of Heraclitus has been dated as late as some time after 478 B.C. by Zeller and Reinhardt (cf. *supra*, Chapter 3, n. 2), and the poem has been considered as belonging to Parmenides' more advanced lifetime by Patin, *Jahrbücher für Class. Philol.*, Supplbd. XXV (1899), 653, and Verdenius (*supra*, n.3). The maturity of Parmenides' metaphysical doctrine, however, need not point to any very advanced age for the composition of the poem. The middle thirties would surely suffice. The profoundly original and mature metaphysics of the *De Ente et Essentia,* for instance, had been developed by St. Thomas Aquinas in his early thirties.

to have been unacquainted with the sayings of the celebrated sage
from the neighboring city of Ephesus.

SELECTED READINGS AND REFERENCES

Parmenidou Peri Physeôs, ed. Jean Zafiropulo (Paris: A. Tallone, 1953).
Contains Greek text, French translation, and notes. The poem has
been rendered in English verse by T. Davidson, in "Parmenides,"
Journal of Speculative Philosophy, IV (1870), 4-8.

Karl Reinhardt, *Parmenides und die Geschichte der Griechischen
Philosophie* (Bonn: F. Cohen, 1916).

F. M. Cornford, "Parmenides' Two Ways," *CQ,* XXVII (1933), 97-111.

A. H. Coxon, "The Philosophy of Parmenides," *CQ,* XXVIII (1934),
134-144.

C. M. Bowra, "The Proem of Parmenides," *Class. Phil.,* XXXII (1937),
97-112.

Willem Jacob Verdenius, *Parmenides: Some Comments on his Poem,*
tr. A. Fontein (Groningen: J. B. Wolters, 1942).

————, "Parmenides' Conception of Light," *Mnemosyne,* ser. 4, II
(1949), 116-131.

G. Vlastos, "Parmenides' Theory of Knowledge," *Transactions of the
American Philological Association,* LXXVII (1946), 66-77.

E. L. Minar, "Parmenides and the World of Seeming," *AJP,* LXX
(1949), 41-55.

E. D. Phillips, "Parmenides on Thought and Being," *Philosophical Review,* LXIV (1955), 546-560.

G. Jameson, " 'Well-Rounded Truth' and Circular Thought in Parmenides," *Phronesis,* III (1958), 15-30.

L. Woodbury, "Parmenides on Names," *Harvard Studies in Classical
Philology,* LXIII (1958), 145-160.

[CHAPTER 5]

The Beginnings of Dialectic

ZENO OF ELEA (*FL. CA.* 465/455 B.C.)

Chronology. Zeno's chronology is determined by the same norms as that of Parmenides. If Plato's account of the meeting of Zeno with the youthful Socrates is chronologically possible, and seventy the age of Socrates at his death in 399 B.C., the dramatic meeting would take place between 455 and 450 B.C. Since Zeno is described as about forty years old at the time, he would have been born somewhere in 495-490 B.C. Some allowance, however, has to be made for possible dramatic liberties. Diogenes Laertius (IX, 29), apparently taking his information from Apollodorus, places Zeno's *floruit* in the seventy-ninth Olympiad (464-461 B.C.), so about a decade earlier. This may not be far wrong, though it seems to have been worked out entirely on artificial grounds, based ultimately on the assumption that the date of the founding of Elea (540-539 B.C.) was the *floruit* of Xenophanes, forty years later (500 B.C.) that of Parmenides, and still another forty years after (460 B.C.) that of the third in "succession," Zeno. Another account, that of Suidas (perhaps tenth century A.D.), would place it for some unknown reason in the preceeding Olympiad, 468-465 B.C. (DK, 29A 1-2).

Life. According to unanimous Greek tradition, Zeno was a pupil and associate of Parmenides. He is described by Plato (*Prm.* 127B; DK, 29 A 11) as tall and handsome in appearance, and as having already acquired a reputation at Athens for the treatises or *logoi* that he had written to defend the doctrine of Parmenides, even though those treatises themselves had not reached Athens before the time of his visit to the city. He is reported to have been active in political life, and to have been put to death in a revolt against the tyrant Nearchus of Elea. However, the details differ widely, and the year of his death cannot be determined. There are indications that he taught for some time at Athens.

Writings. According to Plato's dramatic account, Zeno's defense of his master's doctrine was written when its author was young and eager for controversy, and was copied surreptitiously and published without his consent. Plato, accordingly, seems to be taking Zeno's work rather lightly, while at the same time making plain that Zeno himself meant it seriously as a vindication of Eleatic doctrine. Its method, Plato's account goes on, was the indirect refutation of Parmenides' opponents. These opponents attempted to ridicule the teaching that all things are one. Zeno's tactic was to show how the tenet that things are multiple turns out to be even more ridiculous. Greek tradition does not identify in any definite way the adversaries against whom Zeno directed his arguments.

Plato's description in general is borne out by the extant fragments. This kind of treatment ushers in a new type of rational procedure, the part of logic that Aristotle will later name dialectic, and of which he calls Zeno the founder.[1] The peculiar feature of Zeno's dialectic, however, was seen in his method of arguing from what he himself held to be false but was admitted by his opponent; he would draw directly opposite consequences from the one tenet of his adversary. In this sense Plato (*Phr.*, 261D; DK, 29A 13) called him the "Eleatic Palamedes," apparently emphasizing his cleverness or dexterity in defending either side of an argument; he could make the same things seem like and unlike, one and many, in motion and at rest. This technique, if used against those who made fun of Parmenides' doctrine of the unique being, would mean that Zeno accepted for the sake of argument the hypothesis of his adversaries that things are multiple, and then drew from that hypothesis directly opposite and mutually destructive consequences, so rendering the hypothesis untenable. In a similar way, the third-century B.C. satirist Timon described him as one who could make both sides prevail (D.L., IX, 25; DK, 29A 1).

Plato referred to Zeno's writings as *logoi*. A much later (fifth-century A.D.) writer, Proclus, states that these *logoi* numbered forty (DK, 29A 15). Plato mentions no title, and most likely, according to the usage of the times, none was originally given to them. There does not seem to be sufficient foundation for any later notion that Zeno wrote in dialogue form.

---

[1] This assertion was made in a lost dialogue called the *Sophistes*, 1484b27-38. *Cf.* D.L., VIII, 57; IX, 25 (DK, 29A 1 & 10).

DIALECTICAL ARGUMENTS
A. *Against Plurality*

Finite, Yet Infinite. Zeno supposes that whatever exists is of a quantitative nature. No being can be non-quantitative, "for if it were added to some other being, it would not make it any larger; for if a thing without any size is added, the other cannot at all increase in size. And so what was added would thereby be nothing. But if when it is subtracted the other will in no way be less, nor, on the other hand, will increase when it is added, it is evident that what was added or subtracted was nothing" (*Fr.* 2). This argument presumes as admitted that any addition of being means increase in quantity, and any loss of being involves decrease in quantity. A non-quantitative being could not effect such an increase or decrease. Quantitatively it is nothing; and so it is absolutely nothing. The background of this view may be found quite readily in the outlook of all the preceding Greek philosophers. They thought only in terms of extended things. Zeno merely emphasizes that outlook through the mathematical illustration of addition and subtraction.

In this background, Zeno proceeds to argue that any plurality would render things both finite and infinite in number. Things would be numerically finite, because any given amount of them would always be definite; but they would also be numerically infinite on account of the ever-present dichotomy of each extended part: "If they are many, they have to be just as many as they are, and neither more nor less. But if they are just as many as they are, they must be finite." That is one side of the case. The fragment immediately proceeds to give the other side: "If they are many, beings are infinite; for there are always others in between beings, and again others in between these. And thus beings are infinite" (*Fr.* 3) in number. This argument from dichotomy or bisection[2] presupposes that really existing things, because they

[2] Simplicius (*In Ph.*, 140.33-34; DK, I,258.5-6) explains that this argument is concerned with numerical infinity, and that it proceeds by way of dichotomy. Different versions of the argument seem to have been given in Zeno's treatise. The version found in the present fragment (*Fr.* 3) followed the argument given in *Fr.* 2, that things would be infinite in magnitude. The

are quantitative, are subject in reality to the peculiar characteristics of abstract or mathematical extension. Abstract quantity is infinitely divisible, therefore quantitative things are regarded as similarly divisible and so as composed of an infinite number of constituents. Any spatially extended things, accordingly, are regarded as having parts in between the limits of their extension. These parts will likewise have parts in between their own limits, and so *ad infinitum*. The argument proceeds against a background in which no distinction between real quantity and abstract (mathematical) quantity is as yet recognized. Zeno's adversary is presumed on the one hand to have a conception of things that allows no ultimate units, since each part is always a plurality. On the other hand, the adversary is considered to hold the opposite and contradictory notion that a real plurality is made up of ultimate unitary constituents. Some later Pythagoreans identified the principles of number with the principles of real things; but whether or not this confusion of real and abstract quantity was a specifically Pythagorean notion in Zeno's time is subject to dispute.[3] Zeno's argument, however, clearly assumes that his adversaries, whoever they were, think in terms of two opposed and mutually destructive conceptions of quantity.

No Size, Infinite Size. Further, Zeno argues that if things are a plurality they will have no size at all, and yet will be infinitely large. Because they are spatially extended, they will have parts outside parts and so each part in some way at a distance from the other. The infinite number of parts, shown by the argument from dichotomy, will make each thing infinitely large; on the other hand, things will be so small as to have no size: ". . . each must have some size and thickness and each part of it must be at a

---

notion "in between" may be interpreted in various ways, but in any of these ways Simplicius' explanation that the argument proceeds by way of bisection has to be respected. For a general explanation of the dichotomy argument in both *Frs.* 2 and 3, see H.D.P. Lee, *Zeno of Elea* (Cambridge, Eng., 1936), p. 31.

[3] ". . . 'number atomism' . . . its essential characteristic is its confusion between the attributes of geometrical point, physical atom and numerical unit." Lee, p. 112. For different views on this question, see F. M. Cornford, *CQ*, XVI (1922), 137-150, and XVII (1923), 1-12; W. A. Heidel, *AJP*, LXI (1940), 21-29; N. B. Booth, *Phronesis*, II (1957), 90-103.

distance from the other. And the same reasoning holds good of the one that precedes it; for that also will have size and there will be one preceding it. It is the same, then, to say this once and to say it always; for no such part of it will be the last, nor without proportion to another. So if there are many things, they have to be both small and large; so small, on the one hand, as to have no size; so large, on the other, as to be infinite" (*Fr.* 1).

Simplicius was quoting this passage as an argument for the infinity in size. He does not imply that it contains Zeno's reasoning to prove that things would be "so small as to have no size." It is difficult to see how the latter conclusion could follow from the dichotomy argument, in the setting that Zeno is speaking of real things and attributing to them the features of abstract mathematical quantity. The dichotomy process would go on indefinitely, making each successive part smaller, but at the same time keeping each part quantitative, *ad infinitum*. It shows easily enough in this setting how an unlimited number of extended parts will give an unlimited magnitude. That was the purpose for which Simplicius quoted the argument. But what is the proof for the other member of the total conclusion? Why would a plurality of things have no size whatsoever?

In introducing the passage, Simplicius stated that Zeno had first shown that "if what exists has no size, it would not exist at all" (*In Ph.*, 141.1-2; DK, 29B 1). Apparently there had preceded an argument in which a plurality was shown to have no size. What was that argument? Earlier in his commentary Simplicius had stated that Zeno was equating a unit with a mathematical point: ". . . for he speaks of the point as the one" (*In Ph.*, 99.11; DK, 29A 21). Simplicius also quoted a saying attributed to him, that "if any one could tell him what the unit was, he would be able to say what things are" (*In Ph.*, 97.12-13, 138.32-33; DK, 29A 16). This should mean that Zeno "tried to show that it was impossible for things to be a plurality, since there was no unit in things, whereas 'many' is a number of units" (*In Ph.*, 99.14-16; DK, 29A 21). The argument, accordingly, would be that since things are divisible without limit one can never arrive at a unit, which would have to be indivisible after the manner of a point; so one can never have the units out of which any plurality could be constructed. The smallness that is "so small as to have no size" apparently followed in the argument from what Zeno had stated before, and which Simplicius indicated by saying that Zeno had first shown that "if what exists has no size, it would not exist at all." Simplicius then gave the part of the argument that deals with unlimited size.

By the unit that would form a constituent of plurality, Zeno quite obviously understands something very different from the single being of Parmenides, which excluded all plurality and of its very nature could not be conceived as a constituent of a plurality. Confusion of the two meanings seems to have occasioned Seneca's remark: "If I am to believe Parmenides, there is nothing except the one; if Zeno, there is not even a one!"[4] The "one" that Zeno is showing to be impossible is the unit that for his opponents is the basic constituent of the many. It is represented as a real unit that has the indivisibility of an abstract mathematical point. Again, Zeno's argument is focused upon a view that confused mathematical characteristics with the real constituents of things. It presupposes that the adversary conceives plurality as composed on the one hand of ultimate real units, and on the other hand of indefinitely divisible parts. The fragments seem to indicate, however, that Zeno's basic concern, like that of Parmenides, was with being rather than with unity. They do not support Plato's (*Prm.*, 137B ff.; *cf.* 128AC, DK, 29A 12) representation of it as characteristically a doctrine of "the one."

B. Against Motion

Place.   Diogenes Laertius records that Zeno does away with motion in saying that "that which is moving, is moving neither in the place in which it is nor in a place in which it is not."[5] In the place where the thing is, it is at rest, and so cannot be moving. But it cannot be moving in any place where it is not, for it is just not there to move or to do or undergo anything at all. A moving body, accordingly, is not moving in the place where it is, nor in any other place at all. It is therefore at rest.

[4] *Ep.*, LXXXVIII,45; DK, 29A 21. *Cf.* Simplicius, *In Ph.*, 138.25-26.
[5] *Fr.* 4. On Zeno's notion of place, see DK, 29A 24, and Lee, pp. 38-39.

The argument seems based upon a notion of space that Zeno had already shown to be impossible. Aristotle (*Ph.*, IV 3,210b23; DK, A 24) records the difficulty as "if place is something, in what will it be?" This is quite apparently the conception of place as a material container. It would contain a thing within definite and indivisible bounds, and leave no room for a divisible that would permit motion. Whether any particular adversaries of Zeno expressly taught such a notion of place cannot be determined from the extant testimonia. If this notion of place had been used as an argument against the plurality of things, it would be geared to show the absurdity of saying that space sets up a plurality, namely itself and what it contains.

Zeno's arguments against motion, however, are best known through the summary given by Aristotle (*Ph.* VI 9,239b5-240b7; DK, A 25-28). They are listed by the Stagirite as four in number.

The Racecourse.   The first of these arguments is that a moving object can never cross a racecourse,[6] because it has to arrive at the halfway mark of each successive part before it can arrive at the end of that part. So it can never traverse any given stretch, let alone the whole distance. —This is the dichotomy argument applied as a measure of motion, presupposing that the moving object has to cross separately each abstractly discernible part of the distance. It endows real distance with the requirements of mathematical abstraction, and at the same time subjects it to a unitary measure. In correspondence with the arguments against plurality, it presupposes in Zeno's adversary a notion of distance that consists of two mutually destructive conceptions. On the one hand, each part of a distance is conceived as indefinitely divisible after the manner of abstract extension. On the other hand, each part of the distance is regarded as a definite, unitary, self-contained real length that has to be traversed separately.

The Achilles.   The second argument is called the "Achilles." Achilles, the Homeric symbol for the fastest runner, can never catch the tortoise, proverbial for its slowness. The reason why the

[6] *Cf. Top.*, VIII 8, 160b8-9. On the history of these arguments against motion, see Florian Cajori, "The History of Zeno's Arguments on Motion," *American Mathematical Monthly*, XXII (1915), 1-6. Cajori treats the arguments on the mathematical level. They still occasion lively discussions, e.g., *Mind*, L (1941), 310-311; LI (1942), 89-90; LV (1946), 151-165; 341-345.

quickest runner can never overtake the slowest is that the pursuer must first reach the point whence the pursued started. But in the meantime the pursued has covered some distance, however little. The pursuer, accordingly, has to reach the new point attained by the pursued. While he is doing so, the pursued has advanced further. The same reasoning may be repeated indefinitely, showing that the slower runner will always hold a lead. —This is a variation of the dichotomy procedure, differing only in dividing the parts on a proportional instead of on an equal basis.

The Flying Arrow.   The third argument maintains that a flying arrow is at rest. The reason is that anything in motion has to occupy a given place at any given moment. But this, according to the notion of place that Zeno has presupposed, renders it motionless. The force of the argument, however, is here based upon its notion of time. It presupposes that time is composed of indivisible instants or atomic "nows." The arrow is always contained definitively in just one of those indivisible instants. Consequently the body is always at rest. There is nothing else constituting time besides those indivisibles. The two presuppositions, one regarding place, the other regarding time, require that a moving body be in a given place at any given moment in such a way that it always has to be at rest.

The Moving Rows.   The fourth argument is that a row of moving bodies starting from the middle point of a racecourse would pass a similar row, moving in the opposite direction, in half the time that it would pass a row of similar stationary bodies. This is taken to mean that half a given time is equal to the whole of that time. Aristotle explained the argument by means of symbols and apparently of diagrams. AA represented the stationary bodies, BB the bodies proceeding from the middle point of the racecourse to the goal, and CC the bodies proceeding from the middle point in the opposite direction. The original position was as follows:

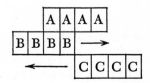

When the motion has ended the respective positions are:

A	A	A	A
B	B	B	B
C	C	C	C

During the time in which the motion took place, the first B passed four C's, but only two A's. Yet each C is of equal length to each A. In exactly the same time, then, the first B, when its traveled distance is measured in units of C, went twice as far as it did in units of A. These units, however, are of exactly the same length. Therefore the first B is traversing the same distance in both half the time (according to the C measure) and the total time (according to the A measure). Half any given time, then, is equal to the whole of that time.

This reasoning has the same presuppositions as the third argument. It follows as though Zeno, after having shown that an alleged moving object does not move at all, proceeded further to argue that even granted that it was moving, further self-destructive consequences would follow—half a given time would become equal to all of that time. Just as in the case of the third, the present argument is directed against a notion of distance as something composed ultimately of extended parts each of which has an absolutely definite length. The moving object is understood as requiring a similarly definite length of time to pass through each part, regardless of whether that part be considered as moving or as at rest.[7] It is definitely contained within the same length of spatial extension for the same length of time. The ultimate parts of both space and time are regarded, in a word, as both extended and indivisible. They are looked upon as definite and indivisible units of length.

The first two arguments against motion presuppose a notion of space, and implicitly also of time, that considers each part indefinitely divisible and yet as a definite unit of length that has to

[7] "The fallacy of the reasoning lies in the assumption that a body occupies an equal time in passing with equal velocity a body that is in motion and a body of equal size that is at rest; which is false." Aristotle, Ph., VI 9,

be traversed separately. The last two arguments make explicit this presupposition in regard to time. Similarly the arguments against plurality are aimed at a plurality constituted of parts that are definite units and yet are divisible indefinitely. All these arguments would hold against anyone who could be first made to admit that a plurality had to be composed of units, and that any given length was indefinitely divisible. The latter tenet could be shown by simple mathematical considerations, the former by a mere common-sense analysis of the notion of plurality. Anyone who maintained plurality in things, whether he were a Milesian cosmologist or a Heraclitean or a Pythagorean or a man of the non-philosophical public, could be easily shown to hold those two presuppositions regarding the composition of extended realities, provided that as yet no sharp distinction between real quantity and abstract mathematical quantity had been established. No other condition is required for the full force of Zeno's arguments. It is hard to see that they have as their target any particular philosophical tendency.

The four arguments against motion are presented very concretely. They envisage a moving object in the racecourse, Achilles and the tortoise, an arrow, and rows of weights rolled in the stadium. The actual arguments, as Zeno conceived them, can hardly be met by raising them to the plane of abstract mathematics. Zeno visualizes the indefinitely continued division of the parts, and so is dealing with an infinite that will never be actually realized. If on the other hand the arguments are encountered, as in Aristotle, by distinguishing the conditions of really extended things from the conditions of abstract (mathematical) extension, they no longer have the same starting point that they had with Zeno, where the conditions of the real and the abstract orders are confused into one common notion of extension.[8]

The Millet Seed. The concrete character of Zeno's reasoning is further illustrated in his argument from the millet seed. A single grain of millet makes no sound when it falls; but a bushel of millet

---

240a1-4 (Oxford tr.). On the presuppositions back of this, see Lee, pp. 100-102. On the text, see W.D. Ross, *Aristotle's Physics* (Oxford, 1936), pp. 660-666.

[8] See L. Malverne, "Aristote et les Apories de Zénon," *Revue de Métaphysique et de Morale*, LVIII (1953), 80-107, esp. pp. 86-92 and 104-105.

does make a sound. The ratio of the bushel to the single grain, however, should be the same as that of the bushel's sound to the sound of each grain and each ten-thousandth part of a grain. Therefore every part of the millet makes a sound when it falls (DK, 29A 29).—This argument quite apparently has as its background the common-sense view of things, and not any particular philosophical tenets.

Zeno's method of arguing, evidently enough, is an application of Parmenides' counsel to follow reasoning no matter how much its results are at variance with sense perception and tradition. The method utilizes to the full Parmenides' observation that the ordinary mortal or common-sense view of things is two-headed—it looks upon everything in opposite ways at the same time. Zeno's arguments capitalize on the two-headed view that ordinary men can be shown to have of extension. They tend to view it as composed of definite parts and yet as indefinitely divisible. The opposite directions that are being followed simultaneously on this reversing way have only to be made explicit. Zeno's mutually destructive conclusions can then be easily deduced.

Unlike Parmenides, however, Zeno does not claim to be arguing from the Truth and reaching true conclusions. Rather, he argues from premises that are admitted by his adversaries, premises that result in contradictory conclusions. Because Zeno inaugurated this method of arguing as a conscious and full-fledged procedure, he is rightly called by Aristotle[9] the founder of dialectic. So understood, dialectic like genuine philosophy, remarks Aristotle,[10] extends to all things, but it is a tentative procedure that always remains on the surface and never gives real knowledge of things. Zeno's fragments, accordingly, offer no evidence of containing any truly metaphysical doctrine. Nor do they present any positive physical teachings. If the report of Diogenes Laertius (IX, 29; DK, 29A 1) is to be trusted, Zeno was already interested in the denial of a vacuum just as though he considered it not-being; and he regarded the things of the cosmos as constituted basically of

[9] References *supra*, n. 1. On the significance, see G. Calogero, "La Logica del Secondo Eleatismo," *Atene e Roma*, XXXVIII (1936), 148-149.

[10] *Metaph.*, Γ2,1004b17-26. The "Dialecticians" were properly the Megarians. These, however, are aptly described as "eredi del verbo e del metodo zenoniano"—Calogero, p. 153.

the opposites hot and cold, dry and moist, and these opposites as changing into one another. This last tenet, if correctly reported, would be radically different from Parmenides' doctrine of the basic cosmic constituents; yet it may refer only to the observed changes of particular things that are characterized by these opposites. In any case, not enough has been reported to allow Zeno any noteworthy stand as a philosopher of nature. His rank as a mathematician is likewise very dubious.[11]

However, even though Zeno cannot be given any notable status as a metaphysician or a natural philosopher or a mathematician, he is not to be denied an outstanding position in the development of Greek thought. He seems to have exercised a profound influence upon the methods of the fifth-century Sophists, the professional teachers of Greece.[12] Plato (*Prm.* 135CD) makes Parmenides say that exercise of the type found in Zeno's arguments is an indispensable preliminary training for dealing with the Ideas. Zeno's procedure, accordingly, could hardly help but focus attention on the different ways in which the human mind can conceive the same things, and so occasion reflexive consideration of the processes of human thought. This reflexion, as far as Greek thought is concerned, came to its full flower in the Aristotelian logic.

MELISSUS OF SAMOS (FIFTH CENTURY B.C.)

Chronology. On the strength of a statement made by Aristotle in the lost work *On the Constitution of Samos* (1567a15-17), the Melissus whose teachings are discussed in the Aristotelian treatises was identified with the naval commander who defeated the Athenians in 440 B.C. Apparently for this reason he had his *floruit* placed in the eighty-fourth Olympiad (444-441 B.C.) by Apollodorus. He was reported (D.L., IX, 24; DK, 30A 1), however, to have "heard" Parmenides, in the sense of having been a pupil of the great Eleatic thinker. In view of the comparatively easy communications between east and west at the time there need be nothing surprising about this contact, but it does suggest that Melissus was born a few years earlier than 480 B.C. For Stesimbrotus, a fifth-century B.C. historian, Melissus the physicist was an

---

[11] See Sir Thomas Heath, *A History of Greek Mathematics* (Oxford, 1921), I,272. Plutarch, *Pericles,* IV, 3, records that Zeno discoursed on "nature," i.e., the physical world.

[12] This influence of Zeno is sketched by Lee, pp. 112-123.

associate or teacher of Themistocles (514-460 B.C.), and so his activity
was viewed as having taken place early in the century (in Plutarch,
Themist., II, 3; DK, 30A 3). Eusebius (*PE,* X, 14, 15) records the
tradition as placing Melissus ahead of Zeno in the Eleatic "succession."
In that order they were in fact treated by Diogenes Laertius.

Writings. Melissus was credited in antiquity with having written
a work called *On Nature* or *On Being.* The titles are most likely of later
origin. Of this treatise ten[13] fragments survive, all taken from Simplicius.

PHILOSOPHICAL TEACHINGS

Temporal Infinity. The first of these fragments reads: "That
which was, was always and always will be. For if it had come into
being, it necessarily follows that before it came into being,
Nothing existed. If however, Nothing existed, in no way could
anything come into being out of nothing" (*Fr.* 1; tr. Freeman).
This seems to be a restatement of Parmenides' reasoning that it
is impossible for (that which) is to come into being. The second
fragment proceeds: "Since then it did not come into being, it is
and always was and always will be and has not beginning or end,
but is unlimited. . . . For it is not possible for anything to be
always, unless it is completely" (*Fr.* 2). Again, the argument
seems based upon the Parmenidean doctrine that (what) is cannot come into being or cease to be, and so has neither beginning
nor end in time; and that (what) is has to possess the total fullness of being, or else it could not be at all. But Melissus goes on
to express his conclusion in a manner that at first sight seems different from that of Parmenides. Melissus concludes that being is
unlimited, using the traditional Ionian term.

The Samian evidently means that being is unlimited in duration, just as Parmenides at one place in his poem (DK, 28B 8.4)
had stated that being is "endless." Being, for Parmenides, was indeed without beginning and without cease (DK, 28B 8.26-27),
but for him this meant that it was held "in the limits of mighty
bonds." To exist eternally implied for Parmenides to be *limited* to
(what) is. It allowed no room for further extension that would
have to mean extension into not-being. There was no not-being

[13] J. Burnet, *EGP,* p. 321, defends as the words of Melissus: "If nothing
is, what can be said of it as of something real?" (Simplicius, *In Ph.,* 103.15-
16). Others consider the sentence to be a paraphrase by Simplicius.

before or after, no non-duration in either direction that would leave being unlimited and so open to further extension. In both directions, being was perfect, complete, and so entirely *limited* as Parmenides used the word. Being could not be conceived as continually filling up successive not-being. Melissus, however, seems to have taken the Eleatic doctrine that (what) is is without beginning and end in time and is completely or all together, and to have expressed that doctrine by means of a term apparently opposite to the one used by Parmenides. Melissus is saying that being is unlimited in time. He is conceiving "beginning" and "end" as implying a *lack* of further being, and in this sense they would have the role of limits to existence. Being has no such limits, and so is unlimited. For Parmenides, on the other hand, "limit" was understood in the sense of definiteness and perfection. For him, (what) is is held within the bonds of a limit, and therefore cannot be boundless (DK, 28B 8.30-32), in the meaning that there is nothing indefinite or imperfect about it.

Melissus, then, is using the term "unlimited" to convey the same notion of eternal duration that Parmenides had expressed by the concept of "limit." Why? Is Melissus, in his more immediate Ionian surroundings, endeavoring to apply the Eleatic doctrine to the "unlimited" basic reality that had been traditional with the Milesian thinkers? In the fragment just considered he has used the notion only in regard to duration. But in the next fragment the term takes on a further application.

Spatial Infinity. The third fragment applies the notion of "unlimited" in the sense of spatial magnitude: "But just as it is always, so has it always to be unlimited in size" (*Fr.* 3). Being is unlimited in extension for the same reason that it is unlimited in time. For Parmenides, (what) is can be lacking in nothing, there is no not-being to prevent it from reaching its fullness in any direction, and so it reaches its *limits* uniformly. For Melissus the same conclusion is expressed as meaning that there are *no* limits to its extension, and so it is unlimited in size. The doctrine is the same as that of Parmenides, but it is expressed by the opposite term. Aristotle outlines the two respective viewpoints as follows: "Parmenides seems to fasten on that which is one in definition, Melissus on that which is one in matter, for which reason the

former says that it is limited, the latter that it is unlimited . . ."
(*Metaph.*, A 5,986b18-21; DK, 21A 30; Oxford tr.). In Aristotelian
language, Parmenides is speaking from a formal viewpoint, in
which the notion "unlimited" would imply indefiniteness and so
a *lack* of perfection; Melissus, on the contrary, is thinking from a
material standpoint, from which a "limit" would mean a *lack* of
further possible matter.[14] Accordingly, "nothing that has a beginning and end is either eternal or unlimited" (*Fr.* 4). The difference in terminology reflects the two different viewpoints.

The Plenum. The unicity of being follows from its unlimited
character: "If it were not One, it will form a boundary in relation to something else" (*Fr.* 5; tr. Freeman). Limit has been
equated with lack; so the first being would be something that is
lacking to any other being, thereby constituting a limit to it.
Being's unlimited nature shows, consequently, that there can be
nothing other than the one reality. It is impossible for there to
be two unlimited realities, for each would thereby limit the other
(*Fr.* 6). For the same reason, being is homogeneous (*Fr.* 7,1),
as though any heterogeneity would similarly constitute a limit.
The least change or rearrangement would destroy the homo-
geneity, and so would mean the complete destruction of what
exists: "Hence if it were to become different by a single hair in
ten thousand years, so it must be utterly destroyed in the whole
of time" (*Fr.* 7,2; tr. Freeman). Therefore pain, which involves
a change in bodily arrangement, is not to be found in being, nor
is grief. Nor can there be a vacuum, for a vacuum is nothing and
so does not exist. Consequently there can be no local motion, for
local motion would require a vacuum into which a thing could
move. For the same reason there can be no rarefaction or condensation. There is only a plenum (*Fr.* 7).

This reads as though some doctrine of a void had already been
in circulation. Being is conceived as a plenum. If the plenum
were conceived as limited, it would be conceived as having a

---

[14] The insistence of Melissus on the unlimited character of being is
usually considered by commentators as departure from, or as a correction
or contradiction of, Parmenides' doctrine that being is limited. For a discussion in terms of alleged Pythagorean opposition, see J. E. Raven, *Pythagoreans and Eleatics* pp. 79-86. On infinity in Parmenides, see R. Mondolfo,
L'Infinito nel Pensiero dell'Antichità Classica (Florence, 1956), pp. 366-367.

void outside it. The plenum, accordingly, has to be unlimited.[15]

Dialectic. Besides the principal line of reasoning that establishes being as one and immobile and a plenum, there are other indications of the same conclusion. As with Zeno, the consequences of the opposite position, that things are many, are drawn out: "If Things were Many, they would have to be of the same kind as I say the One is. For if there is earth and water and air and fire and iron and gold, and that which is living and that which is dead, and black and white and all the rest of the things which men say are real (*alêthê*): if these things exist, and we see and hear correctly, each thing must be of such a kind as it seemed to us to be in the first place, and it cannot change or become different, but each thing must always be what it is. But now we say we hear and see and understand correctly, and it seems to us that the hot becomes cold and the cold hot, . . . it seems to us that they all alter and change from what is seen on each occasion" (*Fr.* 8,2-4; tr. Freeman). Things appear to us as *changing* into their opposites, yet we speak inconsistently of them as *being*. Being, accordingly, is understood by Melissus to denote permanence and complete self-identity. These are excluded by change. So if the supposed changing things are or exist, they have to have the characteristics of Melissus' unique plenum, and so become entirely absorbed into it, just as all things became absorbed in Parmenides' one being. The argument of Melissus seems to be functioning against the whole background of traditional Ionian philosophy, in which opposite changed to opposite in the cosmic processes. The argument shows that the many changing things cannot be genuine: "It is clear therefore that we have not been seeing correctly, and that those things do not correctly seem to us to be Many; for they would not change if they were real, but each would Be as it seemed to be. For nothing is stronger than that which is real" (*Fr.* 8,5; tr. Freeman).

Truth, accordingly, requires that every thing be in a way that is entirely unchangeable, just as the one of Melissus is: "And if it changed, Being would have been destroyed, and Not-Being

---

[15] Such is the reason given by Aristotle for the Eleatic doctrine of unlimited being: "Some of them add that it is 'infinite,' since the limit (if it had one) would be a limit against the void" (*GC*, I 8,325a15-16; Oxford tr. DK, 28A 25).

would have come into being. Thus, therefore, if Things are many, they must be such as the One is" (*Fr.* 8,6; tr. Freeman). Starting from the supposition of many things, and arguing from the aspect of being that is admitted in these things, Melissus has shown that they coincide with the unique Eleatic reality. Similarly from the supposition of change—"if it changed"—he has argued that if the changing things are admitted to exist or to be they have to have the character of the immobile and self-identical Eleatic being. This dialectic is meant to show that the admitted tenets of multiplicity and change are absurd. Even in antiquity, however, a commentator objected that the supposition "beings are many and are in motion" is more reliable than the supposition "nothing can come from nothing," and so should prevail in argument.[16]

Indivisibility. The exclusion of multiplicity renders impossible any bulk or body, for any bulk would be divisible into parts: "If therefore Being Is, it must be One; and if it is One, it is bound not to have body. But if it had Bulk, it would have parts, and would no longer Be" (*Fr.* 9; tr. Freeman). Parmenides had maintained that being is indivisible (DK, 28B 8.22), since it is entirely homogeneous and there is no not-being that could mark off any distinction in it (8.46-49). For any distinction of parts, therefore, Parmenides on account of his basic viewpoint had required a *formal* division; and as there was only being, there was nothing else to make such a distinction in being, and so there could be no other form. Because of this very formal approach, Parmenides was able to accept the notion of an extended being that was not divisible into parts. Melissus, however, is thinking in terms of a plenum that is contrasted with a void, and is forced to approach the problem in a different way. He has to have a plenum that is the opposite of a void, and yet a plenum without the divisibility into parts that goes with the notions of body and bulk. He meets this very real Eleatic problem, to judge from the present fragment, by accepting the notion of an extended plenum that nevertheless is neither body nor bulk, just as Parmenides had accepted the doctrine of an extended being that was not divisible into parts. The denial of the notion "body" to true being

[16] *On Melissus, Xenophanes and Gorgias,* 1; in Aristotle, 974b8-29. DK, 30A 5.

could hardly have appeared at all strange in Eleatic thought. In reporting this fragment of Melissus, Simplicius[17] noted that Parmenides himself had assigned bodies to the realm of seeming. Eleatic being, though conceived as spatially extended, was not conceived as having the divisibility into parts outside parts that is implied in the notion of "body."

However, it seems impossible to determine the exact meaning that Melissus gave to body and bulk in this contrast to the spatially extended plenum. The fragment, nevertheless, shows that Melissus was aware of the fatal problem that confronted any Eleatic doctrine. A doctrine that conceived being as extended in space and yet as indivisible, had to explain how it could be so extended and yet not have parts outside parts.[18] Parmenides had given his own explanation from a purely formal viewpoint. Melissus, apparently, attempted a solution through the exclusion of body and bulk from his conception of the extended plenum. But exactly how he separated the two notions of plenum and body from each other, cannot be determined from the fragment. The awareness of the problem, though, seems to be revealed clearly enough.

The indivisibility of being was further proved by a dialectical argument from the impossibility of motion: "If Being is divided, it moves; and if it moved, it could not Be" (*Fr.* 10; tr. Freeman). A dividing of being is conceived by Melissus as a change from its original status, and so as a motion. Motion, however, has been shown to be incompatible with being. In the sharp Eleatic manner, any becoming or change excludes being. If a thing becomes in any way, and so if it changes at all, it just *is* not. The strange background against which Greek metaphysics will develop has

---

[17] *In Ph.*, 87.5-6. For explanation, see Raven, pp. 87-92. The term used by Simplicius to describe this doctrine of Melissus is "incorporeal" (*In Ph.*, 110.1). "Incorporeal" in Melissus, however, has to be understood in a sense that does not exclude an extended plenum. It is by no means the equivalent of "spiritual."

[18] The problem is stated by Plato, *Sph.* 244E (DK, 28B 7-8). On the problem, see Burnet, *EGP*, pp. 327-328; K. Freeman, *Companion*, pp. 166-168; N.B. Booth, "Did Melissus believe in Incorporeal Being?", *AJP*, LXXIX (1958), 61-65. Though the context from which Simplicius was quoting cannot be determined, he nevertheless reports it as meaning that Melissus himself held that being is incorporeal. The "intellectual error" mentioned by Booth, p. 62, would seem rather to lie in thinking that real extension could be divorced from corporeality.

taken full shape with the Eleatics. Becoming excludes being. Whatever else one may say about a changeable thing, one cannot speak of it as being, or say that it *is*.

The doctrine of Melissus seems to consist in the application of the Eleatic dialectic of being to the unlimited basic reality that had been traditionally taught in his native Ionian surroundings. Explaining the unlimited in terms of the Parmenidean being, it develops the doctrine of the plenum in a way that excludes change and void. It thereby destroys the possibility of the dense and the rare by which Anaximenes had accounted for the cosmic changes. It seems to have enjoyed great prestige and to have appealed more strongly to the immediately following generation than did the poem of Parmenides. Plato (*Tht.*, 180E; 183E; DK, 28B 7-8), in introducing the Eleatic doctrines, names Melissus ahead of Parmenides and has Socrates fall back upon a personal experience to justify his preference for Parmenides. Aristotle, however, dismisses his views as a little too crude to merit discussion (*Metaph.*, A 5,986b25-27; DK, 30A 7) and his reasoning processes as conclusions following from the admission of an absurd proposition (*Ph.*, I 3,186a9-10; DK, *ibid.*).

The fragments seem rather to show a definite basis for the Stagirite's estimate of Melissus. They bear the marks of dialectical reasoning and not of metaphysical penetration. They reveal Melissus as a dialectician who popularized the Eleatic reasoning by developing it against the Ionian background that was more comprehensible to the men of his surroundings. To anyone who admits in the Milesian fashion that there *is* an unlimited primal reality, and who can be brought to concede that being means permanence and complete self-identity, the reasoning of Melissus follows without hindrance. But unlike the keen insight of Parmenides, it does not provide help in probing the inmost nature of being itself.

If Melissus developed a cosmology, no report about it has been handed down, except a quite evidently garbled doxographical statement that nothing is firmly established in nature and all things are potentially corruptible (DK, 30A 12). This, as well as the attention given to pain and grief, might suggest that Melissus assigned to the things of the cosmos an unsubstantial and unstable role of their own, a role that was excluded nevertheless from the status of being. However, no details are available. On the other hand, Aristotle (*Metaph.*, A 5,986b27-33) contrasts Melissus with Parmenides on this point. Parmenides, in contrast to Melissus, was forced in places to follow the observed facts and posited two fundamental principles to explain the cosmic processes. Aristotle speaks as though the Samian's treatise contained only the dialectic of being.

It is hard to see any ground for the claim that Melissus was the first to perceive how atomism would be the only consistent doctrine of plurality. His place in the history of Greek philosophy is secure without that. He systematized in a more popular way the Eleatic dialectic of being, though without adding to it anything profound or very original.

RETROSPECT

Greek philosophy proper, according to all available accounts and evidence, commenced in an endeavor to understand the visible and tangible universe in which men lived and worked. The earliest attempts, those of the Milesians, sought to explain the cosmos and its processes in terms of some basic stuff or plasm that possessed an inherent motion after the manner of a living thing. Such inquiries soon brought to the fore the role that different and opposite formal characteristics played in cosmic development. These opposites were looked upon as inherent in the original matrix, or as developed from it through a process of rarefaction and condensation. Since the intrinsic motion was conceived in a vitalistic fashion, it required no external agent for its origin. It was unoriginated and so was eternal. In these approaches the Milesians bequeathed to succeeding generations in tentative yet solid and clear outlines the way in which the sensible world could be explained on the level of *natural philosophy*. They had sketched the broad lines of an investigation that would continue and would develop eventually into the account of the sensible universe in terms of its substantial principles, material and formal, and of its motion as a process not self-explanatory but proceeding from external causes.

The Pythagoreans seem to have commenced with an account

of the cosmos in terms of two basic opposites, light and darkness or void, limit and the unlimited. This explanation, apparently, was gradually developed in the light of mathematical principles, in such a way that the natures of sensible things became identified with the natures of the mathematical entities. Whether or not the Pythagoreans made any notable contributions to Greek mathematics, they at least used mathematical principles to explain the cosmos as a whole, and in doing so they set afoot, feebly perhaps but lastingly, the quantitative explanation of the universe. It was an account that did not require properly efficient causes, remaining as it did within the realm of mathematical formality. This type of explanation, however, did not receive too much development in subsequent Greek thought. Only in modern times, in the controlling of nuclear energy for use or for harm, has it come to its dazzling and terrifying fullness; but it had its foundations laid firmly and deeply by the daring speculation of these comparatively early Greek thinkers.

Parmenides, deeply impressed by his keen observation of the muddled, inconsistent, and self-contradictory ways in which men ordinarily think, sought his explanation of that disconcerting phenomenon in the mutually destructive opposition of the two basic forms that men combine in the construction of their cosmos. He found his own consistent type of thinking by approaching things from the aspect of their being and only of their being. In this way he inaugurated with astonishing penetration the type of thinking that investigates things from the viewpoint of being, and that later was to be known under the title of *metaphysics*. He left to the multiple and changing things of the cosmos all the reality that appears in them, and so all the reality that men see and feel in them, but he denied to such appearances the far higher status of being. In isolating the aspect of being and making it the standpoint for a new scientific treatment of things, Parmenides opened the way for the science of beings as beings.

Heraclitus, though just as vividly conscious as Parmenides of the contradictory aspects of the cosmos, was struck rather with the role that those opposites played in human conduct. With more sympathetic insight he sought and found consistency in an ever-varying and so apparently inconsistent play and tension of such opposites. In the continually changing tensions all individual polarities had to be brought into the common activity of social or "political" life, a common, in fact, that extended far beyond the limits of the Greek city-state. In that common unity alone could they fulfill their function. Moral life, accordingly, was explained as "political" life, and the problems of finding the unshakeable and abiding measures in the ever-varying circumstances was clearly faced. The foundations for the development of Greek moral science had been laid.

Finally, the followers of Parmenides, Melissus and Zeno, drew from his doctrine of being a dialectic that could hardly help but focus attention upon the different ways in which the human mind can know the same things. The Eleatic dialectic of being may have lacked the insight of a metaphysics, but it was to cause abundant trouble and to result in profound modifications of subsequent Greek natural philosophy. On the other hand, however, it paved the way for the study of the processes of human thought as a special object different from the general cosmic considerations, and so occasioned the development of logic.

SELECTED READINGS AND REFERENCES

Henry Desmond Prichard Lee, *Zeno of Elea* (Cambridge, Eng.: University Press, 1936).

N. B. Booth, "Were Zeno's Arguments a Reply to Attacks upon Parmenides?" *Phronesis,* II (1957), 1-9.

————, "Were Zeno's Arguments Directed against the Pythagoreans?" *Phronesis,* II, (1957), 90-103.

————, "Zeno's Paradoxes," *JHS,* LXXVII (1957), 187-201.

————, "Did Melissus Believe in Incorporeal Being?" *AJP,* LXXIX (1958), 61-65.

Part Two

THE DEVELOPMENTS
OF GREEK PHILOSOPHY

CHAPTER 6

Empedocles of Acragas

Chronology. The considerations entering into the chronology of Empedocles are complicated and difficult.[1] The testimonia are too conflicting to be reconciled. Some have to be rejected in order to permit the acceptance of a definite dating. Any over-all conclusion, consequently, is left highly debatable. The most likely dating is about the year 521 B.C. for his birth, and 461 B.C. or thereabouts for his death. The usually accepted chronology, however, places his *floruit* in 444 B.C. This late dating rests upon indications that are far from compelling, and has been the beginning of a chronological schema that finally results in making Democritus *post*-Socratic, against all the evidence[2] that the Abderite's work was definitely *pre*-Socratic.

Life. No sufficiently established facts are known about the life of Empedocles. The testimonia indicate that he was exiled from his native city. The fragments of his poems may give some hints about his manner of living. Numerous stories concerning him have been handed down in Greek tradition. These, however, even the ones that represent him as taking an active part in democratic political movements, seem to be merely later expansions of notions found in his works. Tradition in general regarded him as belonging to an aristocratic family. From his surviving fragments one can assume safely enough that he was interested especially in natural science, medicine, and religion, and that

[1] See Appendix, *infra* pp. 417-419.
[2] On the testimonia indicating the *pre*-Socratic status of Democritus, see Luigia A. Stella, *Rivista di Filologia e d'Istruzione Classica*, LXX (1942), 21-46. The early datings for Empedocles, Anaxagoras, and Democritus have been dubbed "wild" by critics. Yet they rest on strong evidence, and provide a clear chronological framework in which the course of fifth-century Greek thought can be more readily understood.

he attained considerable fame and popularity. His native city, which he refers to as "yellow Acragas" (*Fr.* 112), was a prosperous Dorian colony slightly west of the middle point on the southern coast of Sicily. It was considered to be one of the most beautiful of the Greek city-states.

Works. About one hundred and fifty fragments remain from two poems of Empedocles. To one of these works was assigned the usual title given to Presocratic writings dealing with natural philosophy—*On Nature.* The other is called *Purifications.* There is no guarantee that these titles were given by Empedocles himself. Like Parmenides, Empedocles wrote in epic verse. Of other works of his mentioned in antiquity, nothing has survived.[3]

PHILOSOPHICAL TEACHINGS

A. On Nature

Apocalyptic Setting. In the initial section of the poem *On Nature* (*Frs.* 1-3), Empedocles addresses himself to a pupil or associate named Pausanius. He emphasizes that men see only a small part during their fleeting lives, though they wish to know the whole. He himself, however, will try, as far as mortal man may know it, to express such comprehensive knowledge to the listener who has come to him in retirement. Accordingly, he beseeches his virgin Muse to convey to him this knowledge, driving his well-harnessed chariot.

This introduction resembles in its general lines the Proem of Parmenides. It presents the doctrine of Empedocles in the form of a revelation from a superior intelligence, as did the introduction in the Eleatic's poem. In regard to this technique, however, it seems obliged to touch a defensive note in commenting (*Fr.* 4) that low minds tend to distrust those above them, and in insisting on the trustworthiness of the Muse as a motive to analyze the message (*logos*) carefully and to grasp it through deep reflection.

The Four Roots. In the fashion of the Ionians Empedocles seeks the ultimate basis of things, and declares it to be fourfold: "Hear, first, the four roots of things: bright Zeus, and life-bearing Hera, and Aidoneus, and Nestis who causes a mortal spring of

---

[3] For a short discussion of these works, see Jean Zafiropulo, *Empédocle d'Agrigente* (Paris, 1953), pp. 64-69.

moisture to flow with her tears."[4] Translated from poetry into more prosaic terms, these four roots of things are called "Fire and Water and Earth and the boundless height of Air, . . ."[5] The form of expression "roots" suggests the conception of cosmic development as a vital process that springs from them. They themselves are not produced by anything else (*Fr.* 7). They have no origin, and so they can function as the absolutely basic constituents of things.

No reason is given in the fragments for choosing the four. Apparently the traditional Ionian opposites—hot and cold, dry and wet—are concretized in these four roots. At any rate, Empedocles does not write as though he encountered any special difficulty in having this general conception of the four roots of things accepted by the public of his day. He speaks as though the fact had merely to be stated and its reasonableness would be evident.

Further precisions regarding the nature of the four roots are not present in the fragments. Aristotle remarks that though Empedocles has four elements he uses them, it is clear from the poem, as though they were two, fire on the one hand and earth, air, and water on the other, and so in this way has one fundamental pair of contraries.[6] The significance of this division cannot be determined from the texts of Empedocles. The Stagirite (*Cael.*, III 6,305a1-4; DK, 31A 43a) further interprets the roots as having the status of smallest particles; and each particle, though divisible, will never be divided. This would imply that Aristotle found no explanation in Empedocles for the baffling problem raised by Eleatic speculation, namely, how something could be extended and yet be immune to division. There is nothing, in fact, to indicate that Empedocles was even aware of the serious problem involved in this tenet.

Change. All things in the sensible universe are but composites of the four roots through a process of mixture: ". . . there is no birth of any of mortal things, nor any end in baneful death, but only a mixing and an exchange of the things that have been mixed, . . ." (*Fr.* 8). Generation and destruction, birth and death,

---

[4] *Fr.* 6; tr. Freeman. Although the meanings have been disputed, Zeus seems to stand for air, Hera for earth, and Aidoneus for fire. See Burnet, *EGP*, p.229, n.3.

[5] *Fr.* 17.18; tr. Freeman. *Cf. Fr.* 38.

[6] *GC*, II 3,330b19-21; *Metaph.*, A 4,985a31-b3. DK, 31A 36-37.

are merely conventional names for this mixing and separating process: "But men, when these have been mixed in the form of a man and come into the light, or in the form of a species of wild animals, or plants, or birds, then say that this has 'come into being'; and when they separate, this men call sad fate. The terms that Right demands they do not use; but through custom I myself also apply these names" (*Fr.* 9; tr. Freeman). Accordingly, men are intellectually shortsighted and foolish when they imagine that anything really comes into being or is destroyed (*Fr.* 11). The reason is that being cannot become or perish: "From what in no wise exists, it is impossible for anything to come into being; and for Being to perish completely is incapable of fulfilment and unthinkable; for it will always be there, wherever anyone may place it on any occasion" (*Fr.* 12; tr. Freeman).

These assertions repeat Parmenides' reflections on the impossibility of generation and perishing, and on the conventional character of the names that designate them. However, Empedocles adheres to plurality as his starting point, and retains one type of change, local motion, as the means of explaining the cosmic processes. But as in Parmenides, reality is distributed evenly everywhere. The impossibility of any true generation or perishing precludes addition to or subtraction from the whole: "Nor is there any part of the Whole that is empty or overfull" (*Fr.* 13; tr. Freeman). A void, accordingly, is impossible.

The Cosmic Processes.   Under the influence of two opposite forces, love and hate, take place the successive union and separation of the four basic roots: "And these never cease their continuous exchange, sometimes uniting under the influence of Love, so that all become One, at other times again each moving apart through the hostile force of Hate" (*Fr.* 17.6-8; tr. Freeman). In the course of the process, the different characteristics of the four roots become successively predominant: ". . . each has its own character, and they prevail in turn in the course of Time."[7] The doctrine is illustrated by the simile of the different pigments that when properly mixed result in the varied products of the painters:

---

[7] *Fr.* 17.28-29; tr. Freeman. *Cf.*: "No, but these things alone exist, and running through one another they become different things at different times, and are ever continuously the same." *Ibid.*, lines 34-35. *Cf. Fr.* 21.13-14.

". . . these, when they take many-coloured pigments in their hands, and have mixed them in a harmony, taking more of some, less of another, create from them forms like to all things, making trees and men and women and animals and birds and fish nurtured in water, and even long-lived gods, . . ." (*Fr.* 23.3-8; tr. Freeman). The cosmic processes, however, are continuous and cyclic (*Fr.* 26). When unified by love, the cosmos is called divine and is described quite after the manner of Parmenides' sphere simile: ". . . equal to itself in all directions and entirely unlimited, a rounded sphere exulting in circular steadfastness" (*Fr.* 28). As a sphere it is ". . . in all directions equal to itself."[8]

Apparently in direct contradiction to Parmenides, for whom the continually changing world processes were "deceptive" (DK, 28B 8.52), Empedocles presents his own account of these processes as "undeceptive" (*Fr.* 17.26). Only at the height of its unity through the predominance of love does the cosmic process reach a state that may be described in terms of Parmenides' sphere. The whole process, though merely one of mixture, can hardly be regarded as mechanical, on account of the two influences under which it takes place, love and hate. Rather, just as with the roots, so with the whole process the notion of a vital functioning is indicated.

Cognition. Thought is regarded as corporeal: ". . . the blood round the heart is Thought in mankind" (*Fr.* 105; tr. Freeman). Thought therefore is one particular function of the four roots: "For from these are all things fitted and fixed together, and by means of these do men think, and feel pleasure and sorrow" (*Fr.* 107; tr. Freeman). This doctrine seems to be a version of Parmenides' views on cognition, now developed in terms of the four roots, and not merely of two basic constituents, light and darkness. Further, as in Parmenides, thought varies according to the changing composition of one's nature: "In so far as their natures have changed, so does it befall men to think changed thoughts."[9] Each force or root is the means by which the same force or root is perceived: "We see Earth by means of Earth,

[8] *Fr.* 29. *Apeirôn* 'unlimited,' in *Fr.* 28, seems meant to describe the endless character of a sphere, and need not indicate any attack on Parmenides' teaching about the limited nature of being.

[9] *Fr.* 108; tr. Freeman. On the meaning, see Verdenius, *Parmenides: Some Comments on His Poem*, pp. 20-22.

Water by means of Water, divine Air by means of Air, and destructive Fire by means of Fire; Affection by means of Affection, Hate by means of baneful Hate" (*Fr.* 109; tr. Freeman). Accordingly, all things without exception are cognitive.[10] Again, this seems to be an application of Parmenides' basic doctrine of cognition, with six ultimate factors instead of two.

All things give off effluences (*Fr.* 89) by which they are known. These, according to Theophrastus' detailed account,[11] are streams of particles that reach the senses and cause the respective cognitions. They fit only the passages of the one particular sense to which they are adapted. Where they are wider than the passage of a particular sense, they cannot enter; where they are narrower, they pass right through without touching it; so in neither of these cases does any sensation take place. That is why one sense cannot discern the objects of another. Empedocles (*Fr.* 84) further speaks of the light or fire going *out* through the passages of the eyes in the act of seeing. This drew Aristotle's query that if such were the case, why do we not see in the dark?[12]

These details indicate a rather primitive notion of cognition. Whether the details were original with Empedocles or borrowed from some contemporary medical source cannot be determined. In any case, Aristotle (*De An.*, III 3, 427a21-25; DK, 31B 106) and Theophrastus (*De Sens.*, 23; DK, 31A 86) both emphasize that Empedocles did not distinguish intellection from sense cognition.

Practical Motivation of Knowledge.   The knowledge imparted by Empedocles is meant to give his pupil control over disease and old age, as well as over the weather and other natural forces, even as far as bringing back the dead to life: "You shall learn all the drugs that exist as a defense against illness and old age; for you alone will I accomplish all this. You shall check the force of the unwearying winds which rush upon the earth with their blasts and lay waste the cultivated fields. And again, if you wish, you shall conduct the breezes back again. . . . And you shall bring out of Hades a dead man restored to strength" (*Fr.* 111; tr. Freeman).

[10] *Frs.* 103 and 110.10. See H. Schwabl, *Wien. Stud.*, LXIX (1956), 49-50.
[11] *De Sensibus,* 7-24. In *Dox. Graec.,* 500-506; DK, 31A 86.
[12] *Sens.*, 2,437b11-14; DK, 31A 91.

This motivation seems to make no specific distinction between the type of knowledge that understands drugs and the type that undertakes wonder-working. There is scarcely any need, therefore, to see a radical difference in the motivation of Empedocles' poem *On Nature* and that of the other work from which fragments have survived, the *Purifications*.

B. *Purifications*

In his other poem Empedocles describes himself going among people in flourishing towns "as an immortal god, no longer a mortal, held in honour by all, . . ." (*Fr.* 112; tr. Freeman). In it he seems to teach quite clearly a doctrine of transmigration of souls: "For by now I have been born as boy, girl, plant, bird, and dumb sea-fish."[13] He also stresses correct knowledge of the gods as being necessary for human happiness: "Happy is he who has acquired the riches of divine thoughts, but wretched the man in whose mind dwells an obscure opinion about the gods!" (*Fr.* 132; tr. Freeman). Yet one cannot grasp the divine by the ordinary path of human cognition: "It is not possible to bring it near within reach of our eyes, nor to grasp it with our hands, by which route the broadest road of Persuasion runs into the human mind."[14] Rather, it has no head, arms, feet, or other organs, but is "Mind, holy and ineffable, and only Mind, which darts through the whole universe with its swift thoughts" (*Fr.* 134; tr. Freeman). Such reflections seem to be merely an echo of Xenophanes. Other fragments[15] indicate that Empedocles condemned the shedding of blood in sacrifices, apparently on account of the transmigration of souls.

From a strictly philosophical viewpoint, Empedocles offers very little that can be called original and profound. He seems rather to have been a successful popularizer of doctrines already worked out by preceding thinkers. In the four roots he stereotyped the basic opposites of the Ionians, but in such a way that the doctrine attained a lasting appeal and went down to posterity under the label of the four Empedoclean elements. He likewise succeeded

---

[13] *Fr.* 117; tr. Freeman. *Cf. Frs.* 115, 118, 119, 120, 126.
[14] *Fr.* 133; tr. Freeman, retouched.
[15] *Frs.* 128, 135, 136, 137, 138.

in having his name attached to the doctrine of the cognition of like by like, even though the conception is fundamentally that of Parmenides. The notion of the effluences, even if it were original with Empedocles, can hardly be placed on a very high level as philosophy. On the other hand, the inspiration of Empedocles' physical doctrines is genuinely philosophical, even though based upon the philosophical reflections of other men. His thought can hardly be explained away as ". . . a religious doctrine, and a translation of it into physical terms, . . ."[16] Rather, the attempt to view the cosmos as composed of primitive constituents, and the Parmenidean argument that those constituents are not themselves subject to generation, are quite apparently on the philosophical level, in spite of the strong mythological background against which these basic tenets are developed. They are evidence of a definitely rational effort to present the pluralistic aspect of the universe as "undeceptive," even while accepting the basic Eleatic reasoning that what truly is cannot undergo change or destruction.

The fact remains, nevertheless, that Empedocles had very little of his own to say, philosophically speaking. Yet he seemed able to enchant his readers with his presentation of philosophical doctrine, and so he has drawn abundantly the attention of historians of philosophy both ancient and modern. Aristotle cited Empedocles as an example of those "who having nothing to say, yet pretend to say something" (*Rh.*, III 5, 1407a33-34; DK, 31A 25). From the viewpoint of poetic composition one can hardly deny the work of Empedocles the merit of a well-rounded, consistent, and vigorously sketched conception of the universe. But in spite of its coherence from that standpoint, its lack of philosophical profundity seems to have justified the criticism of Timon of Phlius, the third-century B.C. satirist who was usually so apt at sighting the basic weakness of any Greek philosophy. Of Empedocles, Timon wrote: ". . . the principles he chose need other principles to explain them" (D.L., VIII,67; tr. Hicks. DK, 31A 1). Yet of all the philosophers he is said to be the only one who enjoys the honor of having a place in Europe named after

---

[16] F. M. Cornford, *From Religion to Philosophy* p. 240. On the mythological background of the *Purifications,* see Kirk-Raven, *The Presocratic Philosophers,* pp. 349-353.

him, Porto Empedocle, situated on the southern coast of Sicily a few miles from the site of ancient Acragas.

SELECTED READINGS AND REFERENCES

G. F. Unger, "Die Zeitverhältnisse des Anaxagoras und Empedokles," *Philol.*, Supplbd. IV (1884), 511-550.

Joseph Bidez, *La Biographie d'Empédocle* (Ghent: Clemm, 1894).

William Ellery Leonard, *The Fragments of Empedocles*, Translated into English Verse (Chicago: Open Court, 1908).

Ettore Bignone, *Empedocle* (Turin: Fratelli Bocca, 1916).

Walther Kranz, *Empedokles* (Zürich: Artemis-Verlag, 1949).

H. S. Long, "The Unity of Empedocles' Thought," *AJP*, LXX (1949), 142-158.

Antonio Traglia, *Studi sulla Lingua di Empedocle* (Bari: Adriatica, 1952).

Empedocleous Katharmoi, ed. Jean Zapirofulo (Paris: A. Tallone, 1954). Contains Greek text of the *Purifications*, French translation, and notes.

H. Schwabl, "Empedokles Fr. B 110," *Wien. Stud.*, LXIX (1956), 49-56.

J. Bollack, "Die Metaphysik des Empedokles als Entfaltung des Seins," *Philologus*, CI (1957), 30-54.

N.-I. Boussoulas, "Essai sur la Structure du Mélange dans la Pensée Présocratique: Empédocle," *Revue de Métaphysique et de Morale*, LXIII (1958), 135-148.

[CHAPTER 7]

Anaxagoras, Diogenes, and
Archelaus

ANAXAGORAS OF CLAZOMENAE (534-462 B.C.?)

Chronology. Among all the Presocratics none has given occasion
for more bewildering chronological reconstructions than Anaxagoras.
He came originally from Clazomenae, an Ionian coastal city on the
gulf of Smyrna, and is placed by unanimous tradition as a pupil, or
at least as somehow associated with the philosophical activities, of
Anaximenes.[1] This Greek tradition, if reliable, should mean that he
came to Miletus well before its fall in 494 B.C. Among his own pupils,
moreover, were numbered Themistocles (514-460 B.C.),[2] Pericles (494-
429 B.C.), Archelaus the teacher of Socrates, and Euripides (484-407
B.C.). He is associated with the story of a meteoric stone that fell about
467 B.C. at Aegospotomi in the Chersonese. This fact would indicate
that he was a well-known figure in the Greek world around that time.
On the other hand, in Socrates' youth—and so by the middle of the
fifth century—he was merely a "book" in Athens, and no longer a living
voice. In the eyes of a contemporary of Socrates, Hippias, he was in
fact represented as one of the "ancients."[3]

The chronological relations in which the activities of Anaxagoras are
placed by these traditions would indicate roughly that he was born

---

[1] DK, 59A 1; 2; 7; 41.

[2] That Themistocles was a pupil of Anaxagoras rests on a statement of
the fifth-century B.C. historian Stesimbrotus. Plutarch (*Them.*, II,3; D.K.,
30A 3), writing more than five centuries later, with the Apollodorian
chronology well established, rejected this testimony on account of Anaxagoras' association with Pericles, who was twenty years younger than Themistocles.

[3] Plato, *Hp. Ma.*, 281C, 283A.

before the last quarter of the sixth century, and that his philosophical career cannot be extended beyond the fourth decade of the fifth century B.C. Yet a report transmitted through Diogenes Laertius states that he was twenty years old at the time of Xerxes' invasion (480 B.C.) and that he lived for seventy-two years. Apparently this had been the basis for the date of his birth taken from Apollodorus and handed down as the seventieth Olympiad (500-497 B.C.; D.L., II, 7; DK, 59A 1). Accordingly, 500-428 B.C. is the dating that has been accepted by the great majority of modern historians as the span of Anaxagoras' life. It seems to agree with the report (D.L., *loc. cit.*) of Demetrius of Phalerum, a pupil of Theophrastus, that Anaxagoras began to lead a philosophic life at Athens when he was twenty, under the archonship of Callias (456 B.C.); for if the name of the archon is changed to read "Calliades" (480 B.C.) this report would likewise indicate the year 500 B.C. as the date of Anaxagoras' birth.

On the other hand, if the Persian invasion originally meant was the one that took place in 513 B.C. and later mistaken for the much better known expedition of Xerxes,[4] then the date of Anaxagoras' birth would be about 533 B.C. This would allow the chronological relations necessary for the facts reported about Anaxagoras' activities, and for Aristotle's assertion that he was older than Empedocles, if 421 B.C. is taken as the year of Empedocles' birth. It would likewise agree with the account that he was forty years older than Democritus, on the acceptance of 494/493 B.C. as the year in which Democritus was born.

Further, Anaxagoras is reported to have lived at Athens for thirty years, and to have been tried and condemned there on charges of impiety and Persian leanings. He was saved by Pericles, and went to Lampsacus, a Milesian colony at the head of the southern shore of the Hellespont. There he died and was buried with public honors (DK, 59A 1; 3; 17; 19). The extant accounts of his trial at Athens are too brief and garbled to be of any help towards arriving at a definite chronology.

From all these considerations the most likely reconstruction is that Anaxagoras was born at Clazomenae in 534/533 B.C., came to Miletus while Anaximenes was still living, and then to Athens after the fall of Miletus (494 B.C.). He stayed at Athens until his trial and condemnation some thirty years later, about 464 B.C. His death in Lampsacus at the age of seventy-two would take place about 462/461 B.C., his fame throughout the Greek world being sufficient to merit the honors paid

---

[4] So G. F. Unger, *Philol.*, Supplbd. IV (1884), 547, Eduard Zeller, *Philos. d. Griechen*, 6th ed. (Leipzig, 1920), I, 1196, states that this interpretation is "naturally" to be rejected, though without offering any special discussion. For the later chronology, see also J. A. Davison, *CQ*, XLVII (1953), 39-45.

him there. Actually, that date has been handed down independently for his death.[5] In this chronology the account of Demetrius of Phalerum that Anaxagoras began his philosophic life at Athens in the archonship of Callias (Calliades) at the age of twenty, will have to be regarded as based on a later assumption that he was twenty years old at the time of Xerxes' invasion.

For those who accept 500-428 B.C. as the dates of Anaxagoras' life, the Athenian period may be located in two different ways. It may be placed at 461-432 B.C. in order to make his trial coincide with the attack on Pericles by the more advanced democrats at the beginning of the Peloponnesian war. On the other hand, it may be taken to extend from 480 to 450 B.C., in order to safeguard his position as the teacher of Pericles and to take at its face value the report that he began to lead a philosophic life at Athens in the year 480 B.C.

Writings.   According to the accounts handed down by Diogenes Laertius (I, 16; II, 6. DK, 59A 1) only one treatise was written by Anaxagoras, and it was composed in an attractive and elevated style. Plato (*Ap.*, 26DE; DK, 59A 35) wrote that at the time of Socrates' trial it was on sale at Athens for one drachma, and that it held the sun to be a stone and the moon earth. This seems to imply that such was the charge of impiety leveled against Anaxagoras at his own trial. If the treatise furnished the occasion for that charge, one may conjecture that it was published not much before 464 B.C. This would permit Aristotle to say that Anaxagoras was "later in works" than Empedocles.

The surviving fragments of the treatise come nearly all from Simplicius, who in the sixth century A.D. still had access to at least the first of its parts.

PHILOSOPHICAL TEACHINGS

The Original Mixture.   The various modern interpretations of Anaxagoras' basic doctrines differ widely and radically. There is special need, therefore, to let the fragments of his work speak as much as possible for themselves. According to Simplicius the

---

[5] See DK, 59A 4;18. The manuscript text of Diogenes Laertius (II,7; DK, A 1) gives 468/467 as the year of his death. The *Marmor Parium*, in inscriptions of the third century B.C., records that Euripides won a prize for drama in 442 B.C., and adds that Socrates and Anaxagoras were his contemporaries (DK, A 4a). This need not mean, however, that Anaxagoras, who had been Euripides' teacher, was still alive in 442. Eusebius, *PE*, X, 14, 14, (504C), regarded him as a contemporary of Xenophanes and Pythagoras, while Hippolytus (*Ref.*, I,8,13; DK, 59A 42), according to the manuscript text, placed his *floruit* in 428/427 B.C.

following lines stood at the beginning of the Clazomenian's treatise: "All things (*chrêmata*) were together, unlimited both in number and smallness; for the small too was unlimited. And when all were together, none was visible on account of the smallness. For air-and-ether prevailed over all, both being unlimited. For in the sum total of things these are the greatest both in number and size."[6]

The opening text, in the solemn manner of the times, clearly referred to a *past* state in which all things[7] were together in a mixture. In it they were unlimited in number. From this standpoint, then, they *all* had the aspect that in the earlier Milesian thinkers characterized the basic stock of cosmic development. They were quantitatively unlimited, and so could be drawn upon indefinitely without fear of exhausting the supply. But they were also unlimited in smallness. The reason offered is that "the small" *too* was unlimited. According to the sequence of thought, "the small" is given the status of one of the things in the mixture, and by its unlimited presence it rendered all other things indefinitely small. A quantity like smallness seems to be regarded by Anaxagoras as a thing. The doctrine would comply with and justify one of the conditions presupposed by Zeno's arguments. It would allow things to be indefinitely small and numerically unlimited.

The express teaching that all things and not just one are unlimited is something new in Ionian cosmology, though it may

[6] *Fr.* 1. Cf. Parmenides, *Fr.* 8.5 (DK, 28B). The words "both being unlimited" are rejected by Jean Zafiropulo, *Anaxagore de Clazomène* (Paris, 1948), pp. 375-376, on the ground that air and ether are limited for Anaxagoras. But in the original mixture, air and ether (like all other things) *were* unlimited, though *now* as separated out in the present universe they are the *largest* components both in number and size. Air and ether, as Cornford, *CQ*, XXIV (1930), 25, notes, take a singular verb, as though they are thought of as a united whole in this regard. At *Ph.*, VIII 1,250b24-26, Aristotle describes the Anaxagorean doctrine as meaning that the things were at rest in the mixture throughout an unlimited time before the separating motion began.

[7] According to the usage of the time, "things" in this context should not have any technical meaning, but need merely signify objects in the vaguest and most indefinite way. Greek tradition gives no evidence of seeing any special technical sense in the Clazomenian's use of the term. However, in the fragments quoted, *chrêma* or *chrêmata* will be added in parentheses whenever the term is expressed in the Greek text. On the initial problematic vagueness of the word in the Milesian background, see Otto Jöhrens, *Die Fragmente des Anaxagoras* (Bochum-Langendreer, 1939), pp. 5-7.

have been implicit in Anaximander. In the present fragment and in others the *numerical* character of the unlimitedness is brought to the fore. This new feature suggests that Anaxagoras is thinking out his doctrine against the same background in which the Eleatic dialectic functioned.

Original Invisibility. Further, in that past state of mixture everything was rendered invisible by the smallness. Why? The reason given is that air and ether, both unlimited, prevailed over all; for at the *present* time these are the two largest components, both in number and size, in the total aggregates of things. The reasoning seems to be based upon an accepted tenet that air and ether at the present time are the most extensive components of the universe. Hence is drawn the conclusion that they likewise dominated in the original mixture, at least in so far as they spread their condition of invisibility over all the things contained in it. They could do this because of their "smallness." They are apparently looked upon as being of a nature so thin and spread out that their constituent parts become small enough to evade detection by the eye.

Against the background of Anaximenes' teaching, there is nothing strange in finding that Anaxagoras regarded air as unlimited and as conditioning the primary source of all cosmic development, and that he stressed its rareness or thinness. These same characteristics are also ascribed to ether, which, according to Aristotle,[8] was identified by Anaxagoras with fire. In the general setting of Greek cosmological notions, the ethereal fire could readily be conceived as invisible. The opening fragment, consequently, reasons quite in accord with the background to be expected in a pupil of Anaximenes who had to reckon with Zeno's dialectic. A thing is looked upon as increasing in smallness as its divisions become smaller and smaller till they finally escape human sight. The preoccupation with the notion of unlimited divisibility in things suggests that this conception is to be manipu-

---

[8] *Cael.*, III 3,302b4-5; *cf.* I 3,270b25 and *Mete.*, II 9,369b14-15 (DK, 59A 73;84). The identification of fire and ether at the time may be seen in Empedocles, *Fr.* 38. Empedocles' (*Fr.* 39) attack on the doctrine of unlimited earth and ether could be directed against *oral* teachings of Anaxagoras, for according to a report (D.L., VIII, 56; DK, 31A 1) that goes back to Alcidamas, a fifth-century writer, Empedocles attended discourses of Anaxagoras.

lated in order to explain the development of the present cosmos.

The Separating Off. Shortly after the initial fragment came the statement: "For air and ether are being separated off from the surrounding multiplicity, and what surrounds is unlimited in number."[9] The two dominating constituents of the original mixture are represented as being separated off from the rest of things, though these latter, numerically unlimited as ever, continue to surround them. Not long after were the following words: "Such being the case, it is necessary to believe that there are many things of all kinds in all composites, and the seeds of all things (*chrêmata*), seeds that have all kinds of shapes and surface characteristics and pleasant sensations."[10] Every composite, accordingly, *now* contains within itself a numerous and wide variety of things, and the "seeds" of all things. As a metaphor, "seeds" would at least indicate something from which the fully constituted things could develop, and would suggest a vital aspect in the process of the development. The differentiated beginnings of all things, then, are present in all composites. The *kinds* of such things, though very numerous, are not indicated as unlimited in number. Instances of composites that Simplicius found mentioned somehow in this connection are men, living things, artifacts, the sun, the moon, and things grown from earth for use in houses. Such composites are "separated off" from the original mixture. Anaxagoras speaks as though all the non-human composites are meant to serve the needs of men.[11]

The fragment continues: "Before these were separated off, all being together, no surface characteristic was visible; for the mixture of all things (*chrêmata*) prevented this, the mixture of the moist and the dry, and the hot and the cold, and the bright and

---

[9] *Fr.* 2. On the resemblance to Zeno's conception of unlimited divisibility in things, see P. Leon, *CQ*, XXI (1927), 140; Cornford, *CQ*, XXIV (1930), 16; J. E. Raven *CQ*, XLVIII (1954), 125-129.

[10] *Fr.* 4. A discussion of this fragment may be found in Leon, *CQ*, XXI (1927), 133-136; G. Vlastos, *Philos. Review*, LIX (1950), 53; Hermann Fränkel, "Review" (of Davide Ciurnelli, *La Filosofia di Anassagora*), *Class. Phil.*, XLV (1950), 190-191. It does not assume a plurality of worlds. Simplicius (*In Ph.*, 460.28-29) notes that Anaxagoras proceeded from the individual mixtures to the original cosmic mixture.

[11] No fragments have been preserved to show whether this anthropocentric tendency was developed in the later books of the treatise. Only the natural philosophy interested the Greek doxographical tradition.

the dark, since there was also much earth therein, and of seeds unlimited in number in no way resembling one another. For none of the other things either resembles any other."[12] Examples of the "things" in the original mixture are here given as qualities like "the hot," "the cold," and so on. These are spoken of in the same manner as was "the small" in the opening fragment.

The way in which the present fragment lists the opposites has suggested the interpretation that a perfect balance of these opposites cancelled out their effects on the senses and so was the reason for the imperceptibility of things in the original mixture. However, no such explanation is given in the fragments, nor is there any evidence that it was so understood by the Greeks who read the Clazomenian's treatise. Rather, the meaning of the text seems to be that the original mixture rendered all things invisible, *even though* the moist and the dry and the cold and the hot and the various seeds had always been differentiated in reality. In the opening fragment the reason had already been given why these things were made indiscernible to human vision by the mixture. It was on account of their smallness, since they were so spread out in the mixture's airlike and etherlike condition.

There is no indication that Anaxagoras is conceiving things like the hot and the cold as substances in the Aristotelian sense. The fragments read as though he is not at all concerned with any need to distinguish things according to their various ways of being, as substances, quantities, qualities, and so on, as the Stagirite later differentiated the kinds of beings. Aristotle, in fact, criticizes the Anaxagorean "separating off" precisely on the ground that it requires the impossible separating of accidents from their substances, since the affections and accidents as well as the substances form the constituents of the Anaxagorean mixture and so are equally the things that are separated off.[13]

Seeds. Nor does the separate mention of "things" and "seeds" in these lines appear to indicate different ways in which as it were two classes of constituents were present in the mixture and in the composites. The mention of "seeds" seems to be merely

[12] *Fr.* 4. On the clause "since there was also much earth therein," see Vlastos, *Philos. Review*, LIX (1950), 33-34, n. 17.

[13] *Metaph.*, A 8,989b2-4. Aristotle speaks as though for Anaxagoras accidents had as independent an existence as substances.

explicative of the way in which some things are contained in the original mixture and in the present composites. Such things are there not as fully developed but as in an already differentiated though still rudimentary guise. The unlimited number of shares and so the unlimited possibilities of different combinations always present in everything allow this way of thinking. It is unlikely that the treatise contained any more precise delineation of what were meant by "seeds" than do the extant fragments. The term, apparently, served merely to emphasize the notion of a source for vital activity and development.

No Becoming or Perishing. Further, the "separating off" does not increase the number of things in the universe: "These having been separated in this manner, it is necessary to know that all things are in no way less or more (for it is not possible to be more than all), but all are always equal."[14] The separating, then, cannot bring anything new into being, nor can it allow anything to perish. This doctrine seems sketched clearly enough against the background of the Parmenidean tenet that change in the order of being is impossible.[15] In true Ionian fashion, however, the cosmic processes are regarded as taking place through circular motion (*Frs.* 9, 12, 13).

Persistence of the Mixture. Even after the separating off, everything continues, as implied in the opening fragments, to contain *shares* of everything else: "And since there are numerically equal shares of the great and of the small, thus also would there be all things in everything. Nor is it possible for them to exist apart, but all things partake of a share of everything. Since there is no possibility for the least to be, it could not be separated or come into being by itself; but as in the beginning so now all things are together. In all things there are many things, and of the things being separated off there are equal numbers in the greater and smaller" (*Fr.* 6). No matter how small or how large a thing is, it contains an equal number of shares in all other things. The language and notion of participation, which will later be given so much emphasis by Plato, is here brought forcefully into play. By means of it the original mixture of all things continues to be present in everything whatsoever, with one exception that

[14] *Fr.* 5. *Cf.* Zeno, *Frs.* 1-3 (DK, 29B).
[15] *Cf.* Aristotle, *Ph.*, I 4,187a26-b2 (first part in DK, 59A 52).

is yet to be mentioned. The reason given for the possibility of such a mixture is the presence of equal shares of the great and the small. Everything is without limit both great and small: "For of the small there is not a 'least,' but always a 'lesser' (for it cannot be that what is should cease to be by being cut [?]). But also of the great there is always a 'greater.' And it is equal in number to the small; and each thing in regard to itself is both great and small" (*Fr. 3*).

The possibility of this whole view, quite apparently, is based ultimately upon the mathematical conception of things that was presupposed by Zeno's arguments. Since each thing shares in the great to the same extent that it shares in the small, no definite amount of shares can be too great for it to contain. It can become indefinitely smaller and smaller, yet never so small that it cannot possess indefinitely shares of everything else. No principle of economy is necessary in this conception. The doctrine means evidently enough that anything sharing in the great and the small, that is, anything that has size and so in this particular background anything that exists, is able to contain a mixture of everything else. The separating off, then, is never complete: "The things in the one cosmos have not been separated from one another nor cut off with an ax, neither the hot from the cold nor the cold from the hot" (*Fr. 8*). Even opposites like the hot and the cold will, accordingly, each contain shares of the other, just as do the great and the small. Each thing, however, is characterized by the shares that predominate in it, somewhat as in Parmenides things were characterized by the different proportions of light and darkness: "And no other thing is like anything else, but each one is and was most manifestly those of which it contains the most" (*Fr. 12*). The number of things separated off, though incalculable, is not described as unlimited: "So that the number of things separated off cannot be known either in thought or in fact" (*Fr. 7*; tr. Freeman).

Cosmology. In view of these doctrines, the original mixture in which air-and-ether predominated seems to be conceived quite within the general ambit of Anaximenes' thought. Somewhat as in Anaximenes, too, the notion of solidification may enter into the process of separating off. First, the simplest and primitive qualities were separated off from the original airlike and etherlike condition of the mixture, and then: "From these, when they are being separated off, earth is compacted; for from the clouds water is separated off, and from the water earth, and from the earth stones are compacted by the cold; and these go outward more than the water."[16] The sun, moon, and stars, apparently, were some of these stones. Aristotle classes Anaxagoras with Empedocles in denying the existence of the void (*Cael.*, IV 2,309a19-21; DK, 59A 68), and states that the Clazomenian's unlimited was "continuous by contact" (*Ph.*, III 4,203a22; Oxford tr. DK, 59A 45). According to Theophrastus, Anaxagoras taught that "the earth is flat in shape, and remains suspended aloft on account of its size and because there is no void, and because the air being very strong carries the earth riding upon it."[17] Again this seems to continue the general conception of Anaximenes, and need not at all run counter to what the same report (I,8,2) notes about Anaxagoras' doctrine of all heavy things going towards the center. In general, the testimonia show that Anaxagoras followed the broad lines of the traditional Milesian cosmogony in explaining the formation of the cosmos through his basic doctrines, and in discussing meteorological, geological, and physiological phenomena.

Change. In his teaching, as in that of Empedocles, change is reduced to the mixing and separating of already existing constituents, now conceived as shares. As with Parmenides as well as with Empedocles, the current terms are considered to be deceptive: "The Greeks are not correct in their recognition of coming-to-be and perishing. For no thing (*chrêma*) comes to be or perishes, but it is mixed together and separated from things (*chrêmata*) that exist. And so they would be correct in calling coming-to-be 'mixing,' and perishing 'separating'" (*Fr.* 17). Nothing new, therefore, ever comes into being. In all natural as well as other processes, the already existing things or shares unlimited in number are merely mixed or separated. These constituents are here expressly called "things," and the resulting composite is also called a "thing." This usage makes it very unlikely that Anaxagoras gave any special technical signification to

[16] *Fr.* 16. *Cf. Fr.* 15.
[17] Hippolytus, *Ref.*, I,8,3; DK, 59A 42; from Theophrastus, in *Dox.Graec.*, 562.5-7.

the word "thing." The qualities like the hot and the cold are given as examples of "things," but likewise the composites about whose coming-to-be contemporary thinkers were arguing can in every case be denoted by the same term, a "thing." At other times, moreover, the qualities as well as the ordinary composites are referred to equally without the use of the noun "things."

The Homoiomeries.   Aristotle, and the Peripatetics after him, interpreted the doctrine of Anaxagoras as meaning that the elements (a term first used in this technical sense by Plato) of all things were *homoiomeries* like flesh, bone, or anything of which the parts have the same name as the whole.[18] Air and ether, for instance, are a mixture of all these homoiomeries.—As usual, Aristotle reports an undoubted fact in Anaxagoras' doctrine, namely, that everything shares in everything else; but he interprets it to mean, from his own viewpoint, that a homoiomery functions as an "element" in the composition of things. The Anaxagorean doctrine, however, as it emerges from the fragments, allows everything to contain a share of everything else, but in such a way that the simplest things were the first to be separated off from the original mixture and then the more complex. This hardly represents a situation that in its own setting should be described as making the more complex things "elements" of the simpler ones. Whether or not Anaxagoras himself used the term "homoiomery" is not known with certainty. The prominence of flesh, bone, marrow, and the like as examples of homoiomeries seems to have been occasioned by his explanation of organic development in terms of his general doctrine of change. The phenomena of growth and nutrition,[19] in fact, pondered over against the Eleatic denial of any true coming-to-be, seem to have led Anaxagoras to the conviction that everything is somehow contained in everything else; and the mathematical conception of extended things provided him with his explanation of the way in which this could be possible, without any need for economy.

Mind.   "In everything there is a share of everything except mind; but in some things there is also mind" (*Fr.* 11). Mind,

---

[18] Aristotle, *Cael.*, III 3,302a31-b4; GC, I 1,314a17-20. DK, 59A 43;46. On the first use of the term "elements" in this sense, see Simplicius, *In Ph.*, 7.13-14.

[19] Cf. testimonia in DK, 59A 45, 46, and B 10.

then, is found shared by some things but not by all. It itself, however, cannot have anything mixed with it. It contains no shares of anything else. The reason given for this is that it may be able to rule over all other things: "All other things partake of a share of everything, but mind is unlimited and self-ruling and is mixed with no thing (*chrêma*), but is alone, itself by itself. For if it were not by itself, but had been mixed with anything else, it would have partaken of all things (*chrêmata*), if it had been mixed with anything; for in everything there is a share of everything, as has been said by me in what has preceded. And the things mixed with it would have prevented it from ruling over anything (*chrêma*) in the same way as when it is alone by itself. For it is the thinnest and purest of all things (*chrêmata*), and possesses all understanding of everything, and is endowed with the greatest power" (*Fr.* 12).

What does this mean? Aristotle testifies that Anaxagoras somehow equates the notions of knowing, ruling, and moving.[20] The fragment does indeed speak as though the three notions meant the same for Anaxagoras. Is this merely a global projection of his own internal experience that human *knowledge* is what commands and sets in motion the members of the body? The fragment reveals nothing about how Anaxagoras arrived at his notion of mind. Mind, though, is conceived at least vaguely after the model of extended things. It is unlimited, apparently in the same quantitative sense as other things, and so can be shared indefinitely by numbers of living beings. As found in these things, it may be characterized in terms of greater and lesser (*Fr.* 12). It is quite evidently looked upon as extended, even though it is the thinnest of all things.

Like any extended thing, mind can be in motion. It is, however, self-ruling, and is therefore self-moving, according to Anaxagoras' equation of the notions of ruling and moving in this regard. It begins to move around at the outset, commencing with what is small and gradually extending its movement: "Mind began to effect the universal rotation, so as to go around at the start. And it first began going around in small extent, but it is going around farther and will go around still farther. And the things that were mixed together, and separated off, and divided, all were known by mind" (*Fr.* 12). By its own movement, then, mind knows, moves, rules and arranges all things in the cosmos. How? No explanation is apparent in the fragments and in all likelihood none was given in the original treatise. Plato (*Phd.*, 97B-99C) represented the youthful Socrates as searching the treatise eagerly and finding no explanation at all on the properly intellectual level. Aristotle (*Metaph.*, A 4,985a18-21; DK, 59A 47), though praising Anaxagoras highly for his intuition that mind had to be the initial cause of motion, concluded that he used mind like a theater machine, dragging it in only when he was at a lose for some other way to explain the necessary character of the world processes; and that in all other cases he accounted for motion through the things that come into being, that is, through the things of the sensible world, rather than through mind.

These indications suggest rather strongly that Anaxagoras did not reach any positive notion of mind that was specifically above the level of extended things; and that the way in which for him mind caused motion was not in any definite manner radically different from the functioning of sensible things. The fragment states that if mind were able to contain a share of anything else, thereby containing shares of all other things, it would not be able to exercise its role of moving them in the way that it actually does. Such a reason seems to imply that mind, when it starts to move, is in no way absorbed into the things around it, as one would expect the purest and thinnest of all things to be absorbed. Rather, mind is resisted by the things that it contacts, and so is able to push them all and set them in motion. Remaining apart from them in this way it is able to know them all and exercise the greatest power over them. However, the nature of such resistance cannot be determined any further from the text, and it does not at all imply an out-and-out mechanical conception. It seems fashioned vaguely after the manner in which cognition attains a thing without in any way being absorbed into that thing, coupled with the experience of the way in which the members of one's own body are moved by one's thought.

Though nothing can mix with mind, mind nevertheless is found in all living things, both animals and plants.[21]

[21] Aristotle, *De An.*, I 2,404b3-5; DK, 59A 100. F. M. Cleve, *The Philosophy of Anaxagoras*, (New York, 1949), p. 115, n. 13, feels that Aristotle is here repeating the words of Anaxagoras himself. On the plants, see testimonia in DK, 59A 117.

Cognition. The senses are not able to perceive the movements of the minute shares that are present in things, and so "on account of their weakness we are not able to judge the truth" (*Fr.* 21). Yet what the senses perceive do give "a view of what are invisible" (*Fr.* 21a). So through sense cognition one is able to arrive at some knowledge of the real but invisible constitution of things. According to Theophrastus,[22] Anaxagoras, in contrast to Parmenides and Empedocles, held that sensation takes place not through the cognition of like by like, but rather of opposite by opposite. The hot, for instance, is recognized by what is cold in the sense. The reason seems to have been the ordinary observation that a physical reaction is caused by the encounter of opposite qualities, and not by that of like ones. Accordingly, all sensation involves pain.

Man, on account of the superior kinds of knowledge that he acquires, is able to subject to his own interests the activities of the lower animals: ". . . through experience and memory and wisdom and art we make use of what belongs to them."[23] Again the anthropomorphic direction of Anaxagoras' philosophy is indicated,[24] but no texts remain to show how this tendency was implemented in the later books of his treatise.

The teachings of Anaxagoras seem to lie quite within the general framework of the Milesian cosmologies. Assumed as the matrix of cosmic development is an original unlimited stock, in which differences are indeed present but are indiscernible to sense cognition. The development itself takes place through local motion, and is viewed after the manner of the vital processes experienced in human growth and activity. But between Anaxagoras and the earlier Ionians lies the Eleatic dialectic of being, coupled with the current mathematical conception of extended things. The unlimited numerical divisibility of all extended things allowed Anaxagoras to see in everything an unlimited capacity for containing invisible shares of everything else, and so to conceive the original stock as a mixture in which many things and

[22] Testimonia in DK, 59A 92, 94.

[23] *Fr.* 21b. It is understood in this way by Fränkel, *Class. Phil.*, XLV (1950), 191a. Burnet, *EGP*, p. 261, translates: ". . . because we use our own experience and memory and wisdom and art."

[24] *Cf. supra*, nn. 10 and 11.

the seeds of all things were contained in an already differentiated but as yet invisible manner. The Eleatic reasoning forced him to explain all change through the separating out and commingling of the things already there in the mixture. In this way he safeguarded qualitative differences while eliminating qualitative change. Apparently he accepted plurality as an initial evidence, and made the size that was discernible by the senses the basic norm for distinguishing the notions of the great and the small. He conceived the whole cosmic process as set afoot and arranged and guided by mind, seemingly after the manner in which the parts of the human body are set in motion and directed by the mind in one's own personal experience.

The intuitions of Anaxagoras, such as that of participation, of the possibilities afforded by the notion of unlimited divisibility when applied to real things, and of mind as the necessary initial cause of motion and as separate from sensible things, were exceptionally profound and fecund. They attained high significance in the subsequent development of Greek philosophy. His insights and his brilliant power of synthetizing them in the explanation of the cosmos rightly entitled him to be called the greatest of the Greek physicists. What is lacking in his treatment, however, as one can judge well enough from the fragments, is a close analysis of the concepts that he was using and of the far-reaching consequences that those concepts entailed. It was still a time in which the "power of dialectic,"[25] as exemplified in Plato's *Parmenides,* had not as yet prompted Greek thought to test the ultimate implications of philosophical concepts.

This deficiency of analytic penetration brought upon Anaxagoras the repeated epithets of "absurd" when the Peripatetics isolated his individual doctrines and in a different setting applied to them new logical tools. It also foredooms to sterility the modern efforts to range Anaxagoras' teaching under later categories of thought, to see in it, for instance, a molecular or nonmolecular doctrine of matter, a mechanical or a teleological conception of the cosmos, a monism, a dualism, or a pluralism. The Clazomenian's treatise lends itself to none of these interpretations in any really definite way. His original mixture, as Simplicius (*In Ph.,* 34.26-27) found it described in the treatise,

[25] Aristotle, *Metaph.,* M 4,1078b25.

seemed indeed meant to be the one reality of Parmenides, but it was a reality that actually and truly contained within itself unlimited numerical plurality and an incalculably wide variety in kinds of things. His distinction between mind and other things is sharp and clear, yet both are on the level of extended reality. His notion of shares and their participation seems to be inexplicable in terms of later notions of matter, whether molecular or non-molecular. Rather, the philosophy of Anaxagoras has to be interpreted in its own Milesian setting and as conditioned by a certain Eleatic and perhaps Pythagorean mathematical background. It is an attempt, carried out with admirable constructive power, to envisage the development of the present universe, by means of motion, from an original matrix in which no differences were visible. It used as its model the vital processes by which seeds and food are the source of things not yet visible within them. In so doing it brought to a much higher peak than had yet been reached the Milesian tradition of a cosmogony explained in rational terms after the model of the vital activity[26] experienced in one's self and observed in the organic functioning present in the outside world.

Anaxagoras was the first known philosopher to work in Athens, which already was the center of Greek culture in drama and art. Before his time philosophical activity had taken place at the periphery of the Greek world, east and west, in Ionia and in the Sicilian and Italian colonies. Now, however, Athens becomes the focal point to which philosophers are drawn, and in a comparatively short time it is established as the center of philosophy as well as of other Greek culture.

DIOGENES OF APOLLONIA (FIFTH CENTURY B.C.)

The Apollonia from which Diogenes came was most likely the Milesian colony of that name in Thrace on the Black Sea. Diogenes is described by Greek tradition as a pupil of Anaximenes and a contemporary of Anaxagoras. This would locate his main activity pretty well in the first part of the fifth century. Like Anaxagoras, he is said (DK, 64A 12) to have mentioned, in explaining his physical doctrines, the

[26] ". . . that reason was present—as in animals, so throughout nature—as the cause of order and of all arrangement, . . ." Aristotle, *Metaph.*, A 3,984b15-17; Oxford tr. (DK, 59A 58).

stone that fell at Aegospotami around 467 B.C. He is reported to have been nearly the last of those who carried on the Ionian tradition of natural philosophy. This statement may be based upon the eclectic character of his teachings, but it concurs with the other reports that he was a contemporary of Anaxagoras and so helps to place him in the second last generation of the Ionian natural philosophers.

A work of Diogenes under the usual title *On Nature* survived to the time of Simplicius, in the sixth century A.D. Simplicius also knew of works of his called *Against the Physiologists, Meteorology,* and *On the Nature of Man.* The last title sounds like that of a physiological or medical treatise. One long passage (*Fr.* 6) testifies to his interest in physiological details.

The philosophy of Diogenes is reported to have agreed in some points with Anaxagoras, in others with Leucippus. As his starting point Diogenes requires something that cannot be questioned; and he wishes the manner of exposition to be simple and dignified (*Fr.* 1). This starting point, like that of Anaxagoras, appears to have been the changes experienced in the sensible world. Things could not change into one another unless they were modifications of the same basic reality (*Fr.* 2). These changes take place according to intelligence and fixed measures (*Fr.* 3). But air is what sustains men and animals, and is their soul and intelligence (*Fr.* 4). "And it seems to me that that which has intelligence is what is called air by men; and that by it all men are steered and that it controls all. For this itself seems to me to be god and to have reached everywhere and to dispose everything and be in everything; and that there is nothing that does not share in it. But no one thing shares in it in the same way as another, but there are many modes both of air itself and of intelligence; for it is manifold in mode, warmer and colder and drier and moister and more stationary or having swifter motion, and in it are many other differentiations, (*numerically*) unlimited, both of pleasant sensation and of surface characteristic. . . ." (*Fr.* 5).

The notions of participation used in this fragment and the general manner of expression are quite close to Anaxagoras, even though intelligence is identified with air. Air functions as soul, and is present in everything. Cosmic development, accordingly, is looked upon as a vital process. All other things are different modifications of this one basic reality, air. The intelligent nature of such a basic reality accounts for the regularity and fixed measures of the cosmic processes. This is traditionally Ionian philosophizing. As with Anaximander, the basic reality steers or governs the universe.[27] It is expressly looked upon as a god.

Diogenes' teaching on cognition is reported to have paralleled that of Leucippus and Democritus in maintaining that the objects of sensible cognition were constituted by convention, in so far as they were appearances resulting from the modifications of the senses themselves (DK, 64A 23). There is no trace, though, of any basic atomism in the extant fragments. The explanation of the regularity and fixed measures through air as an intelligent nature, however, seems to parallel closely enough the teaching of Leucippus that all things take place through reason and necessity (DK, 67B 2), although with Leucippus the intelligent nature is fire.

The fragments of Diogenes, accordingly, bear out the ancient estimate of his thought as a kind of eclecticism. They do not reveal anything very original. They repay careful study, nevertheless, for they are extensive enough to provide closer insight into the way of thinking that was prevalent in the Ionian tradition. They are surprisingly helpful in giving an over-all picture of the dominant tendencies present throughout the early philosophizing on nature. The thoroughly traditional character of his thought, especially from the viewpoint of its immediate background in Anaximenes, is conveyed clearly enough by Simplicius in a brief description of Diogenes' fundamental cosmic reality: "He too says that the nature of the universe is air unlimited and eternal, from which by condensation and rarefaction and change of states the form of other things emerges" (*In Ph.*, 25.4-6; DK, 64A 5).

ARCHELAUS OF ATHENS (FIFTH CENTURY, B.C.)

Archelaus was known as an Athenian, though his name was also associated with Miletus, probably indicating family origin from the noted Ionian city. He was a pupil of Anaxagoras, and

---

[27] See Aristotle, *Ph.*, III 4,203b11-12; DK, 12A 15. *Cf.* Heraclitus, *Frs.* 30 and 64.

"succeeded" the Clazomenian in his philosophical activities at Lampsacus. Afterwards he moved to Athens,[28] where he had Socrates as his own pupil. He is said to have followed the general lines of the Anaxagorean philosophy of nature, although according to a doxographical report (DK, 60A 4,1) he taught that from the start mind contained some mixture. He is also described as being concerned with moral and social questions, distinguishing the morally good and bad on the basis of convention and not of nature. Only one short sentence of his has survived. It seems to imply that coldness as a bond keeps the earth motionless (*Fr.* la).

With Archelaus the center of Greek philosophical activity has definitely shifted to Athens. Here the main interest soon focused on moral and social problems rather than on the Ionian study of nature. The Ionian type of investigation, however, was continued along with traditional moral preoccupations at Abdera in Thrace, and there it reached its most significant and durable stage in the work of the Greek atomists Leucippus and Democritus.

SELECTED READINGS AND REFERENCES

ANAXAGORAS

A. E. Taylor, "On the Date of the Trial of Anaxagoras," *CQ*, XI (1917), 81-87.

A. L. Peck, "Anaxagoras and the Parts," *CQ*, XX (1926), 57-71.

———, "Anaxagoras: Predication as a Problem in Physics," *CQ*, XXV (1931), 27-37; 112-120.

P. Leon, "The *Homoiomeries* of Anaxagoras," *CQ*, XXI (1927), 133-141.

C. Bailey, "On the Theory of Anaxagoras," Appendix I in *The Greek Atomists and Epicurus* (Oxford: Clarendon Press, 1928), 537-556.

F. M. Cornford, "Anaxagoras' Theory of Matter," *CQ*, XXIV (1930), 14-30; 83-95.

Davide Ciurnelli, *La Filosofia di Anassagora* (Padua: Cedam, 1947).

Felix M. Cleve, *The Philosophy of Anaxagoras* (New York: King's Crown Press, 1949). First draft published in German, *Die Philosophie des Anaxagoras* (Vienna: C. Konegen, 1917).

[28] So runs the account of Eusebius, *PE*, X,14,13 (504C).

G. Vlastos, "The Physical Theory of Anaxagoras," *Philosophical Review*, LIX (1950), 31-57.

J. A. Davison, "Protagoras, Democritus, and Anaxagoras," *CQ*, XLVII (1953), 33-45.

J. E. Raven, "The Basis of Anaxagoras' Cosmology," *CQ*, XLVIII (1954), 123-137.

DIOGENES OF APOLLONIA

H. Diller, "Die Philosophiegeschichtliche Stellung des Diogenes von Apollonia," *Hermes*, LXXVI (1941), 359-381.

Jean Zafiropulo, *Diogène d'Apollonie* (Paris: Les Belles Lettres, 1956).

[CHAPTER 8]

The Atomists

LEUCIPPUS (FIFTH CENTURY B.C.)

Chronology. Leucippus is mentioned by Aristotle and Theophrastus as well as by later Greek tradition in a way that marks him as the originator of the atomic conception of the universe, as the notion "atomic" was understood in ancient times. He was variously associated by the doxographers with Abdera, Elea, and Miletus, in such a way that the place of his birth cannot be determined. Nor are the years of his birth and death known. He was said to have been an associate of Parmenides in philosophy, and to have been a pupil of Zeno or (DK, 67A 5) of Melissus. This would seem to place his birth around the beginning of the fifth century or a little earlier. By most modern writers, however, he is placed somewhat later in the century, in order to bring his chronology into line with the late dating usually assigned to Democritus.

Writings. Leucippus was reported to have written a work called *The Great World Order,* a title that was also attributed to Democritus. Whether this title designated two separate works, or a common work of the atomistic school that came down under both names, is not known. The notion of world order, however, is apparent in the one sentence of Leucippus that has survived. The sentence was quoted from a treatise *On Mind,* which may have been either a separate writing or a part of the larger work. It states: "Nothing happens at random; everything happens out of reason and by necessity" (*Fr.* 2; tr. Freeman).

PHILOSOPHICAL TEACHINGS

Necessity. The doctrine of this one extant saying of Leucippus, stressing as it does the reasoned or measured and necessary character of all happenings, would eliminate chance from the cosmic processes. The fragment was quoted as expressing a conception of necessity that was contrasted with the Platonic doctrine of providence.[1] This contrast, as well as the mention of reason before necessity in the fragment, may be taken to imply that necessity was of itself in accord with reason and measure, rather than any notion that reason was an extrinsic force, like art,[2] struggling to overcome necessity. However, nothing further about the context of the fragment has been handed down. In fact, it was noted in antiquity that Leucippus gave no explanation of what necessity was.[3] Against the general Ionian background one may readily presume that it denoted the necessary and intelligible order that had been looked upon traditionally as inherent in cosmic motion.

Atoms and Void. In its Greek philosophical usage the term "atom" was understood according to its etymology. It indicated something that could not be cut or divided, and meant for Greek philosophers an indivisible extended unit. The doctrine of Leucippus in this regard was summed up by Theophrastus: ". . . he assumed elements unlimited (*in number*) and ever moving, the atoms; and in them an unlimited number of shapes, because there was no reason why any should be of one shape rather than another and because he saw unceasing becoming and change in things. He assumed further that *what is* is no more real than *what is not*, and that both are equally causes of the things that come into being. For, assuming that the substance of the atoms was compact and full, he said that they were *what is* and that they moved about in the void, which he called *what is not* and said that it existed no less than *what is*."[4]

For Leucippus, accordingly, the atoms were equated with being and the existing void with not-being. In that way not-being was given an equal status in reality with being. Both the atoms and void really existed. This doctrine has all the marks of an attempt to counter the Eleatic objections against change. The changes in the sensible world were considered to be real, as an

---

[1] See Diels, *Dox. Graec.*, p. 321.

[2] This opposition of art and necessity may be seen in Aeschylus, *Pr.*, 511-518.

[3] Hippolytus, *Ref.*, I,12; DK, 67A 10.

[4] *Phys. Opin.*, *Fr.* 8 (*Dox. Graec.*, pp. 483-484), from Simplicius, *In Ph.*, 28.8-15; DK, 67A 8. *Cf.* Aristotle, *Metaph.*, A 4,985b4-10; DK, 67A 6.

unavoidable starting point. How may they be explained as such, in the face of the Eleatic denial of any existence to not-being? Local motion had been rejected because it required a void, and a void would be not-being. The answer of Leucippus was to maintain that there really was a void into which things could move. That meant endowing the void with real existence, and so admitting that not-being in the Eleatic sense really existed.

Eternal Motion. The reality of observed change required, further, a plurality of particles moving about in the void. In the traditional Ionian fashion of making the stock for cosmic generation inexhaustible, Leucippus posited these atoms as unlimited in number. Similarly, in accordance with the traditional tenet of eternal motion, he looked upon them as always moving. The void was of course regarded as something extended, even though it was not a body. The atoms were compact and of different shapes, and so were extended; but in being declared *atoms* they were explicitly posited as indivisible. In this way the difficulty of explaining how anything could be extended and yet be indivisible was avoided even more dogmatically than it had been by Empedocles. To account for the observable changes there just had to be a void, and there just had to be spatially extended *atoms*, that is, spatially extended indivisibles. Similarly the atoms had to be posited as eternally in motion in order to meet the requirements of the cosmic processes.

Homogeneous Nature. The apparent differences of kind in the composites that result from change were explained by endowing the atoms themselves with different shapes. Since the possible number of shapes was unlimited, and there was no reason for restricting the actual number, the variety of shapes in reality was posited as unlimited. Such is the picture given in the summary handed down by Theophrastus, as quoted above. Except for differences in shape, however, the atoms were all of the same nature, "as if each one of them were a separate piece of gold."[5] According to further testimonia (DK, 67A 7; 13; 14) they were indivisible on account of their smallness and impassible on account of their compact or full nature—they allowed no internal void that would be necessary for change to take place within them. No internal change was possible for them. How their

---

[5] Aristotle, *Cael.*, I 7,275b32-276a1; DK, 67A 19.

"smallness" rendered them indivisible is not explained, though it may have been understood in the sense that they were the smallest possible real bodies, and so were posited as too small to be further divided.

Cosmology. By their difference in shape, arrangement, and position,[6] the atoms constitute in the course of their eternal motion an unlimited number of worlds. Like atoms join with like, in a sifting process, the finer ones tending to proceed outwards. The first conglomeration of atoms that was separated out from the unlimited was in the form of a sphere and was described as though it were a membrane[7] enclosing within itself atoms of all kinds. This analogy with a vital process would indicate that in all the strongly mechanical aspect of his physical doctrine, Leucippus is still thinking closely in accord with the traditional Ionian conception of a cosmic development that was modeled after the growth of living beings. However, from the Peripatetic viewpoint of the doxographical tradition, the atomic structure and necessary motion of the cosmos meant that it was neither animated nor guided by any providence (DK, 67A 22). For Leucippus, soul was constituted of spherical atoms, which on account of their shape were the most mobile of all and so best able to cause motion (A 28). In this way soul was identified with fire and heat.

The earth, formed at the center of the original conglomeration, was described as drum-shaped (D.L., IX,30; DK, 67A 1). This means that Leucippus, in the Milesian tradition, continued to regard the surface of the earth as flat.

Cognition. Cognition was explained somewhat as in Empedocles. Groups of particles called *eidola* or images of the things known were given off by the object of cognition. Both sensation and intellection were explained by these *eidola*. Sensation, however, takes place through the modifications of the senses, and so attains directly only those modifications and does not give true

[6] Aristotle, *Metaph.*, A 4,985b15-19; DK, 67A 6. The doctrine was illustrated by the example of how letters of the alphabet differ—A from N by shape, AN from NA by arrangement, and H from ⊥ (Z) by position. On the reading "Z," see W.D. Ross, *Aristotle's Metaphysics* (Oxford, 1924), I, 141, n. 18.

[7] D.L., IX, 31-32; DK, 67A 1. On the medical analogy, see W. K. C. Guthrie, *CQ*, L (1956), 42.

knowledge of things as they are, that is, as composed of atoms. The *truth*, however, can be discerned in these appearances through the reasoning that shows the atomic constitution of all things. The changes caused by different modifications of their respective senses can make the same thing appear different, and even contrary, to different individuals, just as a tragedy and a comedy might well be composed with exactly the same letters.[8]

All the foregoing doctrines were attributed by Greek tradition to Democritus as well as to Leucippus, and at times when reported under Democritus' name alone they show signs of somewhat greater elaboration. A further development of these teachings and a closer examination of their meaning, accordingly, may be left for consideration in the wider background afforded by the fairly numerous Democritean fragments.

DEMOCRITUS OF ABDERA (494-404 B.C.?)

Chronology. As with Empedocles and Anaxagoras, so with Democritus the chronologies vary widely. The date of his birth has been placed as early as 500 and as late as 460 B.C., and the year of his death as far back as 404 and far forward as 359 B.C. All accounts say that Democritus was a very old man when he died. The lowest figure reported for his age was ninety.

According to Diogenes Laertius (IX,41; DK, 68A 1) Democritus himself in his work *The Lesser World Order* said that he was a young man in the advanced age of Anaxagoras. Democritus either expressly added or was interpreted to mean that he was forty years younger than the Clazomenean sage. He further stated in the same treatise that the book itself was compiled 730 years after the taking of Troy. The Greeks themselves, however, differed in the dates that they assigned for the capture of that famous city. Diogenes went on to say that according to Apollodorus in his *Chronicle* Democritus *would have been* born in the eightieth Olympiad (460-457 B.C.). This is quite evidently a construction based upon the acceptance of the year 1150 B.C. as the date of Troy's fall, and 730 years later, 420 B.C., as the one date available for the *floruit* of Democritus. In spite of its highly artificial character, this is the usually accepted dating. Diogenes, nevertheless, had proceeded at once to mention a different account that placed Democritus' birth in 470-469 B.C. This would be about the same time that

[8] Aristotle, *GC*, I 2,315b6-15; DK, 67A 9. *Cf.* DK, 67A 29-33.

Socrates was born. Another historian, Diodorus of Sicily (XIV, 11, 5; DK, 68A 5), writing in the last half of the first century B.C., added to his account of the events in the year 404 B.C. the fact that Democritus died about that time at the age of ninety. This would give the years 494-404 B.C. as his life span. This dating does not seem to be based on any year assigned for the fall of Troy, though it may well have been taken from Apollodorus.[9]

The best available criterion for judging these different chronologies should be the testimony of Aristotle, who wrote a book on Democritus and who on account of the proximity of Stagira to Abdera was in a position to have accurate information. Speaking of the definition of substance according to its form, Aristotle wrote: "The first who came near it was Democritus, and he was far from adopting it as a necessary method in natural science, but was merely brought to it, in spite of himself, by constraint of facts. In the time of Socrates a nearer approach was made to the method. But at this time men gave up inquiring into the works of nature, and philosophers diverted their attention to political science and to the virtues which benefit mankind."[10] Aristotle, accordingly, looked upon Democritus as having at least commenced his work in a period before the activity of Socrates and the fifth-century Sophists. To judge from Plato's accounts, Socrates in spite of his youth was already busy with problems concerning definition and essence by the middle of the fifth century,[11] and the great Sophists had established their reputation by that time. Democritus' initial work in this regard, then, has to be placed in the first half of the century. His birth, therefore, can hardly have been later than 490 B.C. Diodorus' dating (494-404 B.C.) fits in with Aristotle's manner of speaking, and it keeps the life span of Democritus from running over into the fourth century, which any later chronology has to do in order to respect the unanimous tradition that he died a very old man. It also explains the age presupposed by the report that Democritus was instructed by Persian Magi left behind in Abdera by Xerxes during his retreat in 480 B.C., for it would make Democritus about fourteen years old at the time. Accordingly, it seems by far the most likely of the chronologies, and it allows Democritus to be forty years younger than Anaxagoras, in the case that Democritus himself specified the number of years and that Anaxagoras was born about 533 B.C.

[9] See G. F. Unger, *Philol.*, Supplbd. IV (1884), 545-546.

[10] *PA*, I 1,642a26-31; Oxford tr. *Cf. Metaph.*, M 4,1078b17-21.

[11] For other indications, see Unger, p. 548. For further testimonia that the activities of Socrates came after the work of Democritus, see Luigia A. Stella, *Rivista Critica di Filologia e d'Istruzione Classica*, LXX (1942), 28-29.

In any event, for Aristotle, who was in an excellent situation to judge, Democritus was chronologically *pre*-Socratic. Of the other two chronologies, the first would make him *post*-Socratic, and the second would place him exactly contemporary with Socrates. The chronology of Diodorus is the only one that has him definitely *pre*-Socratic.

Life. Democritus seems to have been born at Abdera, of a family with property, though according to another Greek tradition (D.L., IX, 34; DK, 68A 1) he was from Miletus. His name, however, is regularly associated with Abdera, a seventh-century B.C. Clazomenian colony on the Thracian coast near the mouth of the river Nestos, enlarged by Greeks from Asia Minor who had been forced west under Persian pressure in 544 B.C. According to the accounts, Democritus traveled widely, though details cannot be verified. He himself said (*Fr.* 116) that he visited Athens, but was unknown there. He could hardly have stayed at Athens very long. He is never mentioned by Plato.[12] He seems to have been associated with Leucippus at Abdera, and to have spent his long life in inquiry and teaching and writing. That way of living and working was quite in accord with his reported saying (*Fr.* 118) that he would rather discover one explanation in terms of cause than obtain the kingdom of Persia.

Writings. A long catalogue of Democritus' writings has been handed down through Diogenes Laertius (IX, 46-49) under the general headings of ethical, physical, miscellaneous, mathematical treatises, and works on letters, music, and the arts. How many of these were genuine works of Democritus was open to question already in antiquity. Many of the treatises, it seems to have been understood, were written by his associates and followers. The lexicographer Suidas, probably of the tenth century A.D., accepted as authentic only *The Great World Order,* a work that he calls *On the Nature of the Cosmos,* and some letters (DK, 68A 31). However, the title *The Lesser World Order* may be ascribed to him without hesitation. His style was considered quite literary by the ancients. Over three hundred fragments, mostly from unspecified works, are listed by Diels-Kranz. These fragments are concerned predominantly with the moral sphere, but they testify also to a widespread occupation with astronomy, meteorology, agriculture, medicine, mathematics, music, poetry, painting, and diction. Fragments 35-115 are a collection handed down as "The Maxims of De-

---

[12] A tradition stemming from Aristoxenes in the last half of the fourth century B.C. says that Plato wished to burn the writings of Democritus (D.L., IX,40). Cicero (*Acad. Pr.,* II,17,55; DK, 68A 81) mentions the Abderite among those who were most ridiculed in the Academy. In antiquity it was suggested that the unnamed speaker in the *Rivals* was Democritus (D.L., IX, 37).

mocrates." Stobaeus, a writer probably of the sixth century A.D., quotes many of them as the sayings of Democritus, and on that ground the whole collection is attributed to the Abderite. The history of the collection, however, is unknown.

Since there is no means readily available for distinguishing between what was composed by Democritus himself and what was written by his associates or followers and handed down under his name, the only course acceptable is to regard as at least reflecting his teachings any fragments expressly attributed to him by the ancients, until the unauthentic character of such fragments has been definitely established. Viewed in this way the fragments indicate an all-inclusive interest in the knowledge of his day, and an encyclopedic treatment of the topics under contemporary investigation. The predominance of the fragments dealing with moral matters suggests that Democritus was most widely read and quoted for his moral teachings, and seems amply to justify the first place given to the ethical writings in the list of his works. The other fragments, however, bear sufficient witness to the widespread interests of the author that are presupposed by the varied titles in the list.

PHILOSOPHICAL TEACHINGS

Moral Wisdom. With Democritus the traditional Greek moral wisdom of self-knowledge and moderation is made to bear upon living cheerfully: "He who is to be of good cheer must not undertake a multitude of activities, either in private or public life, and in those that he would undertake he must not choose things above his own strength and natural capacity. But he must be sufficiently on his guard, both to set aside any stroke of fortune coming his way and leading him to excess through its appearance, and not to meddle with things beyond his powers. Moderate bulk is safer than massive bulk" (*Fr.* 3). The sign of this cheerfulness is pleasure: "Enjoyment and lack of enjoyment is the landmark of the profitable and the unprofitable."[13]

In these fragments cheerfulness is represented as the goal towards which one's public and private activities are to be directed. It is attained by learning to know one's own capacities and by living according to those capacities. Deception in this regard can be caused by chance, which is represented as enticing

[13] *Fr.* 4; likewise, *Fr.* 188. *Cf. Frs.* 74, 200, 201.

by means of "appearance," the notion that had been regularly opposed to reality and truth in preceding philosophies. While moderation is set up as the norm of correct conduct, pleasure is regarded as its special mark or sign. Accordingly, these notions of cheerfulness, moderation, pleasure, and chance may be expected to form the leading conceptions in the Democritean ethics. Recognition of one's own deficiencies (*Frs.* 60 and 196) is stressed in self-knowledge.

Cheerfulness. The fragments merely assert that cheerfulness marked by pleasure is the proper goal of human conduct, as though this had only to be mentioned for its desirability to be at once apparent: "The best way for a man to lead his life is to have been as cheerful as possible and to have suffered as little as possible. This could happen if one did not seek one's pleasures in mortal things" (*Fr.* 189; tr. Freeman). Cheerfulness coincides with the state of well-being,[14] imperturbability,[15] and self-sufficiency.[16] Self-sufficiency is grounded on nature and not on chance: "Chance is generous but unreliable. Nature, however, is self-sufficient. Therefore it is victorious, by means of its smaller but reliable (*power*) over the greater promise of hope" (*Fr.* 176; tr. Freeman).

By cheerfulness, then, Democritus understands a stable disposition of mind that is unperturbed by chance events. It grounds itself upon what nature has to offer, and finds therein a never-failing source of pleasure and contentment. It pertains primarily to the soul (*Frs.* 40, 171, and 189), and does not reside in money or material possessions or in the body, for in the soul lies the guiding force[17] of human conduct. The soul, accordingly, is on the level of the divine and is much more estimable than the body,[18] which is its abode[19] and instrument (*Fr.* 159). The soul is therefore responsible for the evils of the body (*Frs.* 159 and 223). Cheerful-

[14] *Frs.* 2c, 140, 257, and the context of Fr. 4. The term "well-being" may have been meant to imply the proper disposition of the atoms, according to the identification of atoms with being.

[15] *Frs.* 215, 216, and the context of *Fr.* 4. *Cf.* Cicero, *De Fin.*, V,29,87 (DK, 68A 169) and Nausiphanes, *Fr.* 3 (DK, 75B).

[16] *Frs.* 209, 210, 246; *cf. Fr.* 231.

[17] According to *Fr.* 171, the *daimon* that is the principle of *eudaimonia* resides in the soul. *Cf. Frs.* 40 and 170, and Heraclitus, *Fr.* 110 (DK, 22B).

[18] *Frs.* 37, 57, 105, 187.

[19] *Frs.* 37, 57, 187, 223, 270, 288.

ness adapts a person to attain the just and lawful as well as the pleasant: "The cheerful man, being carried on towards just and lawful deeds, in both waking and dreaming is glad and strong and free from anxiety" (*Fr.* 174).

Moderation. To acquire cheerfulness, one has to guide one's conduct according to the mean between excess and deficiency: "Cheerfulness is created for men through moderation of enjoyment and harmoniousness of life. Things that are in excess or lacking are apt to change and cause great disturbance in the soul. Souls which are stirred by great divergencies are neither stable nor cheerful. Therefore one must keep one's mind on what is attainable, and be content with what one has, . . ."[20] Using medical terms and analogies, Democritus requires that in the activities of the soul proportion and measure corresponding to the Hippocratic notion of bodily health should be sought: "It is fitting for men to make greater account (*logos*) of soul than of body. For perfection of soul rectifies the misery of body; but strength of body without reasoning (*logismos*) does not make soul a bit better."[21]

Through reason, these statements imply, is the proper *logos* to be attained in human action. Democritus envisages wisdom doing for the soul what medicine does for the body: "Medical science cures diseases of body, but wisdom rids soul of passions."[22] The purpose of knowledge and education, accordingly, is eminently practical: ". . . teaching transforms man, and in transforming him makes his nature."[23] The very nature of man is regarded as brought to its completion through education.

Character. Such wisdom, directed as it is towards action, can hardly be grounded on merely speculative knowledge. Hard work is frequently mentioned as a feature of its acquisition.[24] It is something in which example plays a leading part (*cf. Fr.* 208), and in which imitation of the good man is stressed.[25] The importance

[20] *Fr.* 191; tr. Freeman. *Cf. Frs.* 71, 77, 102, 198, 226, 233, 236, 285, 294.
[21] *Fr.* 187. On the interpretation, see G. Vlastos, *Philos. Review*, LIV (1945), 579.
[22] *Fr.* 31. *Cf. Fr.* 288.
[23] *Fr.* 33. Vlastos, *Philos. Review*, LV (1946), 63, sums up this conception in the words "*Logos* exists for the sake of the deed."
[24] *Frs.* 157, 178, 179, 182, 241-243. *Cf. Fr.* 59.
[25] *Fr.* 39. *Cf. Fr.* 79.

of good desires is repeatedly brought to the fore,[26] and the concept of obligation (*to deon*[27]) is introduced. In these ways character and habituation are the basis for the proper direction of one's life: "For those whose character (*tropos*) is well-ordered, life too is set in order along with it."[28] This correct direction of life is often had without formal learning: "Many who have not learned any *logos* live according to *logos*."[29] Yet "the cause of error is ignorance of the better" (*Fr.* 83; tr. Freeman). These statements envisage on the one hand a type of knowledge that is not necessarily related to good conduct. On the other hand they imply a wisdom that is grounded in the way one's nature is disposed through proper education and habituation, and that results in the morally good. From such practical wisdom proceed correct reasoning and correct talk and action (*Fr.* 2). However, no over-all conception of the difference between theoretical and practical knowledge is found worked out in the fragments.

Pleasure. Though enjoyment is the mark of cheerfulness, pleasures have to be chosen carefully according to the norms of moderation, or they will turn into their opposite: "If one oversteps the due measure, the most pleasurable things become most unpleasant."[30] In particular, reason should derive its pleasures from itself (*Fr.* 146) and from the contemplation of the beautiful or the seemly in works and deeds (*Fr.* 194). It is within the morally good that one should choose one's pleasure: "One must choose, not all pleasure, but that conditioned by the seemly" (*Fr.* 207). Observance of the norm of moderation, far from diminishing pleasure, increases it: "Moderation increases enjoyments, and makes pleasure still greater" (*Fr.* 211). Through being content with what one has, one avoids envy, jealousy, and spite.[31] Anger (*Fr.* 143) and greed (*Frs.* 219, 222, 224, 227) are sharply condemned.

As with Heraclitus, the same things can be either good or evil

---

[26] *Frs.* 55, 56, 62, 68, 70, 72, 73. *Cf. Frs.* 89, 185, 193, 221, 292.
[27] *Frs.* 41, 181. *Cf. Frs.* 2, 42.
[28] *Fr.* 61. *Cf. Frs.* 57, 84, 183, 244, 264.
[29] *Fr.* 53. *Logos* is understood in one sense as the guide of wise conduct (*Fr.* 76) and in another sense as mere speech in contrast to action (*Frs.* 53a, 82, 110, 145).
[30] *Fr.* 233; tr. Freeman. *Cf. Frs.* 71, 189, 214, 231, 232, 235.
[31] *Fr.* 191. *Cf. Frs.* 88, 231, 245.

for men, according to their use in human action (*Fr.* 172). One has to "know how to guide or carry good things successfully."[32] In a varying way, accordingly, the good remains stable throughout all the changes in the pleasant: "For all men, good and true are the same; but pleasant differs for different men" (*Fr.* 69; tr. Freeman). In spite of all individual differences, then, Democritus is able to see a unitary pattern in human nature: "Men shall be one man, and a man shall be all men."[33]

Chance. From a moral viewpoint, Democritus seems to understand by chance all happenings that are not foreseen and reasonably controlled by human understanding. Dependence on chance, consequently, forms the disposition of the man who does not use his intelligence as his guide, the foolish man (*Fr.* 197). Though chance may be generous, it is unreliable (*Fr.* 176). The occasions on which it necessarily runs counter to the intelligent directing of one's life are regarded as comparatively few: "Men have fashioned an image of Chance as an excuse for their own stupidity. For Chance rarely conflicts with Intelligence, and most things in life can be set in order by an intelligent sharp-sightedness" (*Fr.* 119; tr. Freeman). The occasional possibility of intelligent foresight being thwarted, however, seems viewed as giving chance the final word: "Courage is action's beginning, but chance dominates the end" (*Fr.* 269). Yet men can and should benefit always by their misfortunes, so that as far as the properly human good is concerned they have only their own lack of intelligence to blame when things turn out harmful or non-beneficial: "But the gods are the givers of all good things, both in the past and now. They are not, however, the givers of things which are bad, harmful or non-beneficial, either in the past or now, but men themselves fall into these through blindness of mind and lack of sense" (*Fr.* 175; tr. Freeman).

Social Philosophy. The city-state is of the highest importance, for within it are all things and it is their greatest safeguard.[34] The purpose of the law is to benefit the individual men, and it achieves

[32] *Fr.* 173. *Cf. Frs.* 77, 78, 229.

[33] *Fr.* 124; tr. Freeman. This interpretation of the fragment has been suggested by Vlastos, *Philos. Review,* LIV (1945), 591-592. "His physical concept of the soul defines a unitary human nature which affords basis for universally valid judgments." *Ibid.*

[34] *Fr.* 252. *Cf. Frs.* 157, 287.

that purpose through their willing compliance.[35] A man should conduct himself properly, therefore, by inner knowledge and conviction rather than by external complusion (*Fr.* 181). It is in due submission within the social structure that a man brings order into his life: "It is orderly conduct to submit to the law, to the ruler, and to any wiser man" (*Fr.* 47). Yet ultimately, as far as can be gathered from the scattered fragments of Democritus that deal with political life, the purpose of that submission to law and authority and the wisdom of others is always to enable the individual to live a well-ordered and undisturbed life and so enjoy the state of cheerfulness. The right to rule belongs by nature to the stronger (*Fr.* 267), and slaves are instruments to be used for different functions just as are the different parts of one's own body (*Fr.* 270). The spirit of Democritus is broadly cosmopolitan: "To a wise man, the whole earth is open; for the native land of a good soul is the whole earth" (*Fr.* 247; tr. Freeman).

Moral Guidance. A considerable number of moral observations and precepts on the level of moral guidance, for both individual and social life, are found in the fragments. Procreation is necessary according to nature (*Fr.* 278), yet the advice of Democritus is not to have children (*Fr.* 276), or else to get them by adoption so that one can see just what one is getting (*Fr.* 277). The purpose is to spare one's self trouble. Harmful animals are to be killed, apparently in order to promote the state of cheerfulness (*Frs.* 257, 258), and similarly harmful men, within the limits of the protecting law (*Frs.* 258, 259, 260); otherwise, such men are to be punished in various appropriate ways (*Frs.* 261, 262). Reverence (*aidôs*) is strongly inculcated (*Fr.* 179), as is also repentance (*Fr.* 43). The benefits of friendship (*Frs.* 98, 99) and of generosity towards the indigent (*Fr.* 255) are stressed. Prayer seems to be recognized (*Frs.* 166, 234), for instance to Zeus understood as the air (*Fr.* 30).

Running through these and other such moral observations the underlying notion of the Democritean ethics, the attainment of cheerfulness and imperturbability, can be seen with sufficient clarity. This over-all notion of the moral good and most of its particular applications appear as based directly upon Democritus'

[35] *Fr,* 248. *Cf. Fr.* 245. On the dominant individualism in the political philosophy of Democritus, see G. J. D. Aalders, *Mnemosyne,* 4a ser. III (1950), 312-313.

own ethical outlook, though they fit in thoroughly with the atomistic conception of the universe. There need hardly be any question of seeking to derive them from his physical doctrines. They express what he finds desirable for man. The scope of his desires, of course, is limited by his physical conceptions of what there really is to be desired, but the fact that desires exist and require intelligent fulfilment are independent ethical starting-points.

Atomism. Comparatively little about the atomic doctrine is stated expressly in the fragments of Democritus, beyond the fundamental anti-Eleatic position: "Naught exists just as much as Aught."[36] One is dependent largely upon the accounts of Aristotle, in particular, for the Abderite's natural philosophy. Aristotle devoted considerable study to Democritus, wrote a special work upon him, and spoke of him with quite high respect, saying that he was the first to penetrate below the surface in physical problems and that his care and method in treating the problems set him apart from all the other investigators of nature.[37] The work *On Democritus* has been lost, but its account of the atomistic doctrine has been summarized by Simplicius. The nature of the eternal things consisted of small substances unlimited in number. A place unlimited in extent was posited for them. It was called the void, naught (nothing), and the unlimited. Each of the substances was known as reality (aught, the opposite of nothing), the compact, being. They were too small to be distinguished by the senses, but they had all sorts of shapes. Coming-to-be and passing-away were simply the uniting and separating of these atoms both in living and non-living things. The continual motion of the atoms in the void and their innumerable differences in shape account for all the variety in the sensible universe.[38]—The

---

[36] *Fr.* 156; tr. Freeman. *Cf. Frs.* 9, (125), 167, 168. Democritus is said to have used the term *idea* to designate an atom; *cf. Fr.* 141 and the testimonia in DK, 68A 57.

[37] *GC*, I 2,315a34-b2. DK, 68A 35.

[38] *In Cael.*, 295.1-24; DK, 68A 37. The teaching that the atoms had all kinds of shapes seems to have given rise to the interpretation that there were also atoms of huge size (DK, 68A 43 and 47). The testimony of Aristotle in the above passage from Simplicius, however, is definite enough on this point—Democritus held that the atoms were so small that they were imperceptible to the senses. On the Democritean terminology for the collision and interlocking of the atoms, see J. B. McDiarmid, "Phantoms in Democritean Terminology: ΠΕΡΙΠΑΛΑΞΙΣ and ΠΕΡΙΠΑΛΑΣΣΕΣΘΑΙ," *Hermes*, LXXXVI (1958), 291-298.

original cause of the motion was left unexplained, apparently as though no need for explaining it was felt in the Ionian background. The motion was simply reported as having had no origin but as present by necessity from time unlimited.[39] The earth was considered to be oblong in shape (*Fr.* 15). It was still held by Democritus, accordingly, to be flat.

The Soul. The soul was explained in terms of fire atoms: the atoms that are spherical in shape constitute fire and the soul. The reason for requiring the spherical shape is that it renders this type of atom best able to penetrate through everything and to set other things in motion. The conception here, Aristotle explains, is that the soul provides living things with motion.[40] Fire, soul, and mind were in this way identified in nature. They all consisted of fire atoms, that is, the atoms that were spherical in shape. Intelligence and soul were explained by Democritus entirely through atoms and local motion (DK, 68A 101).

Under the aspect of heat, soul is present in all things, for instance in stones (DK, 68A 164) and in dead bodies (A 117). The omnipresent vitalism of traditional Greek philosophy is preserved intact by Democritus, though it is now explained in terms of atoms and void. Composed as it is of atoms, the soul perishes with the body.[41] It is looked upon, however, as pertaining to the divine order.[42] Divine nature likewise consists of spherical fire atoms, though Democritus' particular doctrines on the gods cannot be reconstructed with any certainty.[43] There is no need, however, for seeking any explanation outside the atomistic principles.

Man. For Democritus, man was a universe in miniature: "Man is a microcosm" (*Fr.* 34). The same general disposition can be seen in a man as in the universe as a whole. In man it is directly known to all: "I say the following about the Whole . . . . Man is that which we all know.[44] Democritus seems to be continuing the traditional Ionian procedure of viewing the external universe as paralleling the activities of which man is conscious within himself. The arts are regarded as having been "separated

---

[39] See testimonia in DK, 68A 1, 45 and A 39.
[40] *De An.*, I 2,404al-16; DK, 67A 28. *Cf.* 3,406b15-22; 68A 104.
[41] *Fr.* 297. *Cf. Frs.* Oc and 1, and A 109.
[42] *Frs.* 37, 112. *Cf. Frs.* 18, 21, 129, 189.
[43] *Cf. Frs.* 142, 152, 175, 217, and A 74-79.
[44] *Fr.* 165; tr. Freeman. *Cf.* Aristotle, *PA,* I 1,640b29-33.

off" by necessity (*Fr.* 144), apparently in the sense of man's need to overcome the forces of nature. Music, however, arose not from this necessity but out of a superabundance in man's nature. Words are applied to things by chance and not by nature (*Fr.* 26).

Truth and Opinion. The doctrine of Leucippus that sensation takes place through the *eidola* impinging upon the cognitive organs seems to have been continued by Democritus: "We know nothing about anything really, but Opinion is for all individuals and inflowing."[45] This teaching is understood to eliminate intimate knowledge of reality and to restrict human cognition to appearances, against the background of the Parmenidean contrast between appearance and reality: "It will be obvious that it is impossible to understand how in reality each thing is."[46] All that can be immediately known, according to the Democritean *Canon,* are the conventions set up by human sensation: "Sweet exists by convention, bitter by convention, colour by convention; atoms and Void (*alone*) exist in reality . . . We know nothing accurately in reality, but (*only*) as it changes according to the bodily condition, and the constitution of those things that flow upon (*the body*) and impinge upon it" (*Fr.* 9; tr. Freeman). Truth, then, seems far removed from human achievement: "We know nothing in reality; for truth lies in an abyss" (*Fr.* 117; tr. Freeman).

Only atoms and void, accordingly, exist in reality. They are not perceived by the senses, and so are impervious to direct human knowledge. What they are in themselves, as distinguished from how they appear through sensation, cannot be known. In this way the Eleatic problem, how anything can be extended and yet be atomic or indivisible, would seem to be neatly shelved by placing the real constitution of things outside the scope of human cognition. Human cognition attains merely the effects of the moving atoms upon one's body. These effects vary according to the way in which the body happens to be disposed at the moment. Hence arises the conventional character of the sweet and the bitter and the other sensible perceptions. Against a quite obviously Parmenidean background the world as reported by the senses is regarded as set up by the work of human cognition.

[45] *Fr.* 7; tr. Freeman. *Cf. Fr.* 123, and Leucippus, DK, 67A 29-31.
[46] *Fr.* 8; tr. Freeman. *Cf.*: "It has often been demonstrated that we do not grasp how each thing is or is not." *Fr.* 10; tr. Freeman.

Knowledge, Genuine and Obscure. Yet Democritus does not close the door to all true knowledge. He maintains that sensible cognition, indeed, does not directly attain the real. Yet it provides the possibility for further inquiry that will result in genuine knowledge: "There are two kinds of knowledge, the one genuine, the other obscure. To the obscure belong all the following: sight, hearing, smell, taste, touch. The other is genuine, separated off from this type." Genuine knowledge, accordingly, is regarded as following upon the results of sensation, but by a different and more estimable procedure: "When the obscure type cannot go on either to see more minutely or hear or smell or taste or perceive by touch, but the investigation has to be carried on more finely, then genuine knowledge supervenes as having a finer tool for knowing" (*Fr.* 11).

Genuine knowledge, therefore, is looked upon as following sensible cognition. When the senses reach the point where they can no longer distinguish what is present to them, they have to allow a further type of cognition to proceed with the investigation. This quite apparently means that the senses cannot distinguish the atoms nor perceive the void, which alone are real. The higher type of cognition, however, is able to account for sensible things in terms of atoms and void. The higher type is genuine knowledge, for it explains things in terms of what is real. The report of the senses, on the contrary, is obscure cognition, for it does not distinguish the atoms.

Apparently, then, Democritus maintained that all knowledge depends upon sense reports, yet the senses are incapable of analyzing what they attain. The senses cannot distinguish the extremely fine constituents of which things are composed. They do not give genuine knowledge of things, but only an obscure cognition. Yet the mind depends upon them for all its data. After stressing the conventional character of sensible knowledge, Democritus represents the senses as replying to the intellect: "Miserable Mind, you get your evidence from us, and do you try to overthrow us? The overthrow will be your downfall" (*Fr.* 125; tr. Freeman). The sense constructions, therefore, are actually the appearances of the underlying reality of atoms and void. It is not so much a question of the one kind of knowledge being drastically opposed to the other as of continuing and complementing the work of the other.[47] The genuine carries on the investigation from the point at which the obscure type ceased to penetrate. The function of the one is continuous with the other. There is hardly any question, in the Democritean background, of looking for a difference between them after the manner in which a spiritual is distinguished from a non-spiritual type of cognition. The genuine cognition is not supersensible in that fashion. It could be termed supersensible only in the meaning that it is able to distinguish the extended constituents of things more finely than can any of the senses. It does not, moreover, show how things really are, but undertakes only to explain how their atoms are disposed in the void. To that extent it is genuine knowledge. The report of the senses, in comparison, is obscure cognition, because of the failure to render an account in terms of these atoms. As with Anaxagoras, sensible knowledge is superficial and does not enter minutely into the constitution of things; it does not report correctly how they are disposed. Even genuine knowledge, however, does not explain the nature of the atoms themselves. From that point of view there still remains no knowledge of reality.

Nor is any explanation given of the process by which the various configurations of the atoms allow themselves to be interpreted by the senses in terms of bitter, sweet, and so on. This is dealt with merely as a fact and is relegated to the domain of seeming. The treatment proceeds as though in the Eleatic background no ultimately rational account had to be given for something that pertained not to the order of being but only to the constructions of appearance. Just as in the moral order the starting points of desire and free choice could be accepted by Democritus without any explanation in terms of being, that is, in terms of atoms and void, so in his particular setting could the facts of sensation be likewise accepted without any need for justification on rational grounds.

A consideration of the fragments and the testimonia does not allow any too much philosophic originality in the particular doc-

[47] As Vlastos observes, the sensible qualities for Democritus ". . . are not appearance *against* reality, but the appearance *of* reality." *Tr. Am. Philol. Assn.*, LXXVII (1946), 77.

trines that are credited to Democritus. His moral teaching shows signs of close dependence on Heraclitus.[48] His atomism is but a somewhat further development of the doctrines attributed to Leucippus. His inchoative logic, to judge from Aristotle's remarks, does not seem to have reached any notable status. There is no hint of metaphysical interest, even though he is reasoning against the background of the Eleatic dialectic. But the genius for assimilating current knowledge and organizing it into a consistent whole, and the presentation of it in a way that had a lasting appeal, made up the truly remarkable gifts of Democritus. His was an encyclopedic type of mind, and his pioneer accomplishment of bringing together into a single *corpus* all the knowledge of general interest to his times was in itself an original achievement of high importance in the history of scientific undertakings. It was a task that would be taken up anew and with lasting effects upon European culture by a man from the neighboring Stagira, Aristotle.

The extant fragments of Democritus indicate that he was most widely read and quoted in antiquity for his moral wisdom. The doxographers, however, in accordance with their specific interests, reported mostly upon his natural philosophy. The two outstanding phases of his teaching cohere well enough in one consistent body of thought without any requirement of deriving one from the other. The intimate nature of the atoms could remain unknown to human intellection, which could reason about them only in terms of shape, arrangement, and position. The presence of desires and the possibility of their intelligent fulfilment could be seen as a fact without requiring any more profound explanation on atomistic lines. The Greek atomistic view of reality, therefore, can allow for many things that it cannot undertake to explain. Its over-all consistency does not by any means lie in trying to deduce all knowledge from one starting point, but rather in providing a convenient framework in which all human knowledge can be fittingly located.

With the atomic conceptions of modern chemistry and physics the ancient Greek atomism has nothing in common but the name,

[48] Instances of the influence of Heraclitus on the ethical fragments of Democritus are listed in Eduard Norden, *Die Antike Kunstprosa* (2nd impression, Leipzig and Berlin, 1909), p. 23.

though it has been represented often enough as the ancestor of modern science. It was rather a natural philosophy reached by applying the Eleatic dialectic of being to the traditional Ionian conceptions of cosmic development from the unlimited by means of eternal motion. It remained from start to finish on the plane of natural philosophy, with the help of a dialectic of being. Modern atomic theory, on the other hand, is the result of a process of quantitative measurement, and is based upon the mathematical proportions in which chemical combinations and physical reactions take place. Its procedure is not at all on the level of natural philosophy.

The comprehensive character of Democritus' accomplishment earned for him in Greek tradition the title of "Wisdom" personified. The keynote of his doctrine, cheerfulness, seems to have been expressed in the epithet "The Laughing Philosopher," though the explanation given by later writers for this name is that Democritus was accustomed to laugh at the follies of mankind. Except for the reported hostility of the Platonic Academy, he seems to have been held quite generally in high esteem. The satirist Timon of Phlius, usually so cutting in his remarks about the philosophers, has only admiration for Democritus: "Such is the wise Democritus, the guardian of discourse, keen-witted disputant, among the best I ever read" (D.L., IX,40; tr. Hicks. DK, 68A 1).

RETROSPECT

Well on into the last half of the fifth century the Milesian tradition of natural philosophy was continued in different parts of the Hellenic world. It reached its final stage in the atomistic trend at Abdera. The thinkers throughout this tradition remained within the old Ionian setting of a cosmos that could be explained in terms of development from some basic reality instinct with order and life and motion. From that original matrix, whether it was conceived as water or air or roots or shares or atoms and void or whatever else, they sought to account for the processes by which the present highly developed universe was formed. This way of thinking had continued unbroken from Thales to Archelaus and Democritus. It endeavored to explain the exceedingly complex and differentiated world of sensible experience as the development of a relatively simpler and less differentiated source.

In all these investigators, however, there was never any question of trying to make life and intelligence emerge from brute matter, for intrinsic motion and the principle of intelligible order were regarded as there from the start. There is no trace among them of any conception of matter in its post-Cartesian sense of an inert something in contrast to mind, or even of matter in its Aristotelian contrast to form. The notion of matter as a philosophical concept has not yet appeared. None of these natural philosophers, therefore, can properly be called a materialist, not even Leucippus. None of them attempted to derive life and intelligence from a non-living or non-intelligent source. None of them looked upon life or intelligence as a sort of epiphenomenon arising out of some different and more basic reality. Their original matrix was eternally in motion of itself, and so was conceived by them as something vital in its inmost nature. Intelligence, whether identified with the nature of the unlimited or of fire or of air or of light, was always there at the basis of things. The tendency to regard all things as cognitive, already present in Parmenides, may be seen especially in Empedocles and the Atomists. Only in Anaxagoras is mind regarded as a separate nature, different from though shared by other natures.

The most notable difference in the natural philosophers from Empedocles on is the new Eleatic background against which they have had to reason. They have had to explain the traditional Ionic conception of development in the face of a dialectic maintaining that being cannot change. They met this challenge by positing an original multiplicity of constituents that do not change intrinsically, but mix and separate to give rise to the cosmic processes. There is no hint of any preoccupation with finding a compromise position between Parmenides and Heraclitus. Heraclitus does not enter into their natural philosophy at all. His moral philosophy, however, makes itself felt in the sayings of Democritus. Pythagorean influence, except possibly through the Eleatics, seems to play little or no part in these later natural philosophers, even though it was abroad in the Greek literary world during the third quarter of the fifth century, as may be seen in the fragments of Ion of Chios. The Ionian tradition did not tend to substitute quantitative methods for the ancient type of philosophizing. Even with the Atomists it was not concerned with freeing itself from mythological and metaphysical shackles in order to embark on a positivistic course. Comte's law of the three stages was as yet not known, and these fifth-century thinkers were not aware of any obligation to follow it. The mythological and religious background was part of the culture in which they lived and thought. They do not exhibit any conscious tendency, in their philosophizing, towards getting outside its framework.

On the other hand, however, their philosophy is an essentially different product from their mythology. In their fragments and in the testimonia it shows itself as a genuine effort to start from the physical phenomena and the problems of moral life, and to seek their causes by intellectual intuitions or by reasoning. It made ample use of embryological and other biological analogies that were popular in folklore, like that of the world-egg, and of traditional notions like the origin of men from earth or water, or the mythology of light and darkness. But it based its operative procedure not on any credulity in these themes, but upon what men could perceive with their senses or experience within themselves. It was therefore something radically different from mythology or religious tradition, no matter how much it worked within that cultural setting. Extensive parallels of early philosophical conceptions with mythological themes are easily pointed out. These may help one to see why Greek philosophy tended to think in this or that direction, though definite links are not easy to prove. But they do not furnish any prototype of what is properly Greek philosophy.[49] The explanations of physical change, the distinctions of truth and appearance (*doxa*), the dialectic of being, the understanding of moral life, and other such teachings, resulted from procedures that cannot be characterized as either mythological or religious.

SELECTED READINGS AND REFERENCES

Cyril Bailey, *The Greek Atomists and Epicurus* (Oxford: Clarendon Press, 1928).

[49] On the negative character of the evidence concerning the direct significance of the Orphic and other traditional cosmogonies for the development of Greek philosophical thought, see Kirk-Raven, *The Presocratic Philosophers*, pp. 8-72, especially pp. 8-9 and 46-47.

Maurice Solovine, *Démocrite: Doctrines Philosophiques et Réflexions Morales* (Paris: Alcan, 1928).

Luigia A. Stella, "Intorno alla Cronologia di Democrito," *Rivista di Filologia e d'Istruzione Classica,* LXX (1942), 21-46.

G. Vlastos, "Ethics and Physics in Democritus," *Philosophical Review,* LIV (1945), 578-592; LV (1946), 53-64.

G. J. D. Aalders, "The Political Faith of Democritus," *Mnemosyne,* 4a ser. III (1950), 302-313.

[CHAPTER 9]

Developments of Dialectic and
Practical Philosophy

THE SOPHISTS

The Greek term "sophist" originally meant a skilled craftsman or artist. It was applied to musicians and poets as well as to experts in the various crafts. Even for Plato (*Rep.* X, 596 CD), who in other places uses the term regularly in a derogatory sense, the maker of the universe was a "marvelous sophist." The term continued to bear this original meaning in later Greek literature. It was also used quite early to designate anyone who was eminent for knowledge, either theoretical or practical. The seven sages of Greece, and Pythagoras, Anaxagoras, and the natural philosophers in general, as well as Socrates, were all referred to as sophists. The term, accordingly, meant anyone who devoted himself to the pursuit of *sophia*[1] or wisdom. In the course of the fifth century B.C., however, it came to denote in a special way those who, making a profession of wisdom, earned their living by teaching their own brand of wisdom in their travels from place to place throughout the Greek world.

The Greeks, as far back as the history of their culture can be traced, were keenly interested in the problem of handing down that culture through the education of their young, through *paideia*. In Homeric times the task of education had been confided by the aristocratic families to men specially designated for the work of tutoring. Achilles, for instance, was represented as having been educated by Phoenix.[2]

---

[1] The term *sophia* likewise denoted skill or cleverness in the arts and crafts; e.g., the skill of Apollo in a musical contest, Xenophon, *Anab.*, 1,2,8.

[2] *Iliad*, IX, 443. See W. W. Jaeger, *Paideia* (New York, 1939-1944), I, 23-28; 283-328.

With the increase and spread of wealth through commerce in the days of the Athenian ascendency, opportunities for making a profession out of educating the sons of the rich were opened on a much larger scale. The more democratic institutions of the city-states gave every citizen the right to speak in the public assemblies. The art of swaying these assemblies was the key to political power. Consequently, training in that art was regarded as of prime importance for the sons of the leading families. Such training was predominantly rhetorical, but it had to include the cultural and political knowledge necessary for appealing to the civic consciousness of the public assemblies and courts. It aimed at making a man excel politically. This political excellence or *areté* was the highly prized accomplishment for which the wealthy Greek families were willing to pay generous fees. In undertaking to teach it, accordingly, the great Sophists of the fifth century found a lucrative profession. They journeyed from city to city, acquired wide fame, and accumulated notable wealth, while the less gifted Sophists succeeded in eking out a moderate living. They were the professional teaching class of Greece.

The writings of the fifth-century Sophists, for the most part, did not survive very long. Even of the few treatises that were copied and read for some centuries, only meager fragments remain. This would indicate that there was little of permanent value in their thought, and it renders a correct estimate of their philosophy very difficult. The presumption from their general background would be that their teaching did not bear primarily upon the truth of what was said, but rather upon the art of making it convince others. Like the lawyer's skill in pleading at the bar, it would aim not at the discovery of the objective truth of the question, but rather at a convincing and successful presentation of the case. Hence Plato and Aristotle refused to concede that genuine knowledge was the object of the Sophist's art. They regarded him as content with what passed for knowledge. Plato (*Sph.*, 267E) classed the Sophist among those who imitate but do not know. For Aristotle (*Metaph.*, Γ 2,1004b17-26) the Sophistic teaching *appeared* to be wisdom, but actually *was not* wisdom. Through their influence the formerly revered name "Sophist" acquired the connotation of a quibbler, and has retained that meaning down through the centuries. This adverse judgment of the two most profound of Greek thinkers, however, should not be allowed to settle the issue entirely. The texts that remain have to be examined in themselves and in what is known of their setting in order to determine whether or not at least the greater Sophists possessed a genuine, operative philosophy that guided and justified their teaching.

The two fifth-century Sophists who figured most prominently in the history of Greek philosophy were Protagoras of Abdera and Gorgias of Leontini.

PROTAGORAS OF ABDERA (CA. 490-420 B.C.)

Life. Plato speaks of Protagoras of Abdera as old enough to be the father of Socrates, of the sons of Pericles, and of others of that age.[3] This would place the birth of Protagoras hardly later than 490 B.C. Greek tradition, nevertheless, has him attending discourses of Democritus. Such association with Democritus would be quite possible even though he was only a few years younger than his noted fellow citizen. He is described by Plato as a professional teacher who commanded high fees, and who "died when nearly seventy years old, having spent forty of them in the exercise of his art, and in all that time even down to the present day has in no way ceased to enjoy his high reputation" (*Men.*, 91E). He is reported to have visited Athens three times, and to have taken part in drawing up the constitution for the Panhellenic colony of Thurii.

PHILOSOPHICAL TEACHINGS

Man as Measure. Of the works attributed to Protagoras, only two fragments of philosophical import have been preserved. The first sets up man as the measure of things: "Of all things (*chrêmata*) the measure is man, of the things that are that they are, and of the things that are not that they are not" (*Fr.* 1). This passage occurred at the beginning of one of Protagoras' works, called by Plato (*Tht.*, 161C) *On Truth* and by Sextus Empiricus (*Adv. Math.*, VII,60) *Refutatory Arguments*. Nothing further is known of its context. Plato interprets it as meaning that things actually are different according as they appear different to each individual person, since each individual is equally a man. Sextus presents it as a doctrine of the relativity of truth, for what appears to each individual is relative to him only. Both regard it as giving to "opinion" (*doxa*) the status of truth. Similarly Aristotle[4] explains it as denial of the first principle of demonstration, since it allows the same thing to be and not to be as it appears in opposite

---

[3] *Prt.*, 317C; DK, 80A 5. On the chronologies of Protagoras, see M. Untersteiner, *The Sophists* (Oxford, 1954), p. 6, n. 7; K. Freeman, *Companion* (Oxford, 1946), pp. 343-344.

[4] *Metaph.*, Γ 4,1007b18-23; K 6,1062b12-15. DK, 80A 19.

ways to different individuals. But the Stagirite also understands it to imply that things are perceptible only when they are actually being perceived by the human senses.[5]

The passage has an unmistakable Eleatic background. It is concerned with explaining things in terms of being and not-being. It is saying that man is the measure of both. That could quite readily be a description of the world of seeming (*doxai*) as sketched in Parmenides' poem. There human cognition sets up the two forms. This would explain Aristotle's interpretation of the doctrine as meaning that things are perceptible only while they actually are the object of human perception. It would also locate squarely in the Eleatic background the function of appearance (*doxa*) that both Plato and Sextus found in this teaching. Appearances are given the status of truth. If, as is probable, the word "truth" was used by Protagoras in introducing the passage, it would mean that Protagoras was deliberately suppressing the Parmenidean notion of truth and giving its role to the *doxa*. Not in any eternally stable knowledge but only in the ever-changing *doxai* is truth now to be found. Like his fellow citizen Democritus,[6] Protagoras is reducing all human knowledge to "opinion."

However, not enough is known of the context of the passage to control its meaning more satisfactorily. Viewed in the above way, it does not reveal any deeply original thinking in Protagoras, but rather an adaptation of Parmenides' doctrine of appearance, now substituted for the Parmenidean Truth. To Plato (*Tht.*, 152AE) this conception of Protagoras rightly appeared as the culmination of the "universal flux" doctrine. But as found in Protagoras, if the preceding analysis be correct, the doctrine has its inspiration not from the sayings of Heraclitus but rather from the teachings in the last section of the poem of Parmenides.

Knowledge about the Gods. The other fragment that is of philosophical interest reads: "About the gods I have no way of

[5] *Metaph.*, Θ 3,1047a3-7. DK, 80A 17. In the Eleatic background, the notion "man" in this passage has a general as well as an individual bearing; so K. Reinhardt, *Parmenides* (Bonn, 1916), pp. 242-243. *Cf.* Aristotle, *Metaph.*, Γ 5,1009a6-b25, where the Protagorean relativity is traced back to the doctrine of Parmenides.

[6] *Cf. supra*, p. 147. On the relations of Protagoras' philosophy to that of Democritus, see I. Lana, *Protagora* (Turin, 1950), pp. 77-88. On its development from the Eleatic *doxa* and not from Heraclitus, see Reinhardt, pp. 242-246.

knowing either whether they exist or do not exist, nor what kind they are in form; for many are the things that hinder knowledge, the obscurity and the fact that the life of man is short" (*Fr. 4*). This seems to be merely a practical statement of the difficulties encountered in proving anything rationally either for or against the gods. The further context and development of the theme are not known.

Dialectic. Protagoras was credited with being the first to say that there are two contradictory *logoi* or accounts about everything (DK, 80A 20). This statement, however, merely gives formal expression to an aspect of the Parmenidean *doxa* that had been abundantly exploited by Zeno.[7] Men construct their appearances out of two contradictory forms, hence mutually contradictory aspects can be found and developed in all such constructions. However, the details of the way in which Protagoras explained this doctrine are not available. He is further credited (A 21) with teaching the rhetorical and eristic art of making the weaker *logos* the stronger. This would mean that he claimed sufficient skill to be able to take the account or side of the case that appeared weaker to others, and make it come to appear in their eyes the stronger of the two. But again, the details of this teaching of Protagoras are unknown.

These fragments of Protagoras do not seem to indicate any very original theoretical doctrine. But what they reveal could well provide a consistent basis for his practical teaching. The art of Protagoras, as Plato (*Prt.*, 319 A ff.) has him describe it, aimed at teaching political virtue, the highest and most comprehensive excellence of all. The general conception of the Parmenidean *doxa* was that the world of plurality and change in which men live and act is set up by human cognition in a continually varying way. This background could well serve the interests of one who professed the ability to teach men how to manipulate and control public life. In fact, a more appropriate setting for the claim to that power would be difficult to imagine. But in the light of the sources available, any detailed assertions on the relation of this doctrine to the practical teaching of Protagoras can hardly rank as more than conjecture.

[7] *Cf. supra*, pp. 88-89.

A few maxims concerning education, of popular and practical appeal, have been handed down in Greek tradition as sayings of Protagoras (*Frs.* 3; 10-12).

GORGIAS OF LEONTINI (*CA.* 480-380 B.C.)

The testimonia about Gorgias indicate that he was born around 480 B.C. and lived on into the fourth century, dying at the age of over one hundred years after an extremely successful career as a teacher of rhetoric. He is reported to have been a pupil of Empedocles. One of his own pupils was Isocrates. In 427 B.C. he led an embassy to Athens from his native city, which was located in the eastern fringe of Sicily about twenty-two miles northwest from Syracuse, and accomplished a difficult mission with outstanding credit. The remainder of his life was spent sojourning in different cities in the exercise of his teaching profession.

The only known connection of Gorgias with philosophy is through a work that was called *On Not-being or on Nature.* Its argument has been handed down in two doxographical reports, one by Sextus Empiricus (*Adv. Math.,* VII,65-87; DK, 82B 3), the other by the anonymous author of *On Melissus, Xenophanes, and Gorgias* (5-6,979a11-980b21). It aimed to establish three successive assertions:

1) Nothing is (Nothing exists, there is nothing).
2) Even if anything is, it is unknowable to man.
3) Even if anything is knowable, it is inexpressible and incommunicable to others.

1) The first assertion is established by a dialectic that is modeled upon the Eleatic and draws heavily upon Eleatic sources. If anything is, it will be either being or not-being or both being and not-being. That it cannot be not-being, or being and not-being combined, is shown by the self-contradictory character of the assertions "Not-being is" and "Being, identified with not-being, is." That it cannot be being, is proven by the use of Eleatic arguments. It would have to be either eternal, or something that comes into being, or both. It cannot be eternal, because it would have no limit, and as unlimited it would be nowhere and so would not be at all. It cannot come into being from being, for being already is; nor from not-being, because not-being cannot generate

anything on account of its own lack of existence. Finally, it cannot be both eternal and something that has come into being, because each of those characteristics cancels out the other (*Adv. Math.*, VII,66-72).

The Eleatic sources of these arguments are apparent enough, and were clearly recognized in antiquity. But by way of a special proof of his own, Gorgias is reported to have argued that if not-being *is* not-being, then not-being would *be* no less than being. In this way being is shown to be identical with not-being; and since not-being is not, therefore being, which is identical with it, likewise is not (*MXG*, 5,979a23-33).

Moreover, if it is, it is either one or many. It cannot be one, because it is extended and so is divisible and composed of a plurality; but if in this way there is no unit, it cannot be many, because a plurality is composed of units (*Adv. Math.*, VII,73-74). Nor could it move, because change would mean that what is ceases to be and what is not comes into being; and besides, motion would require a void (*MXG*, 6,980a1-8). These further arguments are only too evidently Eleatic.

2) Secondly, even if anything is, it is unknowable, for being is not a property of things thought. One can think of a chariot running over the sea, or of a chimera, or of other things that have no being. Each sense attains its own object, and only its own object; but one does not reject a visible thing because it is not audible, or vice versa. Similarly, if being were a characteristic of things thought, one would have to say that anything thought is, even though it is not perceived by any of the senses. Being, therefore, is not attained by thought and is not an object of thought. Beings are unknowable.

This argument admits the presence of sensible things, while denying to human cognition the power of recognizing any being in them.

3) Finally, even if beings could be known, they could not be expressed in speech or communicated in speech to others. Speech is different from beings, if by beings are meant the sensible things in the outside world. But speech is not one of those sensible things. Therefore it is only the speech itself that is communicated, and not the beings. Just as the objects of the various senses are different from one another, so are they all different from our speech;

and as they differ in each individual and from moment to moment in the same individual, they provide no object that could remain the same when communicated from one person to another. (*MXG*, 6,980b1-17). The meaning is indicated not by speech, but by the external sensible object itself (*Adv. Math.*, VII,85).

Again, the argument supposes the presence of sensible things in the outside world. It takes for granted that if being is to be found anywhere, it is to be located in those sensible things. Those sensible things are different from speech, and so cannot be expressed or conveyed by speech. They are in continual flux, moreover, and so do not exhibit the sameness that would be required for the communication of a thing from one to another individual.

Parmenides (DK, 28B 2.7-8) had maintained that not-being is neither knowable nor expressible. Gorgias, against the background of the Eleatic *doxa*, has shown the same of being. The arguments from the inability of one sense to attain the objects of another seem to indicate the influence of Empedocles' doctrine of sensation,[8] and the relativity of the objects of sensation is in full agreement with the notion of the Parmenidean world of appearance, especially as reflected in the cognitional tenets of Democritus and Protagoras. Gorgias seems to have used the Empedoclean conclusions about sensation to prove that being is not a characteristic of things known, and that speech is something different from the objects perceived by the various senses. The argument from the relativity of the objects of sensation, coupled with the unhesitating supposition of sensible things in the surrounding world, indicates convincingly enough that the "nature" dealt with by the treatise of Gorgias consists in a universe of sensible flux coinciding in its general effect with the Parmenidean world of seeming.

What is the exact bearing of the long argument of Gorgias? No reliable account of its purpose has been handed down in the doxographical reports or elsewhere in Greek tradition. The reasoning has been interpreted in various ways by modern historians.[9] By

[8] *Cf. supra*, p. 108. Regarding the influence of Empedocles on the second and third parts of Gorgias' reasoning, see O. Gigon, *Hermes*, LXXI (1936), 209-212.

[9] For a summary of these interpretations, see Untersteiner, *The Sophists*, pp. 163-165, n. 2.

some the argument has been regarded as a display of Gorgias' rhetorical ability to prove anything whatsoever, even the most absurd. By others it is looked upon as an anti-Eleatic polemic, or as a parody of Eleatic reasoning, in the sense that the Eleatic arguments can be made to prove the same points about being that they show about not-being, or as an attack on all preceding Greek philosophies. In a more positive fashion it has been interpreted as the tragic view of human life extended now to human thought,[10] or as an effort leading up to the abolition of the copula in regard to phenomenal objects on account of the contradictions that the copula "is" involves.[11] The latter interpretation is supported by Aristotle's assertion (*Ph.*, I 2,185b27-29; DK, 83,2) that a pupil of Gorgias, Lycophron, wished to remove the verb "is" from speech, and that others wished to substitute different verbal forms for it in sentences.

The tone of Gorgias' argument itself seems serious enough, and his reasoning was understood and treated in a serious sense by the doxographers who reported it. Isocrates, Gorgias' own pupil, understood him to mean that there really is nothing.[12] These considerations make it difficult to take the reasoning in any other sense than as meant to prove that there actually are no beings in the world. The conception of being that the argument presumes includes what in English is called real existence, but it also involves inextricably the aspect of something absolutely unchangeable. If either of these characteristics is lacking, the notion of being is destroyed. Being cannot become, for it already is being (*Adv. Math.*, VII,71). "For if Being were to change, it would no longer be Being" (*MXG*, 6,979b28; Oxford tr.). It cannot move, because "it would no longer be in the same condition" (*MXG*, 6,980a2; Oxford tr.). On the other hand, not-being cannot generate being, because not-being does not really exist (*Adv. Math.*,

---

[10] Untersteiner, *The Sophists*, pp. 161-162.

[11] G. B. Kerferd, *Phronesis*, I (1955), 5; 23-25. On the essential agreement of the two extant versions of Gorgias' argument, see *ibid.*, pp. 5-23.

[12] *Helen*, 3; *Antidosis*, 268. DK, 82B 1. On the solidarity of the reasoning of Gorgias with the Eleatic tradition, see Guido Calogero, *Studi sull'Eleatismo* (Rome, 1932), pp. 157-222; E. Bux, "Gorgias und Parmenides," *Hermes*, LXXVI (1941), 402-404. Calogero interprets its motive, however, as anti-Eleatic, in the sense of a reduction to the extreme of absurdity. Also W. Bröcker, *Hermes*, LXXXVI (1958), 427-438, views it as an anti-Eleatic polemic.

VII,71). Accordingly both notions, real existence and absolute unchangeableness, are necessary for this conception of being. Gorgias seriously wishes to remove the aspect of being, understood in the foregoing Eleatic way, from the world in which men live and act. If the caption *On Not-being or on Nature* was meant as a single title, it implies that the world of nature is a world of not-being. This is a world that cannot be understood or explained in terms of being. Its components reveal themselves as sensible things, but not as beings. They communicate themselves through their own sensible reality, and not through any fixed meaning in speech that the aspect of being would require.

Whether this general conception of nature as not-being was intended by Gorgias to clear the way for the supremacy of the persuasive art of rhetoric, can only be conjectured. The removal of the intransigent Parmenidean notion of truth would of course have been an excellent justification for giving a free rein to rhetoric. However, there are no testimonia explaining how Gorgias himself connected his doctrine of nature with his practical teaching. Regarded from a strictly philosophical viewpoint, his reasoning, though cogent, does not exhibit any too much originality. It seems to be merely a special though extreme development of the dialectic inaugurated by the Eleatics and now directed towards removing the aspect of being from the world of human experience. It indicates, nevertheless, a new interest in the problem of the communication of thought from one person to another.

Other outstanding Sophists of the period were Prodicus of Ceos (born *ca.* 470/460 B.C.), Antiphon of Athens (active during the last half of the fifth century), and Hippias of Elis (born about the middle of the fifth century). Only a few fragments, none of much philosophical importance, have survived from their works. An anonymous treatise called *Twofold Arguments* (*Dissoi Logoi*), written probably around the turn of the fourth century B.C., is considered in one way or another to set forth arguments of the Sophists on opposite sides of various questions, for instance that things are both good and bad, or true and false, or that wisdom and virtue are teachable and not teachable. It does not seem to exhibit any original doctrine. It is of considerable importance, however, for a study of the immediate background of Plato's thought.[13]

SOCRATES OF ATHENS (470/469-399 B.C.)

The Socratic Problem. Of all the men whom the Athenians of the late fifth century knew as "Sophists" or teachers of wisdom, the most noted was Socrates. On the stage he was caricatured as combining in one person all the side features of the Sophists that could amuse the Athenian populace. In the writings of his admirers he was held up as the paragon of all the virtues. In the eyes of the restored Athenian democracy he appeared as the corrupter of the city's youth and a menace to the accepted way of life. In the treatises of Aristotle he ranks high as the founder of properly scientific knowledge. In subsequent history he has been viewed in ways that vary just as widely. By Justin Martyr and by Erasmus he was regarded as a pre-Christian saint, and by Nietzsche as the man who ruined European culture in its early formation by breaking up its true balance of Dionysian and Apollonian elements and giving it a rigid intellectual cast.

The difficulties in reaching any considered opinion on this question lie in the nature of the sources at one's disposal. Socrates himself left no writings. He can be known only through the accounts given by others. In these he appears in guises that vary surprisingly. As a result, the amount of reliable knowledge about the historical Socrates that can be gathered from such writings has been estimated all the way from a few isolated facts about his life (Gigon, Chroust)[14] to an extremely great abundance of biographical and doctrinal detail (Burnet, Taylor). The answer to the question will follow upon one's evaluation of the extant sources and decision on the way in which they are to be used. That is what is known today as the Socratic problem.

The Sources. There are four principal sources for the reconstruction of Socrates' life and work. They are:

1) Aristophanes' comedy the *Clouds*, produced in 423 B.C. In it an eccentric Socrates conducts a "thinking house" or "wisdom shop" (*phrontisterion*), and is caricatured as a typical purveyor of the sophistic wares.

[13] On the *Dissoi Logoi*, see A. E. Taylor, *Varia Socratica* (Oxford, 1911), pp. 91-128; Walther Kranz, "Die Sogenannten Δισσοὶ λόγοι," *Hermes*, LXXII (1937), 223-232; E. Dupréel, *Les Sophistes* (Neuchâtel, 1948), pp. 38-43, 89-94, 206-213; Untersteiner, *The Sophists*, pp. 304-310.

[14] O. Gigon, *Sokrates* (Bern, 1947), p. 64; A.-H. Chroust, *Socrates Man and Myth* (London, 1957), p. xii. About Socrates' philosophical doctrine, Gigon (pp. 41; 68) maintained, nothing definite whatsoever can be known.

2) Plato's *Dialogues* (first half of the fourth century), in which Socrates appears as the mouthpiece of true wisdom and the embodiment of the philosophic life.

3) Xenophon's *Memorabilia, Banquet, Apology,* and *Oeconomicus* (first half of the fourth century). These represent a Socrates who exercises an urbane and beneficial influence on all who associate with him, especially the youth. Further, the historical works of Xenophon refer at different times[15] to Socrates.

4) Aristotle's treatises (third quarter of the fourth century), which at times deal briefly with Socrates in the same manner as they do with the other Greek philosophers.

There are further bits of information preserved in ancient literature, but they are either fragmentary or else of very doubtful value. The result is that in the four sources just listed the basic lines for a picture of Socrates have to be found. According to the way in which one or the other of these four sources is selected to control the rest, the portrait of Socrates will differ quite radically. The first part of the problem, then, is to examine the nature of each of these principal sources.

Aristophanes.   The *Clouds* is professedly fiction, and offers a caricature in which certain well-known traits, real but grossly distorted, should be sufficiently discernible. But whether these were all meant to be the traits of Socrates as an individual, or of the Socrates popularly known as a representative of the Sophistic profession, has been a matter of dispute. The professedly fictional character of the *Clouds,* accordingly, demands as its control some information of a more factual nature. If it itself, nevertheless, is made the basic source for judging the other accounts, then Socrates turns out to be a fictitious personage of Attic comedy originally created by Aristophanes, used by Plato at first in a comic sense but gradually changed by him into the mouthpiece of serious philosophy, and finally handed down by Aristotle (who according to this theory knew Socrates *only* through the *writings* of Plato and Xenophon and others) as a real historical person. In this form the legend of Socrates was transmitted to posterity (Dupréel).

Plato and Xenophon.   The dialogue form in which Plato writes is likewise fictional, and does not obligate the author to historical fact. The same has to be said about Xenophon's manner of writing in his

---

[15] *Anab.,* III, 1, 5-7; *Hellenica,* I, 7, 15. On the historicity of these references, see E. de Strycker, "Les Témoignages Historiques sur Socrate," *Mélanges Henri Grégoire* (Brussels, 1950), II, 200-215 (in *Annuaire de l'Inst. de Philol. et d'Hist. Orientales et Slaves,* Vol. X). Similarily the seventh letter attributed to Plato (*Ep.,* VII, 324E-325C) narrates as historic events the treatment of Socrates by the Athenian civil powers, and Aeschines (I, 173) refers to the execution of "Socrates the sophist" as a historic fact.

Socratic discourses, even in the *Memorabilia*.[16] The information obtained from these writings, accordingly, needs to be controlled by accounts whose form is more strictly historical. An extreme view, however, holds that everything found in Plato about Socrates is *in substance* historically true (Burnet, Taylor). In this way one has an exceptionally rich and admirable picture of a man who by preternatural urging was led from early youth to a philosophic life, who without thought of personal remuneration could devote himself to instructing the young, who served his city-state worthily on battlefields and in a term of public office, who heroically suffered death rather than evade the laws of the state to which he owed his culture, and who valued that culture as the one thing that he could take with him after death. The Platonic philosophy of the Ideas becomes the work of Socrates, leaving only particular applications of it to Plato. Taken as authentic, and at its face value at least up to the middle of Plato's life, is the statement of the second among the letters attributed to Plato: "There is no writing of Plato, nor will there ever be. What are now so called belong to Socrates turned young and handsome" (*Ep.* II,314C). One should make his acquaintance with this Socrates directly from the dialogues of Plato, especially the *Apology*, the *Crito*, and the *Phaedo*, and from the Socratic discourses of Xenophon. The picture has been too superbly drawn by its authors to allow it to be conveyed at all adequately at second hand.

Other views maintain that factual but not necessarily doctrinal statements in Plato are to be accepted as historical, or that the earlier but not the later dialogues give historical portraits of Socrates, or that Xenophon's *Memorabilia* but not his other Socratic works give strictly historical information, and so on. Yet the basic consideration that allows these distinctions, namely that the form of the accounts is fictional and so does not obligate to factual history, applies to all the Socratic discourses. The information in these accounts, consequently, needs to be controlled by reports that are presented in the form of historical fact. At the present time Xenophon, though recognized as a valuable source, is no longer used as the basic control for the information on Socrates. Plato is still drawn upon extensively by most modern writers in reconstructing Socrates' life and teachings.

Aristotle. The form of the Aristotelian treatises, in dealing with preceding thinkers, is quite clearly meant to offer as a rule an account of philosophical doctrines that were actually taught by real, historical

[16] See V. de Magalhães-Vilhena, *Le Problème de Socrate* (Paris, 1952), pp. 225-227. On the tendency from the middle eighteenth to the late nineteenth century to give Xenophon the preference as the historical authority for Socrates, see *ibid.*, pp. 135-139.

personages. In this regard Socrates may be found on occasion treated just as any of the rest, though on other occasions the Socrates of the Platonic dialogues is cited. The Stagirite's manner of dealing with his predecessors, as has been seen, is to view their doctrines from the standpoint of his own interest at the moment, and so he is liable to give a very misleading notion of what those doctrines meant in their own setting. However, what Aristotle records turns out in general to be basically factual when it can be checked, even though presented in an alien background. With this important caution the form of the Aristotelian accounts should allow them to be used as strictly historical reports for controlling the other information handed down about Socrates. Of the four basic sources they alone, together with the references in the historical works of Xenophon, are written in the form of strictly factual history.

A further objection against the use of Aristotle as the basic control for extant Socratic information is that he came to Athens some thirty-two years after the death of Socrates. He is giving his accounts at second hand. However, he had ample opportunity, during the succeeding twenty years, of associating with Plato and others who were in a position to know Socrates directly. On account of his keen interest in the development of philosophical doctrines, Aristotle may be trusted to have made full use of his opportunities to learn the facts about Socrates and his teaching. He was in a far better position, accordingly, to acquire reliable information about Socrates than about any previous philosopher. Thirty-two years is in this case a rather short period of time.

Finally, it has been objected that Aristotle provides no essential information regarding Socrates that is not already contained in the Platonic dialogues, and so is worthless as an independent source.[17] This, however, is not entirely true. The crucial Aristotelian report that Socrates did not give the Ideas separate existence, though some of his followers did, is naturally not to be found in Plato. But even if the objection were entirely true, the consideration that some of the Aristotelian accounts are in the form of factual history would indicate that they are to be used for establishing the historical accuracy of the same information found elsewhere in other forms. Consequently the Aristotelian accounts, where they refer to Socrates in the same way as they

---

[17] Vilhena, Le Problème de Socrate, p. 302. Vilhena lists (pp. 259-275) forty Aristotelian references or allusions to Socrates, and discusses (pp. 287-288; 302) those for which he cannot find a corresponding Platonic passage. The view in its extreme form is presented by A.-H. Chroust, "Socrates in the Light of Aristotle's Testimony," New Scholasticism, XXVI (1952), 327-365. See also A. E. Taylor, Varia Socratica, pp. 40-89.

do to other previous philosophers, may be given a "privileged" position as the control for the historicity of what is found in the other main sources. With this criterion a historically acceptable picture of the life and work of Socrates, even though severely limited in extent, may be reconstructed.

Chronology. The first year of the ninety-fifth Olympiad (400-399 B.C.) was the date given in the *Chronicle* of Apollodorus for the death of Socrates. This date is sufficiently attested by fourth-century sources, and was in all likelihood based upon the official record of Socrates' trial on the indictment of refusing to recognize the statutory gods and of corrupting the Athenian youth.[18] There is no reason, then, for questioning the year of his death, which according to unanimous Greek tradition took place by his drinking hemlock in compliance with the sentence passed upon him by the Athenian tribunal. His age at the time was given in different ancient traditions as seventy or as sixty. Since he was a sufficiently established figure by the year 423 B.C. to serve as a personification of the professional teaching class for the *Clouds*, the tradition that he was seventy years old, which goes back to fourth-century B.C. sources,[19] is by far more likely to be correct.

PHILOSOPHICAL TEACHINGS AND METHOD

Definitions. Aristotle, reviewing the philosophies previous to his own, states: "Socrates, however, was busying himself about ethical matters and neglecting the world of nature as a whole, but seeking the universal in these ethical matters, and fixed thought for the first time on definitions; Plato accepted his teaching, but held that the problem applied not to sensible things but to entities of another kind . . . . Things of this other sort, then, he called Ideas, . . . "[20] Here the Stagirite is speaking of Socrates as one of his own predecessors in the actual development of Greek philosophy. He is giving him the same historical status as he gives

---

[18] See D. L., II, 40; 44. The text of the indictment given here (40), and said still to have been preserved in the second century A.D., is except for one word the same as in Xenophon, *Mem.*, I, 1, 1.

[19] Demetrius Phalereus, in D.L., II, 44; Plato, *Apol.*, 17D and *Cri.*, 52E. The exact day of Socrates' birth, as given by Apollodorus (D.L., *loc. cit.*), seems to be an artificial construction of Greek biography; see C. Piat, *Socrate* (Paris, 1900), pp. 54-55.

[20] *Metaph.*, A 6,987b1-8; Oxford tr. *Cf.* M 4,1078b17-19; *P A*, I 1,642a24-31. In all these texts, as well as in those cited n. 22 *infra*, Aristotle speaks of Socrates as a historical figure who played an actual role in the building up of Greek thought.

the Presocratics. He is reporting that Socrates occupied himself with moral questions and not with natural philosophy. His interests centered in the sphere of human conduct. His procedure was to seek the universal in ethical matters, and so for the first time focused attention on definitions.

"Universal" is Aristotle's own term. There is no reason to believe that Socrates or even Plato used the word.[21] To that extent Aristotle is interpreting Socrates' teaching in the light of his own doctrine. But the historical fact to which he alludes is clear enough. Socrates was concentrating on the *nature* of moral entities rather than on their particular instances. He was seeking to establish *what* moral entities are. That is, in fact, just how Socrates speaks in Xenophon's *Memorabilia* (I,1,16) and in Plato's earlier dialogues. He is asking *what* are bravery, piety, justice, beauty, and so on. He is not content with having particular instances of the virtue indicated to him, but is inquiring what the virtue itself is. The "what is" in Aristotelian terminology is the equivalent of "definition," and the definition, of course, is of the universal. To this extent, then, the earlier Platonic dialogues and the *Memorabilia* represent Socrates in fictional form just as Aristotle describes his work in reality. Similarly the *Apology* and the *Phaedo* of Plato stress Socrates' refusal to become interested in natural philosophy. Aristotle, moreover, records Socrates' insistence on the universal in ethical matters as in contrast to the influence of the flux doctrine of Cratylus, and so places the Socratic doctrine in definite opposition to the Sophistic exaltation of the *doxa* or opinion. Again, such is the situation described in the Platonic dialogues. From these angles the dialogues present in general a true though quite apparently expanded picture of Socrates' actual teaching.

Aristotle goes on to say that Plato took over this teaching of Socrates about the universals, but applied it to entities different from those of the sensible world. These Plato called Ideas. The statement means clearly that the doctrine of the separate Ideas was introduced by Plato. Accordingly, the Platonic dialogues that either present or presume the Ideas as a metaphysical doctrine express in this regard Platonic and not Socratic philosophy.

---

[21] At *Men.*, 77A6, however, Plato does put into Socrates' mouth the phrase *kata holou*, which in the form *katholou* became Aristotle's term "universal."

Scientific Induction. In similar vein Aristotle shows that through the method of arriving at the universal from the inductive study of particular things Socrates merits the honor of having assisted at laying the foundations of properly scientific knowledge: ". . . two things may be fairly ascribed to Socrates—inductive arguments and universal definition, both of which are concerned with the starting-point of science:—but Socrates did not make the universals or the definitions exist apart; *they,* however, gave them separate existence, and this was the kind of thing they called Ideas."[22] The notion of induction implied here is that of "bringing to" or "leading to" the knowledge of the universal truth through the consideration of particular instances. It did not involve, though it need not exclude, the elaborate experimental techniques that have been associated with the notion since the time of Francis Bacon.

Virtue as Knowledge. In the three Aristotelian *Ethics,* Socrates is represented as teaching that virtue consists in knowledge. Most of the references seem at least to include the historical Socrates in their scope, even when they bear directly upon passages in the Platonic dialogues.[23] The Stagirite carefully explains the sense in which the Socratic dictum appears to be true: ". . . the position that Socrates sought to establish actually seems to result; for it is not in the presence of what is thought to be knowledge proper that the affection of incontinence arises (nor is it

[22] *Metaph.,* M 4,1078b27-32; Oxford tr. *Cf. ibid.,* 9,1086b2-5.
[23] Passages cited *infra,* n. 24. The *Magna Moralia,* held by some to be the earliest *Ethics* composed by Aristotle, though considered to be post-Aristotelian by most critics, in its opening chapter (I 1,1182a11-30) treats this ethical doctrine of Socrates as that of a historical figure in a brief survey of preceding doctrines, just as is done in the *Metaphysics.* It distinguishes Socratic ethical doctrine from that of Plato. A couple of references in the *Eudemian Ethics* (I 5,1216b2-10; VI 13,1246b34-35) may refer more directly to the legendary figure. Others, like *Rh.,* III 14,1415b30-32 and *Pol.,* II 5,1264b24 refer obviously enough to a fictional Socrates. On the general problem of how the historical Socrates is kept in view in references that recall passages (except in those to the *Menexenus*) in Plato and Xenophon, see T. Deman, *Le Témoignage d'Aristote sur Socrate* (Paris, 1942), pp. 119-120.
As he was definite in rejecting the attribution of separate Ideas to Socrates, even though these are maintained by the Socrates of the Platonic dialogues, so Aristotle presumably would have noted with just as much care the same fact about the ethical doctrines that he mentions, if they had not been taught at least in substance by the historical Socrates.

this that is 'dragged about' as a result of the state of passion), but in that of perceptual knowledge."[24] The contrast is between the universal knowledge of intellection and the particular cognition of sensation. The position of Socrates is that knowledge proper is not overcome by a contrary appetite. This position is represented by Aristotle as correct, because incontinence takes place when the forbidding ethical knowledge is not actually present but only the particular sense opinion.

Aristotle, as may be expected, is expressing himself in the background of his own ethical doctrine. He repeatedly insists in other places that according to the Socratic formulae the virtues belong only to the intellectual part of the soul and not to the appetitive part. Yet he concedes that Socrates was right in maintaining that all virtue necessarily involves wisdom: ". . . Socrates in one respect was on the right track while in another he went astray; in thinking that all the virtues were forms of practical wisdom he was wrong, but in saying they implied practical wisdom he was right." (*E N*, VI 13,1144b18-21; Oxford tr.). Aristotle's point is that the moral virtues, even though they involve knowledge, have to be placed in the appetitive and not in the intellective part of the soul. Socrates, apparently, was not intent upon such precisions but rather upon ranging virtue with knowledge instead of with opinion, in contrast to the teaching of the Sophists. Certainly he did not claim that a man was made virtuous by what Aristotle would call merely speculative knowledge. In fact, as proclaimed by the Delphic inscription, *self-knowledge* was with Socrates the foundation of ethical inquiry.[25] This would be in the Aristotelian sense a practical cognition, for it would be based upon the appetitive side of one's nature, even though Socrates would not have expressed himself in those Aristotelian precisions. It could hardly be thought to consist merely in learning the definitions of the virtues.

From Aristotle's comments, then, it appears that the basic orientation of Socrates' ethical doctrine was the ranging of virtuous conduct with the *knowledge* of what each virtue was rather than

[24] *E N*, VII 3,1147b14-17; Oxford tr. *Cf.* 2,1145b22-28; III 8,1116b3-5; VI 13,1144b17-30. At 1145b24 the metaphor and the simile are those of Plato, *Prt.*, 352C.

[25] Aristotle, *Fr.* 4,1475a2-5. On the reference, see Deman, pp. 44-48, and Vilhena, *Le Problème de Socrate*, p. 293.

with mere opinions on particular instances of the virtue. This teaching can be seen clearly enough underlying the accounts of Xenophon and Plato. Socrates was trying to make men good by getting them to understand, in a practical and not merely theoretical way, what virtue is. By this means he would save them from leading an "unexamined life."[26] Through such knowledge of virtue men would be caring for their souls, just as through knowledge of medicine and gymnastic they take care of their bodies. Obviously a practical knowledge is understood. To the imparting of this type of knowledge the method attributed to Socrates, with its highly personal and emotional stresses, was especially well adapted.

The Socratic Method. According to the accounts of Xenophon as well as of Plato, Socrates' technique consisted in asking questions and drawing out the answers from the other person. Often the other party was made to see that he really knew nothing at all about the subject, as the answers became more and more confused. Socrates himself professed ignorance of the subject.[27] This dissembling procedure, seemingly, earned Socrates the epithet *eirôn*, an adjective that characterized the nature of a fox. Socrates in his conversation was apparently considered to be "sly" or "foxy." At any rate the phrase "Socratic irony," in the sense of understating the truth,[28] has become traditional. Socrates' own purpose, as Plato describes it, was to give the impression that the person answering the questions was learning not from Socrates but from what was already contained in germ in his own mind. The Socratic method of questioning is accordingly represented by Plato as a sort of midwifery—the one being questioned gives birth to the knowledge, Socrates acts only as the obstetrician who assists in bringing it to light (*Tht.*, 149A-151E). But the Socratic questioning could also have the paralyzing effect of the shock associated with the touch of the torpedo fish! (*Men.*, 80AC)

Amplified in the extant portrayals of the Socratic method but resting on the basic authority of Aristotle, then, the general trend

[26] Plato, *Apol.*, 38A.
[27] Aristotle, *S E,* 34,183b7-8.
[28] See Plato, *Rep.*, I,337A; Aristotle, *E N*, IV 7,1127b22-26. On the subsequent developments of the notion *eirôneia*, see W. Büchner, "Über den Begriff Eironeia," *Hermes*, LXXVI (1941), 339-358.

of the Socratic teaching may be grasped in its broadest outlines. It focused inquiry upon moral life, and aimed at a practical *knowledge* of virtue, a knowledge that in fact seems to have been presented as identified with virtue. Such knowledge meant more than an acquaintance with particular instances of virtuous conduct. Rather, it involved arriving at the nature of virtue itself through an examination of its particular instances. Further than that, however, there is difficulty in distinguishing how much has been added in the building up the legendary Socrates, until one comes in Plato to the doctrine of separate Ideas. There one has Aristotle's express testimony that it is Plato himself, and no longer Socrates, who is doing the teaching.

There can be no doubt, though, regarding the profound influence that Socrates exercised upon subsequent Greek thought. He became at once the central figure in a type of Greek literature known as "Socratic discourses." Through their means the name of Socrates seems to have become a byword, and the force of his personality spread throughout Athenian literary circles. According to Aristotle (*Po.*, 1,1447b8-11), these compositions belonged to the same general class of literary products as the mimes of the Sicilians Sophron and Xenarchus, and (*Rh.*, III 16,1417a20-21) they dealt with moral questions. The most enduring and most influential channel for the continuance and spread of Socrates' work, however, proved to be the dialogues of Plato. Plato owes to Socrates the inspiration of his moral and political teaching and the interest in seeking out the true natures of things that led to the doctrine of the Ideas.[29] The concentration on logical questions of definition that appears in the "lesser Socratics," as well as on the over-all concerns of happiness in moral life, stems in the main quite apparently from Socrates. These are factors that play a considerable role in the immediate background of the Aristotelian logical and moral doctrines.

Of Socrates' own deeper thinking, however, and of the considerations that led him step by step to the teachings of which there is record, no indications are available. A man who could

---

[29] Aristotle, *Metaph.*, M 9,1086b3-4. On the "Socratic discourses," see Gigon, *Sokrates*, pp. 42-67 and 179-208; and Vilhena, *Le Problème de Socrate*, pp. 324-353; *Socrate et la Légende Platonicienne* (Paris, 1952), pp. 62-96.

profoundly influence Plato and so many other Athenian intellectuals may be presumed to have thought out his positions over a long period of time and to have developed them in increasing depth through the progress of the years. But Socrates wrote nothing himself, and so has left no means by which history might reconstruct the course of his intellectual strivings. Only the more important of the final results have been recorded. The steps by which these were reached may not have been communicated in detail even orally to his followers. No attempt to reconstruct them can hope to be satisfactory. Just as little is the chance of adequately grasping the peculiar type of thinking that may be presumed to have been Socrates' own, in contradistinction to the ways of Plato and the others who used Socrates as the mouthpiece of their own thought.

THE LESSER SOCRATICS

About men like Phaedo, Simmias, and Cebes, who play the role of Socrates' philosophical disciples in Plato's *Phaedo*, nothing is known with any historical certainty. Aeschines, also present at the death scene in the *Phaedo* (59B), wrote moral discourses centering around Socrates, but he can hardly rank as a philosopher. Other disciples of Socrates, though varying widely in their reported doctrines, are grouped by historians under the title of the "Lesser Socratics," in contradistinction to Plato, the greatest of Socrates' followers.

Aristippus.   One of these disciples, Aristippus of Cyrene, was credited with treatises on virtue and education, and with the doctrine that the goal of human conduct is the attainment of smooth or pleasant sensations (D.L., II,85). Yet he is never mentioned by Aristotle in discussions of the doctrine that pleasure is the supreme good. Doubtful also is his connection with the group of philosophers who took their name from his native city, the Cyrenaics. These men are reported (D.L., II,87) to have taught that pleasure was a smooth and pain a rough motion, and that bodily pleasure is the goal of human activity.[30] However,

[30] Sextus Empiricus (*Adv. Math.*, VII, 191-200) represents the Cyrenaic doctrine as meaning that the sense affections are also the criteria of truth, because they alone are apprehended, and not the things that cause them. This may indicate some influence of the Democritean teaching on cognition upon the Cyrenaic views.

very little is known with certainty about either Aristippus or the Cyrenaics. It is doubtful whether the later biographers had any positive record on which to base their accounts of Aristippus' teachings.

Euclides.   Euclides of Megara is represented by Plato (*Tht.*, 142C-143A) as a member of the Socratic circle. Greek tradition places him in a strong Eleatic background.[31] In this setting he seems to have devoloped a doctrine of the unity of the good, and the non-existence of all that is opposed to it (D.L., II,106). Some logical teachings of his are also reported. But nothing has survived of the writings attributed to him, and the details of all these doctrines remain very obscure.

The followers of Euclides were first known as Megarians, after his native city, and then as Eristics, and still later as Dialecticians on account of their use of the dialogue form of question and answer. His most noted follower in this dialectical development was Eubulides of Miletus, an opponent of Aristotle (D.L., II,106-109). The Megarians acquired a reputation for delight in controversy, but they produced some outstanding logicians like Diodorus Cronus and Philo of Megara, and inaugurated a tradition in logic that was continued in the Stoic school.

Antisthenes of Athens.   Antisthenes is reported to have been first a pupil of Gorgias, and later an associate of Socrates (D.L., VI,1-2). He is credited with a long list of works, predominantly on moral and rhetorical topics. Some of them seem to have been written in the form of Socratic dialogues. No fragments of definite philosophical importance have survived. He is represented[32] as teaching that true wealth is to be found not in property but in the soul, and that a frugal life is most conducive to happiness and actually brings the most enjoyment, with one's leisure and spiritual riches shared by friends. Understood in this way, virtue is teachable and is self-sufficient for happiness (D.L., VI,10-11). However, no connection of Antisthenes with the later Cynic school can be satisfactorily established. His notion of the social

[31] Regarding the Eleatic background of Euclides, see C. M. Gillespie, "On the Megarians," *AGP*, XXIV (1911), 228-232. For a schema of the Megarian school, see K. v. Fritz, "Megariker," in Pauly-Wissowa, *Real-Encyclopädie*, Suppl. V (1931), 720. On the Megarian logic, see I. M. Bocheński, *Ancient Formal Logic* (Amsterdam, 1951), pp. 77-80.

[32] Xenophon, *Banquet*, III, 4; IV, 34-44.

aspect of virtue, moreover, runs counter to Cynic doctrine and practice. Even any association of his with the Cynosarges gymnasium has to be regarded as improbable.[33] According to Cicero (*De Nat. Deorum*, I,13,32), he maintained that the deity was by nature one, in opposition to the commonly accepted polytheism.

In the field of logic Antisthenes looms rather large in the background of some Aristotelian discussions. Against the current Sophistic doctrine that there are two opposite accounts or *logoi* for everything, he seems to have developed the notion of a single *logos* for each thing by making every concept so self-contained that it could be predicated of one thing only and of no other whatsoever: "Hence Antisthenes was too simple-minded when he claimed that nothing could be described except by the account proper to it,—one predicate to one subject; from which the conclusion used to be drawn that there could be no contradiction, and almost that there could be no error."[34] This shows that Antisthenes came to grips with problems concerning the nature of definition and predication, and that his notion of the identity of subject and predicate made error difficult to explain. However, the details of this doctrine and its exact bearing are not known. The doctrine of the isolation of the different sensible objects from one another, as it had been further developed by Gorgias, could have played a role in Antisthenes' restriction of predicability.

Present-day knowledge of the Lesser Socratics, accordingly, is very unsatisfactory. Any special influence of Socrates is hard to discern in what is known of their teachings, and consequently they are of little help in trying to determine the doctrines of Socrates himself. At the most, one can say that their common interest in virtuous life seems to have a Socratic background, and that Antisthenes' concern with predication may well have

[33] See F. Sayre, *Classical Journal*, XLIII (1948), 242a. The suggested derivation of "Cynic" from "Cynosarges" (D. L., VI, 13) seems to stem from an attempt to connect Antisthenes with the Cynics.

[34] Aristotle, *Metaph.*, Δ 29,1024b32-34; Oxford tr. Cf. H 3,1043b23-28; *Top.*, I 11,104b20-21. If Plato's reference at *Sph.*, 251B, is to the school of Antisthenes, it indicates a doctrine of identical predication, similar to the conception described in F. H. Bradley, *Appearance and Reality* (9th impression, Oxford, 1930), pp. 16-20. Only "man" can be predicated of "man," and "good" of "good," but not "good" of "man."

stemmed from Socrates' insistence on the importance of correct definition.

ISOCRATES OF ATHENS (436-338 B.C.)

Life and Work. Isocrates began his career as a teacher of rhetoric and a writer of court speeches. He had enjoyed the best educational opportunities that Athens offered. He seems to have been influenced strongly by Gorgias' rhetorical teaching, and also to have had some fairly close association with Socrates. Early in the fourth century, probably soon after 393 B.C., he founded his celebrated school, and continued throughout his long lifetime to turn out distinguished pupils. His teaching was professedly rhetorical, and, as with the fifth-century Sophists, this meant political training in a whole general culture. Its aim was to educate civic leaders. To the last Isocrates was an outspoken proponent of Panhellenic war against the barbarians, in defense of Greek culture. The exercise of his profession, just as in the case of his great predecessors, brought Isocrates considerable wealth. Twenty-one speeches or discourses, and nine letters, survive from his writings.

PHILOSOPHICAL TEACHINGS

Notion of Philosophy. Not only the founding of a permanent school, in contrast to the wandering life of the fifth-century Sophists, but also an outspoken opposition to eristic (dialectic) as well as to the pursuit of theoretical knowledge for its own sake, give Isocrates a special place in the history of Greek philosophy. This opposition had a deep philosophical background. Plato (*Phdr.*, 279B) remarked that there was a certain inborn philosophy in the mind of Isocrates. Isocrates himself repeatedly professed to be pursuing philosophy and to be a teacher of philosophy,[35] understanding philosophy in the general sense of mental culture (*Antid.*, 183-187). The Isocratean conception of philosophy, in its sharp opposition to the eristic knowledge of his competitors, however, is not developed at any length in his works, but has to be gathered from scattered passages.

[35] *To Demonicus,* 3; *Antidosis,* 50, 162, & passim; *Panathenaicus,* 9. On the meaning of philosophy for Isocrates, see E. Mikkola, *Isocrates* (Helsinki, 1954), pp. 201-203. Even though he attacks his colleagues in the profession, Isocrates does not hesitate to class himself among the Sophists, e.g., *Antid.,* 197; 220; 235.

Supremacy of *Doxa*. In the comparatively early work *Against the Sophists,* written about 390 B.C., Isocrates accuses the eristic philosophers of a false assumption at the very core of their teaching. They pretend to seek the *truth*; and yet as a basis for action such *truth* evidently exceeds the capacity of human nature— men cannot know the future with certainty. The doctrine is summed up in the later (353 B.C.) *Antidosis:* "For, since it is not in the nature of man to acquire a science (*epistêmê*) the possession of which would enable us to *know* what is to be done or to be said, as a result I consider those to be wise who by their *opinions* (*doxai*) are for the most part able to hit on what is best; and philosophers I consider those who occupy themselves with the studies from which they will most quickly gain this kind of intelligence (*phronêsis*)" (271). Philosophy, therefore, is meant entirely for action (*Antid.,* 269). Teachers of eristic, astronomy, geometry, and similar sciences do not indeed harm their students; still such studies are of no help in talking and acting according to the needs of the moment, and so do not merit the name of philosophy. They are a mental exercise and preparation for philosophy, but are not philosophy itself. "I do not, then, think that one should term philosophy a pursuit that is of no help towards either speaking or acting in the circumstances of the moment, but I call such a pursuit rather a gymnastic of the soul and a preparation for philosophy" (*Antid.,* 266).

This categorization covers in general all of what Aristotle would call the theoretical sciences. For Isocrates they are but a mental gymnastic. They may be used as a preparation for philosophy, but they must not be confused with philosophy proper. Philosophy is something that bears directly on speaking and acting, the goal of the traditional aristocratic Greek concept of education. In this conservative notion of Greek culture such sciences can have only a very remote and extrinsic role. Young men, accordingly, may spend some time on them as part of a general education, but they should not allow their minds to become dried up by them (*Antid.,* 268). At least, such studies will help keep young people out of mischief (*Panath.,* 26-27). But in themselves, apart from their propaedeutic value, they are of *no use* except for one who chooses to make his living by teaching them (*Antid.,* 264). The youthful Alexander, who had probably just been placed under the charge

of Aristotle as his tutor, is accordingly urged by the nonagenarian
Isocrates to disregard in favor of rhetoric the eristic[36] that he is
reportedly being taught. In diplomatic style Isocrates represents
as coming from Alexander's own mind the rejection of eristic:
"But this branch of learning, I am told, you are not content with,
but you choose rather the training which rhetoric gives, which is
of use in the practical affairs of everyday life and aids us when
we deliberate concerning public affairs. By means of this study
you will come to know how at the present time to form reasonably
sound opinions about the future, how not ineptly to instruct your
subject peoples what each should do, how to form correct judgments about the right and the just and their opposites and, besides, to reward and chastise each class as it deserves" (*Letter to
Alexander*, 4; tr. Van Hook).

Throughout his writings early and late, therefore, Isocrates is
concerned with defending the philosophy of the *doxa* against the
philosophy of scientific knowledge (*epistêmê*). The overpowering
reason is that only the philosophy of the *doxa* is useful for speech
and action. Up to the very end of his long career, in the *Panath-
enacius* (339 B.C.), Isocrates continues to claim that his philosophy
of the *doxa* comes closer to the truth of things than does the alleged *knowledge* of his competitors (*Panath.*, 9). He represented
his philosophy, in fact, as the commonly accepted wisdom of
Greece: "I maintain also that if you compare me with those who
profess to turn men to a life of temperance and justice, you will
find that my teaching is more true and more profitable than theirs.
For they exhort their followers to a kind of virtue and wisdom
(*phronêsis*) which is ignored by the rest of the world and is disputed among themselves; I, to a kind which is recognized by all"
(*Antid.*, 84; tr. Norlin).

Greek Culture.   Isocrates was evidently intent upon training
leaders who would see to the defence and transmission of the
existing Hellenic culture, rather than upon any innovations of
thought. He maintains the traditional classification of the motives
for human action: "I say that all men do all things for the sake
of pleasure or gain or fame; for outside of these I see no desire

[36] On the Platonic and Aristotelian teaching as the target of the letter to
Alexander, and on the general anti-Platonic bearing of Isocrates' lifelong
polemic against eristic, see P. Merlan, *Historia* (Wiesbaden), III (1954),
61-73.

springing up in men" (*Antid.*, 217). He seems to take for granted, or as obvious, that these ends are properly attained only in the measures provided by the framework of Greek culture. Greek culture itself does not come under the norm of the moral mean. Seemliness, or moral goodness, requires that everything else be pursued according to measure, but Greek supremacy without measure: "To have an insatiate desire for anything else in the world is ignoble (*ou kalon*)—for moderation is generally esteemed—but to set the heart upon a glory that is great and honourable (*kalês*), and never to be satiated with it, befits those men who have far excelled all others . . . Be assured that a glory unsurpassable and worthy of the deeds you have done in the past will be yours when you shall compel the barbarians—all but those who have fought on your side—to be serfs of the Greeks, . . ." (*Second Letter to Philip*, 4-5; tr. Van Hook). Greek culture, accordingly, is regarded as an end to be achieved and perpetuated at every cost. To its interests the hostile barbarians are to be enslaved by war. It is looked upon as something that obviously justifies itself and whatever serves to maintain it, and that merits the sacrifice of everything else in its favor.

Teachability of Virtue. The means for promoting and safeguarding this culture are correct speech and action. For these, scientific knowledge cannot serve as a basis, but only the best opinions about the situation immediately at hand. Isocrates (*Antid.*, 231-235) points out that the greatest men through whose guidance Athens developed and prospered were men of rhetorical proficiency. Genuine philosophy, accordingly, is concerned with the formation of correct opinions. Although admitting that virtue cannot be taught where the disposition to it is lacking, Isocrates claims that this study is the best means of further developing an innate disposition to virtue: "And let no one suppose that I claim that just living can be taught; for, in a word, I hold that there does not exist an art of the kind which can implant sobriety and justice in depraved natures. Nevertheless, I do think that the study of political discourse can help more than any other thing to stimulate and form such qualities of character."[37] Virtue, that is, moral and political excellence, cannot then be taught in the way in which scientific knowledge is communicated from teacher to

[37] *Against the Sophists*, 21; tr. Norlin. Cf. *Antid.*, 274-285.

pupil. It presupposes an appropriate natural disposition as its foundation. But with that disposition present, the study that can arouse and develop it is none other than the rhetorical training of the type imparted by Isocrates. Such training, therefore, is the pursuit of real wisdom. It is the proper care of the soul, it is the only genuine philosophy.

For Isocrates, then, theoretical science may be dismissed as outside the realm of human philosophy proper. For men philosophy consists in correct *doxai* or opinions, and not in scientific knowledge. In the Eleatic background this meant the deliberate choice of opinion against anything modeled even remotely on the paralyzing immobility of the Parmenidean *Truth*. The only philosophy worthy of the name is one concerned with the ever-changing world in which men live and act. The purpose of education is to train men to handle the circumstances of each new day, developing in them an accurate judgment that will hit upon the appropriate course of action (*Panath.*, 30). It is to make them speakers of words and doers of deeds, continuing in the tradition that had built up Greek civilization. Philosophy is meant for living and acting in that civilization, but one lives and acts on the basis of correct opinion and not of scientific truth. Action is concerned with what is to be done, with what is still the future, and the future is not known through any *epistêmê* but can only be gauged by the *doxa*. In this way a vigorous and flourishing mentality on the side of opinion was set up in Athens, clothed in all the traditional appeal of Greek culture. Against it Plato will have a tremendous struggle to maintain the Socratic legacy of the stable and unchanging knowledge of what things are, against the claims of opinion to represent the ultimate in cultural achievement.

RETROSPECT

With the highly developed and enterprising Athenian civilization as the milieu of philosophical endeavor, advanced Greek thought became rapidly focused upon human activity rather than upon the processes of nature. All intellectual undertaking was made by the great fifth-century Sophists to bear upon political and social proficience. As these men were thinking against an

Eleatic background, they could hardly help but exalt to the limit the importance of the Parmenidean *doxa* as the type of cognition necessary for living and acting in the ever-changing practical world. The total elimination of any view of that world in terms of being was the result. No ground was left for any real stability and permanence.

In this situation, however, the problem of the teachability of virtue came to the fore. How can there be any real communication of thought and transmission of acquired excellences if these are not of a stable nature? If they vary from moment to moment and are different in kind in every individual, how can they be passed on in teaching? Against this conception Socrates insisted upon the necessity of attaining to what virtue is, to the nature that remained the same throughout all particular instances and so allowed virtue to be communicated and taught. He struggled for virtue under the aspect of *knowledge,* under the aspect of something stable and abiding. His followers, according to the scanty indications that survive, developed a rather amazing variety of ethical and dialectical teachings. These are impossible now to trace in detail, though they helped provide the complicated background against which Plato and Aristotle worked.

Finally, Isocrates, reacting in favor of the traditional rhetorical training, strove expressly to restrict philosophy to the *doxa,* as the only basis of living and acting. Against the dialectic of his contemporaries, and against the claims of any type of *epistêmê* to possess philosophical worth, he defended effectively the function of rhetoric as the best means of safeguarding and transmitting the invaluable heritage of Greek culture. His appeal was direct. It was to what seemed obvious—men possess no scientific truth about future events, they have only opinions upon which to act; but upon such opinions, correctly formed by its great architects, had Hellenic civilization been raised. In this commonly recognized wisdom of Greece, ranged explicitly on the side of the *doxa,* was the only genuine philosophy, in Isocrates' view, to be found.

Such are the main currents of thought, complicated enough and difficult to trace in their various wanderings, that converged upon the fertile habitat in which the Platonic doctrine of the Ideas emerged.

SELECTED READINGS AND REFERENCES

THE SOPHISTS

Eugène Dupréel, *Les Sophistes* (Neuchâtel: Editions du Griffon, 1948).

Mario Untersteiner, *Sofisti Testimonianze e Frammenti*, 3 vols. (Florence: La Nuova Italia, 1949-1954).

——, *The Sophists*, tr. Kathleen Freeman (Oxford: Blackwell, 1954). In Italian, *I Sofisti* (Turin: Einaudi, 1949).

M. de Corte, "Parménide et la Sophistique," in *Autour d'Aristote*, . . . Offert à Msgr. A. Mansion (Louvain: Publications Universitaires, 1955), pp. 47-58.

PROTAGORAS

A. Neumann, "Die Problematik des *Homo-Mensura* Satzes," *Class. Phil.*, XXXIII (1938), 368-379.

J. S. Morrison, "The Place of Protagoras in Athenian Public Life (460-415 B.C.)," *CQ*, XXXV (1941), 1-16.

Italo Lana, *Protagora* (Turin: Università di Torino, 1950).

Antonio Capizzi, *Protagora: Le Testimonianze e i Frammenti* (Florence: G. C. Sansoni, 1955).

R. F. Holland, "On Making Sense of a Philosophical Fragment," *CQ*, LX (1956), 215-220.

GORGIAS

O. Gigon, "Gorgias 'Über das Nichtsein'," *Hermes*, LXXI (1936), 186-213.

T. S. Duncan, "Gorgias' Theories of Art," *Classical Journal*, XXXIII (1938), 402-415.

G. B. Kerferd, "Gorgias on Nature or that which is not," *Phronesis*, I (1955), 3-25.

W. Bröcker, "Gorgias contra Parmenides," *Hermes*, LXXXVI (1958), 425-440.

SOCRATES

Alfred Edward Taylor, *Varia Socratica* (Oxford: James Parker & Co., 1911).

——, *Socrates* (London: Davies, 1932).

Eugène Dupréel, *La Légende Socratique et les Sources de Platon* (Brussels: Robert Sand, 1922).

Thomas Deman, *Le Témoignage d'Aristote sur Socrate* (Paris: Les Belles Lettres, 1942).

Olof Gigon, *Sokrates: Sein Bild in Dichtung und Geschichte* (Bern: A. Francke, 1947).

V. de Magalhães-Vilhena, *Le Problème de Socrate* (Paris: Presses Universitaires, 1952).

————, *Socrate et la Légende Platonicienne* (Paris: Presses Universitaires, 1952).

Jean Luccioni, *Xénophon et le Socratisme* (Paris: Presses Universitaires, 1953).

William Kenneth Richmond, *Socrates and the Western World* (London: Redman, 1954).

H. Erbse, "Sokrates im Schatten der Aristophanischen Wolken," *Hermes,* LXXXII (1954), 385-420.

Cornelia J. De Vogel, "The Present State of the Socratic Problem," *Phronesis,* I (1955), 26-35.

T. Gelzer, "Aristophanes und sein Sokrates," *Museum Helveticum,* XIII (1956), 65-93.

Anton-Hermann Chroust, *Socrates Man and Myth, The Two Socratic Apologies of Xenophon* (London: Routledge and Kegan Paul, 1957).

LESSER SOCRATICS

Guy Cromwell Field, *Plato and His Contemporaries,* 2nd ed. (London: Methuen, 1948), pp. 158-174. First published 1930.

G. B. Lorenzo Colosio, *Aristippo di Cirene, Filosofo Socratico* (Turin: Edizioni Toffaloni, 1925).

W. H. Reither, "The Origins of the Cyrenaic and Cynic Movements," in *Perspectives in Philosophy* (Columbus: Ohio State University, 1953), pp. 79-90.

C. M. Gillespie, "On the Megarians," *AGP,* XXIV (1911), 218-241.

————, "The Logic of Antisthenes," *AGP,* XXVI (1913), 479-500; XXVII (1914), 17-38.

A. Levi, "Le Teorie Metafisiche, Logiche e Gnoseologiche di Antistene," *Revue d'Histoire de la Philosophie,* IV (1930), 227-249.

F. Sayre, "Antisthenes the Socratic," *Classical Journal,* XLIII (1948), 237-244.

G. M. A. Grube, "Antisthenes was no Logician," *Transactions of the American Philosophical Association,* LXXXI (1950), 16-27.

ISOCRATES

Isocrates, with an English translation by (Vols. 1 & 2) George Norlin; (Vol. 3) Larue van Hook; 3 vols. (London: Wm. Heinemann, 1928-1945).

R. L. Howland, "The Attack on Isocrates in the Phaedo," *CQ,* XXXI (1937), 151-159.

Eino Mikkola, *Isokrates: Seine Anschauungen im Lichte Seiner Schriften* (Helsinki: Finnish Academy of Sciences, 1954).

P. Merlan, "Isocrates, Aristotle and Alexander the Great," *Historia* (Wiesbaden), III (1954), 60-81.

W. I. Matson, "Isocrates the Pragmatist," *Review of Metaphysics*, X (1957), 423-427.

Part Three

THE FLOWERING OF
GREEK PHILOSOPHY

CHAPTER 10

Plato of Athens
—The Ideas

Chronology. Hermippus of Smyrna, a late third-century B.C. historian, related that Plato died when eighty-one in the first year of the 108th Olympiad (348-347 B.C.). The *Chronicle* of Apollodorus, in stating that he was born in the first year of the eighty-eighth Olympiad (428-427 B.C.), accords with this dating.[1] Later accounts that mention the year of his death are unanimous in placing it under the archonship of Theophilus, that is, in the year recorded by Hermippus. This information indicates that Plato died in the first half of the year 347 B.C. The chronological traditions differed somewhat in regard to his exact age and the year of his birth, allowing his birth to be put back with some probability as far as the year 429 B.C.

Biographical Sources. In his dialogue the *Apology* (34A,38B) Plato refers to himself as present at the trial of Socrates. In the *Phaedo* (59B) he mentions that illness kept him from being present at Socrates' death. Aristotle gives a brief sketch of his philosophical formation. A few other details go back to sufficiently reliable sources, for instance, to Hermodorus, an associate of Plato. The anecdotes that come from later Greek biographers are not trustworthy. The story that he was originally named Aristocles and only later called Plato (broad) because of his wide forehead, goes back to Neanthes, a third-century B.C. historian. But the report (D.L., III,4) gives from other sources his robust physique or the breadth of his literary expression as reasons for the change of name, and the epitome of his life by Olympiodorus

[1] D. L., III, 2-3. If the death of Socrates occasioned the withdrawal to Megara, 427 B.C. seems to have been understood by Hermodorus as the year of Plato's birth (D.L., III, 6). For a discussion of the chronological data, see Zeller, *Phil. d. Griechen* (1922), II(1), 390-392, n. 1.

(*In Alc. I*, ed. Westerink, 2,37-41) offers still different explanations, with the result that the whole story is not beyond suspicion on account of the evident confusion in its details. The name Aristocles, though, is reported (D.L., III,43) to have been used in an epitaph inscribed on his tomb.

The main source, however, for the reconstruction of Plato's life are the letters that have been attributed to him. Of these the two most pertinent, the seventh and eighth, are written in a contemporary style by someone apparently well informed, and so are used with little hesitation as sufficiently reliable documents for his biography.

Intellectual Formation.   From these sources the life of Plato may be sketched well enough in its broad outlines. His family[2] on both sides had belonged to the elite of the Periclean age, and continued to play leading parts in Athenian public life. In such an atmosphere Plato naturally grew up with aspirations to political activity. The excesses of the Athenian tyranny and later of the democracy, however, especially in the treatment meted out by both to Socrates, turned him towards the pursuit of philosophy (*Ep.*, VII,324B-326B). His express purpose was to seek in it the remedies for the existing evils of public life. This turning to philosophy, accordingly, is not to be interpreted in any modern fashion as a retreat from practical interests to the isolation of scholarly research, but rather as a step to further and deeper participation in public affairs. Social well-being always remained the predominant motif in Plato, and to the last his philosophical endeavors were wholeheartedly directed to its improvement.

Quite early in his youth, Plato came under the influence of the "Heraclitean" philosopher Cratylus, and through him was deeply impressed by the conception of the sensible world as something in perpetual flux. He continued throughout his life to regard the visible universe in this way. In associating with Socrates, however, his attention was turned to the necessity of seeking stable and abiding grounds for human conduct. He was faced, accordingly, with the problem of looking elsewhere than in sensible things for something permanent and unchanging. Such, at least, is the impression conveyed by Aristotle's brief account[3] of his philosophical formation.

Travels.   Perhaps feeling himself in some danger after Socrates' execution, Plato at the age of twenty-eight, according to Hermodorus, went to Megara and spent some time there with Euclides (D.L., III,6). Nothing definite is known of his activities during the next decade of

---

[2] Plato's family tree may be found drawn up in J. Burnet, *Greek Philosophy*, I (London, 1914), p. 351. On the ancient *Lives, see* F. Ueberweg, *Grundriss*, I, 179-180.

[3] *Metaph.*, A 6,987a32-34. Cf. D. L., III, 5-6.

his life. He may possibly have visited Egypt and Cyrene, but the reports of these journeys are late and unreliable. The large output of his writings, though, would indicate that he devoted considerable time during this period to their composition. The dialogues in which the personality of Socrates shines most clearly could be expected to belong to that time when the memory of the latter's conversations, trial, and death were still fresh in Athenian minds.

At the age of about forty (*Ep.*, VII,324A), Plato visited Italy and Sicily for the first time, perhaps to associate with some Pythagoreans. He became friendly with a young man named Dion, whose sister was married to Dionysius, the reigning tyrant of Syracuse. This friendship had far-reaching consequences in Plato's subsequent life, and occasioned two further visits to Sicily.

The Academy.   Returning to Athens after his first Sicilian journey, Plato inaugurated a school that was destined to have a long history, for it continued its activity until the suppression of the philosophical schools under Justinian in 529 A.D. It became known as the Academy, a name that designated a public park and gymnasium a short distance outside Athens to the northwest, called after a legendary hero Hecademus or Academus. The ancient statements (D.L., III,5;7) that Plato devoted himself to philosophy in the Academy need by themselves mean nothing more than that he engaged in philosophical discussions there as Socrates had in the Lyceum. But in Greek tradition there were associated with these Academic interests a house and a garden, which were owned by Plato and in which he and some of his successors are reported to have lived and worked. Unlike the Socratic circle, moreover, the group around Plato took on very early some definite kind of organization; for the testimonia, though meager, indicate that it held regular social repasts, that Eudoxus of Cnidus substituted as its head while Plato was in Sicily the second time, that a new presiding officer was appointed every ten days, and that Xenocrates, its third head, was chosen by formal election. It kept a shrine of the Muses erected by Plato himself, and could have had the form of a religious corporation devoted to their cult. At any rate, it survived as an organized association, unlike the school of Isocrates, which seems to have centered only around the personality of its head. The details of the methods and activities pursued in the Academy, though, have not been handed down. The few testimonia available seem to show that it was open to all comers, and that Plato himself presided over lively discussions and gave some type of oral instruction. The known interests and accomplishments of some of its members indicate that research was stimulated in mathematical and astronomical fields, in practical legislation, in the art of definition and problems of the type discussed in the

192   THE FLOWERING OF GREEK PHILOSOPHY

Platonic dialogues, and perhaps, though to a lesser extent, in the domain of natural history. A leading mathematician of the time, Euxodus, who had his own school at Cyzicus, became associated with it. But definite information about its original nature and program is lacking. **Political Activities.** After the death of Dionysius in 367 B.C., the influence of Plato's friend Dion over the tyrant's son and successor, Dionysius II, seemed as though it might control the government of Syracuse. Dion, accordingly, wrote to Plato to ask him if he would come to Sicily and make use of this opportunity to bring into realization the union of philosophy and supreme political power in the same persons (*Ep.*, VII,328A). Plato was very doubtful about the prospects of success, and only with great reluctance acceded to Dion's entreaties and went to Sicily again. His efforts to train Dionysius in his philosophical doctrines were unsuccessful, on account of the young ruler's intractable character and of political struggles and court intrigues. In 365/364 B.C., he came back to Athens, though he continued his interest in Sicilian affairs. He went to Sicily once more in 361 B.C., but again his visit was a dismal failure, fraught this time with grave personal danger. He returned to Athens in 360, but continued to keep in touch with Sicilian affairs. This interest continued at least to within a few years of his death in 347 B.C.

Writings. *The Corpus Platonicum.* All Plato's writings[4] that were known to antiquity seem to have been handed down intact. No others than the ones now possessed were cited by the ancients. They consist of *Dialogues* and *Letters.* Recognized as spurious in antiquity, but included nevertheless in the Platonic *corpus,* are a collection of *Definitions* and six non-Platonic dialogues.[5] Catalogued as genuine and arranged in nine "tetralogies" or groups of four by Thrasyllus, a contemporary of the Emperor Tiberius, were thirty-five dialogues and thirteen letters. The *Letters* were regarded as a single unit that constituted the fourth member of the last "tetralogy."

The Dialogues. Of the thirty-five dialogues handed down as genuine, six are rejected by modern scholars, the *Alcibiades II,* the *Hipparchus,* the *Amatores* (or *Rivals*), the *Theages,* the *Clitophon,* and the *Minos.*

[4] Plato's writings are quoted in scholarly works according to page and marginal letter of the Stephanus edition (1578), called after its editor Henri Estienne. Some recent scholars prefer to cite more exactly by adding the lineation of Burnet's edition (Oxford, [1900-1907]), in which around eight or ten lines fall under each marginal letter. In the present chapters on Plato the dialogues, except for the short passages from the *Cratylus,* are quoted according to the Jowett translation with the permission of its publishers, the Clarendon Press.

[5] On these, see J. Souilhé, *Dialogues Apocryphes,* in the Budé edition *Platon, Œuvres Complètes,* XIII, 3e Partie (Paris, 1930).

PLATO OF ATHENS—THE IDEAS 193

Further, the *Epinomis*, according to an ancient report (D.L., III,37), seems to have been the work of Philip of Opus, and its authenticity as a writing of Plato himself has considerable weight of scholarly opinion against it today. There is division of opinion about the *Alcibiades I*. It is quite Platonic in content but is written in a style inferior to though contemporary with that of Plato. It seems to require a relatively late dating. The *Greater Hippias*, according to stylometric tests, is none too early, and is usually treated today as genuine, though scholarly opinion has been divided about its authenticity. The *Menexenus* is now quite generally accepted as authentic, as is also the *Ion*. The rest, including the longer and more important dialogues, are universally[6] recognized today as genuine. In form, the full-fledged Platonic dialogue seems to have been Plato's own development of the "Socratic discourse," against its background in the Sicilian mimes.

Chronological Order. The only method that has proved feasible for determining the order in which the dialogues were written has been that of stylometric tests.[7] The results attained by a number of scholars working independently of one another and using different procedures show in general a remarkable unanimity. According to an ancient tradition (D.L., III,37), Plato left the *Laws* written merely on wax tablets, and the dialogue was copied out by a disciple, Philip of Opus. This is

[6] A recent exception has been the late Josef Zürcher's claim that none of the dialogues were written by Plato, at least in their present form. The *Apology* is of Aristotelian origin, composed by Aristotle himself. The rest in their present form were written by Polemus, head of the Academy 315-270 B.C. Zürcher's arguments, based on linguistic grounds, the position of problems in relation to the Stoics, Epicureans, and Peripatetics, and some alleged historical allusions, are presented in his work *Das Corpus Academicum* (Paderborn, 1954).

On the evidence that the double titles of the dialogues go back to the fourth century B.C., see R. G. Hoerder, "Thrasylus' Platonic Canon and the Double Titles," *Phronesis*, II (1957), 10-20. Regarding the authenticity of the *Alcibiades I*, see Paul Friedländer, *Der Grosse Alcibiades*, 2 vols. (Bonn, 1921-1923); of the *Hippias Major*, G. M. A. Grube, "On the Authenticity of the *Hippias Major*," *CQ*, XX (1926), 134-148; of the *Ion*, H. Diller, "Probleme des Platonischen Ion," *Hermes*, LXXXIII (1955), 171-187; and of the *Epinomis*, see Plato, *Philebus and Epinomis*, ed. Raymond Klibanski (London, 1956), pp. 211-217. For a post-Platonic (*ca.* 343/342 B.C.) dating of *Alcibiades I*, see R. S. Bluck, "The Origin of the *Greater Alcibiades*," *CQ*, XLVII (1953), 46-52.

[7] A detailed survey of the problem is given by W. Lutoslawski, *The Origin and Growth of Plato's Logic* (reissue, London, 1905), pp. 64-193. A shorter history of this stylometric research may be found in John Burnet, *Platonism* (Berkeley, 1928), pp. 9-12. For a comparative table of the results attained by five leading scholars, see W. D. Ross, *Plato's Theory of Ideas* (Oxford, 1951), p. 2.

taken to mean that Plato did not live to publish the *Laws*.[8] The work, accordingly, is placed in the last years of his life. From it as a starting point the other dialogues are arranged chronologically according to the greater or lesser stylistic approximation to it. As a result of this method, the *Philebus*, the *Critias*, and the *Timaeus*, as well as the *Laws*, are dated in the last period of Plato's life. Somewhat before these come the *Politicus*, the *Sophist*, the *Parmenides*, and the *Theaetetus*. To the middle period of the author's literary activity belong the *Phaedrus*, the *Republic*, *Symposium* (*Banquet, Convivium*), and the *Phaedo*. Possibly the *Greater Hippias*, the *Cratylus*, the *Meno*, the *Gorgias*, and the *Protagoras* are to be dated towards the beginning of this period. The rest of the dialogues are assigned to the early years of Plato's writing.

This order fits in with other criteria. The dialogues classed as earlier are more lively and conversational in style, the later ones more didactic. Likewise, Socrates is the main speaker in the earlier ones, but recedes to the background in the later ones, with the exception, however, of the *Philebus*.

The criteria, of course, do not give any absolute datings, nor do they determine the extent of time between the composition of the individual dialogues or even of the groups. There may be a considerable interval, for instance, between the *Theaetetus* and the *Sophist*. A few dialogues can be dated absolutely as after certain events mentioned in them, as the *Apology* after the death of Socrates in 399 B.C., the *Menexenus* as after 390, the *Theaetetus* (142A) as after 369, and the *Laws* (I,638B) as about or after 356 B.C. All these absolute datings are in accord with the results of the stylometric tests. The possibility of later revisions or re-touchings, however, has to be kept in mind when one is assigning a chronological order to the dialogues.

The Letters. Thirteen *Letters* have been handed down with the *Dialogues* under Plato's name.[9] Of these the twelfth was labeled in antiquity as spurious. In the nineteenth century the tendency was to reject them all, and in the first part of the present century to accept as many as possible. Today the first, fifth, ninth, and twelfth are usually recognized as forgeries, and perhaps also the second. The seventh and eighth have the appearance of being the type of "open" letter meant for the general public, and exhibit fairly convincing indications of being

---

[8] On the general problem of the unfinished state of the *Laws*, see M. Van-houtte, *La Philosophie Politique de Platon dans les "Lois"* (Louvain, 1954), pp. 3-56.
[9] There are English translations of the *Letters* by L. A. Post, *Thirteen Epistles of Plato* (Oxford, 1925), and by R. G. Bury, *Epistles*, in the Loeb edition, *Plato VII* (1929).

genuine. However, it is still impossible to be sure of their entire authenticity. With this reservation, the seventh is an important source for confirmation or further explanation of certain doctrines in the *Dialogues*. The authenticity of the other six letters is very doubtful.

Unwritten Doctrines. Ancient Aristotelian commentators speak of a lecture of Plato entitled "On the Good," or of a group of such lectures. However, there is hardly sufficient evidence to affirm positively that any such lecture or lectures ever existed in published form, though records of Plato's oral teaching may well have provided inspiration and material for works like that of Aristotle's *On the Good*.[10] At the same time, there can be no doubt that "unwritten doctrines"[11] of Plato were discussed and commented upon. A number of such doctrines not contained in the dialogues have been handed down by Aristotle, who had every means of knowing at first hand the teachings of Plato in his final years, even though Plato did not set down these doctrines in writing. The works of Aristotle, accordingly, remain a necessary source for Platonic teachings that are not mentioned in the *Dialogues*.

Dialogue Form. The foregoing survey makes evident enough that the *Dialogues* are the principal and basic source from which Plato's philosophy is to be learned. The dialogue form, however, consists in a more or less lively conversation, with an exchange of ideas that progressively penetrate and clarify the subject at issue yet do not seem to result in any definite conclusion. Plato in his dialogues does not as a rule draw conclusions. At times when the dialogue form of question and answer seems to fall short of conveying his message, he bursts into a vivid myth that attempts to drive home his meaning. In this way the myth has an integral and organic function in the Platonic method.[12] The dialogue procedure, accordingly, does not offer results that can be handed down in the manner of a summary of Plato's thought, as cut-and-dried conclusions. His philosophy is expressed in a form requiring that its living development and dynamic emergence be retained in its presentation and in its transmission. It can be assimilated only by following it through as the dialogues unfold it. Any great philosophy, it is true, can be learned properly only from the text of its author, but with Plato a special reason is present in the peculiar literary form of his compositions.

A commentator, of course, may very easily draw conclusions for Plato

[10] See Harold Cherniss, *The Riddle of the Early Academy* (Berkeley and Los Angeles, 1945), pp. 2-4; 12-13.

[11] Aristotle, *Ph.* IV 2,209b15. On the unwritten doctrines as a further source for Platonic teachings, see W. D. Ross, *Plato's Theory of Ideas*, pp. 142-151.

[12] See J. A. Stewart, *The Myths of Plato* (London, 1905), pp. 1-2.

and present them in an easy didactic form. But what assurance is there then, in view of the method found in the dialogues, that Plato is really the one who is talking? In point of fact, such interpretations by commentators have always varied extremely. Rather, the *Dialogues* themselves have to remain the proper vehicle of Plato's thought. They present his philosophy in a way that stimulates and guides one's own thinking. They train the mind to proceed incisively in perennial philosophic questions. They open up vast expanses of intellectual activity. They make one realize the depth of the problems with which one is dealing. Yet they never give a systematic presentation of a philosophy. They may have the answers hidden somewhere in the considerations that they progressively unfold, but those answers, if there, have to be dug out by the reader's own labor. The answers are not given ready-made. For that very reason any synopsis of résumé necessarily gets away from the essential spirit of Plato's exposition, and gives the impression of falsifying more or less his way of thinking. It is easy enough to take a few of Plato's philosophical principles, and with them construct a closed system of reasoning. Such a "system," however, will quickly be found to run counter to other Platonic notions and only with some violence will be made to fit in with different things that Plato has written or with his general norms of procedure. Such, in fact, has been the history of the many attempts to systematize Plato's philosophy. Accordingly, his doctrine is to be learned not from such reconstructed systems but directly from the reading of the dialogues, in accordance with the special form in which Platonic thought received its expression.[13] The other ancient sources can serve only to supplement or help explain what one learns from the dialogues, and the later commentators have the role merely of introductions to or clarifications of the notions found in the dialogues themselves. They will not function as substitutes.

Varying Estimates. In the *Dialogues* of Plato is embodied a philosophy that has ever since been recognized by both friend and foe as one of the greatest and most profound expressions attained by human thinking. It may be accepted enthusiastically, as it has been by generations of Platonic scholars, and even be considered the most beneficent font that western culture has known.[14] It may be decried, in a positivistic outlook, as a great enemy of human freedom.[15] It may be re-

---

[13] On the union of form and content in Plato, see J. Stenzel, *Plato's Method of Dialectic,* tr. D. J. Allan, (Oxford, 1940).

[14] ". . . Plato has been the source of all that is best and of most importance in our civilization, . . ." J. Burnet, *Platonism,* p. 1.

[15] So Karl R. Popper, *The Open Society and its Enemies* (Princeton, 1950), pp. 165-166.

garded as merely a supreme synthesis of materials already fashioned by previous thinkers.[16] It may be admired and yet approached with varying degrees of critical reserve, as has been the attitude of Aristotle and so many in the Aristotelian tradition. Whatever may be one's personal appraisal of it, however, there need hardly be any doubt that the *Dialogues* contain one of the greatest and most inspiring philosophies ever produced in the history of human thought.

The Approach. Though Plato's philosophy has to be learned from the *Dialogues* themselves, a certain amount of help is indispensable for reading these compositions. They may be approached in two ways. The contents of the individual dialogues may be described and explained one by one, as an immediate preparation for reading each dialogue, with the critical information necessary to understand the dialogue in its own original setting. Secondly, an over-all synoptic description of the main themes and trends of Platonic philosophy may be given by noting and explaining the leading topics that run through the dialogues.[17] Both methods of introduction have to be used to a certain extent. A grasp in outline of the contents of the different dialogues and an acquaintance with the historical and biographical details necessary for understanding their dramatic settings are obviously required if one is to read them intelligently. A general acquaintance with the all-pervading and characteristically Platonic themes is also demanded by the dialogue form. Good modern introductions of both types are legion. Yet they should be made use of in such a way that the great preponderance of time at the student's disposal be devoted to the reading of the dialogues themselves, and only a comparatively small part to the secondary and introductory literature. Finally, Plato's intense lifelong interest in knowledge as the means to moral and political welfare should be kept in mind throughout the entire study of his writings.

PHILOSOPHICAL TEACHINGS—
THE DOCTRINE OF THE IDEAS

Terminology. The all-embracing theme that has been associated historically with Plato's name is the doctrine of the Ideas. The Greek term "Idea" is derived from the verb *idein,* which means "to see." The notion conveyed is that of "something seen."

[16] So F. M. Cleve, *The Philosophy of Anaxagoras* (New York, 1949), p. vii.
[17] Introductions of the first type are for instance, A. E. Taylor, *Plato, The Man and his Work* (London, 1926), and Paul Shorey, *What Plato Said* (Chicago, 1933). Of the second type are G. M. A. Grube, *Plato's Thought* (London, 1935), and Joseph Moreau, *La Construction de l'Idéalisme Platonicien* (Paris, 1939).

The word "Idea," accordingly, seems to have meant originally a visible form or character. In Plato's immediate background it had been used to denote the outward form or shape and also the inner structure or nature of a thing.[18] For Democritus (DK, 68B 141) it could mean an atom. In medical literature it signified any kind or class of disease.[19] A Pythagorean background has also been suggested,[20] but this is difficult to establish on the available evidence. In fact, there does not seem to be any one special background for Plato's use of the word. Plato seems merely to have taken the term as it was actually found in various technical and popular significations, and to have used it to express a philosophical notion of his own.

The term *eidos* (Form), also derived from the same Greek verb "to see," and carrying the same meanings as "Idea," occurs continually in Plato as a synonym for "Idea." The terms "being" (*ousia*), "kind" (*genos*), "monad," "unit" (*henas*), or the "nature" (*physis*) of the thing, are also employed more or less indifferently to express the same object. Very often the notion is conveyed by adding "itself" to a word, for instance, "beauty itself." The particular term, accordingly, is of rather secondary importance. Not too much can be gained by trying to attach the Platonic use of the word "Idea" to any particular etymological or even philosophical background. The meaning has to be gathered from the use of the word in the text of the dialogues. The etymological background, though, has at least the helpful function of showing that the word "Idea" did not in Plato's time mean a concept or notion produced by the mind, as it does in English. It meant something outside the mind, in the real world, and presented as such to the mind's gaze. But just what that object is has to be learned from a study of the Platonic text itself.

Moral Interest. In approaching the doctrine of the Ideas as it progressively unfolds in the Platonic writings, one is immediately struck with the consideration that all the earlier dialogues in which it appears are concerned with moral and practical matters, and in particular with the virtues and with education. It

[18] For a survey of the whole problem, see W. D. Ross, *Plato's Theory of Ideas*, pp. 13-16.
[19] See W. Jaeger, *Paideia* (New York, 1939-1944), III, 23-24. *Cf.* Democritus, *Fr.* 11 (DK, 68 B).
[20] See A. E. Taylor, *Varia Socratica* (Oxford, 1911), pp. 178-267.

seems as though Plato's primary concern with the doctrine lay in the development of a sound moral and social outlook. Even though illustrations may be brought in from other fields, they function merely as helps to understand the way in which moral problems are being approached. Socrates had striven to base human conduct on what was *common* to all virtuous acts. He inculcated *knowledge* of what a virtue itself is, as the key to virtuous conduct. The opposite view, popularized by the great Sophists and still more throughout the middle years of Plato's life by the conservative and widely received teaching of Isocrates, was that scientific knowledge of virtue was useless for practical purposes, because such knowledge did not extend to the future and so did not help in mapping conduct. The capacity to form true opinions, as cultivated by rhetorical study, was the really beneficial art in moral and political matters. Against this background the teachings of Plato on the Ideas may be watched gradually developing throughout the dialogues.

Common Characteristic. The *Laches,* considered to be one of the earliest dialogues, asks what courage is. It enumerates various acknowledged instances of courage, but insists that this enumeration does not tell *what* courage *is* (*La.,* 190D-191E). It asks: "What is that common quality, which is the same in all these cases, and which is called courage?" (191E). As an illustration, the notion "quickness" is described in comparison with individual instances of quickness (192AB). The common characteristic that is found in all individual instances of courage, and that allows those instances to be all called by the same name, is clearly being sought.

Knowledge. Further consideration of different instances of courage leads to the suggestion that "courage is the knowledge (*epistêmê*) of the grounds of fear and hope" (*La.,* 196D). It is a knowledge whose presence distinguishes courageous conduct from the daring acts of wild animals or children, a knowledge that comprehends the future as well as the present and the past (198D-199D). The one objection raised against this conception is that it seems to make courage coincide with the whole of virtue instead of with just a part (199E). But the preoccupation clearly bears upon giving courage a common object that extends to the future as well as the past and present, and so comes under the scope of knowledge instead of sensation, as in the case of wild animals and children. By means of such common knowledge one will know how to plan and perform courageously actions that are to take place in the future.

The *Charmides* asks what the traditional Greek virtue of temperance or moderation (*sôphrosynê*) is. It requires that a temperate man *know* that which he is doing temperately. It insists, in fact, that his temperance be based upon self-knowledge, according to the Delphic inscription. The second inscription "Nothing in excess" is not necessary, since "Know thyself" already means "Be temperate" (*Chrm.*, 164B-165C). This knowledge will obviously be a science (*epistêmê*). It is compared with sciences like those of health and of building (165CD). Yet scientific knowledge, whether of present, past, or future things, does not help towards faring well and being happy (*eudaimonein*) unless it is concerned with good and evil (174BE). —Again, the tendency to base virtue on knowledge is apparent. The knowledge meant is expressly a scientific knowledge, but a type of scientific knowledge into whose very object the aspect of goodness enters. This evidently makes it designate a practical kind of knowledge.

Ideas, Forms.   In the *Euthyphro* the same procedure is used to investigate the virtue of piety. Not the particular instances of the virtue are being sought, but that which is the same in all pious actions: "Is not piety in every action always the same? and impiety, again—is it not always the opposite of piety, and also the same with itself, having, as impiety, one notion (*idea*) which includes whatever is impious?" (*Euthphr.*, 5D). That which is the same throughout all pious or impious actions is an "Idea," and its presence in the actions themselves makes them pious or impious. It includes in its own unity everything that is considered to be pious or impious. It is also called a Form: ". . . I did not ask you to give me two or three examples of piety, but to explain the general idea (*eidos* 'Form') which makes all pious things to be pious. Do you not recollect that there was one idea (*idea*) which made the impious impious, and the pious pious?" (6D). Form and Idea, accordingly, are used interchangeably to designate that which is the same throughout all the individual instances of the virtue, and which makes the individual acts be acts of that virtue. It is regarded as something in the acts themselves,

and not just the notion that men obtain of it, as the ordinary use
of the English word "idea" would signify.

Pattern for Conduct. The reason why this Form or Idea is
being sought is that it may serve as a pattern for conduct. By
looking to it one will be able to determine which particular acts
are virtuous and which are not: "Tell me what is the nature of
this idea, and then I shall have a standard to which I may look
and by which I may measure actions, whether yours or those of
any one else, and then I shall be able to say that such and such
an action is pious, such another impious" (6E). The reason for
wishing to know the Idea, then, is to be able to know the kind of
action that is virtuous and by comparison with it to be able to
determine whether various individual actions are virtuous or not.
In this way one is enabled to determine how one should act: "If
you had not certainly known the nature of piety and impiety, I
am confident that you would never, on behalf of a serf, have
charged your aged father with murder" (15D). The Idea, accordingly, should be known in order that one be able to perform
actions according to the virtue. It is a pattern that one has to keep
before one's eyes if one is to act virtuously.

"Itself." The *Greater Hippias*, a dialogue that may be taken as
probably genuine, pursues a like inquiry about the beautiful or
seemly (*kalon*). Along with "Form" (*eidos*, Hp. Ma., 289D,
298B), it uses the expression "the beautiful *itself*" (286D,289CD,
304D) to denote that which is present in all the instances of the
beautiful and makes them beautiful, and by which one may know
which things are beautiful or seemly and which are not. This
mode of expression through the word "itself" continues to be a
fairly regular way of designating the Forms throughout later
dialogues.

Knowledge of the Good. The theme of virtue and its teachability is discussed in much detail in the *Protagoras*. It leads up
to the identification of virtue, which is accepted unhesitatingly
as the most attractive and most seemly of all things, with knowledge of the good (*Prt.*, 349E-360E). Evil is not done knowingly
and willingly: ". . . no man voluntarily pursues evil, or that which
he thinks to be evil. To prefer evil to good is not in human nature;
. . ." (358D). The teachability of virtue, and so the moral and
political education of the young, is made to depend upon this

identification of knowledge with virtue. If virtue is knowledge, it is teachable. If it is not knowledge, it is not teachable (361AC). The desirability of virtue is accepted as only too evident and indisputable. The problem concerns the way in which it is to be attained and transmitted. Virtue consists in knowledge of the good, and as *knowledge* it is teachable. As knowledge of the *good*, it is obviously understood as being a practical knowledge.

Stable Norms. The *Gorgias* shows that the art of rhetoric as taught by the famous Sophist deals with the greatest and best of human affairs (*Grg.*, 451D), yet it imparts only belief (*pistis*) and not knowledge (*epistêmê*). Belief can be true or false, while knowledge can only be true. Rhetoric, however, is the art of persuasion about the just and the unjust (454BD). Since it imparts only beliefs, it can inculcate beliefs that are untrue about the just and the unjust, and so it can be used to accomplish evil. If it gave *knowledge* of what is just, it would thereby make its possessor just and cause him to act in a just manner, and so could not be used for an unjust purpose:

"*Soc.* And he who has learned medicine is a physician, in like manner? He who has learned anything whatever is that which his knowledge makes him?

Gor. Certainly.

Soc. And in the same way, he who has learned what is just is just?

Gor. To be sure.

Soc. And he who is just may be supposed to do what is just?

Gor. Yes" (*Grg.*, 460B).

The political art cares for the soul just as medicine and gymnastic care for the body (464B). The rhetorician who really aims at training and benefiting the souls of the citizens, therefore, should keep before his eyes the virtues of justice and temperance. In point of fact, however, that kind of rhetorician is just not found in practical life (503B). Good action, though, is not performed at random, but by looking to something definite: "Will not the good man, who says whatever he says with a view to the best, speak with a reference to some standard and not at random; just as all other artists, whether the painter, the builder, the shipwright, or any other look all of them to their own work, and do not select and apply at random what they apply, but strive to give a definite form (*eidos*) to it?" (503DE).

The concern is with stable, abiding norms according to which moral and political life can be guided. Philosophy provides these, for it does not speak differently at different times like an Athenian orator or popular leader, but always has the same meaning (482A). Such knowledge is the remedy for the evils that arise from the view that the stronger man has a natural right to seize the property of the weaker, and that a man who has the means may indulge his passions and whims as he pleases, and that such arbitrary indulgence is excellence and happiness. Evidently a practical knowledge, that will make a man virtuous as the medical art makes him a physician, is meant.

Right and Might. The conception that Plato is opposing is summed up sharply in the words of Callicles, the otherwise unknown owner of the house in which the conversation is taking place: ". . . the makers of laws are the majority who are weak; and they make laws and distribute praises and censures with a view to themselves and to their own interests; and they terrify the stronger sort of men, and those who are able to get the better of them, in order that they may not get the better of them; and they say, that dishonesty is shameful and unjust; meaning, by the word injustice, the desire of a man to have more than his neighbors; for knowing their own inferiority, I suspect that they are too glad of equality. And therefore the endeavour to have more than the many, is conventionally said to be shameful and unjust, and is called injustice, whereas nature herself intimates that it is just for the better to have more than the worse, the more powerful than the weaker; . . ." (*Grg.*, 483BD). The sanctions of praise and blame, accordingly, are worked out artificially and set up conventionally by the majority, who are weaklings individually, in order to protect their possessions against stronger individuals who are physically able to seize those possessions and to whom, therefore, such possessions belong by right of nature.[21] According to *natural* right, consequently, "the oxen and other possessions of the weaker and inferior properly belong to the stronger and superior" (484C). This conception of might as right

[21] On the theme of justice as the interest of the stronger, see *Rep.*, I, 338C-344C; *Lg.*, IV. 714BC.

means that one has by nature the right to pursue and indulge one's whims and passions as one wishes, provided only that one has the means to do it: ". . . the truth is this: —that luxury and intemperance and license, if they be provided with means, are virtue and happiness—all the rest is a mere bauble, agreements contrary to nature, foolish talk of men, nothing worth" (492C).

The estimate of philosophy that accompanies this conception of might as right is sketched in a way that corresponds to Isocrates' view of eristic and the mathematical sciences. Philosophy had just been described as having always the same meaning, in contrast to the ever-changing opinions of the populace. In this setting Callicles asserts: ". . . philosophy, Socrates, if pursued in moderation and at the proper age, is an elegant accomplishment, but too much philosophy is the ruin of human life. Even if a man has good parts, still, if he carries philosophy into later life, he is necessarily ignorant of all those things which a gentleman and a person of honour ought to know; he is inexperienced in the laws of the State, and in the language which ought to be used in the dealings of man with man, whether private or public, and utterly ignorant of the pleasures and desires of mankind and of human character in general" (484CD). Philosophy is therefore a pursuit only for the young, as a part of their education, but it is ridiculous in a mature man (485AD). Such a man "creeps into a corner for the rest of his life, and talks in a whisper with three or four admiring youths, but never speaks out like a freeman in a satisfactory manner" (485DE). Plato, apparently, is taking Isocrates' teaching that human conduct cannot be based upon scientific knowledge that would hold for the future, and is showing the extremes to which the conception of acting only upon opinion leads. It opens the way for the arbitrary indulgence of the stronger's wishes. Plato's opponents might claim that they advocated action upon true opinion only; but Callicles is represented as maintaining that his views are the only true ones in practical life. Without a common and obligatory pattern over and above and independent of the wishes of particular individuals, there is no answer to the doctrine that might is right; and there is no rational objection against the tenet that physical force may be arbitrarily indulged as long as the means are at hand.

In this perspective Plato's ardent effort at establishing an Idea or pattern to which the conduct of individuals should conform becomes apparent. It is the search for the basis of common norms of conduct against a conception that results in arbitrary and ruinous indulgence.

Interconnection of the Virtues. The *Gorgias* shows that the common basis for human conduct involves and interrelates all the virtues. The virtues are found to be always associated with one another (507AC), and accordingly "the best way of life is to practise justice and every virtue in life and death" (527E). Again the desirability of virtue is taken as obvious, the problem is to find the stable and permanent something that may be used as a pattern for all virtuous conduct, just as artisans look to a plan according to which they can turn out their products in a definite *eidos* or Form. The preoccupation is more than ever with combatting arbitrary rule or license in human conduct, by showing how human activity has to be carried out according to a common and enduring pattern if it is truly to be virtuous and so be able to attain the good that is the natural goal of every human action.

Recollection. The *Meno* inquires what virtue in general is. It emphasizes that all the virtues have one and the same Form (*eidos*), and that virtue like health has the same Form everywhere (*Men.*, 72CE). By having a servant boy, who has never learned geometry, follow geometrical figures drawn for his aid, it shows that the right answers can be evoked from him (82B-85E). The boy is found to have true opinions (*doxai*) about something of which he *knows* nothing, and by proper questioning these true opinions are changed into knowledge (85CD). This is shown to mean that he already possessed scientific knowledge, geometry, and that he needed only proper questioning to bring it into his recollection. What is teachable is therefore knowledge, and only knowledge; and in this way learning is a process of recollection or anamnesis: "And if there have always been true thoughts (*doxai*) in him, both at the time when he was and was not a man, which only need to be awakened into knowledge by putting questions to him, his soul must have always possessed this knowledge, for he always either was or was not a man?" (86A).

The boy, of course, was looking only at a particular geometrical drawing. Yet he was giving answers that hold for all similar instances. He was recalling truly scientific knowledge. He can do the same for every branch of scientific knowledge as he did for geometry. Plato does not pursue this doctrine of recollection[22] further in the *Meno*, but goes on to the question whether virtue is teachable. According to the anamnesis doctrine, knowledge is the only thing that is teachable (87C). If virtue, by which men are good, is a type of knowledge, then clearly it is teachable; but if it is not a type of knowledge, it is not teachable. Since things are good only when wisely used, and since men are good not by nature but by education, this would indicate that virtue has to be taught and so consists in knowledge (87E-89C).

Causal Basis of Knowledge.   The difficulties urged against the foregoing conclusion lie in the practical difficulties experienced in teaching virtue and in the evident facts where true opinion has been just as good a guide for human conduct and just as useful. The difference, accordingly, is urged that he who has knowledge will *always* attain the right way of doing things, while he who depends upon opinion will sometimes hit it and sometimes not (97BC). True opinions are not as it were fastened in the soul, but come and go. They can be fastened only through reasoning based upon cause,[23] and that process is the process of recollection, by which the true opinions are turned into knowledge and become abiding (97D-98A). Themistocles and the great statesmen of Greek history based their guidance on true opinion only, and so it is hardly surprising that they were not able to teach their abilities to their sons (99B).

The doctrine of the *Meno* indicates that if virtue is teachable and the excellences of Greek culture are able to be transmitted safely through the education of the young, virtuous conduct has to be based upon something abiding, something that remains the same in all individual instances, future as well as past and present. The teaching process is envisaged as occasioning a recollection that fastens true opinions to a firm and permanent basis in the soul through causal knowledge. What is abiding and the same in all the particular instances, that by which anything is virtuous,

---

[22] The anamnesis doctrine is treated in two other places, *Phd.*, 75B-76E, and *Phdr.*, 249B-250A.

[23] On account of this basis in reason, knowledge cannot be overcome by persuasion, but true opinion can (*Ti.*, 51DE).

is regarded as the cause of the virtue in all the particular actions. The function of the Form in making actions virtuous is accordingly viewed as causal, causal of course in a formal way. Once a true opinion has been based upon this permanent and common cause, it thereby assumes the aspect of knowledge.

The importance of a common, abiding basis for virtuous action becomes in this way increasingly apparent. Plato speaks as though education and the future of Greek civilization depended upon the "knowledge" aspect of virtue.

Forms and Being. The *Cratylus*, inquiring whether names have a natural correctness or whether they are purely conventional, and opposing the Protagorean relativity of things, agrees that "it is evident that things are themselves possessors of some stable being (*ousia*) of their own, not in relation to us nor caused by us; . . . but of themselves they are disposed in regard to their own being (*ousia*) as set by nature" (*Cra.*, 386DE). The term *ousia* is here as often elsewhere in the dialogues used to designate the fixed and stable aspect of things that remains the same throughout all the variable instances. It implies that this aspect has the enduring, unchangeable character that had become associated with the term "being" in Greek philosophical tradition. The permanent and identical aspect of things is regarded as not dependent on any relativity to human cognition, nor as caused by the thing's being known, but as by nature present in the things themselves. The carpenter in making a shuttle has to look to the Form (*eidos*) of the shuttle, and this Form is the "shuttle itself" (389AB). All individual shuttles must possess the Form of the shuttle, and the same holds for all other instruments (389BC). So should the lawgiver, in imposing names, keep his gaze fixed upon the proper Form of name (390A). In a similar way there exists the beautiful itself and the good itself and everything else of like nature. Beauty itself is permanent, and always remains what it is in itself (439CD). In this manner it conforms to the notion of being: "How, then, can that which is never in the same state be anything? For if it is ever in the same state, then obviously at that time it is not changing; and if it is always in the same state and is always the same, how can it ever change or move without relinquishing its own form (*idea*)? . . . No, nor can it be known by anyone. For at the moment when he who seeks to know it approaches, it becomes something else and different, so that its nature and state can no longer be known; . . . "(*Cra.*, 439E-440A; tr. Fowler). The general Parmenidean argument for the necessarily unchangeable nature of being is used to establish the permanent character of the Ideas or the things "themselves," against the conception of a universal flux. If a thing changes, it cannot be said to be. For the same reason, an Idea makes knowledge possible, for knowledge requires a fixed object and is itself stable (440AB). The stable natures, accordingly, counter the notion that "all things are flowing like leaky pots, or . . . are just like people afflicted with catarrh, flowing and running all the time" (440CD; tr. Fowler).

The *Cratylus*, accordingly, uses the doctrine of the Ideas to oppose the "Heraclitean" flux. It shows that knowledge has to be based upon the unchanging character of *being*. It requires stable natures not only for the virtues, the good, the beautiful, and things of that kind, but also for the shuttle and all instruments, and finally for anything of which there can be knowledge.[24] The role of the Ideas as the foundation of all *knowledge* becomes uppermost; for the Ideas exhibit the aspect of *being*.

Intuitional Procedure.   In the *Symposium*, which deals with the nature of love, the myth of Diotima describes the way to the perception of the Forms as a series of progressively rising intuitions. The appetitive and affective dispositions enter deeply into the process. It starts from particular sensible things[25] and ascends gradually to other spheres: "For he who would proceed aright in this matter should begin in youth to visit beautiful forms; and first, if he be guided by his instructor aright, to love one such form only—out of that he should create fair thoughts; and soon he will of himself perceive that the beauty of one form is akin to the beauty of another; and then if beauty of form in general is his

---

[24] The most complete list of the things of which there are Ideas is found in *Ep.*, VII, 342D. On the stand that Plato did not reject Forms for any artifacts, see Richard Stanley Bluck, "Aristotle, Plato, and Ideas of Artefacta," *CR*, LXI (1947), 76.

[25] That the Platonic dialectic starts from sensible things and proceeds from them to the Ideas is fully confirmed by Aristotle's assertion that for the Platonists ". . . the Forms are, one may say, more numerous than the particular sensible things, yet it was in seeking the causes of these that they proceeded from them to the Forms" (*Metaph.*, M 4,1078b36-1079a2; Oxford tr.).

pursuit, how foolish would he be not to recognize that the beauty in every form is one and the same! And when he perceives this he will abate his violent love of the one, which he will despise and deem a small thing, and will become a lover of all beautiful forms; in the next stage he will consider that the beauty of the mind is more honourable than the beauty of the outward form." From this stage he proceeds to the contemplation of the beauty or seemliness in laws and institutions, and then to that of the sciences, until "at last the vision is revealed to him of a single science, which is the science of beauty everywhere" (*Smp.*, 210AD).

Having proceeded in this way he will towards the end suddenly perceive "a nature which in the first place is everlasting, not growing or decaying, or waxing or waning; secondly, not fair in one point of view and foul in another, or at one time or in one relation or at one place fair, at another time or in another relation or at another place foul, as if fair to some and foul to others, or . . . existing in any other being, as for example, in an animal, or in heaven, or in earth, or in any other place; but beauty absolute, separate, simple, and everlasting, which without diminution and without increase, or any change, is imparted to the evergrowing and perishing beauties of all other things" (210E-211B).

Participation.   The unchanging nature, reached by this ascending intuitional process, is accordingly regarded as that which all individual instances participate. It is described as existing not in any particular thing but just in itself, with itself, absolutely, in its own formal unicity. This should mean that the absolute nature, for instance of beauty, has its own existence separate from the existence of particular beautiful things. The *Symposium* seems to be the earliest dialogue that implies separate existence for the Ideas, and looks upon the Ideas as being participated by the individual things. The theme of participation, merely mentioned here, will be expanded in subsequent dialogues.

Objects of Intellection.   In the arguments for the immortality of the soul in the *Phaedo*, the Forms play a leading role. They are introduced as knowable by the intellect (*dianoia*) only, and not by the senses (*Phd.*, 65A-66A). They are established by the consideration that a characteristic like equality appears in individual things in greater or less degree, and so falls short of the full nature of such a characteristic. Therefore none of the individual instances can be the characteristic itself (74AE). The Form is regarded as present in the individual thing, and the individual thing as participating the Form (100D-102B). No discrepancy is felt between these two notions. An individual thing is called after the Form and is what it is through the Form, and yet the Form is looked upon as having its own existence. It was "agreed that ideas exist, and that other things participate in them and derive their names from them, . . ." (102AB).

Though moral and mathematical natures are the ones continually in mind throughout the *Phaedo*, the doctrine of the Ideas is extended to all things that can be referred to with the addition of "itself" and about which there can be a dialectical process (75D). The doctrine of recollection is explained in detail as meaning that the soul contemplated the Ideas in a former existence and brought along its knowledge of them; but this knowledge was forgotten at birth, and has to be recalled gradually through the cognition of sensible things that participate them (74E-76E).

Supremacy of the Good. In the *Republic* (V,476AD), the difference between philosophers and non-philosophers is that philosophers know the existence of the Ideas and the distinction of the Ideas from sensible things. Philosophers alone live in a waking world, the others in a dream world. Non-philosophers cannot have knowledge, for knowledge is grounded upon being; they can have only opinion, which is based upon sensible things and artificial products. Particular sensible things are not being; they are only becoming. The Ideas are described as having their being, and their corresponding power of being known, from the Idea of the good: "You would say, would you not, that the sun is not only the author of visibility in all visible things, but of generation and nourishment and growth, though he himself is not generation? Certainly. In like manner the good may be said to be not only the author of knowledge to all things known, but of their being and essence, and yet the good is not essence, but far exceeds essence in dignity and power" (VI,509B). As the sun is the source of growth and change to changing things, so is the good the source of all knowability and of all being; and as the sun is outside the process of growth, so is the good

itself above being. The notion of the good above being is not
elaborated any further in the Platonic dialogues. It quite evidently
means much more than the role of the good as final cause of all
actions that bring things into being. It designates the relation of
the good to the *Ideas,* which do not come into being and which
have no final cause. It makes the good supreme among the Ideas,
and the ultimate condition of all knowability. Knowledge in its
highest aspect, accordingly, seems to be envisaged as practical
and directed towards the good.

   The Divided Line.   To explain the similitude of the good as
the source of knowledge with the sun as the source of light,
the *Republic* proceeds to investigate knowledge and opinion
more closely by using the famous illustration of the divided line
(509D-511E). A line is divided into two unequal sections, the
inequality denoting the greater importance of the top section.
The lower section represents the visible world, the top section
the intelligible. Each of the two sections is then divided according to the same ratio into two unequal subsections, again by
reason of the upper part's greater relative importance in each
case. In the lowest subsection belong shadows, and the reflections
and images of sensible things that appear in water or on polished
surfaces, and the like. The type of cognition that is based upon
these is named conjecture. In the immediately higher subsection
of the line are located sensible things. They are grasped by a
type of cognition called belief. These two subsections taken together form the realm of opinion, which makes up the lower
section of the entire line. As shadows and reflections are images
of the sensible things, so does the whole order of the opinable
stand in relation to the knowable.

   The region of the knowable is in its turn divided into two
corresponding subsections. In the lower of these two subsections
sensible things are used as images, and the procedure is from
"hypotheses" to a conclusion and not to a first principle.[26] It is

   [26] The *Lysis* (219C) called the primary instance of the friendly a "first
principle." On Plato's conception of "hypotheses," see Richard Robinson,
Plato's Earlier Dialectic, 2nd ed. (Oxford, 1953), pp. 93-179; Richard
Stanley Bluck, "ὑποθέσεις in the *Phaedo* and Platonic Dialectic," *Phronesis,*
II (1957), 21-31. The *Euthydemus* (290C) had described how mathematicians hand over their discoveries to the dialecticians for use in dialectical
inquiry.

The Intelligible and Knowable	Ideas	Intelligence (*nous, noesis*) or Reason (*logos*)—Dialectic	Knowledge
	Mathematical Objects	Understanding (*dianoia*)—Mathematics	
The Visible and Opinable	Sensible Things	Belief (*pistis*)	Opinion
	Reflections of Sensible Things	Conjecture (*eikasia*)	

mathematical procedure. Examples of such "hypotheses" are the odd and the even, the various figures of things, the three kinds of angles, and the like. They are obvious to everyone and are accepted by mathematicians at their face value without further question (510CD). The "hypotheses," accordingly, are not assumptions set up tentatively to test their validity, but are the initial mathematical positions that are commonly accepted without any need of further account at this stage of knowledge. The whole mathematical procedure is held down to the lower level of the knowable because of its inability to rise out of the confines of these "hypotheses" and their use of sensible images (511A).

Its objects, however, are described as in "themselves," like "the square itself" and "the diagonal itself" (510DE). They seem still to be represented as Ideas, even though the term "Idea" is not used of them here.

By means of this divided line the relations of knowledge and opinion, and of sensible and intelligible objects, are presented in a synoptic schema. "Conjecture" seems introduced merely to illustrate the basic relation between the different sections of the line. Acquaintance with things just through their shadows and reflections gives a distorted picture in comparison with the direct grasp of those things in ordinary experience. The direct experiential grasp is called "belief" (*pistis*), not in any sense of accepting something on the word of another, but as denoting the comparatively firm assent that the plain man gives to whatever he directly sees or hears or feels. The relation of such cognition to mathematical knowledge, and the relations of the mathematical Ideas to the still higher Ideas, are not explained in further detail. Mathematical treatment, however, is explicitly regarded as something "intermediate" (511D) between opinion (*doxa*) and intelligence (*nous*). It is a clearer type of cognition than opinion, and yet it is more obscure than dialectic (VII,533DE). Mathematical knowledge, therefore, is by no means the highest kind of knowledge, though it seems meant by Plato to be a proportionally higher[27] type of cognition than the kind based upon ordinary sensible perception apart from exact quantitative development. It is a required step in rising to dialectical knowledge. Dialectic, however, uses the mathematical "hypotheses" not as first prin-

[27] "Each higher level is the formal cause and archetype for what lies below it." J. Wild, *Plato's Theory of Man* (Cambridge, Mass., 1946), p. 178. To illustrate this, all segments have to be drawn unequal in the line. On the mathematical equality of the two central subsections in the diagram as "an unintended, and perhaps by Plato unnoticed, consequence of what he does wish to emphasize," see Ross, *Plato's Theory of Ideas*, p. 45. A. Wedberg calls this equality "obviously an unintended feature of the mathematical symbolism to which no particular significance should be attached." *Plato's Philosophy of Mathematics* (Stockholm, 1955), pp. 102-103. For the opposite view, see J. L. Stocks, "The Divided Line of Plato Rep. VI," *CQ*, V (1911), 76-77. While maintaining that the equality is intended and is not unimportant, Stocks nevertheless regards it as "devoid of positive significance" (p. 77). A discussion of the difficulty may be found in R. S. Brumbaugh, "Plato's Divided Line," *Review of Metaphysics*, V (1952), 529-534, and *Plato's Mathematical Imagination* (Bloomington, [1954]), pp. 91-100.

ciples but merely as springboards to the grasp of the first principle of the whole (VI,511B). After the first principle has been attained, dialectic proceeds downward to its conclusion "without the aid of any sensible object, from ideas, through ideas, and in ideas she ends" (511C).

The Cave.   The comparison of the sun and the good is continued through the well-known allegory of the cave. The present state of men is likened to the condition of prisoners in an underground cavern, facing the back wall and chained so that they cannot turn their heads. Behind them burns a fire. Between them and the fire is a smaller wall. By it pass men carrying all sorts of sensible objects, but in such a way that only the sensible objects appear above it and are reflected in the light of the fire on the back wall of the cave. The cognition of the prisoners is therefore based solely on shadows of sensible things. If one of the prisoners be freed from his bonds and made to look at the things themselves in the light of the fire and at the fire itself, he would find his eyes pained and his vision dazzled by the unexpected brightness, and would for the moment consider that his former cognition was the clearer. If he were forcefully dragged out of the cave into the light of the sun, he would have still more difficulty. He would be obliged to habituate himself gradually to the new conditions by discerning first the darker shadows and reflections, then the things themselves by the light of the moon and stars. Finally he would be able to look upon the sun itself. Only at that stage would he understand the whole sensible order in its true perspectives. Returning into the cave to inform the prisoners of the real state of things, he would not be able to adjust his eyes at once to the cave's dim light. He would not be able to discern the shadows as well as his companions do, and would evoke only mockery and violent resistance in telling them that his account of things was superior to theirs (VII,514A-517A).

In this allegory the fire represents the sun and the sun the Idea of the good. The Idea of the good gives birth to the visible sun, and is itself the source of truth and intelligence. Anyone who is to act wisely in private or public has therefore to look upon that Idea. The ascent from the cave is the ascent into the intelligible region. True education, then, consists in rising to the vision of the good. Such knowledge may appear laughable and even pitiable to men accustomed only to experiental cognition, yet it is knowledge based upon being. The best minds, consequently, should be compelled by the state authorities to ascend to the vision of the good, and then to descend into the life of their fellowmen and share with them the benefit of their knowledge (517A-519D). —This means that without philosophy men have a distorted cognition of things, mistaking reflections for the truest reality. Men can learn to know reality as it is in itself only through the pursuit of philosophy, which leads to knowledge of the Ideas. Later in the *Republic*, Ideas are mentioned for a bed and for a table. There is, in fact, a Form (*eidos*) in every case where there is a common name (X,596AB). Participation of the Ideas among themselves, already hinted at in the *Phaedo* (105C), has been taken for granted (*Rep.*, V,476A), though it is not as yet given any development.

The simile of the divided line and the allegory of the cave may be kept in mind profitably throughout the reading of Plato's works. They illustrate vividly the rising degrees of human cognition, which starts from ordinary common-sense acquaintance with things and proceeds through mathematical knowledge to dialectic. Sensible cognition is required for grasping the "hypotheses" of mathematics. These "hypotheses" in turn are the steppingstones to the vision of the Ideas. The two Platonic analogies further show how the worth of these successive degrees is exactly inverted in the ordinary estimation of mankind. Common-sense cognition is regularly given the first place, mathematical knowledge is considered more vague, while dialectical knowledge, when proposed to the ordinary man, seems shadowy and unreal in the extreme. Yet in truth the order is just the reverse.[28] In both analogies the foundation for the comparisons lies in the way images and reflections are formed of sensible things. The reality of sensible things while remaining undiminished in itself is in comparison as the shadow in the water is to the tree. As with Parmenides, the world of the *doxa* keeps all the reality that it has for men in general, while the world of being is shown to be real in a much higher degree. Unlike Parmenides, however, Plato seems intent

---

[28] "The effect can be understood only in terms of its cause, the image only in terms of its archetype, the visible only in terms of its intelligible form or structure." Wild, *Plato's Theory of Man*, pp. 176-177. On the relation to the Aristotelian knowledge *quia* and *propter quid*, see *ibid.*, p. 202.

on making the variable cosmos share in being, since its very nature is a reflection, vague though it be, of the inestimable reality seen in the Ideas. The cosmos in its sensible structure mirrors not only the fixed order of the mathematical proportions but also the wondrous being of the Ideas that are found above the whole mathematical realm.

Region of the Ideas. In the course of a myth the *Phaedrus* describes the object of true knowledge as existing in a supercelestial region: "There abides the very being with which true knowledge is concerned; the colourless, formless, intangible essence, visible only to the mind, the pilot of the soul" (*Phdr.* 247C). It is there that men before birth saw justice itself, temperance itself, and so on (249B-250B). The recollection of these objects takes place through the repeated perception of particular instances in the sensible world. This process results in knowledge according to Form: "For a man must have intelligence of univerals (*kat'eidos*), and be able to proceed from the many particulars of sense to one conception of reason;—this is the recollection of those things which our soul once saw . . ." (249BC).

Difficulties Regarding Participation. In the *Parmenides*, Forms are admitted for motion, rest, unity, and the like, as well as for the just, the seemly, and the good, and apparently, in spite of supposed initial reluctance, for trivial things like hair and mud (*Prm.*, 129E-130E). The difficulties against the participation of the Forms by particular things are then brought forward. The Form remains one; its instances are many. Each individual has to partake of the whole Form, not just part of it. Yet if the whole Form be present in each separate individual, it will, while remaining one and the same, be separate from itself (131AC). Moreover, the reasoning that leads to the existence of the Forms will fall into an infinite regress. If particulars require the existence of an Idea because they share a common character, another Form will be necessary to account for what is common to that Idea and its particulars. Still another will be needed to explain the union of all these Forms and particulars in the one common feature; and so on *ad infinitum* (132AB). This reasoning became known as the Third Man argument.[29]

[29] On Plato's attitude towards this difficulty, see N. B. Booth, "Assumptions Involved in the Third Man Argument," *Phronesis*, III (1958), 146-149.

Further, no way can be found to show how the Form can come into relation with the particulars, even to the extent of being known by men: "But the ideas themselves, as you admit, we have not, and cannot have? No, we cannot. And the absolute natures or kinds are known severally by the absolute idea of knowledge? Yes. And we have not got the idea of knowledge? No. Then none of the ideas are known to us, because we have no share in absolute knowledge? I suppose not" (*Prm.* 134B). Yet as a matter of fact there is knowledge and there is communication of knowledge through speech, and so there must be Ideas (135AC). This means that the difficulties, great as they are, do not suffice for a rejection of the Ideas and their participation by particular things. No way is apparent to show how the Form can be entirely in itself and yet spread out in innumerable individuals, nor how the Form can come into relation with its individual instances. Nevertheless these difficulties cannot set aside the need of the Ideas in explaining knowledge and speech.

Not Thoughts. In the course of the discussion the *Parmenides* shows that the Forms cannot be thoughts of any mind. A thought has to be the thought of something, and, in this case, of something real. That real something, and not the thought of it, will be the Idea. It is through sharing in the Forms that particular things are. If the Forms were thoughts, the consequence would be that "everything is made up of thoughts, and that all things think; or that they are thoughts but have no thought" (*Prm.*, 132C). The Forms, it is agreed, cannot exist in us, because then they would be no longer absolute but relative to us (133C). This reasoning, though meant only of particular instances of the Forms, would seem to exclude the possibility that the Ideas are the thoughts of any mind whatsoever, or that they exist in any mind; for they would thereby, as a mind's thoughts, be relative to that mind and no longer absolute. They have to exist in themselves and in reality,[30] as "patterns fixed in nature" (132D).

Participation Within the Ideas. A further notion, already presupposed in the *Phaedo* (105C) and in the *Republic* (V,476A), is taken up in the *Parmenides*. Not only do sensible things participate the Forms, but the Forms themselves participate one another. To approach this difficult doctrine, long preliminary

[30] *Phd.*, 103B; *Ti.*, 51B-52A.

dialectical exercises are required (*Prm.*, 136AC). These exercises consist in following out in detail the results of internal participations among the Forms. As an instance, the second part of the *Parmenides* takes in turn the hypotheses "A One exists" and "A One does not exist," and reasons out the consequences of the participations of unity with being and with not-being. The results turn out to be self-destroying and impossible. The problem is left unsolved. It seems merely to indicate the need for much closer scrutiny of the ways in which the Forms intercommunicate. This treatment, however, has been given widely differing interpretations in both ancient and modern times. It has been viewed as a parody of Eleatic dialectic, as a refutation of Eleatic doctrine, as an exercise in the detection of logical fallacies, as a development of Idealistic philosophy, or as a metaphysical presentation of the doctrine that the One, like the Idea of the good in the *Republic* (VI,509B), is beyond being. The *Parmenides*, though, characterizes it definitely enough as a preparatory training in dialectic.

The Form of Not-Being. Knowledge had been left by the *Parmenides* as the unshakeable reason for admitting the reality of the Ideas. Its nature is investigated by the *Theaetetus*, against the background of "Heraclitean" flux and Parmenidean immobility. It is not had through any bodily organ, and is grounded on being. It is therefore different from sensation and different from opinion, even from true opinion (*Tht.*, 185C-210A). In the Parmenidean setting, however, foundation in being raises the question of motion and plurality in the objects of knowledge. The *Sophist* takes up that problem. Motion, in spite of its opposition to the Parmenidean conception of being, is shown to exist in the realm of perfect being and therefore to participate being: "And, O heavens, can we ever be made to believe that motion and life and soul and mind are not present with perfect being? Can we imagine that being is devoid of life and mind, and exists in awful unmeaningness, an everlasting fixture? . . . Under being, then, we must include motion, and that which is moved" (*Sph.*, 248E-249B).

Motion as well as mobile things, accordingly, will have to be accepted as somehow sharing in *being*. This establishes motion as one of the Forms or Kinds that make up the world of perfect being. The philosopher, therefore, is not bound by any mutually exclusive alternatives of either Parmenidean immobility or universal flux, but is able to accept both (249D). He can allow the stability of being, and still admit that motion in some way *is* or exists. The two, motion and being, mix with each other or participate each other. Yet motion and being are not the *same*, for the absolutely stable and permanent participates being but does not participate motion. Being, consequently, *is not* motion; it is *other* than motion. In this way it participates otherness or not-being. These considerations show that some Kinds (*genê*) commingle, and others do not. The function of philosophical knowledge or the science of dialectic is to show which ones mix and which do not, and the order and causes of the participation or non-participation (250C-253C). "Then, surely, he who can divide rightly is able to see clearly one form (*idea*) pervading a scattered multitude, and many different forms contained under one higher form; and again, one form knit together into a single whole and pervading many such wholes, and many forms, existing only in separation and isolation. This is the knowledge of classes (*kata genos*) which determines where they can have communion with one another and where not" (253DE). The philosopher, proceeding in the light of the Idea (*idea*) of being (254A), accomplishes through dialectic the task of seeing the divisions and combinations of the various Forms (*eidê*) or Kinds. Most important are the Kinds just mentioned—being, rest, motion, sameness, and otherness, (254C-255E). It was for this work of determining the ways and order in which the various Ideas participate or do not participate one another, that the type of training exemplified in the second part of the *Parmenides* seems to have been intended.

Forms other than being exist. Otherness or not-being, then, evidently participates being. The dialogue has therefore established against Parmenides that not-being actually is or exists, and has accounted for real plurality of beings through participation in this Form. The nature (*physis*) of otherness or not-being, however, is always relative and never absolute like being (255D). In finding this nature among the Forms, the *Sophist* has brought to light both the existence and the Form (*eidos*) of not-being (258D). Not-being by its very presence renders each Kind and each thing other than the rest, and so makes plurality possible (256DE).

Though motion and rest have been repeatedly represented as excluding each other, motion in spite of its "flux" background is allowed to participate sameness—it is the same as itself: ". . . but we call it the 'same,' in relation to itself, because partaking of the same" (256A). It is "motion itself" (256B), a Form with all the sameness that any Form has to have. There is, then, a common Form "motion" that is shared by all particular instances of motion. Plato, however, gives no further explanation of the way in which motion can have the sameness and the being that are proper to the world of Ideas.[31]

Dialectical Division. The *Politicus* takes up the problem of dialectic from the standpoint of proper divisions. Things are not to be divided just any way at all, but according to divisions based on Forms. One should not "cut off a single small portion which is not a species (*eidos*), from many larger portions; the part should be a species (*eidos*). . . . the safer way is to cut through the middle; which is also the more likely way of finding classes (*ideai*)" (*Plt.*, 262AB). One should not, for instance, first divide all mankind into Greeks and barbarians, for the Greeks are only a small part in comparison with innumerable other races (*genê*) of mankind (262D). A Kind (*genos*) or a Form (*eidos*) is necessarily a part, but a part is not necessarily a Form (263AB). Dialectic, therefore, should proceed according to an orderly division. —This procedure with the Ideas fore-shadows the method that will later, using the same terms as Plato, be known as division according to genera and species.

Latest Presentations. In the *Timaeus*, which deals with the production of the visible universe, the Ideas are regarded as really existent models according to which both souls and the whole sensible universe are produced. Pythagorean influence becomes

[31] For the interpretation that motion is present in souls and so in one part of perfect being, see F. M. Cornford, *Plato's Theory of Knowledge* (London and New York, 1935), pp. 244-245, and Ross, *Plato's Theory of Ideas*, p. 110. Souls and Ideas are considered perfect being in contrast to sensible things.—In any case, the procedure of this part of the dialogue is meant to lead up to motion as one of the five most important Kinds or Forms, and to its participation in being. Motion is clearly regarded as a Form in which all mobile things participate. F. H. Anderson, *The Argument of Plato* (London and Vancouver, 1934), p. 193, describes it as "logical otherness."

sharply apparent in the mathematical treatment given to bodies. In the *Philebus*, which treats of the good, the Forms are called monads or units, in seemingly mathematical fashion, on account of their absolute indivisibility. It is an indivisibility that excludes any becoming or perishing. The problems that emerge are to establish the real existence of these monads, and to explain how, if they are indivisible, they can be divided among the indefinitely numerous things that come into being (*Phlb.*, 15B). This objection is mentioned, as in the *Parmenides*, but again is not directly answered. Instead, the process of gradual division, starting with one Idea (16D), into classes and sub-classes is once more illustrated. The division is to be carried on till the total number of formal units is discerned. Then, and then only, is a unit allowed to pass on into the infinity (16E) of the particulars. The Pythagorean background continues to show itself in the explanation of things as composites of a limit and the unlimited. The *Laws* (XII,965B-966A) mentions the pattern or Idea (*idea*, 965C) according to which both guardians and workers should model their activities, and refers occasionally[32] to Form (*eidos*) in the meaning of class or Kind.

The Mathematicals. The *Greater Hippias* (301D-303A) had drawn attention to a peculiarity found in numerical predicates. They apply to groups as such, and not directly to the individuals that make up the group. Because a pair of individuals can be called "two," it does not follow that each of the individuals is two. If the two are said to be just or healthy, on the other hand, it means that both are just or healthy, and that each is so. In the *Phaedo* (74AC) "equals themselves" were mentioned separately as though they were somehow different from sensible equals and from equality.[33] In the *Republic* (VI, 511D) mathematical knowledge is described as "something intermediate" between intellection and opinion, and the Ideas that form its object are located in the divided line between the other Ideas and sensible objects. Aristotle, apparently from his knowledge of the doctrine through his association with the Academy, outlines Plato's teaching as

---

[32] E.g., *Lg.*, III,700AC; VIII,837A; IX,865A; XII,963C.

[33] This indication, just in itself, is not sufficient to allow interpretation in the sense of a fully developed doctrine of an intermediate status for the mathematicals. See Ross, *Plato's Theory of Ideas*, pp. 22-23; 177; A. Wedberg, *Plato's Philosophy of Mathematics*, pp. 95-99.

follows: "Further, besides sensible things and Forms he says there are the objects of mathematics, which occupy an intermediate position, differing from sensible things in being eternal and unchangeable, from Forms in that there are many alike, while the Form itself is in each case unique" (*Metaph.*, A 6,987b14-18; Oxford tr.).

According to Aristotle's testimony, then, the objects of mathematical science, mentioned in the dialogues with the same formula "themselves" that characterizes Ideas, were distinguished by Plato as a distinct and intermediate type of entities. The mathematicals differed from sensible things through their eternal and immobile being. They differed also from the Ideas because they could have many like instances while the Ideas could have only one instance each. That is, there can be many mathematical twos, just as there can be many sensible twos, but there can be only one Idea of two. This distinction seems to show clearly enough that the supersensible reality of the Platonic Ideas rose above any conditions of spatial extension and multiplication, no matter how abstract.

Ideal Numbers. As the Stagirite's account proceeds, however, Plato not only gave the mathematicals an intermediate status, but also explained the Ideas themselves in a numerical framework: "Since the Forms were the causes of all other things, he thought their elements were the elements of all things. As matter, the great and the small were principles; as essential reality, the One; for from the great and the small, by participation in the One, come the Numbers. . . . (for the Forms are the causes of the essence of all other things, and the One is the cause of the essence of the Forms); and it is evident what the underlying matter is, of which the Forms are predicated in the case of sensible things, and the One in the case of Forms, viz. that this is a dyad, the great and the small. Further, he has assigned the cause of good and that of evil to the elements, one to each of the two, . . ." (*Metaph.*, A 6,987b18-988a15; Oxford tr.). Aristotle represents the Platonic Ideas as generated or produced out of two ultimate principles, the One and the matter that participates the One. This matter, he insists, is a dyad, because of the dual character manifested in its very designation, namely the great and the small. It is identified by him with the matter of which the Forms are predicated in sensible things. The One is represented as the cause of good, the matter as the cause of evil. This means that the good was explained by Plato in terms of unity.

The notion of the "generation" or "production" of the Ideas from material and formal cause is of course merely a metaphor. Aristotle acknowledges as much when he endeavors to show that the Platonists should understand this "generation" in a literal sense (*Metaph.*, N 4,1091a28-29). The Ideas are eternal and ingenerate. The metaphor can indicate only a method of understanding and representing their natures. Plato's way of explaining sensible things in mathematical terms, as developed in the *Timaeus,* and in function of the limit and the unlimited, as seen in the *Philebus,* might well be expected to throw the most remote principles of their mathematical structure back through the intermediate mathematicals into the Forms themselves. The elements observed in the structure of all things should somehow find their prototype in the intelligible nature of the Forms. So far there need be nothing surprising in this manner of explanation. But Aristotle, interpreting the Platonic doctrine from the viewpoint of his own four causes, brings Plato's "great and small" under his own notion of "matter," and presents it as identical with the material cause of sensible things. Elsewhere (*Ph.*, IV, 2,209b11-210a2) the Stagirite identifies this "great and small" with the "space" of the *Timaeus,* and declares that it is matter for Plato, since it is a participant. Further, he seems to include Plato among those who identify the "great and small" with not-being, again as a material cause (*Ph.*, I 9,192a6-12). In this way Aristotle extends the one notion of matter, under the guise of the "great and small," to the composition of both sensible things and the Ideas.

That the receptacle (space) of the *Timaeus* does not function as a material cause is clear from the text of the dialogue itself. That space is in no way identified with the Form of otherness or not-being in the *Sophist* is evident from the role of otherness as an Idea, while the receptacle of the *Timaeus* does not proceed from or enter into the realm of the Ideas at all. Aristotle, in fact, reasons that Plato *should* have explained why the Ideas and Numbers are not in place if the participant is place, whether as "the great and the small" or as matter, (*Ph.*, IV 2,209b33-210a2), implying clearly enough that Plato himself did not look upon the "great and small" as their material cause. The Stagirite (*Metaph.*, A 6,988a1) takes advantage of an expression *ekmageion*, "plastic material" (*Ti.*, 50C), that Plato had used along with other metaphors "mother" and "nurse" to describe the receptacle. Aristotle also calls this Platonic "great and small" the "unequal," and complains that its proponent, apparently Plato himself, regarded it as unitary instead of dyadic: "For even the philosopher who says the unequal and the One are elements, and the unequal is a dyad composed of the great and small, treats the unequal, or the great and the small, as being one, and does not draw the distinction that they are one in definition, but not in number (*Metaph.*, N 1,1087b9-12; Oxford tr.).

Because of his manifest effort to bring the Platonic teaching under his own causal doctrine, Aristotle's account of the Ideal Numbers has been viewed in the one extreme as "not a theory of Plato's at all but the result of Aristotle's own interpretation, . . ."[34] Its only Platonic basis is considered to be details found in the dialogues. In the other extreme it has been regarded as a different Platonic doctrine of the Ideas that was taught orally in the Academy and replaced the older presentation of the dialogues.[35] Aristotle's accounts, in fact, seem at times[36] to draw quite evidently upon Platonic sources not contained in the dialogues. Plato's oral teaching on the good, moreover, according to a reported[37] statement of Aristotle, was given in entirely mathematical terms, to the discomfort and chagrin of those who came to listen to him. This was by no means an "esoteric" teaching, for it was

[34] H. Cherniss, *The Riddle of the Early Academy* (Berkeley and Los Angeles, 1945), p. 31. For H. M. Wolff, *Plato* (Bern, 1957), pp. 304-305, it was a doctrine evolved by some members of the Academy, but never accepted by Plato himself.

[35] E.g., J. Burnet, *Platonism*, pp. 120-121; *Greek Philosophy I*, p. 178. A.E. Taylor, "Forms and Numbers: A Study in Platonic Metaphysics," *Mind*, XXXV (1926), 419-420.

[36] See passages listed in Ross, *Plato's Theory of Ideas*, pp. 144-147. The Aristotelian texts dealing with problem are collected and analyzed in Léon Robin, *La Théorie Platonicienne des Idées et des Nombres d'après Aristote* (Paris, 1908).

[37] Aristoxenus, *Harmonics*, ed. H. S. Macran (Oxford, 1902), 30-31. Aristoxenus was a pupil of Aristotle. From what is known of his methods, however, some allowance may be made for exaggeration in the present statement.

the first explanation given to newcomers. It was more than the mathematical preparation envisaged in the *Republic*. It proceeded through geometry and astronomy and culminated in identifying the good and the one. The good, which was the highest of the Ideas in the *Republic*, was therefore presented under its phase of unity. In this setting a less extreme view regards the role now given to the Idea of the one as "not a fundamental change of view, but a difference of standpoint."[38] "Man," "horse," and "white" are suggested by Aristotle[39] as instances of things whose Ideas lent themselves to numerical explanation. This numerical phase may be fully consistent with and perhaps even required by the teachings in the dialogues, but its express development is not contained in them. The gradual unfolding of the doctrine as it emerges in the successive dialogues fully accords with Aristotle's procedure of commencing its study by "not connecting it in any way with the nature of numbers, but treating it in the form in which it was originally understood by those who first maintained the existence of the Ideas" (*Metaph.*, M 4,1078b10-12; Oxford tr.).

In any case, the Ideal numbers attributed to Plato are kept carefully distinct from mathematical numbers. The Ideal numbers are not quantitative.[40] A sensible "two" or a mathematical "two," for instance, is composed of two units. But the Ideal Two is not composed of two units. It is an indivisible unit like any other Form. The Ideal numbers, accordingly, are "not comparable"[41] with one another. They cannot be measured in terms of units or

[38] Ross, p. 242. On the modern theories offered to explain the generation of the Ideal Numbers, see *ibid.*, pp. 187-205.

[39] *Metaph.*, M 7,108a11-12; 8,1084a14-25. On the Platonic identification of the good and the one, with unity as its more fundamental character, see N 4, 1091b1-15; E.E., I 8,1218a24-26.

[40] Aristotle considered as incomprehensible the very notion of nonmathematical number: "Thus if the Ideas are a different sort of number, not mathematical number, we can have no understanding of it; for of the majority of us, at all events, who comprehends any other number?" *Fr.* 11,1475b28-31; tr. Ross (*Select Fragments*, p. 83).

[41] *Metaph.*, M 8,1083a34; *cf.* 6-7,1080a18-1081a21. "The 'inassociability' of Plato's Ideal Numbers, which is here stated, seems to mean that they do not stand in arithmetical relations to one another . . ." A. Wedberg, *Plato's Philosophy of Mathematics*, p. 121. On the problem, see J. Cook Wilson, "On the Platonist Doctrine of the ἀσύμβλητοι ἀριθμοί," *CR*, XVIII (1904), 247-257.

component numbers, as mathematical numbers can. There is an order of prior and posterior[42] among them, and in that order is their difference from one another to be found. But that is not a difference measurable in any kind of units. The Ideal numbers remain above the order of quantity.

In books M and N of the *Metaphysics* Aristotle carries on a continued polemic against the number doctrines of the Academy. He distinguishes a phase in which the Ideas are eliminated and only the Mathematicals remain separate. Through a comparison of Aristotelian passages[43] this doctrine is ascribed to Speusippus, Plato's immediate successor as head of the Academy. Another phase identified the Ideas and the Mathematicals. On account of its prominence in the Aristotelian polemic, it is attributed by historians to Xenocrates, who succeeded Speusippus in 339-338 B.C. Other variants of the doctrine of Ideas, including the assertion of a fourth type of entities that would be located between the Ideal numbers and the mathematicals, are also attacked in these books of the *Metaphysics*. The information given by Aristotle about the teachings in the Academy, however, is difficult to assess and does not seem to provide any very definite and certain picture regarding the details of their development. It shows the prevalent tendency to cast the Platonic doctrine in a strongly mathematical framework, and to give the leading place to the Idea of unity or the one. It illustrates Aristotle's complaint that among his contemporaries philosophy was being turned into mathematics (*Metaph.*, A 9,992a32-33).

Xenocrates was succeeded by Polemon in 315-314 B.C. as head of the Academy, and Polemon by Crates in 270-269 B.C. From Plato to Crates the school is called the Old Academy, to distinguish its original spirit from the trend towards skepticism that it took under Crates' successor Arcesilaus.

The doctrine of the Ideas, as it unfolds gradually through the successive Platonic dialogues, is quite clearly focused upon the virtues by which the care of the soul is exercised and upon their transmission through education. The common, abiding character

---

[42] *Metaph.*, M 6,1080a17-18; b11-14. *Cf. E N*, I 6,1096a17-19.
[43] *Metaph.*, Z 2,1028b21-24; Λ 7,1072b30-1073a3; 10,1075b37-1076a1; and N 3,1090b13-20.

found in all virtuous conduct places virtue or excellence in the sphere of knowledge and not of opinion, even true opinion. Virtuous conduct, accordingly, does not proceed from whims or license or arbitrary physical power, but from knowledge of the common feature pervading all particular virtuous acts, past, present, and future. The common feature is something much deeper than the whole phenomenal order, than the transient sensible world. It is the Idea or Form or Being (*ousia*) of the virtue, or the virtue "itself." It serves as the pattern of virtuous conduct. To it, recognized as a model, all virtuous actions have to conform. On account of the common character of knowledge, virtue can be transmitted. The doctrine of the Ideas, therefore, brings to light a permanent basis for the perpetuation of Greek culture. It seems to have been directed primarily against the chaos and ruin that would follow from conduct based upon each individual's *opinions* and upon the extent of each individual's physical force.

From the start, however, Plato has been conscious that the doctrine of the common feature applies equally in other fields, as the examples quickness, health, medicine, and different mathematical objects show. The doctrine of the Ideas appears gradually in its extension to all sensible natures, to artifacts, and finally to everything for which there is a common name. Upon Ideas all scientific knowledge and all intellectual communication is grounded. Human thinking as well as human living must have an abiding foundation.

The Ideas, therefore, on account of their all-important function for virtuous conduct, for scientific knowledge in general, and for communication in speech, just have to exist for Plato. Their entirely stable nature keeps them from existing as such in sensible things. Their real and absolute character prevents them from being the thoughts of any mind. They have to exist entirely in themselves. What kind of existence is this? It is clearly supersensible and real, yet the common and shared character of the Ideas does not allow it to be the existence of souls or of spirits or of Aristotelian separate substance. It corresponds to no type of existence conceivable by the human mind. Every Idea is an absolute unit in itself, nevertheless it is found spread out and divided in many particulars. No way is ever found by Plato to explain either the existence of the Ideas and their participation by individual things, or the cognition of the Ideas by the human mind. The anamnesis doctrine is offered to account for the presence of knowledge that could not be obtained during the soul's earthly life, but it does not even attempt to explain how any communication could be established between the soul and the Ideas in the previous existence. It undertakes to say *when,* but not *how,* the Ideas are known. The Ideas, though, have to exist, and they have to be known, since thought and speech are facts.

This procedure of the dialogues focuses the reader's close attention upon the extremely difficult considerations that surround any attempt to explain the Socratic problem of *what* things *are,* or, in later terminology, to account for the essences of things. The essence is present in every particular thing, it is somehow completely identical with the particular thing, as predication shows. Yet it extends far beyond the one particular thing to innumerable individuals. It is the same in every instance. It is eternally unchanging, even though the individuals change. The two aspects, immanence and transcendence, are both emphasized. Plato himself shows no consciousness of vacillating between an immanent and a transcendent theory of the Ideas. He persists in recognizing both aspects. Yet only a nature abstracting from all being whatsoever could satisfy these opposite requirements of essence. Any being at all would at once make the principle of contradiction[44] apply, and so prevent an Idea from being one and many at the same time. Platonic thought, however, cannot seek the solution in any such distinction between essence and being. It indicates a problem sharply enough, but has no solution to offer. Against the background of Parmenidean doctrine, Plato's deepest concern is that the objects of knowledge have in themselves the character of being. The whole of his inquiry rolls along that groove. An essence completely abstracting from being could not

[44] The principle of contradiction, called the first principle of demonstration by Aristotle, is not isolated as such by Plato, though it is clearly enough affirmed by him: "But true and exact reason, vindicating the nature of true being, maintains that while two things are different they cannot exist one of them in the other and so be one and also two at the same time" (*Ti.,* 52CD). The principle is regarded, accordingly, as following upon the nature of being. Constantin Ritter, *The Essence of Plato's Philosophy,* tr. Alles (London, 1933) sees it derived from *Sph.,* 230B.

be a Platonic Idea. So the problem continues unsolved. The Platonic Ideas remain inexplicable, both in their own existence and in their relations to particulars and to human knowledge. But knowledge and speech are facts, and so the Ideas and their participation have to be accepted. This doctrine of the *Parmenides* seems to be Plato's final word on the problem,[45] and having stated it he can continue to use the Ideas in his later works. In accord with the whole genius of Platonic thinking, the study of the Ideas through the dialogues leads the mind as few other writings can to penetrate deeply into the problems of essence, but provides no definite solution.

The Parmenidean doctrine of being, however, has been sharply modified by Plato to the extent of allowing plurality through participation in the Form or nature of otherness. Otherness or not-being has been set up by him not as something pertaining to the world of seeming, but as an intelligible Form, and so as an intelligible opposite of being. By its presence it renders things different from one another and different from the Form of being, and so accounts for plurality. The Parmenidean immobility of the world of being, though, is retained in contradistinction to the world of becoming. Yet motion "itself" is allowed to participate sameness and so is given the status of a Form, even though it does not impart any stability to the particular instances of mobile things.

[45] That the Ideas contribute nothing to sensible things or to human knowledge seems to have continued to be the strongest objection against them in Aristotle's time. See *Metaph.*, A 9,991a8-14; M 5,1079b12-18. Nevertheless the Ideas remained the "cornerstone" (Cherniss, *Riddle of the Early Academy*, p. 4) of Plato's thought. Ross notes that one could easily "make a catena of passages drawn from every period of Plato's literary life, in which objective existence is ascribed to the Ideas" (*Plato's Theory of Ideas*, pp. 226-227). In the opposite extreme Burnet (*Platonism*, pp. 40-47) maintained that there is no proof that Plato ever held the doctrine of Ideas, and that if he ever had held it he gave it up definitely and publicly in the *Parmenides*. In a middle position Natorp (*Platons Ideenlehre*, Leipzig, 1903) gave the Platonic Ideas the status not of entities but, in Neo-Kantian fashion, of laws and functions and methods. For the case that as early as the *Euthyphro* Plato located in the apprehension of the Ideas the function of deity, see W. G. Rabinowitz, "Platonic Piety: An Essay Toward the Solution of an Enigma," *Phronesis*, III (1958), 117-120.

CHAPTER 11

Plato—Soul and Cosmos

A. SOUL

Accoroing to Plato's description, the soul has its own proper existence, independent of that of the body: "Do we believe that there is such a thing, as death? To be sure, replied Simmias. Is it not the separation of soul and body? And to be dead is the completion of this; when the soul exists in herself, and is released from the body and the body is released from the soul, what is this but death?" (*Phd.*, 64C) The soul, therefore, is regarded as a thing in itself, endowed with existence and life independent of its union with the body. This notion of the soul is quite in accord with Greek tradition, and in particular with previous philosophical conceptions in which the soul was regarded as a thing constituted by air (Anaximenes, Diogenes) or fire (Leucippus, Democritus). In Plato, however, the soul is represented as something above the whole order of sensible change, even though it is dragged down to that world when it uses the body in sensation: "And were we not saying long ago that the soul when using the body as an instrument of perception, that is to say, when using the sense of sight or hearing or some other sense (for the meaning of perceiving through the body is perceiving through the senses)— were we not saying that the soul too is then dragged by the body into the region of the changeable, and wanders and is confused; the world spins round her, and she is like a drunkard when she touches change? Very true. But when returning into herself she reflects, then she passes into the other world, the region of purity, and eternity, and immortality, and unchangeableness, which are her kindred, and with them she ever lives, when she is by herself . . ." (*Phd.*, 79CD).

Own Life. The kindred region of the soul, accordingly, is the world of stability and being, and not the changing sensible universe. Her proper life is with the Ideas, through knowledge. That life is philosophy. As it is a life led in separation from the body, it is from that viewpoint a death. In this sense philosophy is the pursuit and practice of death.[1] Until the soul is released in this way by philosophy, she is in the body as in a prison: "The lovers of knowledge are conscious that the soul was simply fastened and glued to the body—until philosophy received her, she could only view real existence through the bars of a prison, not in and through herself" (*Phd.*, 82DE). Life in the body prevents in this way the soul from living her own proper life, and only philosophy can release her from that prison. Her true pasturage is found only in the region of the unchangeable Forms (*Phdr.*, 247C-248B). This view quite apparently regards the body as something external to the knowing subject, and merely a receptacle and instrument for the human agent, who is found properly only in the soul. The doubtful *Alcibiades I* states that doctrine explicitly: "*Soc.* And does not a man use the whole body? *Al.* Certainly. *Soc.* And that which uses is different from that which is used? *Al.* True. *Soc.* Then a man is not the same as his own body? *Al.* That is the inference. *Soc.* What is he, then? *Al.* I cannot say. *Soc.* Nay, you can say that he is the user of the body. *Al.* Yes. *Soc.* And the user of the body is the soul? *Al.* Yes, the soul" (*Alc. I*, 129E-130A).

Survival. The survival of the soul after death is implied in the observation that opposites proceed from opposites, and so life from death (*Phd.*, 70C-72E). The recollection or anamnesis of the Ideas requires an existence of the soul previous to its coming into the body (72E-76E). Death, then, means a rebirth of the soul: "For if the soul exists before birth, and in coming to life and being born can be born only from death and dying, must she not after death continue to exist, since she has to be born again?" (77CD).

[1] *Phd.*, 64A; cf. 80E. Cicero expresses this notion as: "Tota enim philosophorum vita . . . commentatio mortis est." *Tusc. Disp.*, I,30,74.
For any one to be called a man, however, the presence of the soul in the body seems to be required by Plato; see *Men.*, 86A; *Phd.*, 76C.

Immortality. The soul, moreover, not only survives life in the body, but is in itself immortal and indestructible. The soul should not be dissoluble, like the body. Her kindred with the Ideas, instead of with sensible things, indicates that she should resemble the Ideas in being indissoluble or almost indissoluble (*Phd.*, 78B-80D). The soul, further, is immortal because her very essence implies life, and so excludes its essential opposite, death (95D-106E).

These arguments are represented as not removing all uncertainty, on account of "the greatness of the subject and the feebleness of man" (107AB). Making liberal use of the affective propensities and the emotional details of the situation in the death cell of Socrates, they have focused attention on the nature of the soul in a progressive series of intuitions, trying to see in its nature the character of immortality. Their meaning is then emphasized by an appeal to the seriousness of the matter: ". . . if the soul is really immortal, what care should be taken of her, not only in respect of the portion of time which is called life, but of eternity! . . . For the soul when on her progress to the world below takes nothing with her but nurture and education; . . ." (107CD). Finally, the whole subject is driven home by a vivid and forceful myth purporting to describe the journeyings of souls after death, their judgment, and their respective punishments and rewards, eternal or temporary.[2] Transmigration of souls, or metempsychosis, had been admitted in the course of the arguments in the *Phaedo*. The soul may as a punishment be required to lead another life, and if necessary a number of lives, in various animal bodies corresponding to the faults of which she has been guilty or the virtues that she has succeeded in practicing without philosophy (*Phd.*, 81D-82B). These transmigrations take place according as the soul gains or loses in wisdom during her various existences (*Ti.*, 91D-92C).

Self-Movent. The soul's immortality is established in the *Phaedrus* through her property of self-motion: "The soul through all her being is immortal, for that which is ever in motion is immortal; but that which moves another and is moved by another, in ceasing to move ceases also to live. Only the self-moving, never

[2] See *Grg.*, 523A-526A; *Phdr.*, 248A-249B; *Rep.*, X,614A-616B; *Ti.*, 42BD; *Lg.*, XII,959B.

leaving self, never ceases to move, and is the fountain and beginning of motion to all that moves besides. . . . But if the self-
moving is proved to be immortal, he who affirms that self-motion
is the very idea and essence of the soul will not be put to confusion. For the body which is moved from without is soulless;
but that which is moved from within has a soul, for such is the
nature of the soul" (*Phdr.*, 245CE).

In the *Laws* the existence of soul is proved by the occurrence
of sensible motion in the world. Inanimate things are being
moved by something else, and so cannot provide a beginning for
motion. Only something that is self-moving can meet this requirement: ". . . when one thing changes another, and that another,
of such will there by any primary changing element? How can a
thing which is moved by another ever be the beginning of
change? Impossible. But when the self-moved changes other, and
that again other, and thus thousands upon tens of thousands of
bodies are set in motion, must not the beginning of all this motion[3] be the change of the self-moving principle?" (*Lg.*, X,894E-
895A). This notion of the soul as by definition the self-moved,
and as the source of all other movement in the cosmos, is developed at considerable length in the *Laws* (X,894B-897C).

Triple Soul. There are three kinds of soul. There is the rational, which is immortal, and is represented as located in the
head. There is also the irascible, which is located in the breast.
Finally there is the concupiscent, located in the abdomen.[4] The
first type is immortal, the other two mortal. Only the third kind
is present in plants (*Ti.*, 77AB). The second kind is present in
brute animals (*Rep.*, IV,441B). Their distinction from one another is shown by their contrary motions: "But the question is
not quite so easy when we proceed to ask whether these principles are three or one; whether, that is to say, we learn with
one part of our nature, are angry with another, and with a third
part desire the satisfaction of our natural appetites; or whether
the whole soul comes into play in each sort of action . . . The

[3] The phrase "beginning . . . of motion" will later be used by Aristotle
to designate an efficient cause. The reasoning of Plato in regard to the self-
movent furnishes an important background for the meaning and bearing of
the arguments that demonstrate the existence of a primary movent in the
eighth book of Aristotle's *Physics*.

[4] *Rep.*, IV,435B-442A; *Ti.*, 69C-70A;89E-90A.

same thing clearly cannot act or be acted upon in the same part
or in relation to the same thing at the same time, in contrary
ways; and therefore whenever this contradiction occurs in things
apparently the same, we know that they are really not the same,
but different" (*Rep.*, IV,436AC). The appetites can desire a
thing that reason forbids, and a man may be angry at the turmoil
of the concupiscent appetite within him (437B-441C). Therefore
each appetite can tend in a direction contrary to one or both of
the others. This indicates that they proceed from three really
distinct souls.

The Platonic arguments have shown that the nature of the
intellectual soul demands immortality. They have not definitely
established, however, that the immortality is guaranteed to it.
That task is left for the more general treatment of the cosmos
and the constitution of its various parts.

B. THE COSMOS

Realm of Opinion.   Plato's description of the visible universe
accords with the general Eleatic background in which cognition
of the sensible world was assigned to the domain of opinion. His
conception of it remains in the Greek philosophical tradition that
regarded the whole cosmos as a living thing. He represents it,
however, as having an intelligent and provident cause: "Wherefore, using the language of probability, we may say that the world
became a living creature truly endowed with soul and intelligence by the providence of God" (*Ti.*, 30B). The sensible universe as such, therefore, has its own proper soul.

The reason why nothing more than probability can be had in
regard to the visible world is that it consists of becoming. It is
something that is always changing. It does not exhibit the unchanging character that is required in an object of knowledge. It
is therefore attained not by intelligence but only by opinion:
"First then, in my judgment, we must make a distinction and
ask, What is that which always is and has no becoming; and
what is that which is always becoming and never is? That which
is apprehended by intelligence and reason is always in the same
state; but that which is conceived by opinion with the help of
sensation and without reason, is always in a process of becoming

and perishing and never really is. . . . As being is to becoming, so is truth to belief. If then, Socrates, amid the many opinions about the gods and the generation of the universe, we are not able to give notions which are altogether and in every respect exact and consistent with one another, do not be surprised. Enough, if we adduce probabilities as likely as any others; . . ." (*Ti.*, 27D-29C). The sensible universe, accordingly, is not an object for strictly scientific study, as are the Ideas or the mathematicals. It is a realm in which only opinion is possible. The goal of anyone who investigates the processes of the cosmos, then, will be to attain as much probability as possible in the results of his research. Nothing more can be expected.

These views are expressed in one of the very late dialogues of Plato, the *Timaeus*. They are put into the mouth of the otherwise unknown and probably fictitious Timaeus of Locri. The doctrine, however, is located squarely enough in the background of Plato's own basic philosophy, in which the world of being is set up apart from the world of becoming, and in which knowledge is based upon Ideas. This conception of the philosophy of sensible nature, consequently, is presented clearly as issuing from Plato's own over-all philosophical doctrines.

The Demiurge. Although Plato's account of the world as animated is fully in line with preceding Greek philosophical tradition, it differs rather sharply in viewing this animation as the work of a provident cause. It arrives at that conclusion by drawing out the implications of generation or becoming: "Now everything that becomes or is created must of necessity be created by some cause, for without a cause nothing can be created."[5] This seems to be the earliest written statement of what will in modern times be called the principle of causality. It is advanced without any other justification than its own plausibility and men's general experience that whatever is found coming into being is always considered to be the result of some causal activity. That, of course, is amply sufficient to make it fit into an explanation of

[5] *Ti.*, 28A; *cf.* 28C; *Phlb.*, 26E. The rendition "creation" is not to be taken as implying any Christian sense of production out of nothing. It signifies merely the general notion of coming into being. Likewise the capitalization of the word "God" is not to be understood as designating or involving a unique and omnipotent nature. The word retains the general sense that it had as used by the ancient Greeks.

the process of becoming when nothing above probability is demanded. It at once directs the inquiry towards a search for the cause that produced the visible universe. This task, however, is seen to surpass the means at human disposal, both as regards the discovery of that cause and the means of expressing its nature and communicating it in speech to others: "But the father and maker of all this universe is past finding out; and even if we found him, to tell of him to all men would be impossible" (*Ti.*, 28C). He is called the demiurge, a term that etymologically meant a "worker for the people" and was used to denote a handicraftsman.

Goodness as Motive. One thing, though, may be accepted without hesitation about the production of the sensible world. The goodness of its artificer or demiurge requires that it be modeled according to the Ideas: "Which of the patterns had the artificer in view when he made the world,—the pattern of the unchangeable, or of that which is created? If the world be indeed fair and the artificer good, it is manifest that he must have looked to that which is eternal; but if what cannot be said without blasphemy is true, then to the created pattern. Every one will see that he must have looked to the eternal; for the world is the fairest of creations and he is the best of causes" (*Ti.*, 28C-29A). Goodness is presupposed as the necessary characteristic of the demiurge, since it would not be right or fitting to think of him in any other way. Nothing more than that quasi-religious motive for so thinking is advanced. In the context of the probable reasoning proper to this type of investigation apparently nothing further is required (*Ti.*, 29C).

What is in this way established, starting now from the goodness of the demiurge, is that the things in the sensible universe are modeled upon the Ideas. That is what the dialogues of Plato's middle period had shown in regard to certain particular things. These had Ideas as their pattern. The doctrine is now being applied to the whole visible world. The demiurge of the sensible universe is represented as making it according to the model of the Ideas. His own goodness is the motive for making the world at all, as well as for making it according to the best of all patterns, the Ideas: "He was good, and the good can never have any jealousy of anything. And being free from jealousy, he desired that all things should be as like himself as they could be. This is in the truest sense the origin of creation and of the world, as we shall do well in believing on the testimony of wise men: God desired that all things should be good and nothing bad, so far as this was attainable" (*Ti.*, 29E-30A). The motive for the production of the cosmos, therefore, was the desire of the demiurge to share his own goodness. Because he was free from jealousy, he wished all other things to be as good as possible, that is, to be as much like himself as he was able to contrive.

Limited Power. The goodness that the demiurge could impart to the world, however, is represented as subject to the limitations of the material with which he had to work. He is not a creator in the sense that he could produce out of nothing the materials with which his craftsmanship is concerned. Rather, he found that material already there, and induced a definite order into it: "Wherefore also finding the whole visible sphere not at rest, but moving in an irregular and disorderly fashion, out of disorder he brought order, considering that this was in every way better than the other" (*Ti.*, 30A). The work of the demiurge, accordingly, was brought into play upon a mass of material that was already there, lying in disorder. It consisted in bringing order and beauty into that chaos.

The World Soul. It is this requirement of order and beauty that indicates the presence of soul and intelligence in the universe as such, and so gives rise to the conception of the whole cosmos as an animated and living thing. The demiurge "found that no unintelligent creature taken as a whole was fairer than the intelligent taken as a whole; and that intelligence could not be present in anything which was devoid of soul. For which reason, when he was framing the universe, he put intelligence in soul, and soul in body, that he might be the creator of a work which was by nature fairest and best" (*Ti.*, 30B). Such is Plato's justification of the traditional Greek view that the universe is something animated. He is content in offering reasons that are fully as probable as any others that have been offered, if not more probable.

The "Body of the World." The body of the universe, because it is visible and tangible, requires fire and earth among its constituents. The fairest bond between these is that of mathematical proportion. Since a solid, unlike a surface, has a double and not just a single mean, two intermediate constituents, air and water, are necessary.[6] Accordingly, "God placed water and air in the mean between fire and earth, and made them to have the same proportion so far as was possible (as fire is to air so is air to water, and as air is to water so is water to earth); and thus he bound and put together a visible and tangible heaven. And for these reasons, and out of such elements which are in number four, the body of the world was created, and it was harmonized by proportion, and therefore has the spirit of friendship; and having been reconciled to itself, it was indissoluble by the hand of any other than the framer" (Ti., 32BC). In this way the four Empedoclean "roots" are justified mathematically as the four primitive constituents of the sensible universe. The reasoning, of course, is not meant to get outside the realm of probability. If the universe is orderly, it will have a basic mathematical framework. In this framework the four traditional basic constituents should fit exactly. In that way the foundation for harmony and friendship in the universe is laid. The bonds of this proportion are so strong that no one but their original framer can loose them.

Global Shape. Further, the most suitable and natural figure for the universe is that of a sphere: "Now to the animal which was to comprehend all animals, that figure was suitable which comprehends within itself all other figures. Wherefore he made the world in the form of a globe, . . . the most perfect figure and the most like itself of all figures; for he considered that the like is infinitely fairer than the unlike" (Ti., 33B). The reasons why the spherical figure was selected as the fairest and most perfect are that of all figures the sphere is most like itself on account of the uniform distance of its extremes from its center, and that it contains within itself all other figures. It is therefore the proper shape for the living body that is to contain within itself all other living bodies. The movement suited to the spherical form, unaltering circular movement within its own limits, was accordingly assigned to the universe as such (Ti., 34A). The universe is in this way one and solitary, but able to converse with itself on account of its excellence, its soul being spread throughout its

---

[6] For a discussion of the background of this doctrine in Greek mathematics, see F. M. Cornford, *Plato's Cosmology* (London and New York, 1937), pp. 45-52.

body and containing its body within itself. It accordingly needs the companionship of no one else, but is a self-sufficient god (*Ti.*, 34B).

A corporeal principle, however, enters in some way into the very constitution of the world soul: "Out of the indivisible and unchangeable, and also out of that which is divisible and has to do with material bodies, he compounded a third and intermediate kind of essence, partaking of the nature of the same and of the other, and this compound he placed accordingly in a mean between the indivisible, and the divisible and material. He took the three elements of the same, the other, and the essence, and mingled them into one form, compressing by force the reluctant and unsociable nature of the other into the same" (*Ti.*, 35A). The detailed meaning of this passage is difficult to grasp.[7] The terminology quite evidently implies as a background the mixing of the very important Forms that was described in the *Sophist*. Being, sameness, and otherness are found participated in the nature of the world soul, a nature that is basically a composite of the unchanging and indivisible character of the Ideas and the divisible character of bodies. Something of a corporeal nature, therefore, is found within even the world soul. The world soul does not rise entirely above the divisible feature that goes with bodies. Accordingly, its constitution can be described at considerable length in terms of mathematical figures and proportions (*Ti.*, 35B-36E). It is in itself subject to quantitative treatment, and to that degree it belongs to the realm of the extended. It is not conceived as something entirely spiritual in itself. It is described as having been generated (34C,37AC). It will be as a matter of fact indissoluble, but only because in the will of its maker it has, like anything else made directly by him (41A), a stronger bond of union than any in its nature. The nature of the soul is indeed such that it calls for immortality, but that immortality seems established as a fact only by the will of the demiurge. In the *Phaedrus* (245C-246A) the self-movent, because it never leaves itself, is always in motion; and so, in comparison with the sensible order, it is by nature ingenerate and immortal. But the natural requirement of immortality is guaran-

---

[7] A careful analysis and discussion is given by Cornford, *Plato's Cosmology*, pp. 59-66.

teed in actual fact, the *Timaeus* shows, only by the will of the demiurge.

Time. The model according to which the universe was constructed, since it consists of the Ideas, is eternal. The demiurge, in his goodness, wished to bestow that attribute of the model as far as was possible upon his work. Since eternity belonged by nature only to the Ideas and was not compatible with anything that had come into being, only another type of duration, time, could be given by the demiurge to his product. This kind of duration was a mobile image of the immobile eternity that belongs to the Ideas in the fullness of all-inclusive durational unity. That unity can be imitated in the sensible world only in a mobile way that spreads the duration in an indefinite plurality of parts outside parts. "Wherefore he resolved to have a moving image of eternity, and when he set in order the heaven, he made this image eternal but moving according to number, while eternity itself rests in unity; and this image we call time" (*Ti.*, 37D). Time, accordingly, was made by the demiurge himself together with the universe, and so would be rendered indissoluble not by nature but by the will of its maker. It will last forever like the universe itself. This quite evidently means that for Plato time, the ordering of motion according to mathematical succession, had definitely a beginning. It was not always present in the motions of the material out of which the universe was constructed, but began only when the demiurge produced it. Such is the explicit testimony of Aristotle (*Ph.*, VI 1,251b17-19), who implies that in this respect Plato differed from all the other Greek philosophers. Plato alone said that time came into being, along with the universe. On the other hand, Aristotle (*Metaph.*, Λ 6,1071b32-33) states that Leucippus and Plato say that motion always exists. If Plato's teaching in regard to motion corresponds in this respect to that of Leucippus, it means that for Plato too there always was motion in sensible things. Plato's express statement, in fact, is that the demiurge found everything that was visible "not at rest, but moving in an irregular and disorderly fashion, . . ." (*Ti.*, 30A). Motion, accordingly, always existed. What the demiurge produced was the order of motion according to number; and that is time. Apparently, then, while motion was regarded by Plato as having always existed, time was not so regarded. Time is a type of duration that began only when the demiurge constituted an ordered universe out of the materials that he found already there and in motion.[8] The orderliness of the motion, and so time, began when the demiurge intervened. For the other Greek philosophers, the order in the cosmic motion was necessary and eternal.

Plato, in accord with the general procedure of his account, makes no attempt to demonstrate any of this doctrine about time. He continues to offer merely probable explanations. Definite, however, is his teaching that the duration of the Ideas is non-temporal, because it is not mobile. It is not spread out in the manner of an extended durational continuum. The existence and nature of the Ideas are regarded as entirely supertemporal.

Other Living Things. The demiurge then proceeded to make the other living things required for the completion of the universe. He modeled them all after the Idea of living thing: "Now as in the ideal animal the mind perceives ideas or species of a certain nature and number, he thought that this created animal ought to have species of a like nature and number. There are four such; one of them is the heavenly race of the gods; another, the race of birds whose way is in the air; the third, the watery species; and the fourth, the pedestrian and land creatures" (*Ti.*, 39E-40A). Apart from the visible manifestations of Earth and the planets and fixed stars, knowledge of the first class, the gods, is beyond the power of men to attain. Regarding them one has to accept the mythological traditions that have been handed down, even though without certain or probable proofs. These gods are immortal not by nature, but only by the will of the demiurge.

In order that the other living things be mortal, they have to be made not directly by the demiurge himself, but by the lesser gods. Only the immortal and divine part is made by the demiurge, out of the same constituents as the world soul but in a more diluted mixture; and it is handed over to the other gods to be interwoven with a mortal nature. The souls were first attached each to a star, where they would all equally see the nature of

---

[8] The tradition of the Academy on this question, though divided, seems to have been preponderantly in favor of the view that Plato meant the becoming in the universe to have a cause, but not a beginning in time. For a discussion of the question, see A. E. Taylor, *A Commentary on Plato's Timaeus* (Oxford, 1928), pp. 66-70.

the universe and its destinies. Then they were implanted by necessity in bodies. He who lived rightly would afterwards return to his star, but he who led an evil life would next pass into a woman and if in that existence he persisted in evil conduct he would pass into a brute animal that resembled his iniquities, until he succeeded in overcoming his irrational tendencies.[9] The two conceptions of why the soul is in the body, both as in a prison in punishment for faults and also as in accordance with the cosmic processes, are in this way combined by Plato.

The Receptacle.   To explain the production of sensible bodies, still according to probable reasoning only, a third type of thing is required, different from the two already considered: ". . . one, which we assumed, was a pattern intelligible and always the same; and the second was only the imitation of the pattern, generated and visible. There is also a third kind . . . , which is difficult of explanation and dimly seen. . . . it is the receptacle, and in a manner the nurse, of all generation" (*Ti.*, 48E-49A). Things that are generated, this reasoning implies, have to have a receptacle in which they are received when they are brought into being, and which as it were nurses them. Since they are always changing, they have not enough stability to be regarded as "this," but only as "such," leaving the term "this" to designate the receptacle in which they are located: "Anything which we see to be continually changing, as, for example, fire, we must not call 'this' or 'that,' but rather say that it is 'of such a nature'; nor let us speak of water as 'this,' but always as 'such'; . . . That in which the elements severally grow up, and appear, and decay, is alone to be called by the name 'this' or 'that'; . . ." (49D-50A). Gold, for instance, remains gold while taking on all sorts of shapes and figures, and what is there is always gold. The gold is looked upon as the "this," and the triangle, or any other shape that it assumes, as only a "such." Similarly the nature that is receptive of all bodies always remains the same: ". . . for, while receiving all things she never departs at all from her own nature, and never in any way, or at any time, assumes a form like that of any of the things which enter into her; . . . But the forms which enter into and go out of her are the likenesses of real existences

<hr>

[9] References *supra,* n. 2.

modelled after their patterns in a wonderful and inexplicable manner, . . ." (*Ti.*, 50BC).

The notion of a "such" as distinct from a "this" is definitely presupposed in this reasoning. Qualities are no longer spoken of just as "things," without any distinction in terminology, as they were among the Presocratics. Plato, in fact, had already introduced the term "quality" as an unfamiliar word in the *Theaetetus* (182A). The doctrine that a quality like "hot" or "white" (*Ti.*, 50A) does not exist in itself but only in something else, and depends upon that other for its existence, is sketched very clearly in the present passage. However, Plato's purpose is to reduce all sensible things, as images of the Ideas, to the status as it were of qualities, just as images in a mirror or reflections on a watery surface do not exist in themselves but only in the reflecting body.

Formless Nature.   Since it is to receive every kind of sensible thing, the receptacle has to be in itself free from any sensible form whatsoever, just as the basic substance from which perfumes are made should be as odorless as possible. Any form would intrude itself and so interfere with the reception of other forms. Therefore the receptacle itself has to be entirely devoid of sensible forms: "Wherefore, the mother and receptacle of all created and visible and in any way sensible things, is not to be termed earth, or air, or fire, or water, or any of their compounds or any of the elements from which these are derived, but is an invisible and formless being which receives all things and in some mysterious way partakes of the intelligible, and is most incomprehensible. . . . fire is that part of her nature which from time to time is inflamed, and water that which is moistened, . . ." (*Ti.*, 51AB).

The receptacle, accordingly, appears continually different as the different forms or images of the Ideas enter and leave it. Each part of it takes on the appearance of the thing that happens to be there at the moment—fire, water, earth, or air, and their compounds. It itself, however, never becomes any of the things that enter into it. It is not a stuff or material that is changed into them. Rather, it merely receives them, as a mirror receives images or the water reflections. The surface of the mirror *appears* different, even though the mirror is not changed in itself at all. The receptacle, correspondingly, never becomes anything else. Similarly, the receptacle alone is a "this." The images that it receives are not to be regarded as substantial, but should be referred to properly with adjectival expressions.

Space. The receptacle, then, always remains the same. It never changes in its own nature. In that way it partakes, though mysteriously, of the intelligible, and is eternal and indestructible. It is known, consequently, by reason, and not by the senses. It is not sensibly perceptible. Yet it is not an object of genuine intelligence like the Ideas, which never receive anything. It is known, therefore, not by genuine intelligence, but by what Plato calls a "spurious reasoning." It is something entirely concerned with the sensible world, and not with the intelligible; yet there is no sense that can perceive it. It shares the eternal and indestructible features of the intelligible world, and so comes under the object of intelligence; yet it is not an Idea that is presented to human understanding as immediately intelligible in itself. The intelligence cannot perceive it directly. One can only reason as to its presence and character and properties from the requirements of the sensible cosmos. It is finally identified with space: "Wherefore also we must acknowledge that there is one kind of being which is always the same, uncreated and indestructible, never receiving anything into itself from without, nor itself going out to any other, but invisible and imperceptible by any sense, and of which the contemplation is granted to intelligence only. And there is another nature of the same name with it, and like to it, perceived by sense, created, always in motion, becoming in place and again vanishing out of place, which is apprehended by opinion and sense. And there is a third nature, which is space, and is eternal, and admits not of destruction and provides a home for all created things, and is apprehended without the help of sense, by a kind of spurious reason, and is hardly real; which we beholding as in a dream, say of all existence that it must of necessity be in some place and occupy a space, but that what is neither in heaven nor in earth has no existence" (*Ti.*, 51E-52B).

Space, therefore, functions as the receptacle of all sensible things. The traditional Eleatic tenet that all reality is extended in space, and contained by a place, is the starting point of the reasoning process. Anything so conceived has to be somewhere, under penalty of not being at all. It has to be in a place. Something, consequently, has to provide the place for all sensible things, and that something is what one calls space. It seems to have hardly any reality. It does not impose its meaning upon the intelligence as does an Idea. One can only look upon it in a dreamlike way and say that it must be there.

The receptacle that is necessary to explain the sensible world is, then, the space that already existed, and into which the reflections of the Ideas that one calls sensible things come and from which they go. There is no question, accordingly, of seeking in Plato's cosmological doctrine a basic material or stock that becomes all other things, after the fashion of the Milesian thinkers. Space receives the images, provides a location for them, and nurses them as a mother, apparently in the sense of filling them out through spatial extension. But it never becomes any of them.

The Ideas, on the other hand, are continually described as being in themselves. They are not in anything else. They are not received into the receptacle. They have, accordingly, no spatial character. They are entirely formal in their nature. They do not exhibit in themselves any non-formal principle that could account for the spreading of a formal characteristic through different parts of space. Their images, the sensible things, are as a matter of fact extended in parts outside parts. The form, then, is reflected by and in a spatial principle, and in that way the image is filled out through the receptacle. This quantitative function of the reflecting principle is a feature that the image cannot bring with it from the Idea by way of participation. Ideas and space remain eternally different from each other. But the image, because it is an image, presupposes the twofold condition of prototype and reflecting principle, neither of which is found within its own nature. An image, since this twofold condition "does not belong to it, and it exists ever as the fleeting shadow of some other, must be inferred to be in another, grasping existence in some way or other, or it could not be at all" (*Ti.*, 52C).

The whole doctrine represents the Ideas as entirely above the spatial as well as the temporal order. It assigns to them a type of being that is fully supersensible, not only excluding all sensibly perceptible qualities, but also rising above the whole quantitative realm. The Ideas have no spatial features. They are not extended in parts outside parts. They cannot be measured in terms of component units, even though they have their own order of prior and posterior. In isolating the Ideas so completely from all spatial as well as temporal characteristics, Plato seems to have been the first Greek thinker to arrive at a notion of truly supersensible being, distinct even from the conditions of mathematical objects. He was not able, however, to give any too positive and definite an account of such a type of existence.

Formation of the Cosmos. Three distinct things, "being and space and becoming," existed accordingly in their respective ways "before the heaven," that is, before the cosmos was formed (*Ti.*, 52D). The basic manifestations of becoming, namely, earth, air, fire, and water, were scattered by a winnowing type of motion to their various places, at first without proportion or measure, but then in an orderly fashion to form the universe, according to basically triangular patterns (*Ti.*, 52E-56C). With this foundation established, the *Timaeus* proceeds to discuss the formation and changes of the various classes of corporeal things, as well as the structure and the functions of the human body (57C ff.).

Necessity. In constructing the universe, the demiurge has to overcome "necessity," that is, the natural tendency of bodies to be in disorder and chaos: ". . . the creation is mixed, being made up of necessity and mind. Mind, the ruling power, persuaded necessity to bring the greater part of created things to perfection, and thus and after this manner in the beginning, when the influence of reason got the better of necessity, the universe was created. But if a person will truly tell of the way in which the work was accomplished, he must include the other influence of the variable cause as well" (*Ti.*, 48A). The natural tendency of bodies, then, works at random and so functions as a "variable cause," militating against perfect order in the universe. It can be overcome to a certain extent by reason, but not completely. There will always remain something irrational in the Platonic cosmos, just as an element that escapes rational control pervades Greek mythology and Greek tragedy.

The demiurge proceeds by "using the necessary causes as his ministers in the accomplishment of his work, but himself contriving the good in all his creations" (*Ti.*, 68E). In human conduct, correspondingly, the necessary causes should be sought "only for the sake of the divine, considering that without them and when isolated from them, these higher things for which we look cannot be apprehended or received or in any way shared by us" (*Ti.*, 69A). Sensible natures, accordingly, are to be used for the purposes shown by wisdom. Without those subservient causes no way lies open for human wisdom to function. But of themselves they are devoid of reason and always produce the accidental and irregular. They can attain what is best only through acting in subservience to intelligent nature. They should never be regarded as other than merely auxiliary causes (*Ti.*, 46CE).

Mathematical Account. As is apparent from the foregoing doctrine of the cosmos, a mathematical account of sensible things was envisaged by Plato in the basic triangular shapes and in the composition according to geometrical patterns and proportions. Yet this is all offered only as probable reasoning, and not scientific demonstration. The fundamental notions of his cosmology in this regard are not based upon any observation or experiment, but upon conjecture. It is merely conjectured that the basic elements should have those shapes and that their transformations proceed according to the geometrical patterns and ratios. No attempt is made to establish by any process of actual measurement that such is the fundamental quantitative character of sensible things.

Not a Science. For Plato, then, the investigation of the sensible cosmos can never reach the status of a science. Because of its object, the ever-changing sensible world, it has to be ranged with opinion (*dox*a) or belief and not with knowledge. Even when it makes use of thoroughgoing mathematical explanations it still remains in the order of opinion. It envisages only a *probable*[10] *application* of mathematical proportions and geometrical forms to the sensible things. It can never attain anything more than probability. Its highest aim, as sketched by Plato, is to give an account more probable than any that has been offered by other thinkers (*Ti.*, 48D).

Reality of the Demiurge. The demiurge seems to be meant by Plato as a real cause, required by the norm that everything com-

---

[10] On the force of the Greek word *eikôs* (probable) as appropriate for describing cognition of the *eikôn* (image) in which for Plato the sensible universe consists, see J. B. Skemp, *The Theory of Motion in Plato's Later Dialogues* (Cambridge, Eng., 1942), pp. 67-69.

ing into being has to be caused. The universe, since it came into being, accordingly demands a cause. The demiurge, it is true, has often been interpreted as merely a dramatic device of the *Timaeus;* but Plato speaks of the demiurge in the same way outside the dramatic setting of this dialogue.[11] He proceeds as though meaning that such a cause really brought the visible universe into its present form. But he ends there. He finds no means to investigate the nature of that cause, and does not think that its nature, even if found, could readily be communicated in speech. But just as there have to be Ideas, even though they are inexplicable, and as there has to be space, though its nature is scarcely intelligible, so if there is a cosmos there just has to be a contriver of it, even though nothing more can be said about him.

The demiurge however, is not envisaged as omnipotent, or as a producer of the basic materials, but merely as a good craftsman who brings the best order possible into the materials[12] at his disposal. These materials retain their natural tendency to disorder, a tendency that the demiurge can never completely overcome.[13]

Non-Spiritual Feature of Soul.   Plato's doctrine of space and time establishes clearly enough that the Ideas are completely superspatial and supertemporal, and so are supersensible in the fullest manner. But in order to distinguish the reality of soul from that of Ideas, Plato introduced into the very nature of soul an element that was incompatible with the kind of reality envisaged for the Ideas. Into the composition of the soul's nature, even in the purest, that of the world soul, there enters a mixture of the otherness that has to do with corporeal nature. The soul can still be treated in terms of mathematical proportions. According to the greater or lesser degree in which this corporeal feature is mixed, can souls be distinguished and graded. The soul is never immortal and indissoluble of itself, but only by the will of its

[11] *Rep.,* VI,507C; VII,530A; *Sph.,* 265C; *Plt.,* 270A; 273AB. See W. D. Ross, *Plato's Theory of Ideas* (Oxford, 1951), pp. 127-128; Skemp, pp. 114-115.

[12] The term *hylê* "wood," which will later become the technical Aristotelian term for matter or material cause, is used in a way that foreshadows this sense by Plato at *Ti.,* 69A. It also occurs in a similar meaning at *Phlb.,* 54C.

[13] On the relation of the Platonic "Necessity" to that of the Greek atomists, see S. Sambursky, "A Democritean Metaphor in Plato's Kratylos," *Phronesis,* IV (1959), 1-4.

maker, the demiurge. It is viewed, accordingly, as sharing in corporeal characteristics. In Plato the conception of soul does not seem to reach an entirely spiritual plane.

The Platonic soul, of course, is a fully constituted thing in itself. It is not just the lifegiving principle of an animate body. It is produced as a complete entity, it comes to be by itself. In this way its nature is not entirely above the order of becoming, in spite of its intellectual kinship with the Ideas. It is investigated, from that viewpoint, by means of probable opinions, and not through scientific demonstration. No very exact conception of it is to be expected, therefore, in the Platonic writings. It is a self-movent, and the origin of sensible motion, and in its highest forms it possesses intelligence. But even in its supreme grade, the world soul, it can hardly be considered a truly spiritual being, on account of the partially quantitative way in which it is conceived and because of its capacity to be generated and its natural dissolubility.

[CHAPTER 12]

Plato—Political Philosophy

A. THE KINGLY SCIENCE

The Political Order. The Platonic dialogues have insisted, more forcefully even than Isocrates, that the most important thing in life is to care for the soul. The art by which the care of the soul is exercised has for Plato a political character: "The soul and body being two, have two arts corresponding to them: there is the art of politics attending on the soul; and another art attending on the body, of which I know no single name, but which may be described as having two divisions, one of them gymnastic, and the other medicine. And in politics there is a legislative part, which answers to gymnastic, as justice does to medicine; . . ." (*Grg.*, 464B). The practice of virtue is in this way given a public setting, fully in accord with the traditional Greek aristocratic notion in which conscience was quite a public matter.[1] The art that looks after the soul is therefore the art that looks after the *polis* or city-state. It is envisaged as having two parts or aspects, legislation and justice. Justice cares for the soul in a way that corresponds to the function of medical art in regard to the body, while the legislative art provides for the soul somewhat as the body is improved and kept in condition by gymnastic. Moral life, consequently, seems to be merged wholly in the life of the *polis*, the Greek city-state. The moral and the political orders coincide.

Justice and Legislation. In Plato's two longest works, the *Republic* and the *Laws*, the combined moral and political order is treated respectively from the viewpoints of justice and of legis-

[1] On the *public* nature of the Greek conscience, see W. Jaeger, *Paideia* (New York, 1939-1944), I, 7-8. Praise and blame were the ethical criteria.

lation. The *Republic,* produced in the middle period of Plato's
literary activity, undertakes to inquire what the virtue of justice
is. It notes that justice is spoken of as the same virtue whether
it is seen in individuals or in the body politic. Since this is the
case, the more satisfactory method of treatment will be to examine
it as it is found in the larger letters of the *polis:* ". . . suppose
that a short-sighted person had been asked by some one to read
small letters from a distance; and it occurred to some one else
that they might be found in another place which was larger and
in which the letters were larger—if they were the same and he
could read the larger letters first, and then proceed to the lesser
—this would have been thought a rare piece of good fortune"
(*Rep.,* II,368D). This happens to be the case in regard to justice:
". . . justice, which is the subject of our enquiry, is, as you know,
sometimes spoken of as the virtue of an individual, and sometimes
as the virtue of a State. . . . Then in the larger the quantity of
justice is likely to be larger and more easily discernible" (368E).
The work, then, undertakes the study of justice both in its moral
and in its political features.

Since the treatment in the *Republic* is based upon the immediate consideration of what justice is, it proceeds directly from
ideal norms. The philosophers destined to govern the city-state
"must raise the eye of the soul to the universal light which lightens
all things, and behold the absolute good; for that is the pattern
according to which they are to order the State and the lives of
individuals, and the remainder of their own lives also; making
philosophy their chief pursuit, but, when their turn comes, toiling
also at politics and ruling for the public good, not as though they
were performing some heroic action, but simply as a matter of
duty; and when they have brought up in each generation others
like themselves and left them in their place to be governors of
the State, then they will depart to the Islands of the Blest and
dwell there; and the city will give them public memorials . . ."
(*Rep.,* VII,540AB). At the same time, however, the rulers have
to keep in mind the human subjects whose actions they are trying
to guide according to the pattern of the Ideas: "And when they
are filling in the work, as I conceive, they will often turn their
eyes upwards and downwards: I mean that they will first look
at absolute justice and beauty and temperance, and again at the

human copy; and will mingle and temper the various elements of life into the image of a man; and thus they will conceive according to that other image, which, when existing among men, Homer calls the form and likeness of God" (*Rep.*, VI,501B).

Since the political organization of the *Republic* is sketched directly according to the Ideas, it is in this way the best polity conceivable. It is presented as the model that other types should strive to imitate as far as possible. It is given the status of an ideal and a pattern. Whether or not it ever will exist in practical life is beside the point. It can exercise its proper function of model without ever having been brought into real existence: "In heaven, I replied, there is laid up a pattern of it, methinks, which he who desires may behold, and beholding, may set his own house in order. But whether such a one exists, or ever will exist in fact, is no matter; for he will live after the manner of that city, having nothing to do with any other" (*Rep.*, IX,592B).

On the other hand, the polity described in the *Laws* is of a kind based directly on set legislation, even though this legislation may have at one time been formulated by lawgivers who could discern the Ideas. The immediately operative principle in such a type of government, therefore, is not scientific knowledge, which proceeds according to the Ideas, but rather is law. Since nothing can be superior to knowledge, a polity based on legislation can be merely a "second-best" civic organization, desirable only on condition that no rulers with the required scientific knowledge are available: "For if a man were born so divinely gifted that he could naturally apprehend the truth, he would have no need of laws to rule over him; for there is no law or order which is above knowledge, nor can mind, without impiety, be deemed the subject or slave of any man, but rather the lord of all. I speak of mind, true and free, and in harmony with nature. But then there is no such mind anywhere, or at least not much; and therefore we must choose law and order, which are second best. These look at things as they exist for the most part only, and are unable to survey the whole of them" (*Lg.*, IX,875CD).

Any type of government, then, in which law is above the actual rulers, is only a "second-best" kind. Such a type is sketched by Plato in the long work of his final years, the *Laws*. The treatment proceeds from a discussion concerning the origin of the Cretan and Spartan legal institutions (*Lg.*, I,624A-625A). It purports to draw up the legislation for a proposed (fictitious) Cretan colony about to be established (III,702CD). It strives to rationalize and soften the rigidity of legislation, however, by insisting that "preludes" to the laws, both in general and in particular,[2] prepare the way for their acceptance (IV,722D-723B). Nevertheless it remains a polity founded upon legislation, and so is necessarily inferior to the ideal state, which is based directly upon knowledge of justice. The relation between the one best type and the "second-best" types of political organization will become clearer from Plato's conception of political science.

Clean Slate. Both the *Republic* (VI,501A), in outlining the ideal state, and the *Laws* (III,702CD), in developing a "second-best" kind, proceed with the understanding that they are constructing an entirely new political entity. They are not attempting to improve any already in existence. In this way they are able to start with the most fundamental of political concepts. They do not have to presuppose any type of civic organization or given geographical situation as present and imposed upon them. Rather, they leave themselves free to choose the social institutions they think best. The *Republic* asks for a clean slate to work with, erasing both existing institutions and men's habituated ways of living (*êthê*): "They will begin by taking the State and the manners of men, from which, as from a tablet, they will rub out the picture, and leave a clean surface. This is no easy task. But whether easy or not, herein will lie the difference between them and every other legislator,—they will have nothing to do either with individual or State, and will inscribe no laws, until they have either found or themselves made, a clean surface" (*Rep.*, VI,501A). Since the projected city-state is to remain a unit in character and organization, it is not to become any larger in popu-

---

[2] For instance, the prelude to the laws against maiming reads: "Mankind must have laws, and conform to them, or their life would be as bad as that of the most savage beast. And the reason of this is that no man's nature is able to know what is best for human society; or knowing, always able and willing to do what is best. In the first place, there is a difficulty in apprehending that the true art of politics is concerned, not with private but with public good (for public good binds together states, but private only distracts them); and that both the public and private good as well of individuals as of states is greater when the state and not the individual is first considered" (*Lg.*, IX, 874E-875A).

lation or in territory than the requirements of common unity permit. It will be "neither large nor small, but one and self-sufficing" (*Rep.*, IV,423C).

In the *Laws* (IV,704A-705C) the proposed colony of the Cretans is given a somewhat inland location, though near good harbors. It is to be more hilly than level. It will be able to produce at home all things necessary but no great abundance of anything, lest export trade arise and it be surfeited with gold and silver money, with their concomitant evils. It will have no neighbors immediately bordering on it. Yet its population has to be determined according to needs of defense against enemies and of aid to allies (V,737CD). The number of landholders is set at 5,040. This figure is chosen because it is adapted to convenient subdivisions.[3] It can be divided by any of the numbers from one to ten (738AB).

Human Element.   The one factor that will inevitably cause difficulties in attaining the required clean slate will be found in the citizens. These, if they come from different races and different cultural backgrounds to a new colony like that proposed in the *Laws,* will lack the friendly atmosphere arising from community of language and usages, and they will not work so well together; but if they are of the same culture, they will be rebellious against change from the ruinous customs they had at home (*Lg.,* IV,708BD). They will not at the start be willing to accept good laws. Only those who have been brought up in good laws from infancy will adhere to them voluntarily and firmly (VI,752CD). A completely new generation is required for the proper functioning of even the second best polity, that based upon legislation.

If the change from rule by bad laws to rule by good laws be so difficult, will not much more drastic means be necessary for change to the ideal state, that is, to rule not by laws but by men of science? The *Republic* (III,415D) implies that the present generation will never be able to see the necessity of accepting the basic teaching that men are endowed in different ways by nature and the office of ruling should be placed in the hands of those

[3] See *Lg.,* V,746D. A table of the fifty-nine divisors of 5,040 is drawn up in R. S. Brumbaugh, *Plato's Mathematical Imagination* (Bloomington, 1954), p. 69. In the imaginary ancient Athens described in the *Critias* (112D), the number of active members of the guardian class, men and women, was kept fixed at about 20,000.

who have a natural aptitude for wisdom. Only their sons and succeeding generations may be educated to accept it. The rulers, in order to have the children accept the ideal state, will have to train them in entire separation from the generation brought up in other habits: "They will begin by sending out into the country all the inhabitants of the city who are more than ten years old, and will take possession of their children, who will be unaffected by the habits of their parents; these they will train in their own habits and laws, I mean in the laws which we have given them: and in this way the State and constitution of which we were speaking will soonest and most easily attain happiness, and the nation which has such a constitution will gain most" (*Rep.*, VII, 540E-541A). The ideal state is presented not as something capable of immediate realization in practice, but as a polity attainable only in a generation that has been completely severed from the influences of its forebears.

Even after the best of training, however, there will always remain a certain irrational nature in all men. This feature is described as though it were a permanent form (*eidos, Rep.,* IX,572B). It can be controlled, but not completely eradicated: "Certain of the unnecessary pleasures and appetites I conceive to be unlawful; every one appears to have them, but in some persons they are controlled by the laws and by reason, and the better desires prevail over them—either they are wholly banished or they become few and weak; while in the case of others they are stronger, and there are more of them" (571B). In every man, however, these lawless tendencies of nature lie latent, revealing themselves in dreams: ". . . in all of us, even in good men, there is a lawless wild-beast nature, which peers out in sleep" (572B).

Variable Nature. The human element, accordingly, is something that Plato does not attempt to idealize. It is a factor that one has always to keep in mind when treating of political science. This condition is stated very clearly in the *Politicus,* a dialogue of Plato's late middle period, between the *Republic* and the *Laws:* "The differences of men and actions, and the endless irregular movements of human things, do not admit of any universal and simple rule" (*Plt.,* 294B). Ideal norms, therefore, have to be applied to human affairs and human individuals in an indefinite variety of ways, according to the ever-differing circumstances of place and time: "A perfectly simple principle can never be applied to a state of things which is the reverse of simple" (294C). The human situation of its very nature is too flexible and varying for adequate grasp by set rules. The legislator, then, can but make his laws in a general form that will hold for the most part and cover only roughly the particular cases: "He will lay down laws in a general form for the majority, roughly meeting the cases of individuals; . . . for how can he sit at every man's side all through his life, prescribing for him the exact particulars of his duty?" (295AB).

Rule by Science. Human activity, however, in spite of its ever-variable nature, has to be guided by a *science* if it is to attain what is best, just as the care of the body requires the science of medicine (*Plt.*, 293BC). Plato's whole doctrine of the Ideas has shown that everything worthwhile and lasting has to be based upon eternal natures and not upon transient circumstances. The highest interest of all, human welfare as such, could hardly be an exception. It will have to be founded upon scientific knowledge. This is the dominant, in fact, the sole consideration in isolating the best type of government. The rulers, "whether they rule with the will, or against the will, of their subjects, with written laws or without written laws, and whether they are poor or rich, and whatever be the nature of their rule, must be supposed, according to our present view, to rule on some scientific principle; . . ." (293A). Scientific knowledge, then, is the determining condition of true government: "Then that can be the only true form of government in which the governors are really found to possess science, and are not mere pretenders, whether they rule according to law or without law, over willing or unwilling subjects, and are rich or poor themselves—none of these things can with any propriety be included in the notion of the ruler" (293CD).

Neither the consent of the governed nor rule according to laws is, in this doctrine, essential to true government. The one necessary condition is the ruler's scientific knowledge of his task. The doctrine of the *Politicus* explains clearly enough why the *Laws* proposes its type of government by legislation as just a second-best polity—mind is lord of all, while laws touch things incompletely and only for the most part (*Lg.*, IX,875CD). Legislation cannot reach down to the details of life's ever-varying circumstances. Therefore "the best thing of all is not that the law should rule, but that a man should rule, supposing him to have wisdom and royal power" (*Plt.*, 294A). Such a ruler is above the law and controls the law. He makes laws, but he remains master of them. He will not hesitate to change or disregard laws as circumstances require: ". . . . he who has knowledge and is a true Statesman, will do many things within his own sphere of action by his art without regard to the laws, when he is of opinion that something other than that which he has written down and enjoined to be observed during his absence would be better" (*Plt.*, 300C).

Political science or art in the ruler, then, is the one basic requirement for the best kind of government. If such an art exists, it will obviously be the most difficult of all accomplishments, and so will be found rarely and even then only in one individual or in very few of the citizens: "Then the royal or political art, if there be such an art, will never be attained either by the wealthy or by the other mob" (*Plt.*, 300E). True government, therefore, will be government by one or at least by very few men who possess the required science and are unhampered by dependence either on laws above them or on the wishes of the citizens subject to them.[4]

"Second-Choice" Rule.   In the best polity of all, accordingly, the ruler is not responsible to his people or to any existing laws, but only to his own clear vision of the good and the just. He will indeed be a lawgiver, but it is he, and not the law, who has the final say. In default of such a ruler, the best form of government is not possible, and so by way of second choice the government has to be instituted on the basis of laws. In this "second sailing" (*deuteros plous, Plt.*, 300BC)—a metaphor taken from the use of

---

[4] Even in the polity of the *Laws*, however, the citizens are presumed to accept the government willingly on account of their training from childhood (*Lg.*, VI,752C) and the evident goodness of the legislation. They live under "a voluntary rule over voluntary subjects" (VIII,832C). Plato's point in the *Politicus* is that willing acceptance by subjects does not enter into the essential notion or definition of true government. Cf. *Rep.*, VI,499B. But it is continually assumed that no one will do wrong when he knows what is good (*Lg.*, V,731C; IX,860D), in the sense of practical knowledge; even though there is a type of knowing (*supra*, n. 2) that does not of itself will the good.

the oars when the wind has died down—nothing contrary to the laws is permitted: "Then the nearest approach which these lower forms of government can ever make to the true government of the one scientific ruler, is to do nothing contrary to their own written laws and national customs" (300E-301A). The ruler himself is bound by the laws in these imitations of true government. Any such polity is necessarily deficient, because fixed laws cannot hope to regulate sufficiently the varying requirements of civil life. Yet the rigid enforcement of such laws is a much lesser evil than any arbitrary disregard of them by a ruler who lacks scientific knowledge. The "second choice" kinds of government, however, should use written laws taken from the model type. It is in this way that they are more or less successful imitations of the best polity (297C-300C). Government on the basis of good laws is accordingly for Plato immeasurably superior to government by an unscientific ruler without laws or with bad laws,[5] even though it is inferior to the model type, that is, to government by scientific rulers who are above the law and are in no way dependent upon the consent of the governed. In this doctrine Plato remains a thorough advocate of the scientific, and not at all of the arbitrary.

The Mean.   The one decisive factor in true government, Plato maintains, is political science. The whole teaching depends on the tenet that there is such a science. But how can political lore achieve the status of a science, if it deals with an ever-varying subject like human activity? How can the unvarying nature of a scientific object be found in such a realm? Plato's answer is that like all other arts, political science can attain consistently the correct mean between excess and defect. By preserving the standard of the mean do all arts achieve the good. Only in this way can there be science in the sphere of human activities (*Plt.*, 284AC). The fact that the arts exist is sufficient to establish the notion of a mean that can be consistently attained: ". . . for if there are arts, there is a standard of measure, and if there is a standard of measure, there are arts; but if either is wanting, there is neither" (284D). Political science, accordingly, will consist in

[5] The practical influence of Plato in this regard is attested by the work of members of the Academy in actual legislation for various peoples, as noted by Plutarch, *Adv. Col.*, 1126BD.

attaining in each instance the correct mean between excess and defect in the moral order. In this way its object continues as something abiding and truly knowable in the midst of perpetual variation, and enables it to have scientific status. The good, then, consists first and foremost in the attainment of the appropriate mean.[6] Such is Plato's development of the traditional Greek moral precept that nothing should be overdone. The theme of the good as the mean is worked out at considerable length in the *Philebus*. It concludes that not just in mind or wisdom or the arts or pleasures but that primarily "in measure, and the mean, and the suitable, and the like, the eternal nature has been found" (*Phlb.*, 66A).

A "Commanding" Science. Plato could hardly be more aware that moral and political norms do not function in the rigidly exact manner of mathematical principles. In seeking the reasons for this difference he distinguishes two types (*eidê*) of science. On the one hand, there are sciences like arithmetic that are devoid of action and furnish *knowledge only*. On the other hand, there are sciences that by their very nature have their knowledge embodied in human actions. These have as their object not things already existing but things that are to be in the future: "Well, and are not arithmetic and certain other kindred arts, merely abstract knowledge, wholly separated from action? . . . But in the art of carpentering and all other handicrafts, the knowledge of the workman is merged in his work; he not only knows, but he also makes things which previously did not exist. . . . Then let us divide sciences in general into those which are practical and those which are purely intellectual" (*Plt.*, 258DE). A basic difference is found between knowledge just for the sake of knowledge and knowledge for the sake of action or production. For Plato as later on for Aristotle this difference is considered to be fundamental in the classification of the sciences.

A science that is restricted merely to *knowing* is therefore dis-

---

[6] For a survey of the Platonic doctrine of the mean, see Rupert C. Lodge, *Plato's Theory of Ethics* (London, 1928), pp. 442-455. Correct order has to place "the goods of the soul first and highest in the scale, always assuming temperance to be the condition of them; and to assign the second place to the goods of the body; and the third place to money and property" (*Lg.*, III,697B). This order is understood in the sense that the lower is on account of the higher: ". . . riches are for the sake of the body, as the body is for the sake of the soul" (IX,870B).

tinguished from a science that deals with something that is to be
done or to be made, and so with something that is future. Such
practical knowledge has to become ingrown in one's actions. It
is not detached from them. It involves not merely a contemplating
of what is true, but a training of one's activities towards the production of a result over and above the knowledge itself. Plato,
however, seems to reserve the term "practical science" to the types
that produce something corporeal, like carpentry and the handicrafts. He is predominantly interested, as has been seen in his
development of the doctrine of the Ideas, in showing that virtue
is scientific knowledge and that moral and social life has to be
based on the common abiding knowledge made possible through
cognition by way of formal causality. He is intent upon having the
political art ranged primarily under the class of knowledge in
its fullest sense: "*Str.* Then, shall we say that the king has a greater
affinity to knowledge than to manual arts and to practical life
in general? *Y. Soc.* Certainly he has. *Str.* Then we may put all
together as one and the same—statesmanship and the statesman
—the kingly science and the king" (*Plt.*, 259CD).

The political art, therefore, partakes of scientific knowledge,
just as does the art of the master builder who himself does not
do the manual labor but directs by his knowledge the actions of
those who do (*Plt.*, 260A-261B). In a similar way the political
science rules over human society and men in general (*Plt.*,
276BC), and is supreme over the activities of all the other arts
and undertakings, even over rhetoric, for it decides what is to
be taught and learned: "*Str.* You mean to say that the science
which judges whether we ought to learn or not, must be superior
to the science which is learned or which teaches? *Y. Soc.* Far
superior" (*Plt.*, 304C). It is even supreme over military art, for
it decides when war is to be waged and when peace is to be
made (*Plt.*, 304E-305A). It has sovereign charge over all the activities of the other arts and sciences, and works them all into
a common unity of direction: "And, therefore, the arts which
we have described, as they have no authority over themselves or
one another, but are each of them concerned with some special
action of their own, have, as they ought to have, special names
corresponding to their several actions. *Y. Soc.* I agree. *Str.* And
the science which is over them all, and has charge of the laws,

and of all matters affecting the State, and truly weaves them all into one, if we would describe under a name characteristic of their common nature, most truly we may call politics" (*Plt.*, 305DE).

The political science, therefore, although ranged by Plato primarily with the sciences that are concerned with knowledge only and not directly with the production of a corporeal object, nevertheless is a "commanding" science. The very nature of such a science is "to command for the sake of producing something" (*Plt.*, 261AB). The terms "art" and "science" are used interchangeably by Plato in this discussion of the relations of the political science and the subordinate arts or sciences. Plato is not intent upon working out a set terminology for the different types of science. He is aiming to show that the political science is in the most complete sense scientific knowledge, and that it is sovereign over all other arts and sciences in virtue of its function of commanding them. Rulers who lack the political science, when by way of second choice they are set up in civil power, should govern according to laws written by those who possessed the science (*Plt.*, 297BD). In this way it continues to remain sovereign, even in the "second-best" kinds of polity.

As a commanding science, then, the political art is evidently concerned with what is to be done, and so is not limited just to knowledge but extends to action. It enables its possessor to implant true opinion in the citizens concerning the seemly and just and good (*Plt.*, 309CD), and so to hold together the varied components of the city-state: "This then we declare to be the completion of the web of political action, which is created by a direct intertexture of the brave and temperate natures, whenever the royal science has drawn the two minds into communion with one another by unanimity and friendship, and having perfected the noblest and best of all the webs which political life admits, and enfolding therein all other inhabitants of cities, whether slaves or freemen, binds them in one fabric and governs and presides over them, and, in so far as to be happy is vouchsafed to a city, in no particular fails to secure their happiness" (311BC). The orientation to action may be expected to make political science depend for its truth not merely on the contemplation of an object, but also upon a certain training and habituation in conduct.

The *Republic* (VII,539E) demands long training in the actual experience of political life as well as dialectic in those destined to rule the city-state. The *Laws* (III,688B) teaches that the statesman should look to "all virtue, and especially that which comes first, and is the leader of all the rest—I mean wisdom and mind and opinion, having affection and desire in their train." The affective side must be included. In all the ramifications of the Platonic doctrine that virtue is knowledge, the severe discipline of early Greek school training has to be kept in mind. The acquisition of either knowledge or true opinions, it was taken for granted, presupposed a suitable disposition of nature and the habituation of the traditional *paideia* (*Plt.*, 308C-309D).

The Philosopher-King. Plato's whole teaching about government by scientific knowledge means that the rulers of men should be philosophers: "*Until philosophers are kings, or the kings and princes of this world have the spirit and power of philosophy, and political greatness and wisdom meet in one, and those commoner natures who pursue either to the exclusion of the other are compelled to stand aside, cities will never have rest from their evils, —no, nor the human race, as I believe,—and then only will this our State have a possibility of life and behold the light of day*" (*Rep.*, V,473CE). This doctrine continues through the *Politicus* (293C) and into the *Laws:* "When the supreme power in man coincides with the greatest wisdom and temperance, then the best laws and the best constitution come into being; but in no other way"[7] In Syracuse Plato's own efforts were directed not to writing a constitution but to training a ruler. Government by a philosopher-king, a man above the laws and ruling according to the Ideas, remained the model polity. Patterned on the Ideas, it was above the arbitrary whims and wishes of any individual in its direction of human life. It was the culmination of the basic tendency in the doctrine of the Ideas, the effort to ground all human action on the permanent and the scientific rather than the ephemeral. But on account of the ever-varying nature of human activity, it had to be government by a man and not by fixed laws.

[7] *Lg.*, IV,711E-712A. The same doctrine is emphasized strongly in the seventh letter (*Ep.*, VII,326AB; 328A; 335D). *Cf. Rep.*, VI,499B; 501E.

B. INSTITUTIONS

Origin of the *Polis*. The city-state arises from the lack of self-sufficiency in the individual when he has to work by himself and live alone: "A State, I said, arises, as I conceive, out of the needs of mankind; no one is self-sufficing, but all of us have many wants. Can any other origin of a State be imagined? There can be no other. Then, as we have many wants, and many persons are needed to supply them, one takes a helper for one purpose and another for another; and when these partners and helpers are gathered together in one habitation the body of inhabitants is termed a State" (*Rep.*, II,369BC). In this way each is able to labor at the product to which his capacity is best adapted, and, by exchanges of products, food and clothing and other necessities are provided for all. This could not be done if every man had to produce everything for himself (*Rep.*, II,369B-371E).

The Three Classes. The city-state, therefore, being formed out of individuals, is but a larger man, and like the individual soul, has three different parts: "Citizens, we shall say to them in our tale, you are brothers, yet God has framed you differently. Some of you have the power of command, and in the composition of these he has mingled gold, wherefore also they have the greatest honour; others he has made of silver, to be auxiliaries; others again who are to be husbandmen and craftsmen he has composed of brass and iron; and the species will generally be preserved in the children. But as all are of the same original stock, a golden parent will sometimes have a silver son, or a silver parent a golden son" (*Rep.*, III,415AB). The first of these classes, the rulers or councilors, are meant to exercise the government and direction of the whole city-state. The auxiliaries or warriors defend it from its enemies with the use of arms, and aid the rulers in preserving internal peace and order. The workers produce the food, clothing, and other means necessary for carrying on civic and individual life. The first two classes are called guardians (*Rep.*, III,414B). Inferior offspring of guardians are to be demoted to the lower class, and naturally superior offspring of the lower classes are to be advanced to the higher (*Rep.*, IV,423CD).

The differences in types of men are accordingly congenital, though the common origin of the race keeps this norm from being absolute. But it provides and preserves in general the three different classes of citizens, corresponding to the three souls, the rational, the irascible, and the concupiscent. From the individuals the three different dispositions pass over into the city-state: "Must we not acknowledge, I said, that in each of us there are the same principles and habits which there are in the State; and that from the individual they pass into the State?—how else can they come there? Take the quality of passion or spirit;—it would be ridiculous to imagine that this quality, when found in States, is not derived from the individuals who are supposed to possess it, e.g. the Thracians, Scythians, and in general the northern nations; and the same may be said of the love of knowledge, which is the special characteristic of our part of the world, . . ." (*Rep.*, IV,435E).

In the same way each class of citizens, just as each soul, has its special virtue or excellence: "Must we not then infer that the individual is wise in the same way, and in virtue of the same quality which makes the State wise? Certainly. Also that the same quality which constitutes courage in the State constitutes courage in the individual, and that both the State and the individual bear the same relation to all the other virtues? Assuredly" (*Rep.*, IV,441CD). Wisdom, therefore, is the virtue appropriate to the governing office of the rulers, courage to the warlike activities of the auxiliaries, while temperance is common to all three classes: ". . . temperance is unlike courage and wisdom, each of which resides in a part only, the one making the State wise and the other valiant; not so temperance, which extends to the whole, and runs through all the notes of the scale, and produces a harmony of the weaker and the stronger and the middle class, . . ." (*Rep.*, IV,431E-432A). Similarly, justice is a common virtue and "is found in children and women, slave and freeman, artisan, ruler, subject,—the quality, I mean, of every one doing his own work and not being a busybody, . . ." (*Rep.*, IV,433C).

Community of Family and Property. Among the guardians at least, the common interest of the model city-state requires that all property, wives, and children be possessed in common: "Both the community of property and the community of families, as I am saying, tend to make them more truly guardians; they will not tear the city in pieces by differing about 'mine' and 'not mine'; each man dragging any acquisition which he has made into a separate house of his own, where he has a separate wife and children and private pleasures and pains; but all will be affected as far as may be by the same pleasures and pains because they are all of one opinion about what is near and dear to them, and therefore they all tend towards a common end" (*Rep.*, V,464CD).

This ideal teaching of the community of family and children is developed throughout the first half of the fifth book of the *Republic*. The *Laws* continues to express the same views, without restriction to any particular class: "The first and highest form of the state and of the government and of the law is that in which there prevails most widely the ancient saying, that 'Friends have all things in common.' Whether there is anywhere now, or will ever be, this communion of women and children and of property, in which the private and individual is altogether banished from life, and things which are by nature private, such as eyes and ears and hands, have become common, . . . I say that no man acting upon any other principle, will ever constitute a state which will be truer or better or more exalted in virtue . . . and therefore to this we are to look for the pattern of the state, and to cling to this, and to seek with all our might for one which is like this" (*Lg.*, V,739BE). Thoroughgoing community of family and property, accordingly, always remained for Plato in the Idea and pattern to which the city-state was as far as possible to conform, even where it could only be approximated in varying degrees according to the capacity and training of the particular citizens. In the second-best polity, as sketched in the *Laws*, houses and land are portioned out for private control and private farming, though the individual must still regard what he has received as the common property of the city-state, and keep it intact for himself and his heir.[8] A third-best type of polity is mentioned but is not presented in any further detail (739E-740D).

Supervision of Marriage. The welfare of the ideal city-state requires that (temporary) marriages be arranged and regulated

---

[8] *Cf. Lg.*, IX,877D. In the ancient Athens of the *Critias* (110C) none of the military class possessed private property.

by the rulers in accordance with the needs of the social organism (*Rep.*, V,458E-460B). The children are to be brought up in common, and the officials will take "the greatest care that no mother recognizes her own child" (460C). Even under the second-best polity, the good of the city-state predominates over individual wishes in the choice of a marriage partner: "Let there be one word concerning all marriages:—Every man shall follow, not after the marriage which is most pleasing to himself, but after that which is most beneficial to the state" (*Lg.*, VI,773B). In this polity, however, exhortation rather than legislation is to be used in effecting the right choice (773CE). In both polities, by way of their respective methods, the procreation of children shall be directed according to best genetic interests and the preservation of the correct average of population.[9] Plato's doctrine in these respects does not advocate license. Rather, it entails the strictest kind of supervision and in the ideal polity an extremely difficult if not impossible denial of some of the deepest and most natural tendencies in mankind.

The common interest of the city-state requires further that women be trained to follow exactly the same pursuits as men—gymnastics, war, and other such traditionally masculine occupations (*Rep.*, V,451D-457C). Indeed, "nothing can be more absurd than the practice which prevails in our own country, of men and women not following the same pursuits with all their strength and with one mind, for thus the state, instead of being a whole, is reduced to a half, . . ." (*Lg.*, VII,805A).

"Noble Falsehood." The common good likewise demands that the ideal city-state use falsehood liberally in its own interests. It is the common good that regulates the morality of deception.[10] The rulers "in their dealings either with enemies or with their own citizens, may be allowed to lie for the public good. But nobody else should meddle with anything of the kind; and although the rulers have this privilege, for a private man to lie to them in return is to be deemed a more heinous fault than for the patient or the pupil of a gymnasium not so speak the truth about his own

---

[9] *Rep.*, V,459A-461E; *Lg.*, V,740DE; VI,773A-775E; 783D-784E. *Cf. Criti.*, 112D.

[10] Falsehood in words, even when beneficial to the one deceived, remains an image of the mental disposition and is considered a lie by Plato, though characterized by him as "not pure unadulterated falsehood" (*Rep.*, II,382C).

bodily illnesses to the physician or the trainer, or for a sailor not to tell the captain what is happening about the ship and the rest of the crew, and how things are going with himself or his fellow sailors" (*Rep.*, III,389BC). Plato means this in the sense "that our rulers will find a considerable dose of falsehood and deceit necessary for the good of their subjects" (*Rep.*, V,459C). As may well be expected, the use of deceit plays an extensive part in the program for the arranging of marriage partners. Noble falsehood (*Rep.*, III,414BC), though, is not mentioned in the polity of the *Laws,* where the rulers themselves are subject to the legislation.

   Education. The dominating Platonic interest in the transmission of culture may be seen from the importance assigned to the function of education in the ideal *polis* (*Rep.*, IV,423E-424B). Of all the offices it is the most worthy of esteem and care, even in the second-best polity, because its effect is so deep: "There remains the minister of the education of youth, male and female; . . . He who is elected, and he who is the elector, should consider that of all the great offices of state this is the greatest; for the first shoot of any plant, if it makes a good start towards the attainment of its natural excellence, has the greatest effect on its maturity; and this is not only true of plants, but of animals wild and tame, and also of men. Man, as we say, is a tame or civilized animal; nevertheless, he requires proper instruction and a fortunate nature, and then of all animals he becomes the most divine and civilized; but if he be insufficiently or ill educated he is the most savage of earthy creatures" (*Lg.*, VI,765D-766A). In this state also, the office of education belongs entirely to the *polis,* since the common good requires that the children be regarded as belonging to it rather than to the parents. The good of the community likewise demands that education be compulsory for all: "In these several schools let there be dwellings for teachers, who shall be brought from foreign parts by pay, and let them teach those who attend the schools the art of war and the art of music, and the children shall come not only if their parents please, but if they do not please; there shall be compulsory education, as the saying is, of all and sundry, as far as this is possible; and the pupils shall be regarded as belonging to the state rather than to their parents" (*Lg.*, VII,804CD).

   Early Training. The training of the child shall begin with his earliest play, teaching him order in it.[11] Customs and usages that imbue him with respect for his elders, and proper deportment and dress, are to be part of his training from the start (*Rep.*, IV,424E-425B). General education has two basic phases, gymnastic and music: "Education has two branches,—one of gymnastic, which is concerned with the body, and the other of music, which is designed for the improvement of the soul."[12] Both these disciplines train the youth to rule over the concupiscent part of the soul (*Rep.*, IV,441E-442A). Neither can be safely neglected: "Did you never observe, I said, the effect on the mind itself of exclusive devotion to gymnastic, or the opposite effect of an exclusive devotion to music? In what way shown? said he. The one producing a temper of hardness and ferocity, the other of softness and effeminacy, I replied. Yes, he said, I am quite aware that the mere athlete becomes too much of a savage, and that the mere musician is melted and softened beyond what is good for him" (*Rep.*, IV,410CD). Music is understood as including literature and poetry, and in general all the culture that came under the patronage of the Muses. In this regard the songs and melodies taught the youth are strictly to be supervised. Only those conducive to the purposes of the city-state are to be selected. All others are to be rigidly excluded. Similarly, strict censorship is to be exercised over all poetry. Even the most highly prized traditional poetry, that of Homer, is to be forbidden when it has a detrimental effect on shaping the youthful emotions (*Rep.*, II, 376E-III,403C). In a word, a complete control of the songs and poetry is placed in the hands of the city-state rulers. A similar policy of supervision is prescribed in the *Laws* (VII,799A-802E).

Mathematics. Besides the two basic disciplines, a certain acquaintance with arithmetic, geometry, and astronomy is proper for freemen: "There still remain three studies suitable for freemen. Arithmetic is one of them; the measurement of length, surface and depth is the second; and the third has to do with the

[11] *Rep.*, IV,425A; *Lg.*, I,643BE; VII,792E-793E; 797AB. The sensations of pleasure and pain are the means by which this earliest training in virtue is accomplished (*Rep.*, III,401C-402A; *Lg.*, II,653A; *cf.* Aristotle, *E N*, II 3,1104b11-13). Men in general are represented as being drawn in different or opposite ways by their affections, as puppets are by strings; and yet men can and should follow the lead of reason and co-operate with the pull of what is best (*Lg.*, I,644C-645C: *cf.* VII, 804BC).

[12] *Lg.*, VII,795D. *Cf. Rep.*, II,376E; III,410B-412B.

revolutions of the stars in relation to one another. Not every one has need to toil through all these things in a strictly scientific manner, but only a few, . . ."[13]

Mathematical study is also meant for military and commercial use, and still further, it serves as an introduction to philosophy by accustoming the mind to reason without the vision of the ever-changing sensible objects: "Then this is knowledge of the kind for which we are seeking, having a double use, military and philosophical; for the man of war must learn the art of number or he will not know how to array his troops, and the philosopher also, because he has to rise out of the sea of change and lay hold of true being, and therefore he must be an arithmetician. . . . and we must endeavor to persuade those who are to be the principal men of our State to go and learn arithmetic, not as amateurs, but they must carry on the study until they see the nature of numbers with the mind only; nor again, like merchants or retail traders, with a view to buying or selling, but for the sake of their military use, and of the soul herself; and because this will be the easiest way for her to pass from becoming to truth and being" (Rep., VII,525BC). However, Plato realizes that a man who is both an expert mathematician and a master of dialectic is very rarely found! (Rep., VII,531E).

Later Training. At the age of thirty, those who have shown the required ability and have proved dependable in war and other duties, are advanced to the study of philosophy, for a period of five years. They are then sent out to put their knowledge to the test of actual experience for the next fifteen years. Only then, at the age of fifty, are they ready to take their places among the rulers (Rep., VII,537C-540A). Great care has to be taken in introducing them to dialectic: ". . . for youngsters, as you may have observed, when they first get the taste in their mouths, argue for amusement, . . . But when a man begins to get older, he will no longer be guilty of such insanity; he will imitate the dialectician who is seeking for truth, and not the eristic, who is contradicting for the sake of amusement; . . ." (Rep., VII,539BC). The Laws (XII,964D-968E) similarly requires in its guardians long training in administration and the higher education (965A) of dialectic.

[13] Lg., VII,817E-818A. Cf. Rep., VII,522C-531D.

Religion. Religion is beyond the sphere of the philosopher and the legislator. Tradition is what has to be followed in this matter: ". . . to Apollo, the god of Delphi, there remains the ordering of the greatest and noblest and chiefest things of all. Which are they? he said. The institution of temples and sacrifices, and the entire service of gods, demigods and heroes; also the ordering of the repositories of the dead, and the rites which have to be observed by him who would propitiate the inhabitants of the world below. These are matters of which we are ignorant ourselves, and as founders of a city we should be unwise in trusting them to any interpreter but our ancestral deity" (*Rep.*, IV,427BC). Plato has no patience with atheism or irreligion.[14] He regards such a state of mind as a passing phase of youthful immaturity. To a youth so deluded should be said, not in anger, but with gentle reasoning: ". . . you are young, and the advance of time will make you reverse many of the opinions which you now hold. Wait awhile, and do not attempt to judge at present of the highest things; and that is the highest of which you now think nothing—to know the gods rightly and to live accordingly. . . . There have always been persons more or less numerous who have had the same disorder. I have known many of them, and can tell you, that no one who had taken up in youth this opinion that the gods do not exist, ever continued in the same until he was old; . . ." (*Lg.*, X,888AC).

Plato, in fact, on account of his whole philosophical outlook had a deep need for personal belief in the providence of higher intelligences in regard to human affairs. According to his pivotal philosophical conceptions, no city-state could attain a high degree of culture unless its rulers patterned it after the Ideas. But Athens and other Greek city-states had as a matter of historical fact reached a high and proud degree of civilization. Yet none of their greatly revered leaders had even heard of the Ideas, let alone being trained in the doctrine. They ruled, according to the Platonic viewpoint, not by knowledge, but by true opinions,

[14] Besides atheism, the tenets that the gods exist but exercise no providence over men, or that they can be bribed, are countered by Plato at considerable length (*Lg.*, X,901C-907B). The amount of attention devoted throughout the *Laws* to religious influence shows how important a topic this was for him. The assertion that god, not man, is "the measure of all things" (IV,716C), is meant in a definitely religious context.

which are undependable and insecure because of the lack of any causal tie. The security and dependability of these opinions in the great Greek leaders required some cause apart from their own thinking, and so inspiration from a higher type of intelligence than the merely human: "And therefore not by any wisdom, and not because they were wise, did Themistocles and those of whom Anytus spoke govern states . . . But if not by knowledge, the only alternative which remains is that statesmen must have guided states by right opinion, which is in politics what divination is in religion; for diviners and also prophets say many things truly, but they know not what they say. . . . Yes, and statesmen above all may be said to be divine and illumined, being inspired and possessed of God, in which condition they say many grand things, not knowing what they say" (*Men.*, 99BD). In the actual condition of human government everywhere, based as it is upon traditionally received notions and not upon philosophical knowledge, the good that is present is due to such higher intervention: ". . . for I would not have you ignorant that, in the present evil state of governments, whatever is saved and comes to good is saved by the power of God, as we may truly say" (*Rep.*, VI,492E-493A). Men so inspired, though few in number, are always to be found.[15]

Constitutions. The different forms of government are listed and described by the *Republic* in order of merit: 1) aristocracy; 2) timocracy; 3) oligarchy; 4) democracy; 5) tyranny. Each is regarded as resulting from the gradual corruption of its predecessor (*Rep.*, VIII,544A ff.). By democracy, basically, Plato understood government by one class of the people, the *demos* or lower class, even though "an equal share of freedom and power" (*Rep.*, VIII,557A) is granted to the other members of the *polis.*[16]

[15] *Lg.*, XII,951B. This divine inspiration of the Greek statesmen has to be interpreted seriously, not ironically; see Zeller, *Philos. d. Griechen*, 5th ed. (Leipzig, 1922), II(1),596, n. 4; J. Adam, *The Republic of Plato* (Cambridge, Eng., 1905-1907), II, 22.

[16] Democracy, like oligarchy and tyranny, is regarded by Plato as a rule over unwilling subjects, always accompanied by some type of force. In the polity of the *Laws*, on the other hand, the citizens are considered to be free from domination of any over the others (*Lg.*, VIII,832CD). In the *Menexenus* (238CD), Athenian democracy is praised because it is really an aristocracy or government by the best. In the *Laws*, the Athenian polity is represented as the extreme type of democratic constitution (III,693D). It was workable because reverence (*aidôs*) in despotic fashion made the

Oligarchy meant government by the wealthy, timocracy government by the ambitious, while aristocracy or government by the best denoted the ideal type. In the *Politicus* (302CE), aristocracy means government by the few with laws, oligarchy government by the few without laws; monarchy with laws is called kingship, without laws tyranny; while democracy has the one name whether with or without laws. These six forms are all different from government by the scientific ruler, and arise because men "can never be made to believe that any one can be worthy of such authority, or is able and willing in the spirit of virtue and knowledge to act justly and holily to all; . . . for if there could be such a despot as we describe, they would acknowledge that we ought to be too glad to have him, and that he alone would be the happy ruler of a true and perfect State" (301CD). Democracy "is in every respect weak and unable to do either any great good or any great evil, when compared with the others, because the offices are too minutely subdivided and too many hold them. And this therefore is the worst of all lawful governments, and the best of all lawless ones" (303A). Monarchy, on the other hand, is of all the imperfect forms of government the best, if it is bound by good written laws, but the worst if it is without laws (302E). Any second best form of government should, according to the teaching of Plato's latest work, partake of elements from each of these basic forms, monarchy and democracy (*Lg.*, III,693DE). The constitution for the proposed Cretan colony is therefore intended as a mean between the two (VI,756E). The best constitution can be brought into being most easily and quickly under a tyranny, because there one man has unimpeded power to make the necessary changes; in the next easiest way, under kingship; in the third easiest, from a form of democracy; while only with the greatest of difficulty can it arise in an oligarchy, on account of the number of different rulers (IV,709E-711D).

In any polity based on legislation the guardians have the task

---

citizens want to live in service to the laws (698B; 699C). The Spartan polity is allowed to be described from one angle as the most democratic of all states, even though from other viewpoints it is of the kingly type and tyrannical and aristocratic (IV,712CE). Accordingly, when Plato maintains that the constitutions sketched in the *Laws* should always keep midway between monarchy and democracy (VI,756E), he need not be expected to mean democracy in the usual modern sense.

of supplying detailed direction that necessarily escapes the general nature of laws. The framers of the constitution can only say: "O friends and saviours of our laws, in laying down any law, there are many particulars which we shall omit, and this cannot be helped; at the same time, we will do our utmost to describe what is important, and will give an outline which you shall fill up. And I will explain on what principle you are to act" (*Lg.*, VI,770B). In regard to any change in the laws themselves, however, a markedly conservative spirit is enjoined. In this second best type of polity the presupposition is that the laws proceed from a wisdom superior to that of the actual rulers. The rulers are not above the law, and so where circumstances require a change they have to proceed cautiously and only with the consent of all the people: ". . . they are never, if they can help, to change aught; or, if some necessity overtakes them, the magistrates must be called into counsel, and the whole people, and they must go to all the oracles of the Gods; and if they are all agreed, in that case they may make the change, but if they are not agreed, by no manner of means, and any one who dissents shall prevail, as the law ordains" (VI,772CD).

The Laws. In the polity described in the *Laws*, the care of the city-state is handed over to a nocturnal synod of rulers who have been given the necessary education (XII,968A-969B). The synod is required to meet every day between dawn and sunrise. It consists of both older and younger men, the younger learning under the guidance of the older (951D-952A). The *Laws* treats of crimes and penalties in considerable detail. Suicide, for instance, when committed apart from the command of the state or intolerable misfortune or disgrace, and through "sloth or want of manliness," is punished by dishonorable burial (IX,873CD). Slavery is prescribed as an institution, on account of "the necessary division of slave, and freeman, and master" (VI,777B), but humane treatment of the slaves is urged (777DE). Slavery, apparently, would be allowed by Plato under any good type of constitution, since the kingly science shows that some kinds of men are not fitted by nature to receive the education proper to citizens, and accordingly "those who are wallowing in ignorance and baseness she bows under the yoke of slavery" (*Plt.*, 309A). Legal reparation of damage is distinguished from punishment for injustice, as though by way of difference between civil and criminal action (*Lg.*, IX,862AC). Private shrines and private cults are forbidden (X,909D-910D), professional beggars are banned (XI,936C), and foreign travel in a private capacity is not permitted (XII,950D).

Throughout its various presentations in widely separated dialogues, as the preceding texts show clearly enough, the political philosophy of Plato retains a marvelous consistence in its inspiration and its aims. Its message is that the proper care of the soul is to be found in scientific knowledge, just as the body is best cared for by the sciences of medicine and gymnastic. Its ideal lies in the direct and unimpeded rule of political science through the person of a ruler endowed with commanding knowledge. In practice the ideal is realized in different degrees of imitation through government by laws stemming in some way from political science and administered by rulers endowed with true opinions. Plato never seems to swerve from these basic notions, applied to men as he knew them in the social life of the Greek city-state. The different attitude of the *Laws* from that of the *Republic* is often interpreted as a change of views resulting from practical experience with the passage of time. Yet the same basic political principles govern both works. The full bloom of life's prime may have made it appropriate for Plato to treat of the ideal polity in the middle period of his writing, and the hardening of arteries with advancing age may have made him better adapted in his later years to deal with government through the comparative rigidity of law. But even the dread of innovation manifested in the *Laws* always permitted change from what was detrimental: "The argument affirms that any change whatever except from evil is the most dangerous of all things; This is . . . true of all things, except, as I said before, of the bad" (*Lg.*, VII,797D). As the texts quoted from the *Laws* make clear, Plato throughout that work allowed for the continual task of supplementing the general nature of the prescribed legislation, and for new circumstances that necessarily would require change in the laws themselves. The note of political science dominates throughout. An extreme interpretation does, it is true, maintain that Plato with the progress of the years completely abandoned his earlier belief in philosophy and the possibility of scientific knowledge, settling for a complete nominalism and a convenient political pragmatism in his final writings.[17] This means that the doctrine of the *Politicus* has to be regarded as a joke, and the last section of the *Laws* as a mask of deliberately intended deception.[18] Taken at their face value, however, the statements of Plato continually attest his adhesion to the grounding of political life on the permanence and intelligibility of the Ideas, which alone can impart the required "irreversible nature" (*Lg.*, XII,960,CE) to human laws and so give them enduring vitality and purpose. His procedure always requires that true government be imposed from above by the superior intelligence of one or of a few, and not that it be worked out from below by way of the opinions and experience of the majority.

Function of the Ideas. Plato's philosophical effort, clearly enough, is directed to the care of the soul through the practice of virtue in the life of the Greek city-state. The science that has this care as its object is political science, the kingly art. It aims to guide human conduct, individual and social, according to the Ideas. This means guidance according to the common essence that is found in all particular acts of virtue, future as well as present and past. The *common* role of the Ideas, of course, readily extends to other orders besides that of moral conduct. It makes possible all scientific thought, as well as communication through speech, and is absolutely necessary for both. It explains whatever order is found in the sensible universe. Yet the modeling of both human conduct and the sensible world upon the Ideas is never complete. In both cases there is always present an irrational element that is never entirely overcome. The necessary or variant cause resists to a certain extent the best efforts of the demiurge,

[17] H. M. Wolff, *Plato: Der Kampf ums Sein* (Bern, 1957), pp. 295-299. This book was also published in the *University of California Publications in Philosophy*, Vol. 30 (Berkeley and Los Angeles, 1957). M. O'Brien, "Modern Philosophy and Platonic Ethics," *Journal of the History of Ideas*, XIX (1958), 472, notes that the differing modern interpretations "whether the dialogues show a unified doctrine, an evolving doctrine, or a set of contradictory doctrines" stem in large measure from the interpolation of modern conceptions into the Platonic problems instead of treating them in their original Platonic terms.

[18] Wolff, pp. 269-270; 303-307.

and the lawless tendencies of human nature persist in a latent
state under the wisest control of the political science. Just as
something inevitably remains unachieved in the artificer's efforts
at bringing the perfection of the Ideas into the sensible world,
so in human conduct, at least while the soul is in the body, ideal
perfection is something to be aimed at and worked for, but
scarcely to be expected in attainment. Plato gives every appearance of meaning seriously that his ideal city-state should really
be the goal of human endeavors. Yet at the same time he keeps
fully aware that it has to be introduced in practice by varying
degrees of imitation according to the immediate disposition of
the human element upon which it is being imposed.

Love of Wisdom. In this Platonic setting philosophy takes on
in a very striking way the notion that its etymology implies. It
is profoundly a love of wisdom, a love of the vision of truth (*Rep.*,
V,475BE). It is a love of the knowledge of the Ideas, rather than
a completely attained possession of knowledge. It cannot adopt
the methods of a dry, intellectually detached study. It has to
make abundant use of the affective propensities of the moment;
it can afford to lose no opportunity of centering all desires upon
its pursuit. It proceeds with urbane and easy humor in pleasant
discussion, raising the soul gradually through successive stages
of its dialectic, and often ending in myth when no further reasoning can sufficiently bring home its point. It is a special kind of
life, a life that can be lived in its perfection only after the soul
has been separated from its bodily prison and lives in itself. The
Ideas are the soul's proper pasture, from which the soul derives
its nourishment imperfectly while joined with the body, perfectly
when it is fully detached by death from its union with the senses.
Sensible cognition always remains a hindrance to philosophy. The
Platonic effort, in freeing men from slavery to the senses, does
not profess to give them wisdom, but only to make them lovers
of wisdom, philosophers: "Wise, I may not call them; for that is
a great name which belongs to God alone,—lovers of wisdom or
philosophers is their modest and befitting title" (*Phr.*, 278D).

In accord with its special character, Platonic philosophy finds
the impersonal medium of the written word a much less satisfactory means of communication than the direct and personal
contact of speech, in which the affective circumstances of the

moment could be so much better exploited. It thrives rather with the "intelligent word graven in the soul of the learner, which can defend itself, and knows when to speak and when to be silent. *Phaedr.* You mean the living word of knowledge which has a soul, and of which the written word is properly no more than an image? *Soc.* Yes, . . ." (*Phdr.*, 276A). The man who has come to know the good and the just and the seemly "will not seriously incline to 'write' his thoughts 'in water' with pen and ink, sowing words which can neither speak for themselves nor teach the truth adequately to others" (*Phdr.*, 276C). In the seventh letter, the difficulty of conveying philosophy through the written[19] word is outlined forcefully: "I certainly have composed no work in regard to it, nor shall I ever do so in future; for there is no way of putting it in words like other studies. Acquaintaince with it must come rather after a long period of attendance on instruction in the subject itself and of close companionship, when suddenly, like a blaze kindled by a leaping spark, it is generated in the soul and at once becomes self-sustaining."[20]

Open Philosophy. Since Platonic philosophy is a life that can be led only imperfectly on earth, it can hardly be expected to give completely satisfactory results in the form of definite and final conclusions. It provides for the highest needs of the soul by opening the way to the vision of true being, and nourishes and sustains the mind by a continually increasing participation in truth and knowledge. It can proceed indefinitely in this way as long as life in the body lasts. It furnishes science meant to guide human life in the best way possible. But it does not, and of its very nature cannot, give final answers to the deepest problems that it encounters. It regularly leaves questions open for further discussion. It does not explain the existence of the Ideas or their participation as found in sensible things and human knowledge. It does not penetrate into the nature of the artificer of the cosmos or the nature of the receptacle, space. It does not say definitely

---

[19] The very doubtful second letter states that Plato has never written anything of his own upon the subject, in order that his doctrine may not unwisely be disclosed to the general public (*Ep.*, II,314AC). This seems to reflect a later tendency of attributing an esoteric teaching to the Academy.

[20] *Ep.*, VII,341CD; tr. Post. *Cf.* 344AC. On the function of moral habituation in regard to knowledge, see R. E. Cushman, *Therapeia* (Chapel Hill, 1958), pp. 57-59; 149-155; 306-308.

278 THE FLOWERING OF GREEK PHILOSOPHY

to just what point human society in general may be molded after the model of the Ideas. It makes no attempt to account for the presence of the irrational factors in the sensible world and in human nature. It indicates the necessity of a mathematical explanation of the cosmos, yet does not itself undertake even the first step towards grounding it on the actually known measurements of sensible things. But it points to all these problems with exceptionally clear vision, and isolates them in a way that has given them in greater or less degree the form in which they have received perennial treatment in subsequent western philosophy. From these viewpoints the philosophy of Plato remains an invitation to think, and not a ready-made system of thought.

In its own immediate setting, however, Plato's teaching was a definite effort to ground human conduct and thinking on a common, enduring basis, rather than upon day-by-day decisions and upon opinions devoid of causal knowledge. It was an uncompromising attack on the supremacy of rhetorical training. The difference between Plato and Isocrates was not at all the contrast between speculative and practical. Both these great teachers were vigorously concerned with bettering human living. In that sense both were eminently practical.[21] The cleavage between them was fundamentally the difference between the scientific outlook and the common-sense mentality. Plato was the thoroughgoing advocate of the scientific, of knowledge (*epistêmê*) against opinion (*doxa*). In the Parmenidean background this meant an effort to bring something of the stable world of being into the ever-changing realm of seeming, through participation. Even though Plato considered the *doxa* to be "Heraclitean," he himself gave new and advanced expression to the Greek conception of political life that had been urged by the Ephesian sage. Like Heraclitus, Plato was intent on striving for the unity of the common in the ever-varying particulars of human conduct, as the difference between living in a waking and in a dream world. Eyes and ears and hands were to see and hear and act in common (*Lg.*, V,739C). Life based upon the Ideas is a waking state, while life based upon particular opinions has only the status of dreaming (*Rep.*, V,476CD). Plato's philosophy, accordingly, is a powerful

[21] The philosopher who lacks contact with public life is sketched in *Tht.*, 173B-176A.

incentive towards conduct based on norms that hold, though in varying degrees, for all; towards government by commonly accepted standards that are above the particular whims of rulers; and towards progress in truly scientific knowledge instead of contentment with a heritage of hit-or-miss conjectures. Plato was the prophet of the stable and the scientific, as opposed to the arbitrary and the superficial.

SELECTED READINGS AND REFERENCES

Plato

Greek text: *Platonis Opera*, 5 vols. in 6, ed. John Burnet (Oxford: Clarendon Press, [1900-1907]). Reprint, 5 vols., 1950, etc.

English tr.: *The Dialogues of Plato*, 4 vols., tr. Benjamin Jowett (Oxford: Clarendon Press, 1871). 4th ed., 4 vols., 1953.

(There are also fine English translations of all Plato's works in the *Loeb Classical Library*, and of individual dialogues or groups of dialogues by Cornford, Rouse, and many other scholars).

Friedrich Ast, *Lexicon Platonicum*, 3 vols. (Leipzig: Weidmann, 1835-1838). Reprint, 3 vols. in 2 (Bonn: R. Habelt, 1956).

Paul Shorey, *The Unity of Plato's Thought* (Chicago: University of Chicago Press, 1904). In *Decennial Publications of the Univ. of Chicago*, First Series, vol. VI.

——, *What Plato Said* (Chicago: University of Chicago Press, 1933).

Alfred Edward Taylor, *Plato The Man and His Work* (London: Methuen, 1926).

Georges M. A. Grube, *Plato's Thought* (London: Methuen, 1935). Reprint, Boston: Beacon Press, 1958.

Francis Macdonald Cornford, *Plato's Theory of Knowledge* (London [Kegan Paul, Trench, Trubner] and New York: Harcourt, Brace, 1935).

——, *Plato's Cosmology* (London [Kegan Paul, Trench, Trubner] and New York: Harcourt, Brace, 1937).

——, *Plato and Parmenides* (London: Kegan Paul, Trench, Trubner, 1939).

Raphael Demos, *The Philosophy of Plato* (New York: Scribner, 1939).

Julius Stenzel, *Plato's Method of Dialectic*, tr. D. J. Allan (Oxford: Clarendon Press, 1940).

Friedrich Solmsen, *Plato's Theology* (Ithaca: Cornell University Press, 1942).

John Wild, *Plato's Theory of Man* (Cambridge, Mass.: Harvard University Press, 1946).

Guy Cromwell Field, *The Philosophy of Plato* (London, etc.: Oxford University Press, 1949).

Richard Stanley Bluck, *Plato's Life and Thought* (London: Routledge & Kegan Paul, 1949).

Neville Richard Murphy, *The Interpretation of Plato's Republic* (Oxford: Clarendon Press, 1951).

William David Ross, *Plato's Theory of Ideas* (Oxford: Clarendon Press, 1951).

Ronald B. Levinson, *In Defense of Plato* (Cambridge, Mass.: Harvard University Press, 1953).

Rupert Clendon Lodge, *The Philosophy of Plato* (London: Routledge & Kegan Paul, 1956).

Robert E. Cushman, *Therapeia*, Plato's Conception of Philosophy (Chapel Hill: University of North Carolina Press, 1958).

[CHAPTER 13]

Aristotle of Stagira
—Logic and the Sciences

Chronology. According to information from Apollodorus' *Chronicle* (second century B.C.) handed down by Diogenes Laertius (V, 9-10) and Dionysius of Halicarnassus (*Ep. ad Ammaeum*, V), Aristotle was born in the first year of the ninety-ninth Olympiad (384/383 B.C.). At the age of seventeen he came to Athens and remained with Plato for twenty years. In the year of Plato's death (347 B.C.) he withdrew from Athens and for the next three years stayed with Hermias the ruler of Atarneus and Assos, towns situated on the coast of Asia Minor opposite the island of Lesbos. In the last year of the 108th Olympiad (345/344 B.C.) he went to Mytilene, on Lesbos. In the second year of the next Olympiad (343/342 B.C.) he journeyed to the court of Philip of Macedon to become the tutor of Alexander. There he passed the next eight years. He returned to Athens in the second year of the 111th Olympiad (335/334 B.C.), where he remained for twelve or thirteen years. He then went to Chalcis, on the island of Euboea, in the third year of the 114th Olympiad (322/321 B.C.), and died there shortly afterwards of sickness, in his sixty-third year. —This information was perhaps gathered by the Peripatetic Philochorus in the last years of the fourth century B.C. It is confirmed by other testimonia and in some details can be made more precise. Aristotle died shortly before Demosthenes, whose death occurred in October, 322 B.C. This would restrict the Stagirite's birth pretty well to the summer of 384, and his death to the very early fall of 322. His first arrival in Athens may have been a little before instead of after his seventeenth birthday, and his departure at the age of thirty-six may have taken place before Plato's death. His second Athenian period lasted about twelve years.[1] The chronological

[1] On this chronology, see I. Düring, *Aristotle in the Ancient Biographical Tradition* (Göteborg, 1957), pp. 249-260.

281

data in regard to Aristotle are exceptionally detailed and so indicate exact documents as their sources.

Lives. The oldest traceable *Life* of Aristotle was written by the Peripatetic Hermippus of Smyrna, towards the end of the third century B.C. It was a leading source for later biographies. It seems to have been based upon documents contemporary or nearly contemporary with Aristotle, some of them arising from controversies in the quarter-century after his death. Though favorable towards the Stagirite it appears to have had no objection to handing down entertaining anecdotes and gossip that stemmed from the anti-Aristotelian side of the controversies and were originally meant to caricature or defame him. The earliest extant account of Aristotle's life, however, is the brief sketch given by Dionysius of Halicarnassus (late first century B.C.) in the fifth chapter of the *First Letter to Ammaeus.* This epitome claims (cc. III; VI) to summarize the information transmitted in the current biographies of Aristotle, thereby indicating that a number of such *Lives* were in common circulation. The next oldest extant and longer biography seems to be that of Diogenes Laertius. A brief epitome known as the *Vita Hesychii* or the *Vita Menagiana* may perhaps be of the fifth century A.D.

The other extant *Lives* all stem from a Neoplatonic biography written by an otherwise unknown Ptolemy, probably of the fourth century A.D. The Neoplatonic tendency and methods of glorifying the philosophers make this source difficult to trust, even though it has preserved some genuine information not found in the other *Lives.* It has come down only in three Neoplatonic school epitomes, the *Vita Marciana*, the *Vita Vulgata* (*Ps.-Ammoniana*), and the *Vita Latina,* as well as in two Syriac epitomes and in Arabic tradition. The *Vita Latina* is a fairly early mediaeval translation of an independent Greek original.[2]

LIFE

Youth. The oldest extant biography that is at all expanded is accordingly that of Laertius (V, 1 ff.). In it, as the first item, Hermippus is quoted as saying that Aristotle of Stagira was the son of Nicomachus, who was descended from Asclepius and who, on account of his knowl-

[2] The Neoplatonic *Lives* may be found in V. Rose, *Aristotelis Fragmenta* (Leipzig, 1886), pp. 426-450; I. Düring, *op. cit.,* pp. 94-163. The biographical testimonia outside the *Lives* are assembled and discussed by Düring, pp. 251-456. For further discussion, see O. Gigon, "Interpretationen zu den Antiken Aristoteles-Viten," *Museum Helveticum,* XV (1958), 147-193.

edge of medicine and his friendship with the king of Macedon, Amyntas (Amyntas III, father of Philip of Macedon), lived at the royal court. This report contains useful information for understanding the background of Aristotle's work. Stagira (earlier Stagiros) was located on the northeast coast of the peninsula of Chalcidice. It was an entirely Greek colony, settled by immigrants from the island of Andros and from Chalcis. Its speech was an Ionian dialect. There is no historical reason, accordingly, for supposing that Aristotle was anything else than Greek in origin. A few miles from Stagira lay the border of the Macedonian kingdom. The position held by his father at the Macedonian court is an important indication regarding Aristotle's cultural background. It means that he was brought up at the royal court and so would be in association with men of the highest political circles in the Macedonian kingdom, and would grow up in an atmosphere of social problems at their top level. It also points to a status of at least moderate wealth and position for the family, explaining how Aristotle could spend the latter part of his youth in Athens at the center of Greek culture and devote himself entirely to rhetoric and philosophy.

Further, the statement that Aristotle's father was a descendant of Asclepius may hint at the custom of practicing Greek physicians to train their sons in their hereditary art of medicine. Although nothing in actual fact is known with certainty of Aristotle's early education in this regard, historians have often pointed to strong tendencies throughout the Aristotelian treatises to interpret things from a biological standpoint,[3] in contrast to the Platonic viewpoint of *logoi* or definitions. Dionysius of Halicarnassus, however, reports that Aristotle's father died before Aristotle himself left Stagira in his eighteenth year for Athens. According to the Neoplatonic *Vitae*, Aristotle was left an orphan and was educated by a certain Proxenus (probably a close relative).

First Athenian Period.   No details are known of Aristotle's twenty-year stay at the Academy. This time is called his first Athenian period. The length of the stay, lasting till Plato's death, certainly testifies to a profound respect for Plato himself, and is ample indication of the deep-rooted influence that the teaching of the Academy must have had upon his intellectual development from his eighteenth to nearly his thirty-eighth year. There is evidence enough that early writings of his were modeled on Plato's dialogues, at least in part. Yet practically nothing is known with certainty about the details of Aristotle's personal relations with Plato. Whenever Plato or the Platonic doctrines are mentioned in the Aristotelian treatises, they are viewed entirely objectively,

[3] E.g., H. D. Hantz, *The Biological Motivation in Aristotle* (New York, 1939).

in the same spirit of objectivity that is exhibited in regard to other leading Greek philosophers. Only in one passage (*E N*, I 6,1096a11-17) does Aristotle speak with warmth and affection of those who had introduced the doctrine of the Ideas. He calls them "friends," and seems to mean friends of himself as well as of his hearers; but he goes on to state that truth is to be preferred to friendship. The passage seems to have the nature of a rhetorical flourish, imitating Plato's (*Rep.*, X,595BC) own treatment of Homer. However, deepest feelings of admiration and friendship and reverence, seemingly for Plato, are unmistakably attested in an altar inscription attributed by Greek tradition to Aristotle (*Fr.* 623,1583a12-18). He consistently opposed the doctrine of Ideas; but the report that he broke away from the Academy during Plato's lifetime and set up a rival school, seems to have been a deliberate misrepresentation circulated in the last decade of the fourth century B.C. to discredit the Stagirite's reputation.

Assos Period. Similarly, there is no certain information about Aristotle's motives for leaving Athens after Plato's death. Hermias, the ruler of Atarneus, had been interested in the work of the Academy and in Plato's efforts to base civil government on philosophy.[4] The position and influence that Aristotle attained while with him is indicated by the Stagirite's marriage to Hermias' niece and adopted daughter, Pythias. Nothing is known of this marriage except that a daughter born of it was called by the same name as her mother. Aristotle's son, Nicomachus, is reported to have been born of a later union with Herpyllis, a member of his household, though in his will the two children seem given exactly the same legal status.

Aristotle's reasons for leaving Assos at the end of three years and going to Mytilene are likewise unknown. He was probably associated during this time with Theophrastus, a native of Eresus on the island of Lesbos, who was eventually to succeed him in his school activities.

Macedonian Period. Whether from old family connections at the Macedonian court, or his reputation at Athens, or, more probably, on account of his association and work with Hermias, Aristotle was invited by Philip to become the tutor of Alexander, then about thirteen or fourteen years old (343-342 B.C.). According to the report of Dionysius of Halicarnassus (*First Letter to Ammaeus*, V), his stay there lasted eight years. In 336 B.C. Philip was assassinated. Alexander succeeded to the throne and soon was in the field at the head of military expeditions. Aristotle's task at the royal court, accordingly, was over, and he returned to Athens in 335/334 B.C. Much of his research

---

[4] See W. Jaeger, *Aristotle* (Oxford, 1934), pp. 111-115. However, the anti-Macedonian feelings spurred on by Demosthenes could easily have been the main reason for Aristotle's departure from Athens.

in natural history seems to have been done during the Assos and Macedonian sojourns.

The Meisterjahre. Xenocrates had succeeded Speusippus, Plato's nephew, as head of the Academy in 339 B.C. This is indicated (D.L., V,2) as the reason why Aristotle began to hold philosophical discussions of his own in the Lyceum. The Lyceum was the name given to a grove outside the city of Athens to the northeast. It took its name from a neighboring temple dedicated to Apollo Lyceus. It was the location of a public gymnasium and had been frequented by Socrates.[5] The etymology and meaning of the word "Lyceum" is uncertain. In various explanations it was said to denote Apollo the wolf-slayer, Apollo the Lycian god (from Lycia in southwest Asia Minor), or Apollo the god of light. At least within Theophrastus' lifetime the school work became associated with a certain *peripatos*. This was some kind of an edifice or at least a covered walk, since in Theophrastus' will it had to be bequeathed separately like a building, along with the houses adjoining the garden (D.L., V,52), and it required a special provision for its upkeep (D.L., V,54). It therefore could not very well have been located in the Lyceum itself. From that *peripatos* the followers of Aristotle received their traditional name of Peripatetics. The term *peripatos* originally meant a walking about or a place to walk about, but already in the latter part of the fourth century it had become connected with school discussions and had acquired the meaning of a school or a place for school activity. In denoting a scholastic discussion or lecture it echoed its old notion of a discussion during a stroll.

The second Athenian period is known as the Stagirite's *Meisterjahre*. At least during its earlier years rhetoric occupied, according to Greek tradition, a prominent place in his teaching. After Alexander's death in 323 B.C. he left Athens, apparently to escape the violence of the anti-Macedonian resurgence that followed the monarch's death. He spent the remaining days of his life at Chalcis where he owned property, seemingly of family heritage on his mother's side. In his will (D.L., V,11-16) he showed himself generous in providing for those dependent on him.

WRITINGS

Various Types. The Initial problems in regard to the works of Aristotle are much more complicated than was the case with Plato. All Plato's writings that were known to antiquity have been handed down in what was their then complete form. On the other hand, the works of Aristotle that were most widely known and read and quoted in

---

[5] See Plato, *Euthphr.*, 2A; *Euthd.*, 271A.

antiquity by the literary public have all been lost.[6] As in the case of
the Presocratics, they are known only through meager fragments and
references found in later writers. These works, according to ancient
testimony, were written in a highly polished and rhetorical style. Cicero,
an able judge in that regard, numbers the Stagirite among those who
were "eloquent, charming, and polished in their language" (*De Or.*,
I,11,49), and speaks of him as "pouring forth a golden stream of
eloquence" (*Ac. Pr., II,*38,119). Cicero, in fact, considered Aristotle
to be *the* fount for the art of rhetoric (*De Inv.,* II,2,6). Quintilian likewise speaks of the "charm of his language" (X,1,83).

Quite different, however, are the treatises that have been handed
down in the traditional *Corpus Aristotelicum.*[7] They bear titles other
than those of the writings quoted in the literary world of antiquity.
They are not composed in anything like the rhetorical style that was
reported for the lost works. On at least one important topic, the personal immortality of the human soul, the fragments of a lost dialogue,
the *Eudemus,* express doctrine that is radically divergent from that of
the treatises. One ancient Aristotelian commentator goes so far as to
say that in his dialogues Aristotle is "versatile in his impersonations"

[6] On this topic see E. Bignone, *L'Aristotele Perduto e la Formazione
Filosofica di Epicuro,* 2 vols. (Florence, 1936); J. Bidez, *Un Singulier
Naufrage Littéraire dans l'Antiquité* (Brussels, 1943). The difficulties facing
attempts to reconstruct these lost Aristotelian works are well illustrated in
the critical study of W. Gerson Rabinowitz, *Aristotle's* PROTREPTICUS *and the
Sources of its Reconstruction* (Berkeley and Los Angeles, 1957).

[7] In scholarly works the treatises are quoted by page, column, and line of
the first two volumes in the Prussian Academy edition (ed. I. Bekker, Berlin,
1831). The fifth volume of this edition contains the surviving fragments of
other works (ed. V. Rose, Berlin, 1870) and Bonitz' invaluable *Index
Aristotelicus.* There are later and better editions of most of the treatises and
of the fragments. Lineation for the alternate text in the first part of the
seventh book of the *Physics,* added to the Bekker lineation, is given in the edition of W. D. Ross, *Aristotle's Physics* (Oxford, 1936). Though the Bekker
pagination continues to be used universally, the numbering of the
fragments and the chapter divisions may be changed in more modern
editions, as in those of the *Nicomachean Ethics.* Papyri found in the sands
of Egypt during the last quarter of the nineteenth century, coupled with
some fragments, have resulted in the recovery of nearly all of what had
been considered a lost work of Aristotle, *The Constitution of Athens,* published by F. G. Kenyon (Oxford, 1891), and in later editions. It was also
edited by J. E. Sandys (London, 1893), and was translated into English by
E. Poste (London, 1891).

The standard English rendition of the treatises and fragments is the
Oxford translation (1908-1952), under the general editorship of W. D. Ross.
All quotations from Aristotle in the following three chapters are according
to this translation, with the kind permission of its publishers, the Oxford
University Press.

and "expresses the false opinions of others,"[8] while Plutarch (*Adv. Colot.*, XX,1118C) mentions the Stagirite's "Platonic writings" as though they formed a special class.

Three different types of Aristotelian writings were, in fact, recognized in later antiquity.[9] One type was called "acroamatic," from the ancient term for a school lecture, *acroasis*. This would indicate works meant directly for use in school activity. A second kind was known to the later writers as "exoteric,"[10] and meant for them works destined for reading outside the school, and so directed to the general literary public. These first two types were called systematic works. The third type was named "hypomnematic," and consisted merely of memoranda to aid the memory or to serve as a basis for further elaboration of a theme. Of these three classes, there have survived only the acroamatic works, and the *Constitution of Athens*, which is generally regarded as belonging to the literary type even though it forms part of a program outlined in the *Nicomachean Ethics* (X 10,1181b14-23). Except for fragments of the works meant for general reading, the other Aristotelian writings have all perished. The acroamatic works are now known as the Aristotelian *treatises*. Further, "particular" works like letters and "intermediate" ones like the *Constitutions* were distinguished from those of "universal" scope.

The Treatises. The indication, implied in the classification "acroamatic," that the Aristotelian treatises were meant for school use is borne out by the character of those that have been handed down. They do not exhibit the features of writings that had ever been intended for the general literary world. They have a style that is as a rule too technical, and a presentation of thought that is too compact, to allow them the role of books destined for an undetermined reading public. Quite often they do not even make an attempt to explain the meanings of technical terms. On the other hand, they are much more than collections of notes meant to aid a lecturer, or to synopsize the contents of a lecture. They show evidence of a careful composition of

[8] Elias, *In Cat.*, 124.5, and (interpreting a statement of Alexander) 115.4-5; Oxford tr. See Düring, pp. 437-439.

[9] See testimonia in Ross's *Select Fragments* (Oxford, 1952), pp. 5-6 (Vol. XII of the Oxford tr.). According to Aulus Gellius (*Noct. Att.*, XX,5,7-12) the distinction between "acroatic" and published works was used by Andronicus of Rhodes.

[10] This later use of "exoteric" (Cicero, *Att.*, IV,16,2) does not necessarily correspond to Aristotle's own understanding of "exoteric *logoi.*" For a discussion of the problem see A. Iannone, *I Logoi Essoterici di Aristotele* (Venice, 1955). The eight instances in which Aristotle uses the term are listed by Iannone, pp. 3-4. Iannone concludes (pp. 26-27) that they refer to preliminary discussions *in the treatises themselves.* Against this view, see Düring, p. 441.

their own kind, they vary in style as occasion requires, they devote great care to precision in language, and they are studded with formal cross-references. They have the appearance of being *logoi,* after the manner of the traditional Ionian *logos,* but now meant entirely for school use. They could be written down by the hearers, perhaps memorized to a certain extent, as illustrated by the function of the *logos* Plato's *Phaedrus* (228BE), and then serve as the basis for lively discussion, as did Zeno's *logoi* in the *Parmenides* (127C ff.). Each *logos* was a treatment of a special topic, complete to a certain extent in itself, but capable of fitting in with larger groupings to form a wider coverage of the general subject.[11]

In this way the same *logos* could be referred to in cross-references in different ways, either singly or as included in a more comprehensive grouping. Further, any *logos* could be added to or changed in details as long as the author continued his teaching activity. Such is the form in which the treatises have been written, and, as usual with Greek philosophical writings, the form has to be kept in mind constantly when interpreting the content. The school *logoi* form, for instance, indicates that where the treatises imply ignorance or express doubt about a particular doctrine, they are presupposing such ignorance or doubt in the minds of the hearers, but not necessarily in the mind of the teacher. Similarly, the cross-references aid in establishing the methodical order of the treatises, that is, the order in which Aristotle wished them to be used in school instruction, but each reference has to be studied very carefully in its own context before one can learn if it may be used as a chronological indication. Dating of the particular treatises is therefore difficult, on account of their form as school *logoi.* As yet, no satisfactory general chronology has been worked out.[12]

[11] On the Aristotelian treatises as school *logoi,* see W. Jaeger, *Studien zur Entstehungsgeschichte der Metaphysik des Aristoteles* (Berlin, 1912). On evidence of lecture-room devices, see Henry Jackson, "Aristotle's Lecture-room and Lectures" *JP,* XXXV (1920), 191-200.
[12] General chronologies have been drawn up on different bases and with differing results by W. Jaeger, *Aristotle* (Oxford, 1934), F. Nuyens, *Ont-wikkelingsmomenten in de Zielkunde van Aristoteles* (Nijmegen-Utrecht, 1939), and P. Thielscher, "Die Relative Chronologie der Erhaltenen Schriften des Aristoteles nach den Bestimmten Selbstzitaten," *Philol.,* XCVII (1948), 229-265. The trend started by Jaeger of seeing a gradual change from Platonic views has been carried to its full extreme by J. Zürcher, *Aristoteles' Werk und Geist* (Paderborn, 1952). Zürcher maintained that the treatises that have been considered genuine were all written after Aristotle's death by Theophrastus, and that not more than twenty or thirty per cent of their doctrine is in substance Aristotelian (pp. 17-18). Zürcher's arguments, based on linguistic and historical considerations, have all proved too weak individu-

In the traditional *Corpus Aristotelicum,* the treatises are grouped in an order that is based upon their subject matter. First come five logical works, the *Categories, De Interpretatione, Topics, Prior Analytics, Posterior Analytics,* and *Sophistical Refutations.* Logic was called an instrument (*organon*) by the Greek commentators, and so this group later became known under the title of the *Organon,* or instrument for the sciences. The longest of the five, the *Topics,* seems to have been an early work of Aristotle.[13] After the logical works come those that treat of natural or sensible things, and so contain the Stagirite's natural philosophy or philosophy of the sensible universe. Of general scope in this field are the eight books of the *Physics.* On more particular topics follow *De Caelo, De Generatione et Corruptione, Meteorologica, De Anima,* a group of shorter treatises known since mediaeval times under the title *Parva Naturalia,* and detailed studies in natural history called *History of Animals, Parts of Animals, Generation of Animals, Movement of Animals,* and *Progression of Animals.*[14] Of these the *De Anima* seems to be chronologically quite late, while the seventh book of the *Physics,* which is detached from the series formed by the other books, seems to be very early. After the physical treatises comes a group that was gathered by the Peripatetics under the title of the

---

ally to have the cumulative effect necessary for making his case convincing. For a coverage of the discussions occasioned by this book, see E. J. Schächer, "War Aristoteles 'Aristoteliker'?" *Salzburger Jahrbuch für Philosophie und Psychologie,* I (1957), 157-238.

[13] The *Organon* has been edited by T. Waitz, *Aristotelis Organon Graece,* 2 vols. (Leipzig, 1844-1846). There are more modern texts of the individual treatises: *Aristotelis Categoriae et Liber de Interpretatione,* ed. L. Minio-Paluello (Oxford, 1949); *Aristotle's Prior and Posterior Analytics,* ed. W. D. Ross (Oxford, 1949); *Aristotelis Topica cum Libro de Sophisticis Elenchis,* ed. M. Wallies (Leipzig, 1923); *Aristotelis Topica et Sophistici Elenchi,* ed. W. D. Ross, (Oxford, 1958). The division of what Aristotle calls simply the *Analytics* into *Prior* and *Posterior Analytics* comes from later editors, and seems to have been based on doctrinal and not chronological grounds. On chronological questions see F. Solmsen, *Die Entwicklung der Aristotelischen Logik und Rhetorik* (Berlin, 1929); P. Gohlke, *Die Entstehung der Aristotelischen Logik* (Berlin, 1936); J. L. Stocks, "The Composition of Aristotle's Logical Works," *CQ,* XXVII (1933), 115-124.

[14] There are some good modern texts of the *Physics,* e.g., W. D. Ross, *Aristotle's Physics* (Oxford, 1936), and of the *De Anima,* e.g., R. D. Hicks, *Aristotle De Anima* (Cambridge, Eng., 1907); W. D. Ross, *Aristotelis De Anima* (Oxford, 1956). Of the *De Generatione et Corruptione* there is H. H. Joachim's *Aristotle On Coming-to-be and Passing-Away* (Oxford, 1922), and of the *Parva Naturalia* W. D. Ross's *Aristotle Parva Naturalia* (Oxford, 1955), and of the *De Caelo* D. J. Allan, *Aristotelis De Caelo* (Oxford, 1936).

Metaphysics[15] and comprises fourteen books. Of these one, book *Lambda*, is completely detached from the series formed by the others. Book *Alpha Elatton* seems to have been added as an alternate introduction to the general subject, while book *Kappa* parallels the teaching found in books *Beta, Gamma,* and part of book *Epsilon*. In the moral field, three Aristotelian *Ethics* have been handed down: the *Nicomachean Ethics* in ten books, the *Eudemian Ethics* in seven or eight, and the *Magna Moralia* in two. The *Magna Moralia* was in all likelihood so called because its books are longer than the books in the other two *Ethics,* and so would be referred to as "the large ethical scrolls." The other two titles indicate some connection with Aristotle's son Nicomachus and with Eudemus of Rhodes, respectively, but what that connection was remains unknown. Dedication was not customary at the time, and there is no evidence that it was a matter of editing. The *Eudemian Ethics* seems to be an earlier treatise than the *Nicomachean*. The stylistics of the *Magna Moralia* place it in a post-Aristotelian period, though its doctrine seems to be earlier than that of the other two *Ethics*.[16] Its authenticity presents a still unsolved

[15] There are modern texts of the *Metaphysics* by W. D. Ross, *Aristotle's Metaphysics,* 2 vols. (Oxford, 1924) and by W. W. Jaeger, *Aristotelis Metaphysica* (Oxford, 1957). The title "Metaphysics" is not found in Aristotle, though it was used regularly by the Greek commentators. It seems to have been coined quite soon after Aristotle's death. In the Greek commentators it is found interpreted as signifying that the primary philosophy is to be studied *after* natural philosophy, or that its subject lies *beyond* the physical order. It may well have implied both meanings in its original use, denoting the one as well as the other side of the notion that what is "first" in itself" is "subsequent" for human cognition. On these points see H. Reiner, "Die Entstehung und Ursprüngliche Bedeutung des Namens Metaphysik," *Zeitschrift für Philosophische Forschung,* VIII (1954), 210-237, esp. pp. 233-235. For other views, see P. Moraux, *Les Listes Anciennes des Ouvrages d'Aristote* (Louvain, 1951), pp. 312-315; I. Düring, *Aristotle in the Ancient Biographical Tradition* (Göteborg, 1957), pp. 286; 423. On the origin in the late eighteenth century and the subsequent history of the hypothesis that the title was coined to denote the order of the treatises in the edition of Andronicus of Rhodes, see H. Reiner, "Die Entstehung der Lehre vom Bibliothekarischen Ursprung des Namens Metaphysik," *Zeitschrift für Philosophische Forschung,* IX (1955), 77-99. For a discussion of the title in relation to the object of the Aristotelian primary philosophy, see P. Merlan, "Metaphysik: Name und Gegenstand," *JHS,* LXXVII (1957), 87-92.

[16] On the three *Ethics,* see A. Mansion, "Autour des Ethiques Attribués à Aristote," *Revue Néoscolastique,* XXXIII (1931), 80-107; 216-236; 360-380. The doctrinal case for the authenticity and the early dating of the *Magna Moralia* is presented by Hans von Arnim, "Die Drei Aristotelischen Ethiken," *Sitzungsberichte der Akademie der Wissenschaften in Wien,* 202.2 (1924) and "Der Neueste Versuch, die Magna Moralia als Unecht zu Erweisen," *ibid.,* 211.2 (1929), and in "Die Echtheit der Grossen Ethik des Aristoteles," *Rh. Mus.,* LXXVI (1926), 113-137; 225-253. As regards the

problem. Continuing the theme of the *Ethics* is the *Politics*. It presupposes extensive investigations of Greek civil constitutions, of which only the *Constitution of Athens* has been recovered. Finally, the *Rhetoric* and the *Poetics* deal respectively with the means of persuasion and with poetry.

Dialogues. Surviving quotations, as well as explicit descriptions in ancient testimonia, show that some of Aristotle's writings were in dialogue form. The works attested in this way to be dialogues occur in the first group of titles, nineteen in number, as found in the earliest list of his writings.[17] Most of these nineteen seem to have been dialogues. Four have the same names as Platonic dialogues—*Menexenus, Symposium, Sophist,* and *Statesman.* The title of the longest, a work in four large books called *On Justice,* indicates that it may have paralleled to some extent Plato's treatment of that virtue in the *Republic.* Other titles, like *On Rhetoric* or *Gryllus,* and *Eudemus* or *On the Soul,* sound as though they designated works that were modeled somehow on dialogues of Plato that treated of the same themes. The *Gryllus,* called after Xenophon's son, should be dated shortly after the latter's death in the battle of Mantinea (362/361 B.C.), and so about five or six years after Aristotle's arrival at the Academy. He would be about twenty-two or twenty-three at the time. The *Eudemus,* similarly, would have been written shortly after the death of Eudemus of Cyprus in 354/353 B.C., when Aristotle was not much more than thirty.

Other Literary Forms. Two or three titles included in those first nineteen seem to denote works written in the form of an exhortation

---

treatment of the virtue of justice and of friendship, the early dating is borne out by the study of M. Hamburger, *Morals and Law: The Growth of Aristotle's Legal Theory* (New Haven, 1951). On the later dating indicated by the linguistics, see K. O. Brink, *Stil und Form der Pseudaristotelischen Magna Moralia* (Ohlau, 1933); K. Berg, "Die Zeit der Magna Moralia," *Wien. Stud.,* LII (1934), 142-147.

There are texts of the *Nicomachean Ethics* by F. Susemihl, *Aristotelis Ethica Nicomachea* (Leipzig, 1887; 3rd ed., rev. O. Apelt, 1912) and by I. Bywater, *Ethica Nicomachea* (Oxford, 1890); of the *Eudemian Ethics* by Susemihl, *Eudemi Rhodii Ethica* (Leipzig, 1884); of the *Magna Moralia* by Susemihl, *Aristotelis quae feruntur Magna Moralia* (Leipzig, 1883); and of the *Politics* by Susemihl, *Politica* (Leipzig, 1872; rev. O. Immisch, 1909; 2nd ed., 1929), and by W. D. Ross, *Aristotelis Politica* (Oxford, 1957).

Editions and translations of all the Aristotelian treatises mentioned in the last four notes, as well as of some other treatises and of the *Constitution of Athens* may also be found in the *Loeb Classical Library.*

[17] D.L., V,22-27. A careful study of this and the other ancient lists is made by P. Moraux in *Les Listes Anciennes des Ouvrages d'Aristote* (Louvain, 1951). *Cf.* Ingemar Düring, "Ariston or Hemippus? A Note on the Catalogue of Aristotle's Writings, Diog. L.V. 22," *Classica et Mediaevalia,* XVII (1956), 11-21.

rather than of a dialogue, as the *Protrepticus* (dated tentatively around 353 B.C. on the basis of its alleged relationship with Isocrates' *Antidosis*), which was addressed to Themiston, ruler of Cyprus; *On Kingship* (dated around 336 B.C.) and *Alexander* or *On Colonists* (dated as after 331 B.C.), both perhaps works addressed to Alexander. *On Philosophy*, in three books, is considered to have been published after Plato's death, because of its critique of the Platonic Ideas. The same way of dating applies to *On the Good*, listed in the group immediately following the first nineteen works, and to *On Ideas*, an important work used by the Greek commentators in explaining Aristotle's treatment of the Ideas. This criterion for dating, however, seems rather weak. Some information has survived about works on other philosophers, *On Democritus*, *On the Pythagoreans*, and *On the Philosophy of Archytas*, all apparently meant for the general reading public; and also about a few logical works like *Divisions* and *On Contraries*, which seem to have been destined rather for school use.

Character of the Literary Works. According to ancient testimonia, the character of the literary works, at least of the dialogues, differed sharply from the didactic presentation that is found in the extant treatises. Cicero mentions that Aristotle developed both sides of every question, even though these were contrary to each other: "But if anyone ever comes forward who can, in the Aristotelian manner, put forward both sides on every subject, and can with knowledge of Aristotle's precepts develop two contrary speeches on every question, . . . he is the true, the perfect, the only orator."[18] Ancient commentators expressed the difference in the two types of works by saying that in the acroamatic treatises Aristotle writes seriously and states what he himself thinks and what is true, while in the other type he aims at a light, graceful style and gives voice to the opinions of others, or uses probable arguments.[19] Cicero (*Att.*, XIII,19,4) further testifies that according to the Aristotelian plan the writer himself has the principal role in the dialogue; and yet he states (*Fam.*, I,9,23) that his own dialogue *On the Orator*, in which the writer does not appear, follows the Aristotelian plan. This may mean that in some dialogues Aristotle himself was the chief speaker, while in others he did not enter in any role. The dialogue form, accordingly, makes it difficult to judge whether a fragment from a writing known to be a dialogue expresses Aristotle's own sentiments and adhesions, or whether it gives voice to a contrary view that is placed in the mouth of one of the speakers. In general, the

[18] *De Or.*, III,21,80; Oxford tr. Aristotle's actual method of teaching seems to have included this eristic art of defending both sides of a question; see P. Merlan, *Historia* (Wiesbaden), III (1954), 76-78.

[19] See testimonia in Ross, *Select Fragments* (Oxford, 1952), pp. 5-6.

forms attributed to these literary works were in common usage at the time, and consequently are what one would expect to find in a writer of that epoch.

Transmission.   As the foregoing survey makes clear, the only works of Aristotle that have survived were all connected with school use. A well-attested story[20] relates that the library of Theophrastus, which contained that of Aristotle, was bequeathed to Neleus, the son of Coriscus, the associate of Aristotle at Assos. Neleus had it transported to Skepsis in northern Asia Minor. There it was buried in an underground hiding place to avoid being seized for the royal library at Pergamum, and lay concealed until the beginning of the first century B.C. At that time the books were bought by Apellicon, a bibliophile. Apellicon made new copies of them, filling with incorrect emendations the gaps caused by damage from moths and dampness. The result was that he published a text full of errors. Afterwards the library was transported by Sylla to Rome, and came into the hands of the grammarian Tyrannion, a man keenly interested in Aristotle. Andronicus of Rhodes (first century B.C.) acquired copies from Tyrannion, and listed and published them. The story takes pains to emphasize that the older Peripatetics did not have Aristotle's works, except only a few, and these mostly exoteric works; while the later Peripatetics had a text that was unreliable because of its many errors.

What can be made of this narrative? It implies that the older Peripatetics did have some of Aristotle's school treatises, and that they had a comparatively larger number of the writings meant for general circulation. There is enough evidence, moreover, to show that some Aristotelian treatises were exercising their influence during the time that the library of Theophrastus lay buried.[21] Besides, the earliest extant catalogues of the Stagirite's works seem to reproduce a list that was made in the third century B.C., and so to represent the books either in circulation among the Peripatetics (Moraux) or collected in the Alexandrian library (Düring) at the time. The list has omissions that give considerable ground for the assertion that the early Peripatetics lacked many of the treatises. Missing are two of the Aristotelian *Ethics* and most of the works concerned with natural science. The *Categories* and the *De Interpretatione* are in the wrong place and would seem therefore to be later insertions.[22] This would indicate that in the last

[20] Strabo, XIII,1,54 (608-609); Plutarch, *Sylla*, XXVI, 1-2(468AB). Strabo (*ca.*63 B.C.-24 A.D.), the first to relate the narrative, was a disciple of Tyrannion and a student of Aristotelian philosophy. There seems little likelihood, therefore, of his being misinformed on its main outlines.
[21] See P. Moraux, *Les Listes Anciennes,* pp. 3-5.
[22] See Moraux, p. 131.

half of the third century B.C. a sizable part of the present Aristotelian Corpus was in some way missing from the accessible works. Would these missing treatises be the ones that were reacquired, at first in faulty copies made by Apellicon from the originals, and later in the corrected edition of Andronicus of Rhodes? Such a conclusion is difficult to draw, because some of the missing ones seem to have been among the treatises that exercised influence during the early centuries. The result is that any conclusions on the transmission of the Aristotelian works during this period remain uncertain and only provisory. On the reasons why later on the writings meant for general circulation ceased to be copied, there are no testimonia at all.

PHILOSOPHICAL TEACHINGS

Division of the Sciences. True to his deeply Platonic training and background, Aristotle in the treatises is primarily concerned with promoting knowledge, in the sense of scientific knowledge both of things that already exist and of things that are to be done. He is accordingly intent not only upon knowing the truth about things that already are, but also upon basing human conduct and undertakings, public as well as individual, upon truly scientific knowledge. A division of the sciences into those that aim at knowledge and those that aim at action had been definitely foreshadowed in Plato (*Plt.*, 258DE). It is explicitly laid down[23] and followed out in actual treatment by Aristotle. At times a threefold division is mentioned: speculative, practical, and productive.[24] The productive sciences have their first principle in the producer. This principle consists of an intuition (*nous*) or an art or some such capacity. The practical likewise have their first principle in the agent, but it consists of free choice, a principle that amounts to the man himself as a human agent.

In spite of this further distinction, however, the truly fundamental contrast remains located in the difference between the speculative and the other sciences. The very first principle or starting point of the speculative sciences lies *in the thing* that is known, and not properly in the speculative scientist. The first principles of the other two types of science, on the contrary, lie

[23] E.g., *Metaph.*, α 1,993b20-21; *E E*, I 1,1214a8-12.
[24] *Top.*, VI 6,145a15-18; E N, VI 2,1139a26-b9; *Metaph.*, E 1,1025b18-26; K 7,1064a10-18. *Cf. P A*, I 1,640a3-4.

within the practical or productive scientist himself, and not in any already existing thing that is being known. Accordingly, the speculative sciences treat of things that already are, while the practical and productive deal with something that as yet does not exist but is to be in the future, something that is to be done or to be made. The goal of the speculative sciences consists in knowledge of truth. That is their good, their purpose. The good of the other two kinds of science, however, lies in something over and above the knowledge that they entail. Their purpose, their good, is respectively action or a product.

Speculative science, therefore, proceeds from principles that are found in the things known. It is directed solely towards the knowledge of things. Practical and productive sciences, on the other hand, proceed from principles found within the knower and aim at something over and above mere knowledge, at something that does not as yet exist. Such are the lines by which the basic Aristotelian division of the sciences is made. The practical sciences bear on conduct and courses of action, while the productive are concerned with things to be made; but in the really fundamental respects just considered, the procedure of both is in radical contrast with that of the speculative sciences.

Introductory Science.   Before anyone can rightly approach a theoretical science, he must first have studied the processes of human reasoning, or, as Aristotle calls this subject, *analytics*: "And the attempts of some of those who discuss the terms on which truth should be accepted, are due to a want of training in logic (*tôn analyticôn*); for they should know these things already when they come to a special study, and not be inquiring into them while they are listening to lectures on it" (*Metaph.*, Γ 3,1005b2-5). An *analysis* of the scientific process of human thought and of knowledge itself is accordingly required by the Stagirite as a necessary preparation for further scientific undertakings. This analysis is called by him "the science which inquires into demonstration and science; . . ."[25] It is a science that has as its object scientific knowledge itself and the processes by which such knowledge is reached. It does not at all imply, however, that thought is the primary or direct object of human knowledge. Aristotle's constant teaching is that sensible things are the original

[25] *Metaph.*, K 1,1059b15-19. *Cf. Rh.*, I 4,1359b10.

and direct object of the human cognitive faculties. Only con-
comitantly with the knowledge or cognition of some other object
does any human cognition attain itself and its own operations:
"But evidently knowledge and perception and opinion and understanding have always something else as their object, and themselves only by the way" (*Metaph.*, Λ 9,1074b35-36). Yet the
sequence in which the sciences are to be studied does not follow
this genetic order. It is rather quite the reverse. The science of
thinking is to be learned before the sciences of things. Apparently
against this background the science of the human reasoning
processes, later called logic, was looked upon primarily as an
introduction to the sciences and was not included by Aristotle in
his schemata of the sciences themselves.

    Role of Logic. The Aristotelian exclusion of logic from the
formal tables of the sciences, however, does not in the least
diminish the momentous role that is played by the preliminary
requirement of this new and introductory science. For the first
time in history a conscious knowledge of what the human intellect is doing is laid down as an accompaniment of all scientific
procedure. The earliest Greek philosophers had worked from
intuition to intuition. Parmenides had introduced a considerable
amount of reasoning, but without demanding any noticeable
conscious effort at keeping aware of the process. The dialecticians
and eristics had made copious use of reasoning processes, and
already in Aristotle's time may have been working out their
schemata of inference, but seemingly without too profound a
study of the intimate nature of predication and demonstration
and their bearing on the various sciences. Plato had sought to
develop an elaborate process of division and composition of the
objects of thought, but again without any prior and thoroughgoing study of the reasoning activities themselves. He remained
content with a dialectical procedure that made ample use of leaps
from one intuition to another. He had insisted on cognition of
the common and abiding features upon which knowledge was
based, but he did not stress the necessity of learning first the
nature of the intellectual processes that allowed the mind to
draw, from objects already known, knowledge of other objects
until then not known. He did not undertake to explain in detail
how such derivative conclusions could remain knowledge in the

full sense of the term. Even Plato was too intent upon the things known to give fully the required reflexive attention to the processes by which those things were being known. "Recollection" was his most plausible explanation.

Aristotle, then, is for the first time introducing rigorous scientific procedure, rigorous because it is conscious of itself and understands itself. Of all his achievements this has had the most lasting effect on subsequent thought. It may well be expected to constitute the particular Aristotelian character that distinguishes his way of thinking from that of all his predecessors. It is the typically Aristotelian procedure. In its completely developed form it is presented in the *Prior* and *Posterior Analytics*.[26] These treatises deal with reasoning in its actual and operative progress. A reasoning process, however, is composed of premisses or propositions, and propositions are complexes that are analyzed into relatively simple terms. The treatment of these two preliminary factors, namely of terms and of propositions, is therefore placed before the *Analytics* in the traditional order of the treatises. It is given in the *Categories* and the *De Interpretatione*.[27] The role of dialectical arguments in regard to reasoning processes is developed extensively in the *Topics*, and faulty procedures are dealt with in the *Sophistical Refutations*.[28] These five treatises contain the Aristotelian logic.

Equivocals, Univocals. A term in any reasoning process, in order to avoid occasioning a faulty conclusion, has to retain the same meaning throughout. The *Categories*, accordingly, opens with the distinction between equivocals and univocals. Equivocals are things that are called by the same name, but have different definitions under that name. One definition will not hold for all the cases designated by the name. The meaning, then,

---

[26] On the general procedure of Aristotelian logic, see Heinrich Maier, *Syllogistik des Aristoteles*, 3 vols. (Tübingen, 1896-1900; reprint, Leipzig, 1936); Jean Marie Le Blond, *Logique et Méthode chez Aristote* (Paris, 1939); and on its relations to modern logic, J. Lukasiewicz, *Aristotle's Syllogistic* (Oxford, 1951); J. T. Clark, *Conventional Logic and Modern Logic* (Woodstock, Md., 1952).

[27] On the doctrine of the categories, see L.M de Rijk, *The Place of the Categories of Being in Aristotle's Philosophy* (Assen, 1952).

[28] Texts of these logical treatises are listed *supra*, n. 13. On the evidence that the *Topics* presupposes the *Categories* and builds upon it, see I. Husik, *Philosophical Review*, XIII (1904), 515-528.

can change, even though the same word is retained. With univocal things, on the other hand, the definition and so the meaning remain always the same. A man and an ox, for instance, are univocally called "animals," while a man and a picture are named *zôia* (the Greek term for "animals" and "paintings") only equivocally (*Cat.*, 1,1a1-12).

The Predicaments. These things constitute the simple terms into which a proposition is analyzed. They may be predicable *of* a subject, as "man" is predicable of an individual or "knowledge" is predicable of grammar. Such predicated things may be present *in* a subject, as "grammar" in the grammarian, or not present in any subject, as for instance "man." An individual instance of grammatical knowledge, on the other hand, is *in* the grammarian but it is not predicable *of* anything. These considerations give rise to the doctrine of the categories or things predicated.[29] Things that are not *in* any subject are called *ousiai*. This term is traditionally translated "substances," although it is an abstractive form of the Greek word for "being." It denotes therefore the things that truly are, in contrast to the various ways in which they may be. A man, for instance, is pale, two-legged, courageous. under all these ways it is the man who really *is*—white, two-legged, and so on. The other characteristics, accordingly, are not designated by the notion of being (*ousia*), but are referred to as "going with" what is already there, that is, with the substance. In contrast to the substance they are called "accidents." Here (*Cat.*, 4,1b25-27) and in the *Topics* (I 9,103b22-23) Aristotle lists nine categories or predicaments that are accidents—quantity, quality, relation, location, time, position, state, action, and passion. Elsewhere, however, he does not include all nine. There seems to be no compelling reason for placing the number of the predicaments at ten.

Substance. Substance is twofold, either primary or secondary. A primary substance is the ultimate subject of all predication. It is the individual substance, for instance a particular man like Socrates. All substantial and accidental categories are predicated of or are present in the individual substance. The individual

---

[29] The Greek term *katêgoria* meant a charge laid against someone. The verbal form was used also in the meaning of "assert." The technical sense of "predicate," however, seems to have been first introduced by Aristotle.

substance is therefore the most fundamental "being" (*ousia*) with which the logician is concerned, and so for logic the individual concrete substance is the primary being or primary substance. Substances like "man" and "animal" are predicated of the individual, as when one says that Socrates is a man or is an animal. These substances, so predicated, are for the logician secondary substances.

The secondary substances, because predicable of *all* the individuals that share them, are called "universals," a word that does not occur as a technical term before Aristotle. Universals may be either species or genera, the species being narrower than the genera and so nearer to the primary substance and to that extent more truly substantial. Any given substance, however, cannot admit varying degrees within itself, for any such substantial change would make it a different substance. Substance, further, has no contrary of its own, but is capable of possessing contrary qualities, like black and white (*Cat.*, 5,2a11-4b19).

Accidents.   Accidents also may be taken universally, and when so taken are predicable of substance or of another accident, as for instance "grammar is knowledge." Individual accidents, on the contrary, though always found *in* some substance, are not predicable *of* anything whatsoever, either substance or accident. An individual instance of grammatical knowledge is *in* a man, but is not predicated *of* that man (*Cat.*, 2, 1a20-b9). Quantity may be discrete, as in a number, or continuous, as in a line. Qualities may be habits, like the virtues; dispositions like heat, cold, health, disease; capacities or faculties, like the capacity to be healthy or to be a boxer; affective qualities, like heat, cold, whiteness, blackness; or the figure and shape of a thing, like straightness or curvedness or triangularity. Most qualities admit of variation in degree, for instance, whiteness; but some, like triangularity, do not.

The *Categories* proceeds to investigate these and other characteristics of the various predicaments, and then examines some features that run through different categories, namely, opposition, priority, simultaneity, motion, and possession. Later these five became known as the post-predicaments, because they were treated after the predicaments in the Aristotelian treatise.[30]

---

[30] On the authenticity of the last chapters (10-15) of the *Categories*, see I. Husik, "On the Categories of Aristotle," *Philosophical Review*, XIII

Propositions. The second logical treatise, *De Interpretatione,* deals with propositions. The terms or simple elements that were treated in the *Categories* are neither true nor false. Truth and falsity involve combination and separation. When the simple elements, accordingly, are coupled with some finite form of the verb "to be" they form a proposition, and the proposition is true or false, the verb carrying with it the implication of time. The proposition affirms or denies a predicate of a subject in time, past, present, future. Propositions may be simple or composite, that is, compounded of two or more simple propositions. Propositions are contradictory when they affirm and deny the same predicate of the same subject with reference to the same time, provided the terms are not equivocal and other necessary qualifications are met. Propositions may be universal or particular, positive or negative, necessary, impossible, or contingent. According to these characteristics they present different kinds of opposition to one another even though they have the same terms.

Syllogism. The *Prior Analytics* shows that reasoning (*syllogismus*) is composed of propositions. As parts of a reasoning process the propositions are called premisses. A demonstrative premiss is a proposition that is laid down by the demonstrator as true, while a dialectical premiss is a proposition that is accepted by one's adversary and so may be used in discussion aside from one's own adhesion to its truth. Reasoning or syllogism—the Greek word "syllogism" means "reasoning"—is "discourse in which, certain things being stated, something other than what is stated follows of necessity from their being so" (*APr.*, I 1,24b18-20). The *Prior Analytics* examines the different forms in which propositions can be brought to bear upon each other in such a way that this discourse takes place. The two propositions together must have three and only three terms: major, minor, and middle. The middle term is common to both premisses. The major and minor are called the extremes. Correct relation of the extremes to the middle term is required for a syllogism. The treatise proceeds accordingly first to examine this relation in the different possible types or figures of syllogism, and then to

---

(1904), 514-528; "The Authenticity of Aristotle's Categories," *Journal of Philosophy,* XXXVI (1939), 427-431; L. M. de Rijk, "The Authenticity of Aristotle's *Categories," Mnemosyne,* 4a ser. IV (1951), 129-159.

determine the truth or falsity of a conclusion in relation to the truth or falsity of the premises.

Demonstration. While the *Prior Analytics* is concerned only with the formal nature of the syllogism, the *Posterior Analytics* investigates the conditions under which the syllogism gives *knowledge* in the strictest sense of the word. Scientific knowledge is defined, as in Plato (*Men.*, 98A), through its causal basis and through the necessity that it involves. This is the necessity of *being*, the necessity that in the Parmenidean background distinguished knowledge from opinion: "We suppose ourselves to possess unqualified scientific knowledge of a thing, as opposed to knowing it in the accidental way in which the sophist knows, when we think that we know the cause on which the fact depends, as the cause of that fact and of no other, and, further, that the fact could not be other than it is" (*APo.*, I 2,71b9-12). The process that reveals the cause as cause and as necessarily so, is called demonstration: "By demonstration I mean a syllogism productive of scientific knowledge, a syllogism, that is, the grasp of which is *eo ipso* such knowledge" (*APo.*, I 2,71b17-19). In order to give this knowledge, the premises must have certain definite conditions: ". . . the premises of demonstrated knowledge must be true, primary, immediate, better known than and prior to the conclusion, which is further related to them as effect to cause. Unless these conditions are satisfied, the basic truths will not be 'appropriate' to the conclusion" (*APo.*, I 2,71b20-23). The scientific knowledge contained in the conclusion is regarded, accordingly, as the effect of the premises when one premiss is submitted to the other. The effect in this case follows with necessity. The premises therefore must themselves be true, since they are the proper cause of the truth in the conclusion. They must be primary and immediate and so indemonstrable, else they would require another process of demonstration to establish them. They must be better known than the conclusion, for knowledge of them is to result in the as yet unattained knowledge of the conclusion (*APo.*, I 1-2, 71a1 ff).

Propter Quid and **Quia Knowledge.** There is another sense in which the premises of a syllogism may be called "immediate." This occurs when they give the proximate cause of the conclusion (*propter quid* knowledge, "knowledge of the reasoned fact") and not merely a remote cause or something that is reciprocally entailed by the conclusion without being properly a cause (*quia* knowledge, "knowledge of the fact"): "Knowledge of the fact differs from knowledge of the reasoned fact. To begin with, they differ within the same science and in two ways: (1) when the premisses of the syllogism are not immediate (for then the proximate cause is not contained in them—a necessary condition of knowledge of the reasoned fact): (2) when the premisses are immediate, but instead of the cause the better known of the two reciprocals is taken as the middle; for of two reciprocally predicable terms the one which is not the cause may quite easily be the better known and so become the middle term of the demonstration" (*APo.*, I 13,78a22-30). Both types, the *propter quid* and the *quia*, are demonstrative knowledge. An instance given of the former is that the planets do not twinkle because they are near. The nearness is considered, against the background of ancient physics, to be the proximate cause for their failure to twinkle. The demonstration that they are near because they do not twinkle is considered to be conclusive, but not to give the proximate cause of the conclusion; it is therefore only *quia* knowledge.

Similarly if a cause is given, but only a remote cause, the demonstration yields only *quia* knowledge. The proof that a wall does not breathe because it is not an animal is demonstrative. It gives a cause, but not the proximate cause. Animality is not the proximate cause of respiration, because some animals do not breathe. The remote cause, accordingly, serves for demonstration in negative reasoning, but not in positive.

The *propter quid* procedure, which furnishes the exactly fitting cause, yields the superior type of knowledge; for knowledge is cognition through causes. Mathematical knowledge of sensible phenomena, accordingly, is a higher type of knowledge than the kind given by merely empirical observation of those same phenomena. Mathematical investigation, approaching the phenomena from the quantitative viewpoint, is able to manifest the exactly fitting causes under that aspect of the phenomena, and so provides *propter quid* knowledge of them. Empirical observation, when restricted to a qualitative procedure, gives only *quia* knowledge (*APo.*, I 13,78a22 ff.).

Induction. The "immediate" character of the indemonstrable knowledge given in the primary premisses means that those premisses allow no middle term by which they might be demonstrated. The primary premisses, however, furnish a better kind of knowledge than any obtained through demonstration, since as the *cause* of the conclusion the indemonstrable knowledge is "better known" than the conclusion itself. This knowledge of the indemonstrable premisses is not had by any innate possession, but by induction from sensibly perceived objects: "We conclude that these states of knowledge are neither innate in a determinate form, nor developed from other higher states of knowledge, but from sense-perception. It is like a rout in battle stopped by first one man making a stand and then another, until the original formation has been restored. The soul is so constituted as to be capable of this process" (*APo.*, II 19,100a10-14). By this process of induction, accordingly, the soul is "led to" or "brought to" the universal as present in the particular: "When one of a number of logically indiscriminate particulars has made a stand, the earliest universal is present in the soul: for though the act of sense-perception is of the particular, its content is universal— is man, for example, not the man Callias" (*ibid.*, a15-b1).

In the flux of the particulars, therefore, the soul is gradually able to perceive the first constant and unchanging universal. It proceeds further to see still wider universals, until it reaches the highest universals. These are no longer divisible into superior genera, but themselves constitute the highest genera, the categories: "A fresh stand is made among these rudimentary universals, and the process does not cease until the indivisible concepts, the true universals, are established: e.g. such and such a species of animal is a step towards the genus animal, which by the same process is a step towards a further generalization" (*ibid.*, b1-3).

Sensible Origin of Knowledge. The original premisses from which all demonstrative knowledge is derived are therefore obtained through induction from sensible particulars. On this point Aristotle's doctrine is explicit. All human knowledge, consequently, originates in sensible experience. As the metaphor of the army rout shows, the universal is first seen in one particular, in a single individual. The plurality of individuals, it seems, is required to focus the mind's vision gradually on that universal, which is present in all the individuals but is finally perceived as such by the mind in one particular instance. In that way the flux appearance is stopped. This is the "intuition (*nous*) that apprehends the primary premisses" (*Apo.*, II 19, 100b12). Accordingly, "intuition (*nous*) will be the originative source of scientific knowledge" (*ibid.*, b15).

In the context of the logical treatment Aristotle does not attempt to give any analysis of the capacity of the soul to perceive the universal in the particular, nor does he explain how the universal can be present in a particular. He merely observes that "the soul is so constituted as to be capable of this process," and that the universal "man" is present in the individual Callias. He leaves the further investigation of these facts to the theoretical sciences that treat of the soul and of being.

Dialectic. The *Topics* deals not with demonstration, which proceeds from truth known as such, but with reasoning from opinions (*endoxa*). Such a process is genuine reasoning. It is not demonstrative, however, but is *dialectical*. It reasons from opinions that are generally accepted, though not recognized definitely by the reasoner as true on the strength of their own proper evidence. Though the dialectic itself does not yield knowledge in the full sense of the term, it is of the utmost importance for the acquisition of knowledge and for meeting other people on their own ground. Not only is it useful as an intellectual training, but it is required in order to focus the mind on the first indemonstrable principles from which all demonstration proceeds. These indemonstrable principles are by no means the conclusions of the dialectical reasoning. Rather, they become apparent to the mind, on their own proper evidence, in the course of the dialectical inquiry.

In so helping the mind to focus on the evident truth of the first principles, dialectic may be said to contain the path to the first principles of all the sciences. Hence arises its indispensable function "in relation to the ultimate bases of the principles used in the several sciences. For it is impossible to discuss them at all from the principles proper to the particular science in hand, seeing that the principles are the *prius* of everything else: it is through the opinions generally held on the particular points that these have to be discussed, and this task belongs properly, or most appropriately, to dialectic: for dialectic is a process of criticism wherein lies the path to the principles of all inquiries."[31]

Dialectical procedure, then, has a role of primary importance for Aristotle. It is the discussion that brings to light the indemonstrable first principles of scientific demonstration. Of itself it does not yield knowledge, yet it is a necessary step in the quest for knowledge. It shows how deeply for Aristotle the scientific starting points were engaged in the complexities of experience. The *Topics*, accordingly, examines at great length various dialectical procedures, and explains the technique of dialectical discussion in regard to reaching the definition, properties, genera, and accidents[32] of the things under investigation. The Platonic dialectic is regarded as one such procedure for dividing the genera,[33] but as only a small part of dialectic taken as a whole (*APr.*, I 31,46a31-b37).

The general treatment undertaken in the *Topics*, and in particular its discussion of fallacies, are concluded in the *Sophistical Refutations*. This book deals with fallacious arguments that have the appearance of being genuine proofs but actually are not. In contradistinction to dialectic, however, such fallacious reasonings when deliberately undertaken to gain a point or to make a show of an unreal wisdom, are termed sophistic (*SE*, 1,165a17-33). Sophistical arguments may be occasioned by modes of expression, such as equivocity, or may be independent of the mode of expression, as for instance confusing the accidental with the essential (fallacy of accident) or missing the point (*ignoratio elenchi*) and so on (*SE*, 4,165b23 ff.). The *Sophistical Refutations* examines these arguments and shows how to detect and how to counter their fallacies.

Various types of dialectic had been developed by the Eleatics, the Sophists, and the Eristics, as well as by Socrates and by Plato. Against the background of these continued endeavors Aristotle has consciously centered attention upon the thinking processes that have made them possible. This reflexive analysis of human thought

[31] *Top.*, I 2,101a36-b4. *Cf.* VIII 1,155b12-156a11.
[32] *Top.* I,5 ff. These four, with the differentia, were later known as the "predicables."
[33] *Top.*, VI 6,143a29 ff.; 10,148a14-22. The Platonic method of division is called a "weak syllogism" (*APr.*, I 31,46a32-33).

has resulted in a new science—logic. As a preliminary training for science, logic shows the way to the rigorous and orderly procedure of all the other sciences. It is therefore the first of the philosophic sciences in the order of learning. Yet it has been explained by Aristotle in a way that leaves the objects of the other sciences entirely independent of any creative activity on its part. It does not at all produce those objects. It finds them already awaiting its work, work that consists merely in understanding and directing the processes of the human mind investigating them.

Though logic is accordingly the first philosophical science in the pedagogical order, it is far from being primary in the order of science as such. Rather, because it deals merely with *logoi* ("forms of reasoning,"—*Rh.*, I 4,1359b16) and not with definite things, it is not given and will not attain a place in the formal ranks of the Peripatetic sciences. Its role is envisaged not as giving knowledge for its own sake, but only as a training for acquiring the knowledge furnished by the sciences that treat of definite things.

[CHAPTER 14]

Aristotle—Theoretical Science

THEORETICAL SCIENCE is found by Aristotle to be of three different kinds, namely, physical, mathematical, and theological. There is, first, a theoretical science of sensible or mobile things. This takes as its first principles the basic elements of the sensible things themselves, and in the light of these principles investigates the visible universe. Such a science clearly has its starting point in the things known, and not in the knower. It is therefore a theoretical, not a practical, science. It is called natural philosophy, or "physics" in the ancient sense of the term. There is also a type of theoretical science that considers quantitative abstractions drawn from sensible things. It treats of these quantitative properties not as in any mobile existence but as taken abstractly in an immobile state. This is mathematics. Finally, knowledge of things that exist in separation from sensible matter, that is, the knowledge of things entirely supersensible, constitutes a third and higher type of theoretical science: "That physics, then, is a theoretical science, is plain from these considerations. Mathematics also, however, is theoretical; but whether its objects are immovable and separable from matter, is not at present clear; still, it is clear that *some* mathematical theorems *consider* them *qua* immovable and *qua* separable from matter. But if there is something which is eternal and immovable and separable, clearly the knowledge of it belongs to a theoretical science—not, however, to physics (for physics deals with certain movable things) nor to mathematics, but to a science prior to both."[1]

The broadest division of the objects that lend themselves to

[1] *Metaph.*, E 1,1026a6-13; *cf.* K 7,1064a2-b6.

the consideration of theoretical science is developed quite noticeably by the Stagirite against a general Platonic background. It
follows the grades of the Platonic division into the purely intelligible, the mathematical, and the sensible, as had been illustrated
by the simile of the divided line. The basic division into the mobile and the immobile goes back of course to Parmenides. Mobile
things are those of the sensible cosmos. Separate immobile things
are those that, like the Platonic Ideas, have real existence in
themselves apart from the sensible order and are entirely incapable of any change. If such immobile things do exist, they will
have to exist in complete separation from any intrinsic principle
of change, and in this sense they have to be characterized as
separate as well as immobile.

Between these two orders, the sensible and the entirely supersensible, are found the objects of mathematics. As the quantitative dimensions of sensible bodies, the mathematicals exist *in*
sensible things, and so are not "separate." Yet they are considered
by the mathematician as though they were found in separation
from any mobile principle. In this way they offer an immobile
object for his treatment. All the branches of mathematics are
regarded by Aristotle as a theoretical philosophy. Taken together
they in fact constitute one of the three theoretical philosophies.

Theoretical philosophy in general is given a higher rank as
knowledge than any practical or productive philosophy, because
it is an end in itself and so is not directed towards anything else
in a way that would give it a subordinate status. Among the theoretical sciences themselves, however, theology occupies the highest place of all, since it deals with the highest type of things:
"There must, then, be three theoretical philosophies, mathematics, physics, and what we may call theology, since it is
obvious that if the divine is present anywhere, it is present in
things of this sort. And the highest science must deal with the
highest genus. Thus, while the theoretical sciences are more to
be desired than the other sciences, this is more to be desired
than the other theoretical sciences" (*Metaph.*, E 1,1026a18-23).

A. NATURAL PHILOSOPHY

Natural Science.   The treatment of natural things in general is
undertaken by Aristotle in the eight books of the *Physics*. The

term "nature" in this respect is restricted somewhat arbitrarily but very effectively by the Stagirite to the sensible world. The etymology of the Greek word for nature (*physis*) allows the significations of either being or becoming. In its usage in the Presocratic fragments the term is found in both significations, though predominantly in the meaning of the fixed and stable constitution of a thing. It denotes most frequently what the thing *is*. In Plato the Ideas were similarly found "in nature," in the sense of immobile and permanent reality. Aristotle himself (*Metaph.*, Δ 4, 1014b18-1015a13) lists meanings of "nature" signifying a permanent principle, and acknowledges that by extension it may designate any kind of being; but in his own usage he prefers to restrict it to the sensible order. In accordance with the meaning "to grow," which the verb *phyomai* had taken on in regular Greek usage, he regards the notion of "becoming" or "birth" as primary in the term *physis,* and its extension outside the world of becoming as merely secondary. In this way "nature" as a technical term became restricted to the visible and tangible universe, and "natural" science or philosophy was limited to the investigation of the sensible world.

Dialectical Approach. Since a theoretical science proceeds from first principles that are found within the thing under investigation, the initial task of the philosophy of nature will be to discover its primary principles in the sensible things themselves. In accordance with the general directives of the Aristotelian logic, the process of their discovery will be dialectical, not demonstrative. The dialectical procedure, under the guidance of the logical knowledge that is presupposed in the hearers, investigates the labors of previous philosophers in their attempts to isolate the first principles of natural things. The discussion brings out many points of note about the physical universe. That universe is a plurality. It consists of substance and accidents. Sensible substance itself is found to be a plurality. Change is seen as a process from one contrary to the other, as from black to white, from sweet to bitter, from hot to cold. All the preceding philosophers appear to have agreed that contraries are in one way or another the principles of natural change. The primary contraries, therefore, may be expected to function as the first principles of natural things. But, according to the logical teachings, contraries do not constitute the substance of anything. They

310 THE FLOWERING OF GREEK PHILOSOPHY

are accidents, and so should require a substrate. Such a substrate, whether water, fire, air, or something intermediate, was in fact assumed by the early thinkers. The study of previous doctrines shows in this way that at least two basic elements, the primary contraries, are required to explain the sensible cosmos; and that at all events three, the primary contraries and the substrate, will be sufficient (*Ph.*, I,1-6).

Privation, Matter, Form. Having elucidated the pertinent problems through this dialectical survey, Aristotle proceeds to develop his own account. In any observable change there is always something underlying the change, *something that changes* from one characteristic to another. This is clear in all accidental changes. There is always a man, for instance, who becomes cultured. It is stone or bronze or gold that changes in shape to become a statue. The contraries in each case are the form to be acquired and the privation of that form on the part of the subject. A man who is *un*cultured becomes cultured. The subject, in this case a substance, man, changes from one contrary to the other.

The Aristotelian account is obvious enough in cases of a substance changing from one accidental contrary to another. It establishes the general nature of change. Change *within* the order of substance, however, cannot be observed directly, for its substrate is not immediately observable. It can be illustrated, though, by analogy with accidental change. Just as the bronze is to the statue or the wood to the bed, so within the order of substance itself there must be a matter (*hylê* 'wood') that has no form whatsoever. The bronze while changing preserved its own proper form of bronze, but when one substance changes into another it cannot preserve any form at all. There is no form whatsoever in the thing prior to the form by which it is a substance. In this way the Eleatic difficulties are solved. A thing comes to be, neither from being nor from not-being absolutely, but from qualified not-being, that is, from privation (*Ph.*, I 7-8).

While privation is of its very nature not-being (in the qualified sense just explained), matter in general is not-being only accidentally, since of itself it approaches in a way the permanence implied by the notion of substance (*ousia* 'being'). In one sense, of course, it does come to be and cease to be, but in another sense it does not. As containing the pertinent privation, it ceases to be in any change; but in its own nature, as potency to change, it does not cease to be and so is outside the order of becoming and ceasing to be. The substrate of generation and corruption—that is, of change within the category of substance—will accordingly in its own nature be potential and yet ingenerate and incorruptible. If it could come to be, it itself would have to have underlying it a first or primary substrate as one of its intrinsic principles. Such matter, then, is the primary and intrinsic substrate of generation. Out of it a thing is generated, in the sense of change that is not in the accidental order but in the substantial (*Ph.*, I 9). This is a radically different notion of substrate from that of the Platonic receptacle, which was not intrinsic to sensible things and was not a principle out of which they were made.

The only kind of forms with which natural philosophy deals are forms that are perishable by reason of having matter as their substrate. Forms that have no matter fall within the scope of the primary philosophy,[2] which is the Aristotelian theology.

Nature.   In the light of these considerations, natural things, or things constituted by nature, are those that have within themselves their principle of motion and of rest. Such things are, for example, animals, plants, earth, air, fire, and water. Artificial things, on the contrary, like a bed or a coat, do not have as such that principle within them. Only the wood or the fibre, that is, the material of which they are composed, has such a principle. The term "nature," then, properly designates the intrinsic principles, in the substantial order, of motion and rest. Nature is defined as "*a source or cause of being moved and of being at rest in that to which it belongs primarily*, in virtue of itself and not in virtue of a concomitant attribute" (*Ph.*, II 1,192b21-23). Everything that "has a nature" or is "by nature" is therefore in the category of substance. The absolutely primary and formless substrate or *matter* that is the subject of change in the order of substance is "nature." Likewise the *form* that is given in the definition of any sensible substance is "nature." These two alone are properly called "nature." The composites that they constitute, like man, are "by nature" or "natural things." Of the two constitu-

---

[2] *Ph.*, I 9,192a34-36. *Cf.* II 2,194b14-15. For a general study of the Aristotelian physical doctrine, see Augustin Mansion, *Introduction à la Physique Aristotélicienne*, 2nd ed., (Louvain and Paris, 1946); for a study from the viewpoint of development, see H. E. Runner, *The Development of Aristotle Illustrated from the Earliest Books of the Physics* (Kampen, [1951]).

ents, the form is more properly nature than the matter, because it is the actuality, while the matter is only the potency; and anything is more properly said to be its actuality rather than its potentiality. "Nature," accordingly, is twofold—form and matter (*Ph.*, II 1). In this way the term "nature" is restricted by Aristotle to the sensible world, and yet is made to denote fundamentally the stable and incorruptible principles that are intrinsic to the things of that changing cosmos.

The Four Causes.   Matter and form, therefore, are the two intrinsic causes of a sensible substance. Extrinsic causes are the primary origin of change or of coming to rest, as for instance the father is the cause of the child; and that for the sake of which something is done, as health is the cause of taking a walk (*Ph.*, II 3). These two extrinsic causes became known in Peripatetic tradition as the efficient and final causes, and the other two as the material and the formal.

Chance, Spontaneity.   Chance is not the cause of anything whatsoever, if one understands "cause" without qualification. By way of accident, though, it can be a cause. It consists merely in the occurrence of some unforeseen causality that changes a planned course of action. A man, for instance, may go to a place for an entirely different purpose, but may thereby meet a man from whom he collects money. In that way, because of his journey, he gets the money by chance. Chance, accordingly, is reserved for the sphere of deliberately planned actions. Corresponding to it in the lower orders of activity is spontaneity. Both chance and spontaneity, because they are causes only by way of accident, presuppose intelligence and nature as *per se* causes (*Ph.*, 5-6).

Motion.   Since nature is the principle of motion, it requires for its understanding a sufficient grasp of the meaning of motion or change. Motion or change is found in all the categories of being. It is the passage from the potential to the actual. It is an actuality, for it means more than just the potential subject of change. Yet it is an actuality that does not at all remain permanent as that actuality, even for the smallest part of time, but is actual only in so far as it is passing into further act, that is, in so far as it is potenital to something more. Hence arose the celebrated though cryptic Aristotelian definition of motion: *"The fulfilment of what exists potentially, in so far as it exists poten-*

tially, is motion . . ." (*Ph.,* III 1,201a10-11). In the category of
quality motion or change is called alteration; in the category of
quantity, increase and decrease; and in the category of place,
locomotion (*Ph.,* III 1-3).
The Unlimited. Time and magnitude, both found in the
sensible world, are divisible without limit. This introduces the
problem of the unlimited or infinite, the problem so tellingly exploited by Zeno. The unlimited is shown to be an attribute of
number or magnitude. It therefore belongs to the category of
quantity, and so cannot in Pythagorean fashion be the substance
of things. One may ask, though, whether any body can be unlimited in extent. A compound body cannot be unlimited in this
way, if its elements are all limited; and if any one of its elements
were unlimited, that element would annihilate all the others. The
simple bodies, on the other hand, are all observed to be limited.
By the simple bodies are quite evidently meant the Empedoclean
elements, air, earth, fire, and water. A further argument, based
similarly upon ancient concepts, shows that the accepted notions
of the absolute differences of place—up-down, before-behind,
right-left—are incompatible with the existence of an unlimited
body (*Ph.,* III,4-5).

On the other hand, time and magnitude are divisible without
limit, and number may increase without limit. Yet actually one
will always have a limited magnitude, and a limited number of
divided parts: "Yet the sum of the parts taken will not exceed
every determinate magnitude, just as in the direction of division
every determinate magnitude is surpassed in smallness and there
will be a smaller part" (*Ph.,* III 6,206b18-20). In this way the
definition of the unlimited is reached: "*A quantity is infinite if it
is such that we can always take a part outside what has been
already taken*" (*Ph.,* III 6,207a7-8). Precisely as unlimited it is
incomplete. It pertains accordingly to matter rather than to form
and as such is unknowable. Consequently, a body unlimited by
way of increase cannot actually exist, for it could not have a
form: "For the matter and the infinite are contained inside what
contains them, while it is the form which contains" (*Ph.,* III
7,207a35-b1). Any body that would be unlimited in extent (unlimited by way of increase) would have to have some form containing it; but a form is definite, and so would render the un-

limited impossible. Number, moreover, is a plurality of "ones," and so must consist in a certain definite quantity of them. Therefore it will always be actually limited, though potentially unlimited, since a greater number than any definite quantity can always be thought. The fact that the infinite can be used in mathematics and can be the object of thought does not at all require the actual existence of anything unlimited in extent, because the potentially unlimited character of magnitude and number suffices as a foundation for that way of thinking (*Ph.,* III, 7-8).

The notions of matter and form used in this discussion show that for Aristotle matter as such is unknowable. The form is considered to be definite and knowable. This means that the whole intelligible content of a sensible thing is its form. Form for Aristotle, consequently, means content. The Aristotelian contrast between form and matter, therefore, is not to be understood as a contrast between form and content. Rather, "form-content" is contrasted with unintelligible matter. One should be careful not to equate the Aristotelian matter with the notions of matter prevalent since the time of Descartes, in which matter is regarded as extension or as something extended of itself, and so knowable in itself. Matter in the substantial order for Aristotle is not of itself extended and is entirely unknowable in itself. Modern conceptions of matter are, from the Aristotelian viewpoint, conceptions of something already possessing form.

Place.   The Stagirite finds that preceding thinkers, except in a way Plato, left no doctrine on place, either as regards its problems or as regards their solution. He accepts the notion of the six absolute directions—"up" is the direction in which fire and light things are borne, "down" is that in which earth and the heavy naturally tend, and so on. This conception involves different places, absolutely distinct from one another, and distinct from the bodies that are necessarily in some place but may enter or leave any particular place. Place is accordingly separate from the sensible things and contains those things. It has to be immobile, on account of its absolute character—a place remains always the same. It is therefore the innermost containing boundary, considered as absolute and unchanging. Consequently *"the innermost motionless boundary of what contains is place"*

(*Ph.*, IV 4, 212a20-21). The sensible universe, which has no containing surface surrounding it, is according to this conception not in place. Indirectly, though, it may be said to be in place because its parts are in place. Similarly the soul may be said to be indirectly in place, because its body is in place (*Ph.*, IV 1-5).

The Void. The void is conceived as a place with nothing in it. It is not, as the Eleatics claimed, required to account for movement, "for bodies may simultaneously make room for one another, though there is no interval separate and apart from the bodies that are in movement" (*Ph.*, IV 7,214a29-31). In fact, the movement of things excludes a void, for the void as void admits no differences of place; and different places are required to explain the movement of sensible things. Nor do the rare and the dense indicate that there is a void, since the ultimate matter is potentially the same in both cases, even though found respectively under the two opposite accidental characteristics, rare and dense (*Ph.*, IV 6-9).

Time. The nature of time is found to be divisible, and therefore to consist of parts. Always "one part of it has been and is not, while the other is going to be and is not yet" (*Ph.*, IV 10, 217b33-34). The "now," which divides the past from the future and limits them both, is not a part. It is an indivisible, in contrast to a part that is always divisible. Time cannot be the same as movement, because any movement can become faster or slower and is found only where the moving thing is; but time is everywhere, and is what defines fastness and slowness. Yet time cannot exist without movement and change. Time, in fact, is a numbering of motion. It is the "number of motion in respect of 'before' and 'after'" (*Ph.*, IV 11,219b2). Accordingly, where there is no motion there is no time. But only through the indivisible "now" do the parts of time exist, just as motion exists only through a body: "But the 'now' corresponds to the body that is carried along, as time corresponds to the motion. For it is by means of the body that is carried along that we become aware of the 'before and after' in the motion, and if we regard these as countable we get the 'now.' Hence in these also the 'now' as substratum remains the same (for it is what is before and after in the movement), but what is predicated of it is different; for it is in so far as the 'before and after' is numerable that we get the 'now'" (*Ph.*,

IV 11,219b22-28). The "now," accordingly, both divides and continues time, somewhat as a point may be both end and beginning in a line. Time as the measure of motion is continuous, and is divisible without limit. It will last as long as motion. It is best computed from the regular circular motion of the heaven, because as a measure this is the most readily known (*Ph.*, IV 10-14).

The Primary Movent. The last four books of the *Physics* discuss problems concerning motion. The seventh and eighth books seek the highest efficient cause of motion in the sensible universe. Everything that is being moved, they show, is being moved by something else. This is proved in Book Seven by the essential divisibility of motion. Motion depends essentially on its parts, and so nothing can be in motion essentially and primarily, that is, of itself: ". . . for that which is in motion will always be divisible, and if a part of it is not in motion the whole must be at rest" (*Ph.*, VII 1,242a14-15). The eighth book establishes the same proposition by induction. Further, in point of time there cannot be an absolutely first movent, because time, which is dependent on motion, is eternal. Any given "now" is the end of a preceding part of time, and so always presupposes a preceding time. It is similarly the beginning of the future and so always involves a future time. Correspondingly, every motion requires a preceding process and results in a subsequent process.

Since the original cause of any motion cannot be something that is being moved by another, it has to be a self-movent; and within it, what primarily imparts motion has to be a part that is immobile. These immobile movents are as a rule perishable.[3] Because motion is eternal and continuous, the first movent or first movents will have to be eternal. Movents that are able to be or not to be could not either singly or in their sum total account for the necessary continuous and eternal motion of the cosmos; for there would have to be something else to explain their coming to be and perishing. The first movent or movents, accordingly, will be the cause of the motion of the other movents. One such movent is preferable to many, and a limited number of them to an unlimited (*Ph.*, VIII 1-6).

---

[3] As the immobile part of a self-movent, Aristotle understands the souls of plants and animals, and finally the imperishable souls of heavens; see *Ph.*, VIII 6,258b16-259a2; 9,265b32-34.

The Primary Motion. The primary motion is local motion, because local motion is always presupposed by the other kinds, that is, by alteration, augmentation, and generation and perishing. The only single and continuous eternal motion, however, is circular motion; for circular motion is the sole motion that never varies in direction. The only motion of an absolutely primary self-movent, therefore, will be a circular motion. This motion requires that the primary immobile movent be without parts and without magnitude. Any magnitude that it had would have to be either limited or unlimited. But its magnitude cannot be unlimited, for an unlimited magnitude cannot exist; nor can it be limited, for a limited magnitude cannot possess the unlimited power necessary to cause eternal motion, motion throughout unlimited time. Circular motion is fastest at the circumference, and so locates the primary movent in the circumference of the universe (*Ph.*, VIII 7-10).

The primary immobile movent that Aristotle has in mind is evidently enough the soul of the outermost heaven. Any animated thing, plant or animal, is a self-movent and its soul originates motion. Such perishable self-movents, however, require a higher and imperishable efficient cause to account for the eternal series of generations and passings-away. The operative notion in the Aristotelian demonstration of the primary efficient cause is therefore the *eternity* of the cosmic processes. The first efficient cause is necessary, not to explain the existence of things, but to account for the eternal character of their motion. The argument is based clearly upon the eternity of cosmic motion and of time. Without that basis it is no longer the Aristotelian proof.

Though the sensible world as such is not animated for Aristotle, yet it is contained within an animated sphere, and all its motions are affected by the soul of that sphere. To this limited but noteworthy extent is the Stagirite still thinking in the framework provided by the ancient Milesian thinkers—the sensible universe as a whole does not require an *efficient* cause outside itself, and there is no temporal origin of its motion.

The Heavens. The unchanging circular motion of the heavenly bodies, considered as established by ages of recorded observation, shows that this is the type of motion proper to them. Circular motion, however, has no contrary. The nature to which circular motion is proper will, accordingly, be exempt from contraries. It is therefore not subject to generation or perishing, or to quantitative or qualitative changes, because all these require contraries, as has been shown. The nature of the heavenly bodies, then, will be different from any of the basic sublunary elements, fire, air, earth, and water, all of which are subject to alteration and to generation and perishing. It will be a nature over and above those four, and it is identified by Aristotle with the *aither* of Greek tradition, now sharply distinguished from fire. Besides being ingenerate and incorruptible and unalterable, it is neither light nor heavy, because it is subject to neither upward nor downward motion (*Cael.*, I 2-5).

The Soul.   The fragments of the lost dialogue *Eudemus* seem to represent Aristotle's earliest known discussion on the soul. The dramatic setting of the *Eudemus* is related by Cicero (*Div. ad Brut.*, I,25,53). Eudemus of Cyprus, a friend of Aristotle, was apparently dying of sickness. In a dream he was told that he would soon recover, that in a few days the local tyrant would die, and that in the fifth year after this sickness Eudemus himself would return home. The first two predictions were immediately fulfilled, but at the end of the fifth year Eudemus fell in battle without having come back to his native city. The dream was interpreted, accordingly, as prophesying the return of his soul to its home after it left the body in death.—This implies the notion of a soul that survives the body and can live its true life apart from the body, quite in Platonic fashion. Other testimonia[4] speak of the soul existing before the body and of its remembering after death its experiences in the body, and of metempsychosis in general. One of the speakers in the dialogue quotes, apparently with approval, a saying "that not to be born is the best of all, and death better than life; . . . the next best, and the best achievable for men, is, having been born, to die as soon as may be."[5] Aristotle, in fact, is reported as teaching that life apart from the body is

---

[4] See Ross, *Select Fragments* (Oxford, 1952), Eudemus 4,5,11,12 (pp. 17-23.).

[5] *Fr.* 40,1481a43-b16; tr. Ross, *Select Fragments*, Eudemus 6.

natural to souls, like health, while life in the body is unnatural, contrary to nature, like disease.[6]

On the other hand, the Stagirite is reported to have said in the same dialogue *Eudemus* that the soul is a form.[7] This expression suggests a doctrine quite different from the Platonic. The doctrine is developed carefully in the treatise *De Anima.* After pursuing the regular introductory dialectic (*De An.*, I) and noting that "by life we mean self-nutrition and growth" (*De An.*, II 1, 412a14), the notion of the soul reached by the treatise is "a substance in the sense of the form of a natural body having life potentially within it" (a19-21). As a form in the order of substance the form will be the very first actuality of the matter that it informs, and with that matter it will constitute an organic body as a single whole. Every soul, accordingly, is "the first grade of actuality of a natural organized body" (b5-6). This means definitely that the soul and the matter that it informs are not two different substances each complete in its own order, as the Platonic and all previous Greek conceptions of soul and body would imply, but that together they constitute only one substance, the living body. Their union is but another instance of a first form and absolutely formless matter constituting a single natural entity (b5-9). To inform and constitute a body, then, is the very nature of soul. In no sense could its presence in the body be described, according to this doctrine, as "unnatural." Rather, separate existence for a soul would seem unnatural and impossible.

Further consideration extends the notion of "life" to sensation and thinking. Of these the soul is the first principle. It is the essential form "by or with which primarily we live, perceive and think" (*De An.*, II, 2, 414a12-13). Its powers or faculties are "the nutritive, the appetitive, the sensory, the locomotive, and the power of thinking" (*De An.*, II 3, 414a31-32). Plants have the first kind, animals the second and third and some the fourth, and man has the last. These classify *all* the types of soul (a32-b22).

Knowledge. Knowledge is described in terms of identity of

[6] *Fr.* 35,1480b14-15. On the interpretation of these fragments in a Platonic sense, see W. W. Jaeger, *Aristotle* (Oxford, 1934), pp. 39-53. For the case against the presence of any doctrine of Ideas or of anamnesis in them, see R. Phillipson, "Diogene di Enoanda e Aristotele," *Rivista di Filologia e d'Istruzione Classica,* LXVI (1938), 242-245.

[7] *Fr.* 42,1482b36-38.

knower and thing known: "Actual knowledge is identical with its object: potential knowledge in the individual is in time prior to actual knowledge . . ." (*De An.*, III, 7,431a1-2). In the potential state things known are in the mind "just as characters may be said to be on a writing-tablet on which as yet nothing actually stands written" (*De An.*, III 4,430a1-2). The mind therefore "is in a sense potentially whatever is thinkable, though actually it is nothing until it has thought" (429b30-31), that is, it is actually none of its objects before it knows them. The same doctrine holds correspondingly for sensation. Accordingly, "the soul is in a way all existing things" (*De An.*, III 8,431b21).

Aristotle finds that in point of fact the presence of an image is always a condition of human thought: "To the thinking soul images serve as if they were contents of perception. . . . That is why the soul never thinks without an image" (*De An.*, III 7, 431a14-17).

Mind.   Mind is shown to be separate from matter because it is not hindered by strong stimulation as in the case of the senses, because it can think itself reflexively, and because it can attain the essential character of things and the abstract mathematicals (*De An.*, III, 4,429a18-b22). However, the preceding doctrine of cognition requires that mind be twofold: "And in fact mind as we have described it is what it is by virtue of becoming all things, while there is another which is what it is by virtue of making all things: this is a sort of positive state like light; for in a sense light makes potential colours into actual colours. Mind in this sense of it is separable, impassible, unmixed. . . . When mind is set free from its present conditions it appears as just what it is and nothing more: this alone is immortal and eternal (we do not, however, remember its former activity because, while mind in this sense is impassible, mind as passive is destructible), and without it nothing thinks" (*De An.*, III 5,430a14-25).

This short and extremely difficult passage has given rise to the traditional distinction between the active and the passive intellects and the many controversies concerning the two. Aristotle's assertion that the passive mind is perishable and that the other alone is immortal, is explicit. However, if the notion of "remember" has the same sense here as it seems to have had in the *Eudemus* (*Fr.* 35,1480b9;18), it means that all remnants of life on earth are entirely erased from the surviving mind, and that for the Stagirite there is nothing one could call personal immortality. The separate mind would be a "part of the soul" (*De An.*, III 4,429a10) only in the fashion of an extrinsic efficient cause necessary for thinking. It alone of all things pertaining to man is divine and it alone enters from outside (*GA*, II 3,736b27-28). The difficulties in the Aristotelian notion of the human soul remain quite evident. As a soul it is of its very nature an actuality of matter, and so cannot have existence apart from matter. On the other hand, its intellectual operations require an active principle that exists separately from matter and independently of matter. No satisfactory solution of these difficulties is found in the Aristotelian text. The fragments of the *Eudemus* present a conception of personal immortality that is apparently in irreconcilable opposition to the doctrine of the *De Anima*. In the *Nicomachean Ethics* (I 13,1102a23-1103a3) Aristotle does not hesitate to make use of, for his purposes of the moment, what seem to be Platonic conceptions of the soul that were familiar to his hearers. To what extent the dialogue form of the *Eudemus* allowed him to put into the mouths of the speakers notions to which he himself did not adhere, is a point on which the fragments do not provide sufficient information.

B. MATHEMATICS

The next type of theoretical philosophy, mathematics,[8] deals with the quantitative properties of sensible things as considered by the mind in abstraction from the things in which those properties exist. Accordingly, "the mind when it is thinking the objects of Mathematics thinks as separate elements which do not exist separate" (*De An.*, III 8,431b15-16). This process renders the mathematical objects immobile. Their nature is such that they are in no way falsified by such separation and immobility, "for

[8] On the Stagirite's mathematical views, see T. L. Heath, *Mathematics in Aristotle* (Oxford, 1949); H. G. Apostle, *Aristotle's Philosophy of Mathematics* (Chicago, 1952). W. D. Ross, *Aristotle's Prior and Posterior Analytics* (Oxford, 1949), p. 59, shows the falsity of the rather usual view that Aristotle was lacking in mathematical ability. Works with mathematical titles are listed in the ancient catalogues, but no genuine Aristotelian treatise on a mathematical subject has survived.

in thought they are separable from motion, and it makes no difference, nor does any falsity result, if they are separated" (*Ph.*, II
2,193b34-35). Although the mathematicals, on account of this
separation from sensible things, have no physical matter, they
nevertheless admit plurality—there can be many semicircles, for
instance, of the same size. The mathematicals have therefore
what Aristotle calls intelligible matter (*Metaph.*, Z 11,1037a4-5),
just as in the logical order the genera function as intelligible
matter to the species (*Metaph.*, H 6,1045a7-35).

Even though the procedure of mathematics is through abstractions, it admits application to the things of the sensible
world from which the mathematicals were originally taken. In
this way it gives rise to the "more physical" of the mathematical
sciences, like optics, harmonics, and astronomy (*Ph.*, II 2,194a7-
12). These sciences, then, are for Aristotle essentially mathematical, not physical. They treat of the same things as do the
physical sciences, but they subordinate them to mathematics, and
in that quantitative fashion provide *propter quid* knowledge of
them (*APo.*, I 13,78b34-79a3). The case is the same for the science of mechanics, and apparently will be the same for any
similar science that is based upon quantitative measurement.

C. THEOLOGICAL SCIENCE

Science of Beings *qua* Beings.   The highest type of theoretical
science, treating as it does of things that are both separate and
immobile, is called by Aristotle theological or primary philosophy.
It is presented by the Stagirite in the treatises that were later
collected under the title *The Metaphysics*.[9] In the main series of
these treatises it is introduced by the usual dialectical consideration of preceding efforts (*Metaph.*, A), issuing into an especially
elaborate listing of the *aporiae* or difficulties that hinder one's
approach to the science (*Metaph.*, B). The motive urged for its
pursuit is the natural desire that all men have to *know*, a desire
that can be satisfied only through understanding things by means
of their highest principles and causes, and that is aroused by

[9] On the order of this collection, see A.-H. Chroust, "The Composition
of Aristotle's *Metaphysics*," *New Scholasticism*, XXVIII (1954), 58-100;
for a doctrinal introduction, W. Marx, "The Meaning of Aristotle's 'Onto-
logy,'" (The Hague, 1954).

wonder at things of which the cause is not apparent (*Metaph.*, A 1-2). The highest causes are shown to be the causes of things according to their universal aspect of being. The primary philosophy, accordingly, will be the science of being *qua* being (Γ 1,1003a21-32). It will be a science that treats of things not in the light of physical principles like matter and form, or of quantitative principles like numbers and dimensions, but of principles that extend universally through and beyond the physical and mathematical orders to all things that have the aspect of being.

Parmenidean Background. In so designating the science, Aristotle implies that his predecessors who sought the elements of things were in reality seeking these highest principles. In another metaphysical treatise, that seemingly is not part of the main series, he brands as obsolete the method of thinkers who tried to account for plurality by setting up in opposition to the "being" of Parmenides a single nature that was called "not-being," even though it was endowed with existence: "They thought it necessary to prove that that which is not is; for only thus—of that which is *and something else*—could the things that are be composed, if they are many" (N 2, 1089a5-6). Aristotle regards this way of placing the problem as outdated. In the light of his own established doctrine of the *Categories*, which shows that there are various types of being, he objects that just *one* single nature, like the alleged "not-being," could not account for so many different kinds of being: "But it is strange, or rather impossible, that the coming into play of a single thing should bring it about that part of that which is a 'this,' part a 'such,' part a 'so much,' part a 'here'" (a12-15). What is opposite to being, then, cannot consist in just one single nature. Rather, such "not-being" will be as multiple in nature as the categories of being—for instance, "not being a man" (substance), "not being straight" (quality), and so on. The Platonic Form "not-being" would merely provide one more type of being. It itself would be a different type of being, just as substance and quality are different types of being. Being may also be considered as the true. In this sense it has a corresponding "not-being" in the false, for what is false is said not to be. Further, being may be taken in the sense of the actual. The opposite "not-being" in that case is the potential, the principle from which generation and change proceed, as for instance man proceeds from what is actually not man but is potentially man, and white proceeds from what is not white actually but is so potentially (N 2, 1089a15-b8).

These three senses of "not-being" correspond to three of the four ways in which being was signified for Aristotle. The four ways were: 1) being *per accidens,* for example in "The musician builds a house," where it is merely accidental or just happens that the builder in this case is a musician; 2) being as distributed in the categories, which is being *per se;* 3) being as the true; and 4) being in the sense of the actual as compared with potential being (Δ 7,1017a7-b9). Of these the first way, being *per accidens,* is itself regarded as something quite close to "not-being," because it lacks the necessity and definiteness implied by "being," and so cannot be an object of knowledge (E 2, 1026b21-1027a26). It therefore need not be set up in contrast to not-being. Being as the true is not in things but in the mind, and accordingly is not the principal type of being. Like being *per accidens,* it connects or separates the kinds of being that are found in the categories. The actual and the potential are found spread throughout the various predicaments. Being as expressed in the categories will consequently provide the fundamental way for understanding how things can be different and yet all come under the one designation of being.

Beings Through Reference. The doctrine of the *Categories* had shown that "being" is predicated of a number of things in various ways. Yet, Aristotle finds, being is always expressed in reference to a certain definite nature: "There are many senses in which a thing may be said to 'be,' but all that 'is' is related to one central point, one definite kind of thing (*physin*), and is not said to 'be' by a mere ambiguity. Everything which is healthy is related to health, one thing in the sense that it preserves health, another in the sense that it produces it, another in the sense that it is a symptom of health, another because it is capable of it" (Γ 2,1003a33-b1). Just as health itself is present only in the disposition of a living organism, so, according to this doctrine, being will be present as a nature only in its primary instance. Health itself is not present in the food that causes it or in the exercise that preserves it. These secondary instances are not healthy in themselves, but are called healthy because of the relation they bear to the health in the living organism. Similarly the nature of being is found only in one category, substance (*ousia*). The other categories, the accidents, are called being because they are affections of substance. Motion likewise may be called being because it is an affection of being *qua* being (K 3,1061a8-10), that is, of substance or of things named being through reference to substance. Privations and negations may also be called being on account of their relations to the nature of being; even not-being is in this way expressed in terms of being. Accordingly, the science that treats of the nature of being will treat of all these things, just as the science of health treats of all things that are called healthy. It will likewise treat of the "forms" of being, such as unity, sameness, likeness, and their contraries (Γ 2,1003b5-1004a1).

The whole problem is quite clearly drawn up against the Parmenidean background. As with the Eleatics and with Gorgias, there is no thought of denying the presence of qualities and so on in the sensible cosmos. The question centers on the right of such things to be called being. Being is understood in Parmenidean fashion to denote the immobile, the permanent, and the positive. The substance remains, while its accidents come and go. Considered in relation to its accidents, substance exhibits the permanence that characterizes being; and in contrast to privations and negations, it designates a positive nature. In substance, then, as its Greek name *ousia* implies, is to be located the nature of being, being *qua* being.

These considerations suggest, however, that the nature of being cannot primarily be located in sensible substance. Sensible substances are subject to generation and passing away. Even though they are permanent relatively to accidents, they are not absolutely permanent. They are not the entirely immobile and separate entities with which the theological science proposes to deal. Is there then within substance itself a corresponding order of reference, in such a way that material substances will be only secondary instances while the absolutely separate and immobile constitutes the primary instance of substance? There are suggestions in the Aristotelian text that such is the case.[10] Before this question can be approached, though, the existence and nature of the separate substances have to be established. In the meantime, the principle

[10] Γ 2,1004a3-4; 3,1005a33-35; Λ 7,1072a31-32.

that the science that treats of the primary instance treats likewise of all the secondary instances, has been made clear. If the
separate substances are the absolutely primary instance of being,
the science that has as its subject the separate entities will be by
that very fact the science that treats universally of beings as
beings.[11]

Sensible Substance. The central books of the *Metaphysics*
deal with sensible substance from the viewpoint of being. Because
form means determination and actuality, matter indeterminateness and potentiality, they find that in such composites of form
and matter the form is prior in the order of being to both matter
and composite: "Therefore if the form is prior to the matter and
more real, it will be prior also to the compound of both, for the
same reason" (Z 3, 1029a5-7). From the standpoint of the primary philosophy the form, and not as in a logical context the
composite individual, is the primary substance: ". . . for there is
no formula of it [the concrete substance] with its matter, for this
is indefinite, but there is a formula of it with reference to its
primary substance—e.g. in the case of man the formula of the
soul—, for the substance is the indwelling form, from which and
the matter the so-called concrete substance is derived; . . ." (Z
11,1037a27-30). On account of its actual and definite character the
form is the primary cause of the thing's being, just as it is the
cause of the thing's unity: ". . . it is the *cause* which makes *this*
thing flesh and *that* a syllable. And similarly in all other cases.
And this is the *substance* of each thing (for this is the primary
cause of its being); . . ." (Z 17,1041b26-28). As the form is the
actuality and perfection of the thing, it is in this way the end or
final cause of the process of becoming: "Further, matter exists in
a potential state, just because it may come to its form; and when
it exists *actually*, then it is in its form. . . . For the action is the
end, and the actuality *(energeia)* is the action. And so even the
word 'actuality' is derived from 'action,' and points to complete

[11] E 1,1026a29-32; K 7,1064b11-14. For this interpretation of the texts,
see P. Merlan, *From Platonism to Neoplatonism* (The Hague, 1953), pp.
132-181; against it, A. Mansion, "L'Objet de la Science Philosophique
Suprême d'après Aristote, Métaphysique, E,I," in *Mélanges . . . Offerts à
Mgr. Diès* (Paris, 1956), pp. 151-168. Of the basic opposites stressed by
Merlan, pp. 135 ff., "not-being" is reduced by reference, like the accidents,
to the primary instance of being (Γ 2,1003b7-10).

reality *(entelecheia)"* (Θ 8,1050a15-23). These two words "act" *(energeia)* and "perfection" *(entelecheia)* are the peculiarly Aristotelian terms for form.

Definiteness and actuality, according to this reasoning, are the marks of being. Both are given to the matter and also to the composite by the form. In this way the form is the primary entity in the sensible thing and the cause of its being. It is also the principle by which the thing is known, in conformity with the Parmenidean and Platonic tenets that knowledge is grounded upon being. Actual knowledge, therefore, will always be of something definite. It will always be of a "this" *(tode ti)*, an Aristotelian term that designated primarily the form and secondarily the composite individual as made definite by the form.[12] This knowledge is found *able* to be applied to indefinitely numerous individuals of the same species, and so is potentially universal: "For knowledge, like the verb 'to know', means two things, of which one is potential and one actual. The potency, being, as matter, universal and indefinite, deals with the universal and indefinite; but the actuality, being definite, deals with a definite object,—being a 'this', it deals with a 'this'" (M 10,1087a15-18). The one Aristotelian term *eidos*, accordingly, can when taken in an actual sense mean the definite *form*, and when taken in a potential sense can mean the indefinite and universal *species*. Because a universal lacks the definiteness and actuality that characterize being, it cannot from the viewpoint of the primary philosophy be *ousia* or substance, even though in the logical order it functions as a secondary substance: "But man and horse and terms which are thus applied to individuals, but universally, are not substance but something composed of this particular formula and this particular matter treated as universal; . . ." (Z 10, 1035b27-30).

Separate Substance. Definiteness and actuality, by which being is characterized in the Aristotelian inquiry, can hardly allow sensible form to be the absolutely primary substance or primary instance of being. As act of a potency sensible form is not pure actuality, and as capable of indefinite multiplication in matter it involves the indefinite universal. The whole movement

---

[12] See *De An.*, II 1,412a8-9. For discussion of this topic, see A. Preiswerk, "Das Einzelne bei Platon und Aristoteles," *Philol.*, Suppl. XXXII, 1 (1939); A. M. de Vos, "Het 'Eidos' als 'Eerste Substantie' in de Metaphysica van Aristoteles," *Tijdschrift voor Philosophie*, IV (1942), 57-102.

of the primary philosophy points in the direction of substances entirely separate from matter and so purely actual and definite. But the main series of the treatises in the *Metaphysics* does not contain this further development of the theme. Instead, a detached treatise, Book Lambda, proves from the necessarily eternal cosmic motion established in the *Physics* the existence of separate substance. A thing whose nature is potential may possibly not be, and so could not be the cause of the necessity in the eternal movement: "Further, even if it acts, this will not be enough, if its essence is potency; for there will not be *eternal* movement, since that which is potentially may possibly not be. There must, then, be such a principle, whose very essence is actuality. Further, then, these substances must be without matter; for they must be eternal, if *anything* is eternal. Therefore they must be actuality" (Λ 6,1071b17-22).

The separate substances, then, are entirely immaterial, for they have no potency whatsoever. They are by no means hypostatized universals, but are definite forms, different in their very nature from sensible things that are capable of universalization. Act, accordingly, is equated with form by Aristotle, and matter is equated with potency. As entirely immaterial act, separate substance is cognitive; for cognition means having a form in some way without matter. Separate substance possesses itself in this way, and so may be described as a "thinking on thinking" (Λ 9,1074b34-35), since with it the thinking subject and the object that is being thought are one and the same (7,1072b20-23). As "the actuality of thought is life" (1072b26-27), this highest and pure actuality of separate substance is the best and most divine eternal life. It consists entirely in self-contemplation. Thinking about any other object would mean dependence on that object. It would introduce potency into the nature of separate substance and so destroy its pure actuality (9,1074b18-35).

Pure actuality, then, is for Aristotle finite immaterial form. Its unicity or plurality is not of major concern to the primary philosophy. The number of separate substances is determined on the findings of the astronomers. Separate substance moves the spheres through being desired (7,1072b3), that is, by way of final causality. No other way of causing motion is possible for it, because efficient causality would bring it in some way outside itself and destroy its finite perfection. Every original motion in the heavens, accordingly, will require a special separate movent. The number of such original motions is left to the astronomers, who are found to place it at forty-seven or fifty-five. There is of course strict order in these motions, and the cause of the simple movement of the outermost sphere will be the primary movent, another will be the second, and so on, according to the movements of the stars (8,1073a14-1074a14).

Incomplete Treatment. The *Metaphysics*, as should be evident enough, does not give a complete and fully organized treatment of its subject. But it makes fairly clear the general movement of the Aristotelian theological science. Being is taken against the immediate historical background as denoting the permanent, the unchangeable, the definite. The problem is how the passing, changing, partially indefinite things of the sensible universe are beings. The primary philosophy shows first that within sensible things substance is the primary instance of being, and the accidents and privations and negations and changes are secondary instances. Further, within sensible substance itself, form is the primary instance, matter and the composite are secondary instances. The final step would be that as regards form the primary instance is separate form. Separate form would thereby be the absolutely primary instance of being, and all other things would be beings on account of their reference to it through final causality. In any case, the primary instance of substance and so of being is for Aristotle form as finite act. In form alone is to be found the true nature of being, with its permanent and definite characteristics. All else is being through reference to form.

Being and the Mobile. From the things that are beyond the order of place and time, things that are divine and absolutely immobile and eternal, being is derived for Aristotle in varying degrees to all other things.[13] These latter attain as best they can the permanence of being through imitating, by the perpetuation or cyclic continuation of the same species in perishable and changing individuals, the abiding formal character of immobile substance. By way of this continuity the status of being is achieved in things that do not of their own nature have being, things in

[13] *Cael.*, I 9,279a17-30. *Cf. GC*, II 10, 336a31-337a17; *GA*, II 1,731b31-35; *De An.*, II 4,415a26-b7.

the realm of generation: ". . . but not all things can possess 'being,' since they are too far removed from the 'originative source.' God therefore adopted the remaining alternative, and fulfilled the perfection of the universe by making coming-to-be uninterrupted: for the greatest possible coherence would thus be secured to existence, because that 'coming-to-be should itself come-to-be perpetually' is the closest approximation to eternal being" (*GC* II 10,336b30-34). In this way the eternally stable characteristic of the Parmenidean being is retained by Aristotle, and yet is carried over in various degrees to the world of sensible things. Instead of setting up an unintelligible opposite of being, like darkness for Parmenides, or a physical opposite of being, like the void for the atomists, or a single intelligible opposite like the form of otherness for Plato, the Stagirite has in effect ranged all changeable natures under the opposite of being, and has found them sharing in being to the extent in which they seek and imitate the permanent. Being, accordingly, is participated by the mobile in varying degrees. Accidents are being in comparison with accidental motion, substance is being in comparison with accidents, imperishable bodies in comparison with the perishable.[14] Sensible substance (*Metaph.*, K 3,1061a8-10) and also being as spread throughout the categories (E 4,1027b31-1028a4) may therefore be regarded as being *qua* being, in comparison with what is subsequent to them, respectively, in the derivation of being. But being *qua* being in its primary instance, absolutely speaking, and as the subject of the primary philosophy, is the eternal and entirely immobile nature of the separate substances (E 1,1026a10-32).

Being and Plurality.   The Aristotelian doctrine of form as act is based upon the forms perceived in the sensible universe. These are all definite natures, each differentiated in itself from other forms. From a study of them is evolved the tenet that being is primarily located in form as act, with the result that the primary instance of being is placed in finite form. This understanding of

[14] In the second book of the literary work *On Philosophy*, Aristotle is reported to have developed a proof of a supreme instance of being from the grades of goodness found in the things that exist: "In general, where there is a better there is a best. Since, then, among existing things one is better than another, there is also something that is best, which will be the divine." *Fr.* 15,1476b22-24; tr. Ross, *Select Fragments*, On Philosophy 16 (pp. 87-88). This proof was considered to have been taken from the second book of Plato's *Republic*.

form as finite act allows each form to be by its very nature different from other forms, and so safeguards doctrinally the manifest
plurality of forms in the universe. Nothing else is required for
the philosophical justification of plurality in being. The doctrine
of matter or potency then explains the multiplication of the form
within the same species. But even in forms without matter,
namely, the Aristotelian separate substances, a plurality is possible because of the nature of form as finite act. The absolutely
primary instance of being may be found in a multiplicity of pure
acts.

Primacy and Universality.   The many things in the sensible
universe may be logically united in gradually widening unities,
specific, generic, and analogical (Λ 6,1016b31-1017a3). Analogies
run through all the categories of being; for instance, as the
straight is in length, so the white is in color (N 6,1093b18-21),
or as is sight in eyes so is mind in the soul (*Top.*, I 17,108a11),
or as accidental differences modify their subjects so do substantial
differences specify matter (*Metaph.*, H 2,1043a4-9). Because it
extends in these ways across the categories, analogy is a wider
unity than any generic unity. But it is not used in Aristotle to set
up the widest unity of all, that of being. The universality of being
is explained only in terms of reference to a primary instance. In
studying being in its primary instance, one is studying the nature
of being, being as being, and so is treating universally of all
beings. In this way the universality of being as the subject of the
most universal science continued to be viewed by the Greek commentators down to the twelfth century. With Avicenna and the
Scholastics, however, the subject of metaphysics became common
being as sharply distinguished from the primary being, though
common being was made to include in one way or another all the
differences of being and so was by no means an empty concept.
In the late nineteenth century, against an Idealistic background,
the object of the Aristotelian metaphysics came to be interpreted
as the most abstract and the most empty of concepts. In the
present century a widely prevalent tendency has been to regard
the Stagirite's metaphysical doctrine as having undergone a
drastic evolution from its earlier to its later stages. In his younger
days Aristotle is considered to have held that the primary philosophy had as its subject the immaterial substances, somewhat

as the highest science for Plato was concerned with the supersensible Ideas. In his later and more independent years, on the
other hand, he is regarded as having changed to the view that
the object of the primary philosophy is being in general, as distinguished from all particular beings, even the immaterial substances.[15] Another interpretation maintains that in his final stage
of development Aristotle gave the primary philosophy a double
object, the immaterial substances *and* being in the highest degree
of abstraction. At the cost of sacrificing rigorously scientific exactitude, he united the science of the immaterial with the general
science of being, and so was able to claim that the primary philosophy was *also* the universal philosophical science.[16]

In the text of the *Metaphysics,* however, no such contrast between universality and the definite nature of the primary instance of being is permitted to stand. Because it is primary in
relation to all other instances, the nature of the highest instance
is thereby universal to them all. In this way the theological science is universal by the very fact that it deals with immobile
substance. It is universal because it is primary, and so deals with
being as being.[17] However, although the nature of being is distinguished from the natures of the secondary instances, they
are not at all regarded as two intrinsic entitative constituents,
for the Aristotelian primary philosophy does not lead in the
direction of a first cause that creates other things from nothing.
But in its own setting the science offers its solution to its proper
problem. Men by their very nature desire to know. The Aristotelian theological science claims to present them with the highest
object of this desire.

For the Stagirite the goal of theoretical science has remained
throughout as he had described it. It is truth for the sake of truth
itself. Even where utilitarian purposes are obvious, as for instance in mechanics, these are not mentioned by Aristotle as the

---

[15] W. W. Jaeger, *Aristotle* (tr. Robinson), pp. 167-227.

[16] A. Mansion, "Philosophie Première, Philosophie Seconde et Métaphysique chez Aristote," *Revue Philosophique de Louvain,* LVI (1958), pp.
171-173; 209.

[17] cf. *Metaph.,* Γ 3,1005a33-b1; E 1,1026a27-32; K 7,1064b6-14. See
P. Merlan, "Metaphysik: Name und Gegenstand," *JHS,* LXXVII (1957),
89-92.

proper goal of the science. In the sensible world the priority of substance in regard to the accidents has led him to find the highest physical science in the procedure from the principles of sensible substance, that is, from matter and form. The Aristotelian natural philosophy still has its place in accounting for the possibility of motion and change, and in explaining how a formal characteristic can remain the same even though it is spread out in spatial extension or multiplied in singulars. The entirely potential principle, matter, because it has absolutely no formal characteristic of its own, and so is unknowable in itself, allows change from one nature to another, as well as extension and multiplication without formal change.

The troubles commence when substantial form is used for explaining particular natures. Aristotle's identification of form with final cause tended to make him proceed as though knowledge of a natural thing's purpose gave insight into its form (*PA*, I 1,640a-13-b4). Qualities and activities were supposed to provide knowledge of the substantial nature, for instance that fire is a substance and that stellar substance is different from any sublunar substance. The endeavor to explain specific sensible things in the light of their substantial forms became a stumbling block in the Peripatetic tradition for centuries. Its sterile attempts were superseded by the quantitative procedures of modern physics and chemistry. These, though giving their ultimate explanations only in the accidental order of quantity, have attained undreamt-of success in furnishing a truly scientific account of the material world. Aristotle's schema of the theoretical sciences certainly has a place for such procedures. They fit in perfectly with the "more physical" of the mathematical sciences, like optics and astronomy. But it never became the destiny of the *Peripatos* to develop them.

In the realm of metaphysics, the deficiencies of the primary philosophy are equally noticeable. Knowledge of its object, the separate substances, is established through the Aristotelian natural philosophy. The necessity of eternal cosmic motion and the animation of the heavens are essential tenets for the demonstration. Once they are discarded the whole argument falls to the ground. The existence of separate finite forms that are their own ultimate actuality cannot be established any more than can the existence of Platonic Ideas. Yet such were the objects of the Aristotelian theological science. Nor is there any hint in that science of the possibility of a properly existential procedure.

In spite of these defects, however, the broad outlines of the Aristotelian schema for the theoretical sciences have never lost their basic validity. They still lie at the root of current distinctions between natural philosophy, modern science, and metaphysics. They give a profound insight into the different ways in which sensible things may be known. They show that besides the descriptive procedure based upon qualities, there are three truly scientific approaches to things, from the viewpoints respectively of a thing's ultimate physical principles, of its quantitative principles, and finally of the principles of its being.

CHAPTER 15

Aristotle—Practical Science

The Supreme Good. In the *Nicomachean Ethics* Aristotle bases his inquiry upon the observation, so strongly signalized in Platonic circles, that every deliberate human action is done for some good: "Every art and every inquiry, and similarly every action and pursuit, is thought to aim at some good; and for this reason the good has rightly been declared to be that at which all things aim" (*EN*, I 1,1094a1-3). This assertion strikes the keynote of the whole Aristotelian ethical doctrine, just as the opening sentence of the *Metaphysics* expressed the motif of the primary philosophy. The many goods or goals of human actions, however, are not all co-ordinate. Some are subordinated to others, just as bridle-making and the arts of producing equipment for horses are subordinated to the goal of riding, and this and all other military actions to the art of generalship. In such subordination the lower end is desired for the higher. But the process of desiring goods for some still higher good cannot go on indefinitely, for in that case all desires would have no genuine goal or purpose. They would be in vain. If, then, there is one such good that is desired for its own sake and all other things are desired on account of it, this will be the supreme good. Knowledge of it will of course have great influence on one's way of living, and knowing it clearly one will be able to attain it more readily. The paramount importance and necessity of this study is accordingly beyond doubt.

The Political Science. If there is such a supreme good, it will naturally be the end and good of the highest art, the art that directs all the other arts and techniques and all human actions.

As a matter of fact, there is such an art, namely, the political science: ". . . for it is this that ordains which of the sciences should be studied in a state, and which class of citizens should learn and up to what point they should learn them; and we see even the most highly esteemed of capacities to fall under this, e.g. strategy, economics, rhetoric; now, since politics uses the rest of the sciences, and since, again, it legislates as to what we are to do and what we are to abstain from, the end of this science must include those of the others, so that this end must be the good for man" (EN, I, 2,1094a28-b7). The reasoning is that as a matter of fact there exists a supremely authoritative science; its end therefore must be the supreme human good, to which all human actions are to be directed. The good of the individual is in this way identified with the good of the city-state. As with Plato, there is no human good outside the civic good. Just as for Plato, moreover, the virtue of justice was best studied in the larger letters of the body politic, so for Aristotle the human good is best studied in the greater vision of the political good: "For even if the end is the same for a single man and for a state, that of the state seems at all events something greater and more complete whether to attain or to preserve; though it is worth while to attain the end merely for one man, it is finer and more godlike to attain it for a nation or for city-states" (EN, I 2,1094b7-10). The investigation of the supreme good is accordingly a political inquiry (EN, I 1-2).

Aristotelian political science, therefore, is the science of living in a *polis,* a Greek city-state, even though the same general principle is seen applying also to a non-Greek nation. In this sense it is the science of moral living. The Stagirite is very evidently drawing up the basic notions of the science against a strong Platonic background.[1] He is proceeding as though he can take for granted that notions like the universal finality of the good, the hierarchic subordination of different arts and pursuits to still higher ones,

[1] The indications of the Platonic background are noted especially throughout the first book of the *Nicomachean Ethics* by John Burnet, *The Ethics of Aristotle* (London, 1900). John Alexander Stewart, *Notes on the Nicomachean Ethics of Aristotle,* 2 vols. (Oxford, 1892), provides a running commentary on the text, and similarly on its more important parts there is the postumous work of H. H. Joachim, *Aristotle, The Nicomachean Ethics,* ed. D. A. Rees (Oxford, 1951). The influence of the *Laws* on many passages in the *Ethics* is particularly noticeable.

and the identity of the individual good with the good of the Greek city-state, are familiar to his hearers and accepted by them without question. The notion that the individual man can find his good and perfection only in the life of the city-state, was, of course, familiar enough to Platonic hearers,[2] and carried with it the overtones of the Greek cultural superiority in respect to the barbarian world. The necessity of merging the life of the individual into the common had indeed been stressed long before by Heraclitus. But the immediate background of these Aristotelian assertions, as is apparent by the wording and the examples, is the Platonic teaching. The presumption that this Platonic background is operative in the hearers throughout the entire first book of the *Nicomachean Ethics,* and will make itself felt sufficiently in the subsequent books, is quite clearly indicated.

Fluctuating Subject-Matter.   The subject matter of the political science is described in the accepted phraseology of the epoch as "the seemly (*ta kala*) and the just." This is an object that admits of much fluctuation, and in fact seems to vary from city-state to city-state: "Now fine and just actions, which political science investigates, admit of much variety and fluctuation of opinion, so that they may be thought to exist only by convention and not by nature" (*EN,* I 3,1094b14-16). That, of course, holds in general of things that are good: wealth may ruin some people, courage may result in death. The same thing becomes good or bad in different circumstances. The objects investigated by the political science, therefore, are not rigid like those of mathematics. Premisses and conclusions alike will hold "roughly and in outline" and "for the most part" (b20-21). Aristotle makes no special effort to prove any of these conceptions. They are all quite Platonic. He speaks as though they needed only to be mentioned and would obtain ready acceptance from Platonically trained hearers.

The First Principles.   Since the political science deals with all the actions of human life in general, it is not a proper study for a young man. A youth lacks the necessary experience of these actions. Habituated and mature control of passion, moreover, is necessarily required in the student of this science: "Hence a young man is not a proper hearer of lectures on political science; for he is inexperienced in the actions that occur in life, but

[2] See Plato, *Lg.,* IX,875AB; X,903BD.

its discussions start from these and are about these; and further, since he tends to follow his passions, his study will be vain and unprofitable, because the end aimed at is not knowledge but action. And it makes no difference whether he is young in years or youthful in character; the defect does not depend on time, but on his living, and pursuing each successive object, as passion directs."[3] Sufficient personal experience and mature habituation are therefore indispensable conditions for studying the political science. The science in this case cannot be divorced from its order to action. Its purpose is not just to acquire knowledge, but to make men good. It has to be rooted in good ethical habits (*êthê*), in the correct way of living. Its very starting points or first principles, in fact, have to be acquired through such habituation. Without these first principles one is not equipped even to begin the study of the science: "Hence any one who is to listen intelligently to lectures about what is noble and just and, generally, about the subjects of political science must have been brought up in good habits. For the fact is the starting-point, and if this is sufficiently plain to him, he will not at the start need the reason as well; and the man who has been well brought up has or can easily get starting-points" (*EN*, I 4,1095b4-8).

As in natural philosophy the starting points were attained by sense perception and induction, so in the political science the first principles are acquired by correct habituation. In this way they are able to produce the type of scientific *knowledge* that is proper to the fluctuating nature of the subject matter (*EN*, I 7,1098a26-b8). The child has to be brought up correctly, apparently in accord with the Greek traditions of *paideia*, in order to develop into a fit student of practical science. If he is brought up correctly, he will know that some actions are right or seemly and that other actions are wrong. He will know the fact in such moral matters, and knowledge of the fact (*hoti, quia*) is all that is required for the starting point of this science. He does not have to know the reason (*dioti, propter quid*) at the beginning. As long as he can tell the difference between right and wrong actions, he is equipped for the study. In some actions he will see the difference right away, simply on account of his habituation. In others he may have to inquire and listen to men who are able to give counsel;

[3] *EN*, I 3,1095a2-8. *Cf*. II 1-2,1103b23-31; VI 8,1142a11-20.

and in this second case he will be enabled by his habituation to seek and receive and absorb the proper instruction. In either case, then, it is by means of habituation that the first principles of the political science are acquired.

Eudaimonia. Through one's habituation, accordingly, one chooses the kind of actions or life in which one locates one's highest good. This is a first principle of human action; for one's supreme good will necessarily be the common and very first principle of all one's actions (*EN*, I 12,1102a2-4). Men agree on the name for that highest good. It is *eudaimonia*, a word that in Greek suggests the notion of being well directed by a superior *daimôn* or preternatural power, that is, the notion of being fortunate. It involves the conceptions of happiness, prosperity, and full contentment. Yet, on account of the differences in disposition and habituation, different types of men seek that highest good in widely differing things, and in different times and circumstances the same individual may locate it differently—when he is sick, health will seem the greatest good, and when he is poverty-stricken, wealth. Most men, to judge by the way they live, place it in sensible pleasure. This holds especially for the less educated people, and is an attitude fitting for slaves and beasts. Others, those who engage in political activity, seek it in honor and fame. This view is shown to be superficial, because honor and fame depend upon those who bestow rather than on the one who receives, and so it is too fickle a thing to be chosen as one's highest good. Moreover, such men wish to be honored on account of their virtue or excellence, and so virtue is in this way tacitly acknowledged as the higher good. But even virtue or excellence does not exclude inactivity and misfortune, and so in itself alone it can hardly be *eudaimonia*, since the very term implies good fortune. Thirdly, there is the life of contemplation. The type of life directed to gain or moneymaking is evidently on account of something else, namely, on account of that for which the money will be useful. It itself, therefore, is not aimed directly and immediately at the highest good (*EN*, I 4-5).

Aristotle is making the three types of life, traditionally attributed to Pythagoras, illustrate the function of habituation in determining one's chief good. The life of gain, however, is in the Aristotelian treatment relegated to a subordinate position. The life of pleasure is restricted to that of sensible pleasure, and so is separated from the life of contemplation, which forms the third member of the Aristotelian division.

Not an Idea.   An entirely separate good like the Platonic Idea, even if it existed, could not function as the good sought in human actions. The good, in point of fact, is not an object that appears identical in all its instances in the way that whiteness appears identical in snow and in white lead. Goodness, rather, is an object that varies as it is seen in the useful, in pleasure, in honor, in wisdom, and so on. It has a different definition in each of these cases. It is not something that corresponds to one single Idea. It functions as an Aristotelian equivocal, and seems to be analogical in its different instances.

If it were a Platonic Idea, moreover, the good could never be attained by men or brought into relation to individual men. It could not therefore be the human good. In point of fact, again, no such Platonic Idea enters into any of the arts or sciences that work out the various goods. The supreme human good, on the contrary, will have to be something that is sought in every human action. For its sake all other things are done.

Self-sufficiency.   Accordingly, no one chooses the supreme good for anything over and above itself; and all other things are chosen for its sake. This is illustrated by a commonly accepted characteristic of the supremely final good, its self-sufficiency. That self-sufficiency, however, has to provide not only for one's self, but also for parents, family, friends, and civic life, since man is by nature social or political. Human life requires all these associations and has to be able to provide for them, if it is to attain its fullness.

Complete Life.   *Eudaimonia,* moreover, will have to consist in activity, for it is a life in the sense of action. The proper function or activity of man, as distinct from plants and beasts, is reasonable activity of the soul. That means "activity of the soul in accordance with virtue" (*EN,* I 7,1098a16), and not only for a short time but "in a complete life" (a18), just as one swallow or one day does not make the spring. A normal life span, therefore, is a necessary condition for attaining the supreme goal of human nature.

Traditional Notions.   The Aristotelian outline of the highest good is easily shown to be in harmony with traditionally accepted notions. As the highest *activity* of the *soul*, it fits in with the philosophical conception of *eudaimonia* as a good of the soul rather than a good of the body or an external good, and also with the conception that *eudaimonia* consists in "living well" and "doing well." The Aristotelian conception of it as reasonable activity in accordance with virtue agrees with views that place it in virtue or in wisdom; and in requiring that *eudaimonia* include accompanying pleasure, external goods, and good fortune, the Aristotelian doctrine takes account of the views that place it in these. Pleasure, in fact, belongs to things of the soul, and virtuous life is in itself pleasant. To it pleasure is not something adventitious, but is necessarily found in good action. To be good one must enjoy performing good actions. The most pleasant actions for the good man are those he judges to be good and seemly. Virtuous actions, accordingly, are in themselves most pleasant; for in these matters the morally good man judges correctly. In a word, what the morally good man judges to be seemly he finds also most pleasant.

In the Aristotelian notion of *eudaimonia*, therefore, the best, the most seemly, and the most pleasant coincide, while friends and external goods and prosperity are required accompaniments. The latter conditions make a certain amount of good fortune either by gift of the gods or by chance enter into *eudaimonia*, in accordance with the etymology of the word. The requirement of a complete life excludes from *eudaimonia* children and those who later in life meet with great misfortunes, as for instance Priam (*EN*, I 6-12).

Virtue. Basically, however, *eudaimonia* or the highest human good is "activity of soul in accordance with perfect virtue" (*EN*, I 13,1102a5-6). The political science, therefore, has to make a study of virtue. Its purpose in doing so, as a practical science, will be to make the citizens good and obedient to the laws. Since properly human virtue is virtue of the soul, some knowledge of the soul is necessary, just as knowledge of the body is necessary for the healing art of medicine. That knowledge, though, is limited to what is necessary for the practical purposes of the political science. Further theoretical knowledge of the soul is outside its requirements. The student of the political science has to know, for instance, that the soul has both irrational and rational aspects;

but whether these are separate parts or merely distinct features of the same soul does not enter into his needs. He has to know just enough to understand how the virtues of the soul are distinguished according to these two aspects, some virtues being intellectual, like philosophical wisdom, and others being moral, like liberality and temperance (*EN*, I 13).

Dialectical Procedure.   With only one or two exceptions, the notions that are laid down in the opening book of the *Nicomachean Ethics* prove to be the conceptions that could be expected in Platonically trained hearers. Aristotle does not have to labor these notions. He has to emphasize, however, the practical character of the science. Its first principles are obtained through habituation by proper education according to the Greek culture, and they are in this way adapted to a fluctuating subject matter. They are not rigid like the principles of mathematics, but cover particular instances only roughly and for the most part. On the judgment of the correctly habituated man, the good man, depends the determination of the seemly and just, that is, of the morally good. In this way the first principles of the science, including the supreme human good, *eudaimonia,* are established. The dialectical procedure required by the Aristotelian logic has accordingly a specially important function in reaching the first principles of the political science. It has to seek out in its investigation what morally good men consider good actions and good goals, and present these to the judgment of the correctly habituated hearer, who is thereby able to see them in the role of first principles just as the hearer in a speculative science is through dialectic brought to the intuition of speculative principles. Customary praise and blame in circles of Greek culture will, therefore, be the regular criteria in discriminating between good and bad actions in the moral order.

The requirements that men usually include in their own notions of *eudaimonia* have consequently their important role in establishing the Aristotelian notion of the highest human good, even though the practically operative judgment is that of the correctly habituated hearer. All this makes abundantly clear how very fundamental and very operative is the Aristotelian distinction between speculative and practical science. Practical science has a radically different procedure from that of any speculative science. As science, it will have to be of the universal. Through its dialectic it will be able to find true universals in a subject matter that is always fluctuating, but universals that are not rigid in their application like the universals of the speculative sciences. The ethical universal will have to respect the fluctuating nature of its subject matter and at the same time meet the requirements of scientific universality.

Moral Virtue. Moral or ethical virtue, as the derivation of its name implies (*ethos* 'habit'), comes through habituation. No moral virtue, therefore, is innate. It has to be acquired by performing acts of the virtue, just as lyre-players acquire their art by playing the lyre. A good constitution of a city-state, therefore, aims to make its citizens good by directing their actions in a way that will form good habits in them. Good conduct and proficiency in virtue, accordingly, will be based upon the early formation of good habits: "It makes no small difference, then, whether we form habits of one kind or of another from our very youth; it makes a very great difference, or rather *all* the difference" (*EN*, II, 1,1103b23-25). This requirement of good habits holds likewise for the acquisition of the science itself, since its purpose is not a theoretical knowledge of what virtue is, but rather to make men good. Good action is action according to the right rule or reason or proportion (*logos*), as is commonly admitted. In moral matters the right norm will have to be applied in a variable way, according to the nature of the subject matter: ". . . . matters concerned with conduct and questions of what is good for us have no fixity, any more than matters of health" (*EN*, II 2,1104a3-5). In this sphere there is nothing rigid or stabilized after the manner of theoretical truth. The universal account (*logos*) is of this ever-variable nature, and all the more so will particular accounts be "lacking in exactness; for they do not fall under any art or precept but the agents themselves must in each case consider what is appropriate to the occasion, as happens also in the art of medicine or of navigation" (a6-10).

The ethical universal is indeed a universal, according to this doctrine, but it applies in a different way in each instance. In each particular case it has to be determined by the judgment of the individual good man. With this understanding of the variable character of ethical universals in their application to each particular case, one may proceed to investigate the way in which these universals are determined.

The Moral Mean.   In general, virtuous action will be according to a mean between excess and defect. In any virtue, for instance temperance or courage, one can easily see that the virtue is destroyed by either excess or defect. Secondly, virtue is produced by repeated acts and increases one's capacity to perform those acts. Thirdly, virtuous actions will be performed with pleasure. Plato is quoted for the saying that correct education consists in being brought up from early years to find delight in the things in which one should find delight and pain in the things at which one should be pained. Every action, in fact, is accompanied by either pleasure or pain, and the desirability of actions is as a rule estimated or measured by the yardstick of pleasure and pain. Hence arises the importance of being trained to find pleasure in the things that should cause pleasure and pain in the things that should cause pain. The authority of Heraclitus is also quoted as well as that of Plato for the important role of pleasure in ethical striving. The conclusion is that the man who uses pleasure and pain correctly will be good, the man who uses them incorrectly will be bad. In this sense both virtue and the political science are concerned with pleasures and pains (*EN*, II 1-3).

Unlike a product of the arts, a virtuous act can never be constituted in independence of the agent's momentary disposition. If a product of the arts is constituted in accordance with the rules of the art, it is thereby good, regardless of the artisan's own disposition when making it. Although Aristotle does not give any examples here, he makes his meaning clear enough. A house is a good house if as a finished product it conforms to a correct blueprint, regardless of the carpenter's personal disposition. As long as the knowledge represented by the blueprint is worked into the product, the product is good. In the moral sphere such is not the case. What determines the goodness of the act, for instance of justice or temperance, is the moral habituation of the agent: ". . . as a condition of the possession of the virtues knowledge has little or no weight, while the other conditions count not for a little but for everything, i.e. the very conditions which result from often doing just and temperate acts" (*EN*, II 4,1105b2-5). The determination, then, of virtuous actions cannot be made independently of the agent's disposition. They have to be defined in terms of a man's habituation: "Actions, then, are called just and temperate when they are such as the just or the temperate man would do; but it is not the man who does these that is just and temperate, but the man who also does them *as* just and temperate men do them" (b5-9). The way in which actions are performed is therefore essential to their constitution as virtuous actions, and that way is finally determined not by any characteristic of the actions as such but by the habituation of morally good men. An individual, nevertheless, can perform a just or temperate action by chance or at the suggestion of another, even though he himself does not already possess the virtue. In this way he can commence to acquire the virtue. Virtues, accordingly, are neither passions nor faculties, but are *habits,* in the sense of stable and voluntary habituation (*EN*, II 4-5).

Therefore the mean according to which a virtuous action avoids excess and defect is not fixed and rigid like a mathematical mean. It cannot be determined independently of the individual's disposition at the moment. What is too much food for one person may not be too much for another. The mean, then, has to be sought ". . . not in the object but relatively to us" (*EN*, II 6,1106b7). The mean in each case will be determined by the judgment of the morally good man, the man who is capable of judging in moral matters. It is ". . . the mean relative to us, this being determined by a rational principle, and by that principle by which the man of practical wisdom would determine it" (*EN*, II 6,1107a1-2). The rational principle (*logos*) or proportion in which the moral mean consists, therefore, is set up in each case by the judgment of a wise man (*phronimos*), in the sense of a man who has what is called practical wisdom.

Extreme of Goodness. The doctrine that virtue consists in a mean does not, however, involve any notion of what in English is called the mediocre. Virtue, as its name in Greek implies, always signifies excellence. From that viewpoint it is an extreme, for it is what is best. In its case, though, what is most excellent consists in a mean between excess and defect: "Hence in respect of its substance and the definition which states its essence virtue is a mean, with regard to what is best and right an extreme" (*EN*, II 6,1107a6-8). The mean, accordingly, is in virtue the extreme of goodness. The excess and deficiency constitute opposite vices. These considerations become evident through a study of the different virtues and the application of the criteria of praise and blame that are given to the various kinds of human actions. In combating a vice, however, one has to aim sometimes a little beyond the mean in order to attain the virtue most easily (*EN,* II 6-9).

The Voluntary. The indications of praise and blame show that only voluntary actions are virtuous. Compulsion from an external principle, to which the agent contributes nothing, destroys the voluntary character of an action. Likewise ignorance destroys it. Acts that proceed from anger or concupiscible appetite, though, are not involuntary: "Since that which is done under compulsion or by reason of ignorance is involuntary, the voluntary would seem to be that of which the moving principle is in the agent himself, he being aware of the particular circumstances of the action. Presumably acts done by reason of anger or appetite are not rightly called involuntary" (*EN,* III 1, 1111a22-25).

When deliberation precedes, the voluntary becomes an object of choice. Choice, accordingly, is "deliberate desire of things in our own power; for when we have decided as a result of deliberation, we desire in accordance with our deliberation" (*EN,* III 3,1113a11-12). The end sought is an object of a *wish,* the means are the object of deliberation and *choice.* Since the activity of the virtues is concerned with means, virtue and vice are voluntary. But the end is also fundamentally voluntary, since it is wished in accordance with habituation that may be controlled: "Now some one may say that all men desire the apparent good, but have no control over the appearance, but the end appears to each man in a form answering to his character. We reply that if each man is somehow responsible for his state of mind, he will also be himself somehow responsible for the appearance; . . . But actions and states of character are not voluntary in the same way; for we are masters of our actions from the beginning right to the end, if we know the particular facts, but though we control the beginning of our states of character the gradual progress is not obvious, any more than it is in illnesses; because it was in our power, however, to act in this way or not in this way, therefore the states are voluntary" (*EN*, III 5,1114a31-1115a3). Even though the type of life that one leads, the life of pleasure, the life of honor, or the life of contemplation, is wished as a result of one's habituation or disposition, the habituation or lack of habituation was in one's power at the beginning of its formation, and so in that way is voluntary.

The Particular Virtues. In accordance with these teachings, the different virtues are investigated in detail. Courage "is a mean with respect to things that inspire confidence or fear, . . ." (*EN*, III, 7,1116a10-11). The mean is chosen because it is seemly (*kalon*). Temperance makes the concupiscible appetites conform with correct proportion or rational principle (*logos*), again in order to attain the seemly: "Hence the appetitive element in a temperate man should harmonize with the rational principle; for the noble is the mark at which both aim, and the temperate man craves for the things he ought, as he ought, and when he ought; and this is what the rational principle directs" (*EN*, III 12,-1119b15-18). Liberality, similarly, regulates conduct in regard to wealth, with the seemly always as the motive: "Now virtuous actions are noble and done for the sake of the noble. Therefore the liberal man, like other virtuous men, will give for the sake of the noble, and rightly; for he will give to the right people, the right amounts, and at the right time, with all the other qualifications that accompany right giving; and that too with pleasure or without pain; . . ." (*EN*, IV 1,1120a23-26).

A corresponding account is given of the related virtue of magnificence, concerned with expenditure on a large scale; of loftymindedness, the crowning virtue of Greek aristocratic tradition, which is concerned with honor on a grand scale; of the unnamed virtue that regards honors on a lesser scale; and of good temper, the mean with respect to anger; and of other virtues required for harmonious social life (*EN*, IV).

Justice. Justice is "that kind of state of character which makes people disposed to do what is just and makes them act justly and wish for what is just; . . ." (*EN*, V 1,1129a7-9). In a wider sense justice is used to mean virtue in general, and in this meaning it of course includes all the virtues. In the narrower sense of a particular virtue it is concerned with honor or money or safety. The justice concerned with the distribution of common possessions

follows a geometrical proportion, while that concerned with transactions between individuals has to observe an arithmetical proportion (*EN*, V 1-5).

Household or economic justice is that of the householder in
regard to the household or family. It is different from political
justice, which is regulated by law: "For justice exists only between men whose mutual relations are governed by law; and law
exists for men between whom there is injustice; for legal justice
is the discrimination of the just and the unjust. . . . This is why we
do not allow a *man* to rule, but *rational principle*, because a man
behaves thus in his own interests and becomes a tyrant" (*EN*, V
6,1134a30-b1). Political justice, then, is "according to law, and
between people naturally subject to law, and these as we saw
are people who have an equal share in ruling and being ruled"
(*EN*, V 6,1134b13-15).

Political justice is partly determined naturally, partly by convention: "Of political justice part is natural, part legal,—natural,
that which everywhere has the same force and does not exist by
people's thinking this or that; legal, that which is originally indifferent, but when it has been laid down is not indifferent, e.g.
that a prisoner's ransom shall be a mina, . . ." (*EN*, V 7,1134b18-
22). It is determined by nature not in the rigid sense in which
natural things are determined, as fire for instance burns the same
way both in Greece and in Persia, but in a way that is variable:
". . . with us there is something that is just even by nature, yet
all of it is changeable; but still some is by nature, some not by
nature" (b29-30). Even though constitutions differ in different
city-states, therefore, "there is but one which is everywhere by
nature the best" (1135a5). Aristotle merely states that, once their
variable nature is granted, the things naturally just are evident
(1134b30-33). He does not give any further explanation of the
meaning of the naturally just and its ever-variable character, or
any explicit development of this doctrine in the direction of the
distinction between natural law and positive law.

Equity. Law, then, is required for justice. But because a law
is universal, it can often cover only the usual cases, and will be
incorrect in certain particular cases. For this reason the law has
sometimes to be corrected by equity. The fault is not in the law,
but in the very nature of the subject matter found in the moral

or practical order: "When the law speaks universally, then, and a case arises on it which is not covered by the universal statement, then it is right, where the legislator fails us and has erred by over-simplicity, to correct the omission—to say what the legislator himself would have said had he been present, and would have put into his law if he had known" (*EN*, V 10,1137b19-24). Equity, therefore, is "a correction of law where it is defective owing to its universality" (b26-27). Where the subject matter is indeterminate, the rule cannot be rigid, just as the rule used for Lesbian molding is not rigid but adapts itself to the shape of the stone. The equitable man, accordingly, is ready where circumstances require to take *less* than the law would allow him if he insisted on its letter (*EN*, V 10). Equity, in consequence, may work to one's own immediate disadvantage as well as to one's advantage, and the equitable man gladly accepts either.

The Right Rule.   Since all virtuous conduct is determined by the right rule or proportion (*logos*), it requires knowledge of this rule in each particular case. What then is the right rule and how is it laid down? Being a rational principle, it has to be attained by the rational part of the soul. This rational part, however, has in its turn two parts, one by which are contemplated things whose principles are invariable, and another by which are contemplated things whose principles are variable. Through the latter part the right rule in moral matters will have to be grasped. When concerned with action in this sphere the intellect is called practical, and the truth involved is practical. The truth of the practical intellect will consist in conformity with right desire, in contrast to theoretical truth into whose determination the desire or disposition of the knower does not enter. Just as the speculative intellect can be developed and directed by theoretical wisdom (*sophia*) and the productive intellect by art, so the practical intellect has its corresponding state in "a true and reasoned state of capacity to act with regard to the things that are good or bad for man" (*EN*, VI 5,1140b5-6). This state is a virtue called practical wisdom (*phronêsis*). It requires excellence in deliberation, good understanding and judgment in practical matters, and correct discrimination of the equitable. Since it is concerned with things to be done, it will be dealing not only with particulars but with things that are variable; and in these variables it must intuit its universals: ". . . the intuitive reason involved in practical reasoning grasps the last and variable fact, i.e. the minor premiss. For these variable facts are the starting-points for the apprehension of the end, since the universals are reached from the particulars; . . ." (*EN*, VI 11,1143b2-5). It can be greatly helped, therefore, by the experience of these variable things that has been had by older and experienced people and people of good practical judgment (*EN*, VI 1-11).

Interdependence of the Virtues. The commonly accepted definitions indicate that practical wisdom sets the right rule for any virtuous action: ". . . even now all men, when they define virtue, after naming the state of character and its objects add 'that (state) which is in accordance with the right rule'; now the right rule is that which is in accordance with practical wisdom" (*EN*, VI 13,1144b21-24). Practical wisdom is, in fact, the right rule in moral matters. The moral virtues therefore all involve practical wisdom as the determination of the rule by which they avoid excess and defect. But reciprocally, practical wisdom involves the moral virtues, for it makes its judgment in accordance with right desire, and right desire is determined by the moral virtues. The virtues of the practical intellect, consequently, involve one another: "It is clear, then, from what has been said, that it is not possible to be good in the strict sense without practical wisdom, nor practically wise without moral virtue" (*EN*, VI 13,1144b30-32). With practical wisdom, then, all the moral virtues are given (*EN*, VI 12-13).

The stress on the interdependence of the moral virtues, the description of the soul as having parts, and many of the conceptions of the different types of cognition presupposed in the foregoing treatment, continue to show a strongly Platonic background, and to indicate that the whole procedure is directed towards Platonically trained hearers. Against this background the nature of the ethical universal has been made sufficiently clear. It is a universal that remains the same, even though it is set up differently in every particular instance. Temperance, for example, remains temperance universally in all its instances, even though the amount of food or drink concerned is different in every particular instance, and in every instance the mean determining that amount is set up according to the particular circumstances by the judg-

ment of the man of practical wisdom. Temperance remains universal, even though the mean that determines it is in this way
variable and not rigidly applicable like a mathematical universal. A very small amount of food may be temperate for an
ailing person, and a huge quantity for an athlete like Milo of
Croton. As is the case with the yardstick for the Lesbian molding,
the ethical universal has to bend and adapt itself to the nature
of its subject matter; nevertheless it remains the same rule and
the same universal.

Incontinence. One may, however, act wrongly without being
habitually wicked. This condition is named incontinence. It is
possible because a man may preserve his direction towards the
good universally, while he acts for a particular that is evil:
"Further, since there are two kinds of premisses, there is nothing
to prevent a man's having both premisses and acting against his
knowledge, provided that he is using only the universal premiss
and not the particular; for it is particular acts that have to be
done" (*EN*, VII 3,1146b35-1147a4). A man can have habituated
knowledge that he is not actually using. He need not be knowing the forbidding moral premiss actually, but only possessing
it in a habitual state, like men asleep, mad, or drunk. Such men
may recite the verses of Empedocles or utter scientific statements,
without thereby actually understanding them, just as a beginner
in a science may rattle off its formulae, and likewise actors on the
stage. Passion has a corresponding effect in regard to one's
knowledge. The man who acts incontinently, therefore, either
has not the ultimate particular premiss that directs to virtuous
action or else at the moment has it in a merely habitual state:
"Now, the last premiss both being an opinion about a perceptible
object, and being what determines our actions, this a man either
has not when he is in the state of passion, or has it in the sense in
which having knowledge did not mean knowing but only talking,
as a drunken man may mutter the verses of Empedocles" (*EN*,
VII 3,1147b9-12). For Aristotle, it should be remembered, knowledge of the universal is not actual knowledge (*Metaph.*, M 10,-
1087a16-18).

In this light the Socratic position that virtue is knowledge, or
that no one sins knowingly, has a restricted justification; for knowledge of the good in the highest sense of the term "knowledge"

is not present and so is not overcome. The particular opinion according to which the action takes place, e.g., "This is sweet," is not *per se* contrary to the right rule. It is the passion, not the opinion, that runs contrary to the right rule. The right rule in this case would be, as a particular premiss, "I should not taste this," and the incontinent man in the moment of deciding has not that rule actually in regard to himself. He may recite it, but that means no more than an actor on the stage who recites lines in the first person without applying them to himself. How the passion is to be removed and the man's normal state restored is a matter for natural science (*EN*, VII 1-3).

The man of practical wisdom, however, cannot be incontinent: "Nor can the same man have practical wisdom and be incontinent; for it has been shown that a man is at the same time practically wise, and good in respect of character. Further, a man has practical wisdom not by knowing only but by being able to act; but the incontinent man is unable to act . . ." (*EN*, VII 10,1152a6-9). The necessary order of practical knowledge to action is operative in this reasoning. The incontinent man, though, is not a wicked man, for his usual inclination and the type of life that he would choose are good. But he may be termed "half-wicked" (*EN*, VII 10). Continence and incontinence, accordingly, are not identified with virtue or wickedness, though they are concerned with the same subject matter (*EN*, VII 1,1145a36-b2).

The discussion on continence and incontinence helps to make clear how deeply and how essentially practical knowledge is implanted in a man's disposition to action. Cognition of the moral right and wrong in a man who is not himself morally good is not scientific *knowledge*, but merely the recitation of norms learned by rote from others. It is not knowledge in the light of the basic moral principles, for these depend upon one's own habituation. In a word, a man who is not morally good cannot have the first principles of moral science, and so cannot have the scientific knowledge that proceeds from those principles.

Friendship. Friendship[4] is necessary for human life. It is

---

[4] The problems concerning friendship were outlined in Plato's *Lysis*. Notions developed by Aristotle on the theme continued to make themselves felt to a considerable extent in Cicero's *De Amicitia* and against a Christian background in the twelfth century in the *De Spirituali Amicitia* of St Aelred of Rievaulx. On the Platonic gradation of friendships, see R. G. Hoerder, "Plato's Lysis," *Phronesis*, IV (1959), 23-28.

praised as something seemly in itself, and is regarded as the highest form of justice. It may be for one's own pleasure or utility, or for the sake of the good. In its perfect state it presupposes virtue and has the good of the friends themselves as the motive for wishing them well: "Perfect friendship is the friendship of men who are good, and alike in virtue; for these wish well alike to each other *qua* good, and they are good in themselves. Now those who wish well to their friends for their sake are most truly friends; for they do this by reason of their own nature and not incidentally; therefore their friendship lasts as long as they are good . . ." (*EN*, VIII 3,1156b7-12). Such friendship requires equality in the parties concerned. In friendships where there is inequality, as between father and son, elder and younger, husband and wife, ruler and subject, the love has to be proportional to the inequality, and in this sense attains the equality necessary for friendship. Some sort of friendship is present wherever there is any community of men, from the political community down: "For in every community there is thought to be some form of justice, and friendship too; at least men address as friends their fellow-voyagers and fellow-soldiers, and so to those associated with them in any other kind of community. And the extent of their association is the extent of their friendship, as it is the extent to which justice exists between them" (*EN*, VIII 9,1159b26-31).

Ultimate Source of Friendship. No matter how much one may make a friend's personal good one's own good and wish a friend well for the friend's sake, the ultimate source of friendship is always one's own proper good: "Friendly relations with one's neighbors, and the marks by which friendships are defined, seem to have proceeded from a man's relations to himself. . . . he wishes for himself what is good and what seems so, and does it . . . for his own sake . . . and he wishes himself to live and be preserved, and especially the element by virtue of which he thinks" (*EN*, IX 4,1166a1-19). It is for his own good, then, that the good man, who is the judge and measure of all moral matters, engages in friendship. To that extent the Aristotelian conception of friendship is radically self-seeking. Basically it looks to one's own good, no matter how much that good is placed in the good of another.

Pleasure. The importance of pleasure becomes manifest from its role in shaping the moral habits of the young[5] and from its relation to virtue throughout life: ". . . in educating the young we steer them by the rudders of pleasure and pain; it is thought, too, that to enjoy the things we ought and to hate the things we ought has the greatest bearing on virtue of character. For these things extend right through life, with a weight and power of their own in respect both to virtue and to the happy life, since men choose what is pleasant and avoid what is painful; . . ." (*EN*, X 1,1172a20-26). Pleasure, in fact, is something that completes cognitional activity: "For, while there is pleasure in respect of any sense, and in respect of thought and contemplation no less, the most complete is pleasantest, and that of a well-conditioned organ in relation to the worthiest of its objects is the most complete; and the pleasure completes the activity" (*EN*, X 4,1174b20-23). Various pleasures are bound up with their respective activities and intensify them: "This may be seen, too, from the fact that each of the pleasures is bound up with the activity it completes. For an activity is intensified by its proper pleasure, since each class of things is better judged of and brought to precision by those who engage in the activity with pleasure; e.g. it is those who enjoy geometrical thinking that become geometers and grasp the various propositions better, and, similarly, those who are fond of music or of building, and so on, make progress in their proper function by enjoying it; . . ." (*EN*, X 5,1175a29-35). Pleasures vary according to the different dispositions of different persons, and according to the different disposition of the same person at different times, like sweet things to a sick man and to a healthy man. The proper judge in matters of pleasure is therefore the good man, the man who is correctly disposed towards his proper activity as man: "If this is correct, as it seems to be, and virtue and the good man as such are the measure of each thing, those also will be pleasures which appear so to him, and those things pleasant which he enjoys" (*EN*, X 5,1176a17-19).

The Life of Contemplation. Since *eudaimonia* or the highest human good is desirable for its own sake, it will consist in an activity that is sought for nothing beyond the activity itself. Virtuous actions are of this nature: "Now those activities are desirable in themselves from which nothing is sought beyond the

[5] *Cf. MM*, II 7,1206b17-29.

activity. And of this nature virtuous actions are thought to be; for to do noble and good deeds is a thing desirable for its own sake" (*EN*, X 6,1176b6-9). The seemly has its own desirability, independently of anything else, and all seemly actions share in this desirability. But among these the highest and best will naturally be the chief good. The highest activity is that of the highest faculty, the intellect, contemplating its highest and best object. It is philosophical contemplation. That is the complete happiness of man, if it continues with the things necessary for it like friends and external prosperity throughout a complete lifetime. It is likewise the most pleasant of lives (*EN*, X 7). Life in accordance with the other virtues gives happiness, but only a secondary kind (*EN*, X 8).

Political Constitution. In order to acquire the proper ethical formation, so necessary both for happiness and for practical knowledge, one should be brought up under right laws. Accordingly, the Aristotelian *Politics*[6] professes to be a direct continuation of the ethical investigations. It forms part of the same science. It undertakes a study of the constitution of the body politic. For this purpose Aristotle proposed to use materials from the constitutions that he had collected,[7] along with the details of their history.

In the *Politics*, slavery is found to be natural, because some men are adapted by nature to work with their bodies under the direction of others, as instruments (*Pol.*, I 4-5). Private property and families are necessary, contrary to the Platonic teaching which would destroy natural affection and interest and would cause dissension instead of removing it (*Pol.*, II 2-5). Monarchy, aristocracy, and constitutional government are good constitutional forms, for they have in view the *common* good. The perversions of these, tyranny, oligarchy, and democracy, respectively, are bad forms, since they aim at the interest of the monarch only, or the wealthy only, or the needy only, and not at the common welfare (*Pol.*, III 7). Constitutional government is defined as that in which "the citizens at large administer the state for the common interest . . ." (*Pol.*, III 7,1279a37-39). This conception is

[6] For a running commentary on the *Politics*, see William Lambert Newman, *The Politics of Aristotle*, 4 vols. (Oxford, 1887-1902).

[7] *EN*, X 9,1181b12-23. Of the one hundred and fifty-eight mentioned in the ancient lists, only the *Constitution of Athens* has survived.

closer to the modern notions of democracy than were the types
of government that Aristotle knew under the name "democracy,"
since these all meant rule by a *part* of the citizenship only, the
demos, that is, the poorer classes. Government by the majority was
for him not necessarily democracy, since it could happen that the
majority would be the rich, and not the *demos* (*Pol.*, IV 4).

Aristotelian ethical doctrine, as is clear from the foregoing survey, means seriously that its first principles are obtained through
habituation. They are not intuited in existing things, as in the
case of the speculative sciences, but are seen in the conformity
of certain actions with the habituation received through a correct
education. The general character of actions that conform with this
proper habituation is called the seemly (*to kalon*). It appears as
something eminently desirable in itself, and more desirable than
anything else. It imposes itself on the intellect in an obligatory
form expressed by the notion "should" (*dei*). One should do
what is seemly, and for the sake of the seemly. That is the only
motive given in the Aristotelian *Ethics*. The seemly appears,
not in anything rigidly established in the nature of things, but in
the conformity of an action with one's own correct moral habituation.

Among human actions that are seemly the highest is the chief
human good, *eudaimonia*. It consists in the use of the highest
faculty, the intellect, in the contemplation of its highest object,
throughout a complete lifetime and accompanied by the excellences of soul, the external goods and prosperity, and the
friends that are necessary for its attainment and continuance. This
contemplation can take place only at intervals and for a short
time on each occasion; but it is eminently worth while to subordinate everything else to its achievement in the favored few.

In any case, *eudaimonia* is the very first principle of one's
activity, no matter in what one places it. It is properly chosen on
the basis of correct habituation. Similarly individual actions appear brave, temperate, just, and so on, through their conformity
with one's ethical habituation. In the choosing neither of the
highest good nor of individual seemly actions is scientific or
demonstrative (*propter quid*) knowledge required. The fact that
one sees the end and the individual actions as conforming with

one's moral habituation suffices. One sees that this is right and that is wrong, without knowing the reasons scientifically. The good man does not have to be an ethician. Scientific ethical knowledge, however, helps him in his conduct, since of its very nature it tends to make a man good. To be healthy, one does not have to know medicine; yet knowledge of medicine promotes health. Practical knowledge, similarly, helps action. In the Aristotelian *Ethics* it exhibits the most highly developed expression of the traditional Greek precepts "Know thyself" and "Nothing in excess." It uses the knowledge of the other sciences in so far and only in so far as such knowledge is useful for directing human conduct to its proper end.

Approached from the viewpoint of theoretical scientific procedure, the Aristotelian ethical doctrine is obviously circular. The seemly is determined on the basis of one's habituation, but one's habituation is determined by the practice of seemly acts. Good habits are formed by correct education, but the very notion of "correct" in this case depends upon the seemly, which in its turn is determined by the judgment of the correctly habituated man. Similarly, the moral virtues depend upon the practical wisdom that sets their mean in each particular case; but practical wisdom depends upon the moral virtues in order to determine the mean. Viewed theoretically, the circular dependence would be evident enough. But for Aristotle the procedure of practical science is not that of the theoretical sciences. The starting points are not obtained by speculative intuition of an object, but are realized in the living man who acts. The human agent is not born in an ethical vacuum. He is as a matter of fact brought up in a civilized environment. He is already habituated before his actions become the object of his ethical considerations. His actions proceed from himself with reciprocal interdependence of moral virtue and practical wisdom, and as such they are studied by the ethician. The purpose of the ethician is not to generate moral action from speculatively determined principles, but to produce good conduct through knowledge of it in the light of its own livingly engaged and concretely grasped starting points.

In scope, the Aristotelian ethics is quite apparently this-worldly, and is thoroughly pagan. It seeks and locates supreme human happiness in a life of philosophical contemplation on earth.

It is not concerned in any important way with activity after death. It is fundamentally self-seeking, since it sees even the highest type of friendship proceeding from the radical desire of self-perfection. It allows one to place one's own good in the good of another basically because it is for one's own good to do so. It justifies slavery. It is an ethics severely limited by the natural philosophy and the metaphysics upon which it draws for knowledge of the soul and of the highest type of being. It is an ethics adapted to the outlook of life in a Greek city-state.

In spite of the closely knit relations of its various parts, however, the philosophy of Aristotle is not presented as a system, and does not lend itself readily to systematization. From this standpoint it has been treated in various ways. Efforts have been made to systematize it in spite of itself, or to explain its seeming contradictions by development theories, or to brand it as a hopeless collection of radical inconsistencies, or to explain the situation by maintaining that Aristotle as a contemplator was not at all interested in eliminating the divergencies that he encountered.[8] There is a fifth possibility, arising from the form of the Aristotelian treatises as school *logoi*, and seeing in the apparent inconsistencies Aristotle's technique of adapting his instruction to and making use of the various conceptions actually present in the minds of his hearers. There is still no general agreement upon an over-all method of interpretation.

In its own historical setting, though, the Aristotelian philosophy may with little hesitation be recognized as a continuation and a culmination of the general Platonic lines of thinking. An older attitude was expressed by Coleridge: "Every man is born an Aristotelian, or a Platonist. I do not think that any one born an Aristotelian can become a Platonist; and I am sure no born Platonist can ever change into an Aristotelian" (*Table Talk*, July 2/1830). In view of their common insistence upon universal and necessary knowledge, on supersensible entity as the ground of being, on the foundations of moral and political life in abiding philosophical wisdom, the two philosophies seem closer to each other than they are to the many others that have appeared in the

---

[8] For a short discussion of these four possibilities, see P. Merlan, *From Platonism to Neoplatonism* (The Hague, 1953), pp. 182-184.

history of western thought. From these they both are much more radically separated than from each other. In fact, it has been said that in face of their community of thought the disagreement on the Ideas "seems almost to be a question of words."[9] However, the radically new Aristotelian analysis of sensible things and sensible change results in a fundamentally different natural philosophy and a fundamentally different metaphysics, though both these sciences function in the broad area of Platonic inspiration. The Aristotelian logic, moreover, gives a profoundly new cast to human thought. Yet these sharp and deep differences remain quite within the orbit of the highly intellectual tradition that had been so well developed by Plato.

The Aristotelian wisdom, accordingly, continues the best traditions of Greek thought. Its metaphysics, even though drastically limited by the natural philosophy that furnishes the basis for arriving at the existence and nature of separate substance, provides insights and methods that are of perennial worth in dealing with being. In the analysis of the virtues and in the general notions of practical science and its procedure, the ethics of Aristotle is a lasting heritage from which much can be learned in any age. His philosophy has by no means exhausted its influence today. It can still furnish guidance and inspiration as it continues to be more thoroughly investigated and better understood—"For the wisdom of Aristotle grows on the mind as one ponders upon it, and the future will be all the better if it continues to digest his wisdom."[10]

SELECTED READINGS AND REFERENCES

Aristotelis Opera, 5 vols, ed. Academia Regia Borussica (Berlin: Reimer, 1831-1870). The fifth volume contains Hermann Bonitz' *Index Aristotelicus,* which has been reproduced separately by the Akademische Druck- u. Verlaganstalt, Graz, 1955.

The Works of Aristotle Translated into English, 12 vols., ed. W. D. Ross (Oxford: Clarendon Press and Oxford University Press, 1908-1952). There is an index to this translation by Troy Wilson Organ, *An Index to Aristotle in English Translation* (Princeton: University Press, 1949). There are more recent translations of individual works, e.g. of the *Metaphysics* by Richard Hope (New York, 1952) and by

[9] W. D. Ross, *Plato's Theory of Ideas* (Oxford, 1951), p. 226.
[10] E. Barker, *The Politics of Aristotle* (Oxford, 1946), p. v.

John Warrington (London and New York, 1956), of the *Nicomachean Ethics* by J. A. K. Thomson (London, 1953), and of the *Politics* by Ernest Barker (Oxford, 1946), and editions and translations in the *Loeb Classical Library*.

M.-D. Philippe, *Aristoteles* (Bern: A. Francke, 1948). This bibliography of Aristotle forms number eight in the series *Bibliographische Einführungen in das Studium der Philosophie* (ed. I. M. Bocheński).

Werner Wilhelm Jaeger, *Aristotle, Fundamentals of the History of His Development,* tr. Richard Robinson (Oxford: Clarendon Press, 1934). Published in German 1923.

William David Ross, *Aristotle,* reprint, 5th ed. (London: Methuen, 1956). First edition 1923. Published also by Meridian Books, New York, 1959.

————, *Aristotle's Metaphysics,* with Introduction and Commentary, 2 vols. (Oxford: Clarendon Press, 1924).

————, *Aristotle's Physics,* with Introduction and Commentary (Oxford: Clarendon Press, 1936).

————, *Aristotle's Prior and Posterior Analytics,* with Introduction and Commentary (Oxford: Clarendon Press, 1949).

P. Merlan, "Aristotle's Unmoved Movers," *Traditio,* IV (1946), 1-30.

————, "Metaphysik: Name und Gegenstand," *JHS,* LXXVII (1957), 87-92.

Jean Léonard, *Le Bonheur chez Aristote* (Brussels: Palais des Académies, 1948).

Donald James Allan, *The Philosophy of Aristotle* (London, etc.: Oxford University Press, 1952).

————, "Aristotle's Account of the Origin of Moral Principles," *Proceedings of the XIth International Congress of Philosophy,* XII, 120-127.

Ingemar Düring, *Aristotle in the Ancient Biographical Tradition* (Göteborg: Elanders Boktryckeri Aktiebolag, 1957).

[Part Four]

THE MIDDLE AND
FINAL YEARS

CHAPTER 16

Peripatetics, Cynics, Skeptics

and the Academy

PERIPATETICS—THEOPHRASTUS OF ERESUS
(*CA.* 370-285 B.C.)

Chronology. According to Apollodorus' *Chronicle* Theophrastus, Aristotle's successor, was himself succeeded some time during the 123rd Olympiad (288-285 B.C.) by Strato of Lampsacus (D.L., V, 58). He died shortly after at the age of eighty-five (V, 40). This would place his birth around 370 B.C., making him about fourteen years younger than Aristotle.

Life. Nearly all that is known about the life of Theophrastus comes from the accounts preserved in Diogenes Laertius' *Lives* (V, 36-57) along with the text of his will and a list of his works. According to those accounts, Theophrastus was a native of Eresus on the island of Lesbos, the island to which Aristotle went after his stay at nearby Assos. As a very young man, he is reported to have attended Plato's discourses, and so would have had the opportunity to meet Aristotle in Athens. Afterwards he became a disciple and close associate of the Stagirite. He had originally been called Tyrtamus, but was named "Theophrastus" by Aristotle on account of his gift of eloquence. He became the head of the school when the Stagirite left Athens for Chalcis (322 B.C.). He was the owner of the famed *Peripatos* and he acquired possession of Aristotle's library. He was a man of great industry and of a kindly disposition, attracting large numbers of hearers to his school. He bequeathed the *Peripatos* with garden and adjoining houses to a specified group of his associates, in communal ownership and for use in the pursuit of philosophical studies. All his books were willed to Neleus.

Works. Of the treatises designated by the two hundred and twenty titles handed down in the long list of Diogenes, comparatively little[1] has survived. There remain two botanical works, the *Enquiry into Plants* and *On the Causes of Plants*, together with some shorter physical writings, all composed in the manner of the Aristotelian treatises on natural history; an ethical work, *Characters*, giving a study of different moral types somewhat after the fashion of such sketches in the Aristotelian *Ethics;* a sort of introductory essay known under the later title *Metaphysics*, which poses a number of aporiae that arise from the doctrine of the Stagirite's primary philosophy, here understood as the science of separate entities; and numbers of fragments, including those from his *Physical Opinions*, the account that began the long tradition of the Greek doxographers.

Doctrines. The remnants of Theophrastus' work show industry and intelligence, but testify to a seemingly complete lack of speculative originality in their author. They contain no genuinely new philosophical notions. As regards his logical doctrines this has been shown by recent study.[2] As regards the *Metaphysics* and the *Characters*, it is quite evident from a reading of those works. The botanical treatises merely continue, with great observational detail, the type of study initiated by Aristotle in natural history.

The work of Theophrastus indicates how the Peripatetic tradition was formed in the spirit of remaining closely within the lines sketched by its founder. Very little, however, is known about the school and its history.[3] After Andronicus' edition of Aristotle

[1] The text of Theophrastus has been edited by Fridericus Wimmer and published by Teubner, *Theophrasti Eresii Opera quae supersunt Omnia*, 3 vols. (Leipzig, 1854-1862), and Didot (Paris, 1866; 1931). There is a text of the *Characters* by H. Diels, *Theophrasti Characteres* (Oxford, [1909]); of the *Metaphysics*, with English translation, by W. D. Ross and F. H. Fobes, *Theophrastus: Metaphysics* (Oxford, 1929); and some editions of different fragments or groups of fragments. The *Loeb Classical Library* has an edition and translation of the *Enquiry into Plants*, 2 vols., Sir Arthur Hort, (London and New York, 1916) and of *The Characters of Theophrastus* (John Maxwell Edmonds, London and New York, 1929). There are other English translations of the *Characters*, notably that of Richard Claverhouse Jebb, *The Characters of Theophrastus* (London and Cambridge, 1870; 1919).

[2] See I. M. Bocheński, *La Logique de Théophraste* (Fribourg, Suisse, 1947), pp. 125-126.

[3] The fragments of the Peripatetics may be found in Wilhelm August Mullach, *Fragmenta Philosophorum Graecorum*, 3 vols. (Paris, 1860-1879), III, 206 ff.; F. Wehrli, *Die Schule des Aristoteles* (Basel, 1944—). Their names are listed in W. D. Ross, *Aristotle* (London, 1953), p. 296. For their *Lives*, see D.L., V, 58-93.

in the first century B.C. the period of the Greek commentators on Aristotle commences, and continues down to the fourteenth century A.D.[4] The most important of them is Alexander of Aphrodisias (*fl. ca.* 200 A.D.).[5]

CYNICS—DIOGENES OF SINOPE (*CA.* 410-320 B.C.)

Chronology. According to the best historical evidence, the Cynics originated with Diogenes of Sinope. Sinope, a colony from Miletus, was a commercial city in Pontus on the southern coast of the Black Sea, and so was located on the furthest eastern fringe of the Greek world. From this his native city Diogenes was exiled and went to Athens. If the date of his exile is fixed, on the basis of coinage happenings at Sinope, as after 350 B.C., he would arrive in Athens an elderly man some time close to the death of Plato. On the other hand, stories told about him associate him with Plato at Athens. During Aristotle's time, at any rate, he was well-known in Athens as "the dog" (*ho Kyôn*), being so designated by the Stagirite without explanation or apology (*Rh.*, III 10,1411a24). He was an old man in the 113th Olympiad (324-321 B.C.), and died at the age of nearly ninety (D.L., VI, 76; 79) Roughly, then, he was an older contemporary of Aristotle, and lived at Athens at least some time during the Stagirite's second Athenian period.

Writings. According to the list preserved by Diogenes Laertius (VI, 80), both dialogues and tragedies were attributed to Diogenes of Sinope, though there was also a tradition that he left nothing in writing. In point of fact, no writings of his have survived, and his actual teachings cannot be determined satisfactorily. During the two hundred years after his death, a copious literature arose concerning him; but of this only quotations in later authors have survived. No complete treatises of any of the Cynics are extant. Their fragments have been collected by W. A. Mullach, *Fragmenta Philosophorum Graecorum*, II, 295-395.

---

[4] The standard text of the Greek commentators is the Prussian Academy edition, *Commentaria in Aristotelem Graeca*, 23 vols. (1882-1909) and *Supplementum Aristotelicum*, 3 vols. (1885-1903). A list of the commentators may be found in Ross, *Aristotle* p. 296.

[5] For a study of Alexander, see Paul Moraux, *Alexandre d'Aphrodise* (Liège and Paris, 1942).

PHILOSOPHICAL TEACHINGS

Way of Life. It seems impossible to piece together with certainty any consistent philosophical doctrine that might be called the philosophy of the Cynics. Even in antiquity some maintained that Cynicism was not a philosophy at all, but just a manner of living.[6] At least, the Cynics are reported as having wanted to do away with logic and physics and the ordinary Greek educational studies of mathematics and music, and center their whole attention on the teaching and practice of virtue (D.L., VI,103-105). The Greek epithet "Dog" from which the term "Cynic" comes, was given them clearly enough as a mark of contempt. In Homeric usage it signified "shamelessness." The main reason for applying this epithet to Diogenes and his followers, according to Greek tradition, was that they lived like dogs. But they took it up themselves and kept it in the meaning of the watchdogs of philosophy, the ones that guarded true wisdom.[7] The adjectival form "Cynic" goes back as far as Menander (ca. 343/2-291/0 B.C.), who used it to designate the philosophical affiliation of his contemporary, Crates of Thebes.

Self-Sufficiency. According to the account in Diogenes Laertius, the bronze statues honoring the memory of Diogenes of Sinope bore the inscription: ". . . thou alone didst point out to mortals the lesson of self-sufficingness and the easiest path of life" (VI,78; tr. Hicks). If this testimony represents correctly the substance of Diogenes' teaching, it would mean that the notion of self-sufficiency lay at the basis of his views on living. Self-sufficiency (*autarkeia*), of course, was a familiar enough notion. It was stressed by both Plato and Aristotle in their doctrines on the good and happiness. There is nothing surprising about Diogenes' use of the notion, though there is no evidence that the Cynics gave it any philosophical explanation or development, and even their use of the term has been questioned.[8] At any rate, this notion of the easiest path of life, whatever it may be called,

---

[6] D.L., VI,103; St. Augustine, *c. Acad.*, III, 19,42. Lives of some of the more prominent Cynics may be found in D.L., VI,82-102.

[7] *Cf.* D.L., VI,33;40. The mediaeval Dominicans punned somewhat similarly on their own name to call themselves the "watchdogs of the Lord."

[8] See F. Sayre, *Diogenes of Sinope* (Baltimore, 1938), p. 23.

consisted in doing away with the desire for superfluities and getting back as close to nature as possible: "Through watching a mouse running about, says Theophrastus in the Megarian dialogue, not looking for a place to lie down in, not afraid of the dark, not seeking any of the things which are considered to be dainties, he discovered the means of adapting himself to circumstances" (D.L., VI,22; tr. Hicks).

Anti-Conventional. The life according to the simplicity of natural wants meant in practice a disregard for all social standards and conventions. "Change the currency" was the motto attributed to Diogenes. This meant altering the political currency (D.L., VI,20), that is, doing away with the accepted norms by which social life in the Greek world was led. Even the structure of the Greek city-state itself was reprobated. The only true body politic, according to Diogenes, embraced the whole world (D.L., VI,72). When asked where he came from, accordingly, he replied that he was a "cosmopolitan," a citizen of the world (D.L., VI,63).

Asceticism. To live the life advocated by Diogenes, however, an ascetic training was required. "Nothing in life . . . has any chance of succeeding without strenuous practice (*askêsis*); and this is capable of overcoming anything" (D.L., VI,71; tr. Hicks). The term "ascetism" seems to have been taken by Diogenes from the Spartans, whom he admired greatly.[9] As examples of what training or "ascetism" will accomplish, he mentions athletes, fluteplayers, and craftsmen (D.L., VI,70). The Cynic asceticism meant getting used to physical hardships, poverty, contempt, insults, and so on. It appears to have been quite negative in character and limited to a preparation for living in freedom from the restraints of social life. It was not at all envisaged as a help towards practicing more positive virtues like honesty or chastity, virtues for which the Cynics appear to have had little regard.

The Cynic short cut to virtue and happiness, accordingly, consisted in living as far as possible without the benefits of civilized life. It continued in varying degrees of popularity throughout the long middle centuries of Greek philosophical activity and well into

[9] *Cf.* D.L., VI,27; 59. On the Cynic asceticism, see Sayre, pp. 7-11; D. R. Dudley, *A History of Cynicism* (London, 1937), pp. 32-34.

its final years. The last known Cynic, Sallustius, probably died early in the sixth century A.D., not so long before the official closing of the philosophical schools. It was therefore one of the most long-lived of the Greek philosophical movements, in spite of the antisocial character that was in such sharp contrast to the average Greek mentality.

SKEPTICS AND THE ACADEMY

The Term "Skeptic." The origin of the term "Skeptic," a term not found in the earlier testimonia, is recorded by Diogenes Laertius (IX,69-70). Skeptics were so called, he reports, because they were always looking for the truth and never finding it. The term comes from *skeptesthai,* meaning to look carefully at, examine, consider. Diogenes and Sextus Empiricus (*Pyrrh. Hyp.,* I,7) note that they were called also Aporetics and Ephectics (*epochê*). These terms indicate that they deliberately suspended their judgment and so remained in a state of *aporia,* the state that the Aristotelian scientific procedure was meant to remove, but which the Skeptics accepted as ultimate (*epochê* or suspension of judgment). They were further called Zetetics or seekers, because they were always *seeking* truth. Again, this attitude was in contrast to the Aristotelian conception, in which the *zêtêsis* or seeking led up to a solution of the *aporiae* and to definite conclusions. Of these names, "Skeptic" was the only one that survived. The others serve to indicate, however, the way in which the term "Skeptic" was applied. It meant that the careful examining and considering never reached any further than just that stage. In a properly scientific question the original Aristotelian state of *aporia* was deliberately and consciously accepted, after the careful examination, as the resultant state of mind. The merely initial state in the Aristotelian procedure becomes indicated as also final in the Skeptical inquiry, as far as philosophical thinking is concerned.

Types of Greek Skepticism. There were two traditional lines of Greek Skepticism, each hostile to the other, but finally converging in Aenesidemus. The older, called Pyrrhonism, lasted from the fourth century B.C. to the third century A.D. The slightly later type, the Academic, flourished in the Platonic Academy from the third to the first century B.C., its procedure being then absorbed by the Pyrrhonic tradition. No works of the original Skeptics have survived. The oldest source for their teachings is Cicero, whose accounts are often difficult to interpret. Sextus Empiricus, the last of the Pyrrhonic writers, has left much detailed information about the nature of the Skeptic movement. He wrote probably towards the end of the second century A.D., perhaps a couple of generations earlier than Diogenes Laertius. Only in the later phases of the movement are to be found the term "Skepticism" and the highly refined philosophical conception that it denotes. The progress towards it was gradual.

A. PYRRHONISM—PYRRHO OF ELIS
(CA. 365-275 B.C.)

Chronology. Diogenes Laertius records that Pyrrho of Elis was first a painter, and then undertook the pursuit of philosophy, journeying in the East with Anaxarchus of Abdera and associating with Magi and Indian Gymnosophists, and living to the age of nearly ninety (IX,61-62). Anaxarchus flourished in the 110th Olympiad (340-337 B.C.) and was a companion of Alexander (D.L., IX,58). There were active schools of painting in the Peloponnesus during the last part of the fourth century B.C., and Elis was situated in the northwest corner of the peninsula. On these indications the dates for Pyrrho's life are conjectured as around 365-275 B.C.

Philosophical Teachings

Virtue the Sole Good. Through his association with Anaxarchus of Abdera, who had been taught by the followers of Democritus, and on account of his own attention to the works of Democritus himself (D.L., IX,58; 67), Pyrrho seems to have been situated in the Democritean tradition, as distinct from that of the Athenian schools. However, he left no writings (D.L. IX, 102), with the result that his philosophical formation cannot be traced with any certainty. According to the more ancient testimony[10] he lived piously, maintaining that virtue was the only good. All other things, even life or death, were *indifferent*.[11] In so

[10] Timon of Phlius, as reported by Aristocles of Messina (first century A.D.) in Eusebius, *P E*, XIV,18,3, and as quoted by Sextus Empiricus, *Adv. Math.*, XI,20; Eratosthenes of Cyrene (third century B.C.) in D.L., IX,66; and Cicero, *De Fin.*, III,4,12; IV,16,43.

[11] *Adiaphoria*, D.L., IX,66. Cicero, *Acad.*, II,42,130, reports it in still stronger fashion as the "insensibility" (*apatheia*) of the wise man to all else but virtue and its opposite, vice. Intermediate things do not move him either way.

On the essentially *moral* character of Pyrrho's teaching, see V. Brochard, *Les Sceptiques Grecs*, 2nd ed. (Paris, 1923), pp. 59-76; L. Robin, *Pyrrhon et le Scepticisme Grec* (Paris, 1944), pp. 20-22.

placing the eternal nature of the good above the vicissitudes of extrinsic things and happenings, he claimed to find a tranquil state like the imperturbability of the Democritean ethics. In the Pyrrhonian tradition this state was called *ataraxy*.

Abstention from Truth Judgment. The indifference of things, seen so sharply in the moral order, meant for Pyrrho that in their being and truth they present nothing definite to human cognition. They allow no sensations or opinions that could give rise to truth or falsehood. Hence there is not a single thing about which one can say "it is" rather than "it is not," or "it both is and is not," or "it neither is nor is not." This teaching of Pyrrho's was known as the *ou mallon*, "not more" (this than that). In its sense things were uncertain (*astathmêta*) and indeterminate (*anepikrita*). So one must remain steadfastly without opinion, not inclining to any side. In this *abs*tension from judgment of truth or falsity, the Pyrrhonists of a later age saw their own *epochê* or *sus*pension of judgment in all philosophical questions. But in Pyrrho himself it seems to have been merely a refusal to rely on any power of human cognition to attain the truth about things, that is, to know them as they are or as they are not. Upon such abstention, according to Timon, an immediate disciple, ataraxy followed "like its shadow" (D.L., IX,107). Sextus Empiricus (*Pyrrh. Hyp.*, I,28-29) represents this sequence as known merely by fortuitous experience, and illustrated by the case of Pyrrho's contemporary, the painter Apelles, who after failing in his efforts to paint a horse's foam threw his sponge at the picture and found it left the exact impression that he had been trying to paint.

Moral Conduct. Although one abstains from all truth judgments, one continually faces decisions in practical life. These are to be made according to the usages of place and epoch. Right and wrong, accordingly, are determined by convention and custom (D.L., IX,61; *cf*.108). In this way there is no abstention from decision in the sphere of action, but only in that of truth. It need not be surprising, then, that in the eyes of Cicero, Pyrrho seemed a rigid moralist rather than a Skeptic, that to a certain Numenius he appeared to dogmatize (D.L., IX,68), and that for Sextus' teacher Theodosius Skepticism did not originate with Pyrrho (IX,70). In any case, Pyrrho's blunt agnosticism in regard to truth seems a far cry from the highly refined philosophical Skepticism to which later followers gave his name.

The most noted of Pyrrho's immediate disciples was Timon of Phlius. Like Pyrrho, he lived to the age of nearly ninety (D.L., IX,112). His dates are placed at about 325 to 235 B.C.[12] He wrote extensively in verse, and was noted especially for three volumes of satires (*silloi*) in which "from his point of view as a Sceptic, he abuses every one and lampoons the dogmatic philosophers" (D.L., IX,111; tr. Hicks). He seems to have systematized Pyrrho's teachings in writing. Anyone who is to be happy (*eudaimonêsein*) has to consider, first, the nature of things, secondly, how one should be disposed towards them, and finally what is attained by proper disposition in regard to them. To these questions he gave Pyrrho's answers. Things are by nature indifferent, we have nothing to express about them (*aphasia*), and the reward is ataraxy.[13] Appearances and the customary prevail everywhere (D.L., IX,105). The tradition of Pyrrho (D.L., IX,115-116) continued till the beginning of the third century A.D.

B. ACADEMIC SKEPTICISM

The second main line of Greek Skepticism began in the Platonic Academy early in the third century B.C. Sextus Empiricus (*Pyrrh. Hyp.*, I,220) relates that as viewed by most writers there were three Academies. The Old Academy was that of Plato himself and his immediate successors. The Middle Academy was that of Arcesilaus and his group. Finally, there was the New Academy, that of Carneades of Cyrene and his successor Clitomachus of Carthage. Some writers, Sextus noted, add a Fourth and Fifth Academy, while Cicero (*Acad.*, I,12,45-46) reports a tradition that styled as the "New Academy" that of Arcesilaus.

The Middle Academy. Arcesilaus of Pitane (in Asia Minor), the founder of the Middle Academy, was represented as an admirer of Plato but also a devoted follower of Pyrrho, and as having adopted the methods of the Megarian dialectical tradition.[14] According to information taken from Hermippus by Diogenes Laertius (IV,44), he was seventy-five when he died, and he had enjoyed unprecedented popularity among the Athenians. He was succeeded, Diogenes further reports without mentioning his source, in the fourth year of the 134th

[12] On the chronology, see Brochard, p. 79, n. 7.
[13] Aristocles, in Eusebius, *P E*, XIV,18,2-4.
[14] D.L., IV,32-33; Eusebius, *P E*, XIV,5,12; 6,4 (from Numenius of Apamea).

Olympiad (241-240 B.C.) by Lacydes, the founder of the New
Academy. This would give the years 316/315-241/240 B.C. as his
dates. Apollodorus, though, in giving the 120th Olympiad (300-297
B.C.) as his *floruit*, seems, if correctly reported,[15] to have placed him
some twenty-five years earlier. In spite of his association with Pyrrho,
he was considered an opponent by Timon. There are indications
enough to show that he regarded himself as a follower of Plato rather
than of Pyrrho. Greek tradition claimed that he did not write any
books. At least there are no fragments of any philosophical content,
though a few epigrams and sayings attributed to him have been preserved by Diogenes Laertius.

Accepting, as did Pyrrho, the stand that things are unintelligible, Arcesilaus denied, according to Cicero's account (*Acad.*,
I,12,45), that there was anything that could be known, even the
Socratic proposition that one knows nothing. Equally strong reasons could be adduced for either side of any question. Therefore
assent should always be withheld. Such an attitude was the
ultimate purpose or end[16] envisaged by the wise man. From this
viewpoint Arcesilaus was considered to have been the first to
practice the *epochê* (D.L., IV,28). For decisions in practical life
he required as a canon the *eulogon*. The *eulogon* (reasonable)
seems to have referred to actions that one could, apart from any
dogmatic commitment, justify with good reasons and fit into a
wise course of conduct.[17] Such teaching appears to have been a
development of Platonism, but in genuinely Skeptical direction.[18]
It is reported as having been projected mainly against Stoic
assertiveness.[19] Sextus (*Pyrrh. Hyp.*, I,232-234), while accepting

[15] D.L., IV,45; *cf.* 59 and 61.
[16] Sextus Empiricus, *Pyrrh. Hyp.*, I,232.
[17] See Sextus, *Adv. Math.*, VII,158; Brochard, pp. 111-112; Robin,
Pyrrhon, pp. 61-67.
[18] See Cicero, *Acad.*, I,12,46. For an interpretation of Plato himself as
finally a skeptic, see Hans Matthias Wolff, *Plato* (Bern, 1957). The stand
that both sides of a question are open to philosophical defense had been
familiar enough from the *Dissoi Logoi*. As applying to all propositions, even to
the proposition that asserts it, it is expressly attributed by Seneca (*Ep. Mor.*,
LXXXVIII, 43) to Protagoras, while Metrodorus of Chios, said by some to
be a pupil of Democritus (D.L., IX,58), denied that one can know anything, even the fact that one knows or does not know, or whether anything
exists or does not exist (DK, 70B 1).
[19] According to the Academic tradition known to Cicero (*Acad.*, I,12,44),
Arcesilaus directed his attack entirely against Zeno's Stoicism. For a detailed
study of this polemic, see Robin, *Pyrrhon*, pp. 49-66; M. dal Pra, *Lo Scetticismo Greco* (Milan, 1950), pp. 83-110.

Arcesilaus as a Skeptic on account of his *epochê,* notes that some considered him as really a dogmatist because he continued to hand on Platonic doctrine.

The New Academy. About Lacydes and his first two or three successors very little is known. The next, Carneades of Cyrene, according to Apollodorus,[20] died at the age of eighty-five in the fourth year of the 162nd Olympiad (129-128 B.C.). He would therefore have headed the Academy about a century after Arcesilaus. From the accounts he appears to have been a remarkably gifted man, but he did not leave any writings. He maintained that there is absolutely no criterion of *truth.* In this he directed his arguments against all his predecessors.[21] Appearances, which are basic for cognition, are affected by subjective conditions; and there are no means of distinguishing absolutely a true appearance from a false appearance, in normal as well as abnormal states.[22] The most one can have is probability, and one must be content with its various degrees.[23] This was known as the *pithanon* (probable, persuasive). It avoided commitment to any dogmatic truth, since what is only probable might turn out to be false.[24] Yet it appeared to Sextus (*Pyrrh. Hyp.* I,226-227) as a positive assertion of the existence of probability and degrees of probability, unlike the undogmatic stand of a Skeptic. It seems to have been developed in conscious rejection of the *eulogon* of Arcesilaus, though there is not enough evidence to determine satisfactorily the exact differences.[25] The fairly regular usage in the Platonic dialogues of leaving questions open could no doubt be taken to allow a doctrine that was content with anything for which reasonable justification could be offered; and from that view it would be scarcely more than a step to conclude that all motives for action, and for assent in general, present only probability of various degrees. However, the details of this development cannot now be traced historically.

[20] D.L., IV,65. Cicero (*Acad.,* II,6,16) states that he lived ninety years.
[21] Sextus Empiricus, *Adv. Math.,* VII,159; 166.
[22] Sextus, *Adv. Math.,* VII,159-165; 402-414. Besides the example of the oar appearing broken in the water, Cicero (*Acad.,* II,25,79) mentions the one color on the pigeon's neck appearing multiple.
[23] Sextus, *Adv. Math.,* VII,166-175. *Cf.* Cicero, *Acad.,* II,10,32; 32, 103-105.
[24] Cicero, *Acad.,* II,32,103.
[25] See Brochard, pp. 110-111.

The Fourth Academy, under Philo of Larissa (*ca.* 147/40-79/77 B.C.), seems to have continued the Skeptical trend in a considerably milder way. In the Fifth, Antiochus of Ascalon (*ca.* 128-68 B.C.) gradually brought the teaching of the Academy back to the assertion of definite knowledge, stemming finally the course of Skepticism within its domain. The Platonic tradition continued, with a strong tendency to incorporate teachings from other philosophical schools, through the period known as Middle Platonism. This period comprised the first two centuries of the Christian era, and in its last years it led up quite noticeably to the final phase of ancient Platonic thought, Neoplatonism. Efforts to revive Pythagorean teachings became mingled with the Platonic tradition during this time in the tendency called Neopythagoreanism. The first to undertake the revival of Pythagorean doctrine is considered to have been Nigidius Figulus, who was active in the first half of the first century B.C. Plutarch of Chaeronea (*ca.* 46-120 A.D.) and Numenius of Apamea (second century A.D.) were influential representatives of the tendency.

The use of Platonic teachings to help interpret the Scriptures was commenced at Alexandria by Philo Judaeus (active in first half of first century A.D.). Philo drew heavily upon the *Timaeus* in explaining the Mosaic account of the world's creation in his *De Opificio Mundi*. The place in which the Ideas are located, however, becomes the mind of God, which Philo, using the Stoic term and notion, calls "the divine Logos" (*De Opif.*, V,20). Later at Alexandria Christian writers continued the use of Platonic philosophy in the service of divine revelation. The most outstanding were Clement of Alexandria (second and third centuries A.D.) and Origen (*ca.* 185-254 A.D.).

C. LATER GREEK SKEPTICISM

The Pyrrhonic tradition seems to have continued at Alexandria. It received new development during the first century B.C. in the writings of Aenesidemus, who appears to have been a contemporary of Cicero, and to have been used by Philo in the early first century A.D. as though he were already well-known at that time. Aenesidemus of Crete, it seems, had been trained in Academic Skepticism. This kind of Skepticism, however, he attacked as dogmatic, and in its place sought to revivify and organize the agnostic attitude of Pyrrho in the mold of the Academy's refined systematic procedure. None of his works has survived. The following titles are known: *Pyrrhonic Discourses*, advocating a thoroughgoing and radical type of Skepticism; *Against Wisdom; On Investigation; Pyrrhonic Outlines*, explaining the ten tropes of the *epoché;* and what seems to have been an introductory treatise on the *Elements.* Five more tropes were added by Agrippa, who was active probably in the middle of the first century A.D. The last of the Pyrrhonic writers was Sextus Empiricus, whose dates are likewise unknown but whose work is indicated as belonging to the late second century A.D. The name "Empiricus" suggests connection with medical activity, a profession in which Sextus engaged. Of his extant works one bears the same title as that of Aenesidemus, *Pyrrhonic Outlines.* The other is called *Against the Mathematicians,* a term that covers the different types of scientists and teachers, such as physicists, logicians, and so on. Five of its eleven books went originally under a separate title *Against the Dogmatists.* Other titles, except for a couple that denote a medical treatise, may refer to parts of these works.

The Tropes. The term "trope" as used by the Skeptics meant a way or form of argument that showed the necessity of the *epoché* or suspension of judgment. The ten systematized by Aenesidemus are based upon the variable nature of their subjects (D.L., IX,79) and seem to have been grounded in the flux doctrine attributed to Heraclitus. They present the arguments that are stock-in-trade for Skeptics everywhere—the easily detected deceptions and relativity of sense impressions, the difference in judgments made by madmen whose state should not be judged less normal than that of anyone else, and the wide variation in tastes and ethical judgments.[26] Of the eight further tropes against the doctrine of causality, as they are attributed to Aenesidemus, the first is based upon the consideration that causality is imperceptible; the other seven stress the deficiencies of the various attempts at explaining causality.[27] Of the five tropes added by Agrippa, the first was based upon the *discord* that arises among men when they try to evaluate the human cognitive processes; the second, on the *infinite regress* in always proving one thing by another; the third, on the *relativity* of perceptions; the fourth, on the impossibility of establishing satisfactory *hypotheses* to serve as principles for demonstration; and the fifth, on the *circularity* involved when the thing to be proved enters into the proof itself.[28]

The Skeptic attack on knowledge of causality was not at all

[26] Sextus, *Pyrrh. Hyp.,* I,36-163; D.L., IX,79-88.
[27] Sextus, *Pyrrh. Hyp.,* I,180-186. *Cf.* D.L., IX,97-99.
[28] Sextus, *Pyrrh. Hyp.,* I,164-177; D.L., IX,88-89.

meant to do away with scientific pursuits in so far as they were useful to life. Rather, the arts were to be cultivated from this viewpoint of their utility, but not for the purpose of knowing the nature of their subjects.[29]

Greek Skepticism, accordingly was a general attack upon the certainty of any of the teachings (*dogmata*) of the philosophers. Those who proclaimed such certainty were in consequence named "dogmatists." In this sense the Skeptics themselves claimed to have no *dogmata*,[30] not even the proposition that nothing could be laid down as certain (D.L., IX,74). Their Skepticism was aimed only at philosophies, and was never intended to curtail action in the sphere of practical life.[31] They are represented as replying to their critics: ". . . for we recognize that it is day and that we are alive, and many other apparent facts in life; but with regard to the things about which our opponents argue so positively, . . . we suspend our judgement because we are not certain, and confine knowledge to our impressions" (*D.L.*, IX,103; tr. Hicks).

SELECTED READINGS AND REFERENCES

PERIPATETICS

Die Schule des Aristoteles, Texte und Kommentar, ed. Fritz Wehrli (Basel: Benno Schwabe, 1944—): 1, Dikaiarchos (1944); 2, Aristoxenos (1945); 3, Klearchos (1948); 4, Demetrios von

[29] Sextus, *Adv. Math.,* I,49-53; *cf. Pyrrh. Hyp.,* II,102.

[30] The Skeptical philosophic formulae like "We determine nothing" were meant as doing away with themselves along with all other positive statements, just as a medicine eliminates itself along with what it is meant to drive out; *cf.* Sextus, *Pyrrh. Hyp.,* I,13-17; 206; D.L., IX,74-76.

[31] For a discussion of this topic, see Phillip De Lacy, "οὐ μᾶλλον and the Antecedents of Ancient Scepticism," *Phronesis,* III (1958), 67-71. The attitude of philosophical Skepticism but at the same time practical acceptance is aptly illustrated by Sextus in his description of the Skeptic's conduct in regard to the Greek gods: "For perchance the Sceptic, as compared with philosophers of other views, will be found in a safer position, since in conformity with his ancestral customs and the laws, he declares that the Gods exist, and performs everything which contributes to their worship and veneration, but, so far as regards philosophic investigation, declines to commit himself rashly." *Adv. Math.,* IX,49; tr. Bury). Greek Skepticism remained in this way from start to finish in the philosophical order. M.dal Pra, *Lo Scetticismo Greco,* p. 217, notes that Skepticism cannot live of its own proper life, but of its very nature is a parasite that lives on other philosophies and so dies with them.

Phaleron (1949); 5, Straton von Lampsakos, 1950; 6, Lykon (1952); 7, Herakleides Pontikos (1953); 8, Eudemos von Rhodos (1955); 9, Phainias von Eresos, Chamaileon, Praxiphanes (1957).

George Malcolm Stratton, *Theophrastus and the Greek Physiological Psychology before Aristotle* (London [Allen & Unwin] and New York: Macmillan, 1917).

Joseph H. H. A. Indemans, *Studiën over Theophrastus* (Nijmegen: Janssen, 1953).

Edmond Barbotin, *La Théorie Aristotélicienne de l'Intellect d'après Théophraste* (Louvain and Paris: J. Vrin, 1954).

Theophrastus On Stones, Introduction, Greek Text, English Translation, and Commentary, ed. Earle R. Caley and John F. C. Richards (Columbus: Ohio State University, 1956).

CYNICS

Donald R. Dudley, *A History of Cynicism from Diogenes to the 6th Century A.D.* (London: Methuen, 1937).

Farrand Sayre, *Diogenes of Sinope, A Study of Greek Cynicism* (Baltimore: J. H. Furst, 1938).

SKEPTICS

Sexti Empirici Opera, 3 vols., ed. Hermann Mutschmann (Leipzig: Teubner, 1912-1954). There is a Loeb Classical Library edition, *Sextus Empiricus*, with an English Translation, 4 vols., by R. G. Bury (1933-1949).

Victor Brochard, *Les Sceptiques Grecs*, 2nd ed. (Paris: J. Vrin, 1923). First published 1887.

Mary Mills Patrick, *The Greek Sceptics* (New York: Columbia University Press, 1929).

Léon Robin, *Pyrrhon et le Scepticisme Grec* (Paris: Presses Universitaires, 1944).

Mario dal Pra, *Lo Scetticismo Greco* (Milan: Fratelli Bocca, 1950).

PLATONISM

Reginald Eldred Witt, *Albinus and the History of Middle Platonism* (Cambridge, Eng.: University Press, 1937).

Harry Austryn Wolfson, *Philo: Foundations of Religious Philosophy in Judaism, Christianity, and Islam*, 2 vols. (Cambridge, Mass.: Harvard University Press, 1947).

Charles Bigg, *The Christian Platonists of Alexandria* (reprint, Oxford: Clarendon Press, 1913). First published 1886.

CHAPTER 17

Epicureans and Stoics

EPICURUS OF ATHENS (341-270 B.C.)

Chronology. According to Apollodorus' *Chronicle,* Epicurus was born in the third year of the 109th Olympiad, on the seventh day of the month of Gamelion, in the seventh year after the death of Plato. The tenth day of Gamelion was assigned in his will to be celebrated each year by his followers as his birthday (D.L., X, 15; 18). This information places the birth of Epicurus around the beginning of 341 B.C. The same account states that when he was thirty-two he founded a school of philosophy first in Mytilene and Lampsacus, and then five years later moved to Athens, where he died in the second year of the 127th Olympiad (271-270 B.C.), in his seventy-second year. Accordingly, he began his school at Athens while Theophrastus was head of the *Peripatos* and Polemon of the Academy.[1]

Life. Epicurus was the son of Athenian parents, and was brought up on the island of Samos, though the place of his birth is unknown. At the age of eighteen he came to Athens, apparently in fulfilment of civic duties. After the death of Alexander (summer, 323 B.C.) the Athenian settlers were expelled from Samos, and Epicurus left Athens for Colophon to join his father. He had become interested in philosophy, perhaps through the works of Democritus, at the age of fourteen. At Colophon he first gathered disciples around him. Later at Athens he acquired a property outside the city. It was known as the Garden. In it he lived for perhaps some thirty-five years a frugal and communal life with his disciples, apart from the political and social activities of the world around him. He bequeathed the Garden to Hermarchus of Mytilene and his successors in the direction of the

[1] A synoptic table of the scholarchs or heads of these three schools, together with those of the Stoa, is given in Ueberweg-Praechter, *Grundriss* (Berlin, 1926), I,663-666.

school, with provision for the celebrating of Epicurean festivals. Women as well as men, and apparently (D.L., X,3; 10) even slaves, were all admitted to membership in the philosophic community. According to the best testimony, Epicurus was of a kindly and likeable disposition. He was able to attract and hold the friendship of those with whom he associated, though he was abusive of other philosophers and outspoken in asserting his own independence of them. He advocated simple living, and claimed himself to be content with plain bread and water—"Such was the man who laid down that pleasure was the end of life" (D.L.,X,11; tr. Hicks).

Writings. Epicurus is reported to have been a prolific writer, surpassing all his predecessors in the number of volumes produced. These amounted to three hundred rolls, all filled with his own thought and without a single quotation from any one else. The best are listed by Diogenes under about forty titles (D.L., X,26-28). Only three letters, lists of forty "Principal Doctrines" and of eighty or eighty-one aphorisms, and various fragments, survive.[2] The first and third letters are accepted today as genuine, and the second, if not genuine, is at least regarded as containing authentic Epicurean doctrine.

PHILOSOPHICAL TEACHINGS

Canonic. The introduction to Epicurean philosophy was called *Canonic,* and was contained in a single work of its founder entitled *The Canon* (D.L., X,30). Dialectic was rejected as superfluous, on the ground that ordinary terms are sufficient for physical inquiries. The criteria of truth are three: sensations, preconceptions, and feelings. Every sensation stands absolutely on its own footing. It is evident in itself, guarantees its own truth, and cannot be refuted by anything whatsoever, not even by another sensation. On these sensations all further knowledge, by reasoning, is based. A preconception (*prolêpsis*) is a sort of universal notion stored in the mind from previous sensations of something external that had often been perceived, and is recalled by

[2] The text of these, with English translation and commentary, may be found in C. Bailey, *Epicurus* (Oxford, 1926). There is a Teubner text of the *Letters* and *Principal Doctrines* and the *Sententiae Vaticanae*, by P. von der Mühll (Leipzig, 1922). Fragments of another letter, from a Herculanean papyrus, were edited by Christian Jensen in *Ein Neuer Brief Epicurs* (Berlin, 1933), and the ethical texts by C. Diano, *Epicuri Ethica* (Florence, 1946).

a new sensation.[3] Feelings are twofold—pleasure and pain. Pleasure is favorable to animate nature, while pain is hostile. They are the criteria by which actions are either chosen or avoided (D.L., X,33-34).

Philosophy of Nature. The first letter of Epicurus, written to a disciple, introduces itself as an epitome of his longer works on nature. In a straightforward and compelling style it explains very dogmatically that the universe consists of void or space, and bodies. If there were no void or space, bodies would have nothing in which to be and in which to move. But it is evident through sensation that there are bodies and that they are in motion. Those bodies are unlimited in number. Anything limited has to be marked off by something else; but the sum total of things leaves nothing else by which it could be marked off. The void, too, has to be unlimited in order to provide place for the unlimited number of bodies. Composite bodies are formed from atoms and dissolve into atoms. The atoms vary indefinitely in their shapes, even though the number of shapes is not absolutely unlimited. The like atoms of each shape, however, are unlimited in number. There is nothing, therefore, against an infinity of worlds. The atoms are in perpetual motion. They go onward to the utmost, so in fact the number of worlds is unlimited. Images of the same shape as solid bodies, but thinner than any visible object, are given off by the bodies, reach the senses, and make perception possible. On account of their thinness these *eidôla* or images can travel through the void at great velocities. The soul is something corporeal, and is spread throughout the body, being composed of fine particles. The frame or body loses the power of sensation when the soul departs. The soul likewise loses this power, for sensation requires both body and soul. If the soul were not corporeal, it would be merely empty space, and so could not act or be acted upon. Accidents have no separate existence, but belong to bodies just as the senses show them. Time is a very special kind of

[3] Cicero (*De Nat. Deorum,* I,17-19,44-49), however, describes these preconceptions as innate, and not perceived by the senses, as though they consisted of streams of finer atoms that escape the sense organs. The other interpretation is defended by C. Bailey, *The Greek Atomists and Epicurus* (Oxford, 1928), pp. 418-421; 568-576; that of Cicero, by N. W. DeWitt, *Epicurus and His Philosophy* (Minneapolis, 1954), pp. 142-150. Neither explanation, however, is found in the extant text of Epicurus himself.

accident, and on account of its nature it cannot be investigated by means of the preconceptions already existing in the mind.

Natural science, accordingly, shows the cause of things. Understanding the universe in this way, as something composed only of atoms and void, one will be delivered from the principal cause of disturbance, namely that the heavenly bodies have wills and activities that affect one's life. In basing all one's knowledge on the senses as the criteria of truth, one thereby attains peace of mind or ataraxy. The summary concludes: "Wherefore we must pay attention to internal feelings and to external sensations in general and in particular, . . . and to every immediate intuition in accordance with each of the standards of judgement. For if we pay attention to these, we shall rightly trace the causes whence arose our mental disturbance and fear, and, by learning the true causes of celestial phenomena and all other occurrences that come to pass from time to time, we shall free ourselves from all which produces the utmost fear in other men" (D.L., X,82; tr. Bailey).

This epitome reveals clearly enough that Epicurus had taken over the thoroughgoing atomistic docrtine of Democritus, with a number of minor changes in detail. He is using that doctrine as a means of securing peace of mind. Such is the whole purpose of natural philosophy and the only need for it. This is stated explicitly in the *Principal Doctrines*.[4] Apparently in opposition to the Skeptical search for ataraxy in the denial of any criterion of truth, the clear evidence of sensation is propounded as the basic criterion of the truth that frees from fear and brings peace of mind.

The second letter offers a summary of the Epicurean teaching on the celestial phenomena, for a disciple. The whole purpose of that study, again, is to acquire ataraxy and unshakeable confidence (D.L., X,85) by escaping the influence of myth (X,116).

Moral Philosophy. The third letter is likewise addressed to a disciple, but seems to have been intended for the general reading public. In true Democritean[5] fashion it represents philosophy as the health of the soul. It requires the cultivation of that health

[4] *Principal Doctrines*, XI; *cf.* XII. For the differences in detail between the atomism of Epicurus and that of Democritus, see Bailey, *Greek Atomists*, pp. 529-531.

[5] *Cf. supra*, Chapter VIII, nn. 21-23.

of the soul from youth to old age, if one is to achieve *eudaimonia* (D.L., X,122). It sketches the basic elements of right and seemly living, and urges their observance—"... these do and practice, considering them to be the first principles (*stoicheia*) of the good life" (X,123; tr. Bailey).

Piety and Impiety. The first element of good moral life is to have the correct attitude towards the gods: "First of all believe that god is a being immortal and blessed, even as the common idea of a god is engraved on men's minds, and do not assign to him anything alien to his immortality or ill-suited to his blessedness; but believe about him everything that can uphold his blessedness and immortality. For gods there are, since knowledge of them is by clear vision" (D.L., X,123; tr. Bailey). The word for "believe" is the official word *nomizô*, designating the honors to be paid to the gods in a Greek city-state. Epicurus is clearly requiring conformity to that official practice. The real impiety, however, is to believe that the gods have any influence on the good and bad fortunes of men: "And the impious man is not he who denies the gods of the many, but he who attaches to the gods the beliefs of the many. For the statements of the many about the gods are not conceptions derived from sensation, but false suppositions, according to which the greatest misfortunes befall the wicked and the greatest blessings (the good) by the gift of the gods." (123-124; tr. Bailey). There is enough evidence to establish the sincerity of Epicurus' belief in gods and the necessity of paying them the customary civic honors.[6] The type of knowledge by which the gods are immediately known cannot be determined satisfactorily from the extant text.[7] In the text Epicurus is intent rather on emphasizing that the gods cannot influence human life one way or the other, and so their existence need not be the cause of any mental disturbance to men.

Death. According to the physical doctrine of Epicurus, all sensation ceases with death, as sensation required union of body and soul. This means that all pain and so all evil will cease with death. Death therefore is not an evil to be dreaded, though the

---

[6] On this subject, see A. J. Festugière, *Epicurus and His Gods* (Cambridge, Mass., 1956), pp. 58-62. The charge of impiety urged against the Epicureans may be compared with the judicial charge of impiety brought against Socrates.

[7] See Bailey, *Epicurus*, p. 330, n. 8; *Greek Atomists*, pp. 438-467.

fear of it has to be overcome by correct thinking: "Become accustomed to the belief that death is nothing to us. For all good and evil consists in sensation, but death is deprivation of sensation. And therefore a right understanding that death is nothing to us makes the mortality of life enjoyable, not because it adds to it an infinite span of time, but because it takes away the craving for immortality. For there is nothing terrible in life for the man who has truly comprehended that there is nothing terrible in not living. . . . So death, the most terrifying of ills, is nothing to us, since so long as we exist, death is not with us; but when death comes, then we do not exist" (*D.L.*, X,124-125; tr. Bailey).

Pleasure. Since the aim of living is to produce peace of mind, one must always act in such a way as to avoid pain and fear. Absence of pleasure, though, makes one feel pain. Pleasure, accordingly, is the first good: "And for this cause we call pleasure the beginning and end of the blessed life. For we recognize pleasure as the first good innate in us, and from pleasure we begin every act of choice and avoidance, and to pleasure we return again, using the feeling as the standard by which we judge every good." (*D.L.*, X,128-129; tr. Bailey). Just as sensations are the criteria of scientific truth, so then are the feelings of pleasure and pain the criteria of what is good and bad in the moral order.

Prudence. As there are many pleasures, however, and some are incompatible with others, one has to calculate the advantages and disadvantages in choosing pleasures, yet always with the view of obtaining on the whole the greatest possible pleasure: "Every pleasure then because of its natural kinship to us is good, yet not every pleasure is to be chosen: even as every pain also is an evil, yet not all are always of a nature to be avoided. Yet by a scale of comparison and by the consideration of advantages and disadvantages we must form our judgement on all these matters. For the good on certain occasions we treat as bad, and conversely the bad as good" (D.L., X,129-130; tr. Bailey). For instance, simple diet, even of bread and water, produces the highest pleasure when one is accustomed to it and needs it. A profligate life does not result in a pleasant life. Since the choice of pleasures depends upon prudence (*phronêsis*), this virtue is the very foundation of the most pleasant life: "Of all this the beginning and the greatest good is prudence. Wherefore prudence is a more precious thing even than philosophy; for from prudence are sprung all the other virtues, and it teaches us that it is not possible to live pleasantly without living prudently and honourably and justly, (nor, again, to live a life of prudence, honour, and justice without living pleasantly). For the virtues are by nature bound up with the pleasant life, and the pleasant life is inseparable from them." (X,132; tr. Bailey). The letter ends with an exhortation to meditate on these things day and night.

The mutual accompaniment of virtue and pleasure is understood by Epicurus in a setting quite different from the Aristotelian. For him the basic pleasure is of a lower order: "The beginning and the root of all good is the pleasure of the stomach: even wisdom and culture must be referred to this" (*Fr.* 59; tr. Bailey). This outspoken doctrine makes contentment of the stomach the first need in the pursuit of a philosophic life.[8] The only ethical reason for the virtue of justice is the avoidance of the fear attached to lawbreaking: "Injustice is not an evil in itself, but only in consequence of the fear which attaches to the apprehension of being unable to escape those appointed to punish such actions" (*Principal Doctrines,* XXXIV; tr. Bailey). The motive for obeying the law, accordingly, is to keep free from mental disturbance. Self-sufficiency is stressed (*Sententiae Vaticanae,* LXXVII; *Fr.* 70). This self-sufficiency is placed in living unknown (*Fr.* 86), released from the prison of public affairs and politics (*SV,* LVIII). The abstention from public life, so different from the attitude of Plato and Aristotle, seems to reflect the spirit of Athens under its later rulers. Yet the wise man will not "turn dog," that is, will not become a Cynic (D.L., X,119). The Epicurean, therefore, will live according to social standards and conventions, but will be self-sufficient as an individual, not as a citizen. Friendship, though, was stressed in the philosophy of the Garden.[9] The motive throughout all this, of course, remains pleasure (*Fr.* 10; 12); and among pleasures there is no essential difference (*Principal Doctrines,* IX). The lack of any specific difference in pleasures as such sharply distinguishes the Epicurean notion from the Aristotelian, where pleasure is distinguished according to the specifically different actions that it accompanies.

---

[8] See Bailey, *Epicurus,* pp. 397-398.
[9] See Festugière, pp. 27-50.

Solely on the basis of the *amount* of pleasure obtainable does the Epicurean prudence make its decisions. This is considered to be living according to nature.[10]

The extant texts show that Epicurus was familiar with the other current philosophies of the age. He combatted Skepticism and Cynicism, though taking over the concepts of ataraxy and self-sufficiency and claiming that they were to be attained only on the basis of the Garden's dogmatic atomism. His ethical terminology shows a close acquaintance with the work of Plato and with the phraseology of Aristotle.[11] The appeal of his teaching was direct and popular. Base knowledge on evident sensation, direct conduct according to the obvious motives of attaining pleasure and avoiding pain: in this simple way one lives according to nature and acquires peace of mind and *eudaimonia*. All available evidence shows that followers of Epicurus like Diogenes of Oenoanda (second century A.D.) propagated their philosophy with a missionary zeal. As a result it became the most widespread of the ancient Greek philosophies, lasting over six centuries, and fading out in the middle of the fourth century A.D.[12] Its best-known Latin exponent was Lucretius, in his poem *De Rerum Natura,* written some time between the years 59 and 54 B.C. It was accused by its enemies of atheism on account of its teaching about the gods, and of effeminacy because of its doctrine on pleasure. It was a highly coherent and closed system of thought, its natural philosophy being developed according to its logic or Canonic, and its ethics following cogently upon its conception of nature.

ZENO OF CITIUM (*CA.* 362/357?-264/259 B.C.)

Chronology. A decree of the Athenians under the archonship of Arrhenides in the 129th Olympiad (264-261 B.C.) stated that as Zeno of Citium had devoted many years in the city to philosophy and to teaching the youth virtue and temperance, it seemed good to the people to bestow praise upon him and to build him a tomb at public

[10] See *Principal Doctrines,* XXV; *Fr.* 85. *Cf. Fr.* 57.

[11] For a study of the Platonic and Aristotelian background in the formation of Epicurus, see E. Bignone, *L'Aristotele Perduto e la Formazione Filosofica di Epicuro,* 2 vols. (Florence, 1936).

[12] A synopsis of the history of the Epicurean movement may be found in DeWitt, pp. 328-353.

expense (D.L., VII,10-11). Other testimonia indicate the first year of that Olympiad as the date of his death. His fellow citizen and disciple, Persaeus, is reported to have said that Zeno came to Athens at the age of twenty-two and that he "completed seventy-two years in the ethical schools" (D.L., VII,28). This would seem to mean that he lived at least ninety-four years, and so would have been born about 358/357 B.C., some seventeen years earlier than Epicurus. The chronology, however, is far from being certain, especially as regards the date of Zeno's birth. Lucian (*Macr.*, 19) and Diogenes Laertius (VII,28) say that he lived ninety-eight years, but the testimony of Persaeus has usually been read to mean that he died at the age of seventy-two. A couple of testimonia would suggest that he lived a few years beyond 263 B.C. Diogenes (VII,2), moreover, indicates that Zeno commenced to associate with Crates the Cynic at the age of thirty, and his report (VII,28) from Apollonius of Tyre (first century B.C.) has been interpreted to mean that Zeno inaugurated his own school at the age of fifty-eight.

Life.   According to all available indications,[13] Zeno was of Phoenician and not Greek descent, though everything known about his doctrine points to a thoroughly Greek education. He was a native of Citium in Cyprus, a Greek colony that had Phoenician settlers. Coming to Athens while still in early manhood, he became a pupil first of Crates the Cynic (*fl.* 328 B.C.) and then, for twenty years, of Stilpo the Megarian and of Xenocrates and Polemon (D.L., VII,2; 4). Probably around the end of the fourth century, and so about the same time or a very few years after Epicurus had commenced teaching in Athens, he inaugurated a school of his own in a colonnade known as the Painted Porch or the Portico of Pisianax. He would be close to sixty years old at the time. From the Porch (*stoa*) in which he held his discussions the name Stoic had its origin. Of the four principal philosophical schools at Athens, the Academy, the Peripatos, the Garden, and the Stoa, it was the only one that was located from the start within the city walls.

Works.   Titles of twenty works written by Zeno were recorded by Diogenes Laertius (VII,4). Of these, as well as of the writings of the other ancient Stoics, only fragments survive, mostly in indirect quotation or in paraphrase.[14] The scarcity of direct quotations and the

---

[13] For these, see M. Pohlenz, *Die Stoa* (Göttingen, 1948), I, 22-23. On the chronology, see C. B. Armstrong, *Hermathena*, XX (1930), 360-365.

[14] The fragments have been collected and edited by H. v. Arnim, *Stoicorum Veterum Fragmenta*, 4 vols. (Leipzig, 1903-1924). On the history of the Stoic philosophy, see Pohlenz, *op.cit.* There were disagreements from the start, SVF, II, 10 (*Fr.* 20).

eclectic character of later reports render a consistent detailed picture of Stoic philosophy very difficult. The general outlines, however, appear clearly enough. Though these are found attributed to Zeno himself, it may well be that their systematized form is the work of the third head of the school, Chrysippus.

PHILOSOPHICAL TEACHINGS

Division of the Sciences. The Stoic division of philosophy into physical, ethical, and logical corresponds to the general lines of the Epicurean division, and is attributed (D.L., VII,39) to Zeno himself. Through the influence of the Stoics this threefold division was to have a long history, side by side with the Peripatetic division of the sciences. The order in which the different branches were to be studied, however, varied among the Stoics. According to some, no one part was independent of the others, but rather all blended together. Logic was given the same status as the other two divisions, and not the role of a mere instrument of the sciences proper, as in the Peripatetic schema. For some of them, logic included both rhetoric and dialectic (VII,40-41), though dialectic occupied most of the attention.

Logic. Stoic logic, stemming largely from a Megarian background, seems to have attained the general lines of its full development in the numerous works of Chrysippus, and to have been diffused widely in handbooks called introductions to logic. These writings have all been lost. Their doctrine can be known today only through the accounts of Sextus Empiricus (*Adv. Math.*, VIII; *Pyrrh. Hyp.*, II) and Diogenes Laertius (VII,41-83), and a number of scattered and often confused statements in other ancient authors, mostly unsympathetic. According to these reports the Stoics distinguished the meaning (*lekton*) of the sounds uttered in speech from the sounds themselves (the signs) and from the externally existent object (*to tynchanon*) to which they referred. The sign and the external existent were both corporeal. The meaning (*lekton*) was what was understood by a person who knew the language and missed by a person ignorant of the language, when both heard the same sounds. It was not perceived, for instance, by the barbarians when they heard Greek. Unlike the other two it was not considered to be a body, just as the void, place, and time were not bodies, though how anything could be incorporeal in the general framework of the Stoic philosophy seems to have made some Stoics deny the existence of the *lekta* (*Adv. Math.,* VIII,258) and to have caused unending controversy (262).

A complete *lekton* had both subject and predicate, and consisted of a proposition, question, command, wish, and the like. The subject alone, or the predicate alone, was an incomplete *lekton.* The Stoics had a doctrine of categories, though there is no evidence that it was treated in connection with the incomplete *lekta,* and it has given rise to doubts whether it belonged in their logic at all, and not in their physics. It taught that there was a supreme genus, "something" or "being," and four main categories, 1) substrate, 2) quality, 3) state, and 4) relation. Each category contained and determined its predecessor according to the above order. The function of the categories in Stoic teaching has not yet been determined satisfactorily.

Propositions for the Stoics were simple or compound. A simple proposition had one subject and one predicate. A compound proposition was composed of two occurrences of the same proposition or of different propositions, joined by a logical connective. Compound propositions were conditional if joined by the connective "if," disjunctive if joined by "either—or," conjunctive if joined by "and." Inferential (connected by "since"), causal (connected by "because"), and other types are mentioned but do not seem to have played an essential role in Stoic logic.

With propositions, arguments were formed. Arguments were studied from the viewpoints of validity, truth, and demonstration. An argument could be valid or invalid. A valid argument could be true or false, and a true argument could be demonstrative or non-demonstrative. A demonstrative argument was one that brought to light a true conclusion not already known. "If it is day, it is light; but it is day; therefore it is light" is valid and true but not demonstrative, because "it is light" was already known. On the other hand, "If sweat drops flow through the surface, knowable pores of the flesh exist; but the first; therefore the second" (*Adv. Math.,* VIII,305-306) is demonstrative because the conclusion was previously unknown. There were five (or for some Stoics more than five) basic modes or *schêmata* of non-demonstrable arguments that have no need of demonstration because they are obviously conclusive. These were accordingly accepted as axiomatic. They were:

1) If the first, then the second; but the first; therefore the second.

2) If the first, then the second; but not the second; therefore not the first.

3) Not both the first and the second; but the first; therefore not the second.

4) Either the first or the second; but the first; therefore not the second. The fifth seems to have been:

5) Either the first or the second; but not the first; therefore the second. To these basic modes all other forms of valid argument could be reduced. The Stoics had four rules (*themata*) for this reduction, of which only two, or at most three, can be determined today. The exact nature of these rules and the manner of their application, however, remain obscure. Invalid arguments and paradoxes seem to have been discussed at great length. The most noted was that called "The Liar." It seems to have been expressed in different ways, for instance that the man who says he is lying is both telling the truth and lying.

The Stoic logic seems to have dealt at considerable length with impressions, criteria of truth, terms, definitions, genera and species and classifications, contraries and ambiguities. Nevertheless its truly distinctive feature lay in its character as a propositional logic instead of a class logic. The steps of its procedure were accordingly expressed in ordinal numbers (if the first, then the second) and not, as with the Aristotelian, in letters of the alphabet (every B is A). In later antiquity, syncretism of the Stoic and the Peripatetic logical traditions was prevalent, though the earlier Stoics seem to have made a point of using different terminology from the Aristotelian. There is not enough left of Stoic logic, however, to evaluate it at all adequately. Mathematical logicians are able to see in it anticipations of modern theories in semantics and implication, and so consider it the highest form attained by ancient logical endeavor. Yet the wide disagreement on vital questions among the Stoics and their Megarian predecessors, and the ancient complaints that their leading exponent Chrysippus was repetitious and haphazard in his presentation, suggest that Stoic logic never reached the degree of scientific unity and organization found in the Aristotelian *Analytics*. But it did make significant additions to logical research among the Greeks. It likewise included in its scope what today is called grammar.

Cosmology. The Stoic natural philosophy or account of the cosmos (*logos peri tou kosmou*) had a twofold division, corresponding to the Aristotelian mathematical and physical treatments of natural things. There was for the Stoics on the one hand a mathematical account of the universe, as may be seen for instance in the study of the size and movements of the celestial bodies. On the other hand there was another type of inquiry that was solely physical, and that treated of the substance (*ousia*) of the cosmos, of its beginning or lack of beginning in time, of its animation, of its government by providence, and such questions (D.L., VII,132-133). From this viewpoint there are two original principles, a passive principle named matter and an active principle called god, mind, fate, Zeus, and many other names. This active principle was conceived as a sort of cosmic fire or fiery breath (*pneuma*). It was called "the seminal reason (*logos*) of the cosmos" (D.L., VII,136). It is the artificer of everything, producing the basic elements and all the bodies in the universe, pervading them all and governing them all according to reason. In this way the whole cosmos is a living being and the "substance of God is declared by Zeno to be the whole world and the heaven, . . ."[15] The earlier and most of the subsequent Stoics taught a periodic return of all things to the primitive state and a repetition of the development process (*ekpyrôsis, palingenesis*).

Ethics. For Zeno the goal of human striving was life according to nature. This was the same as a virtuous life. The reason was that any individual nature is a part of the nature of the whole cosmos, and so life according to nature means life according to right reason; and living according to right reason is living virtuously. In such virtue does *eudaimonia* or human happiness consist (D.L., VII,87-88). The basic impulse of an animal is towards self-preservation, and not, in Epicurean fashion, to pleasure.

---

[15] D.L., VIII,148; tr. Hicks. For testimonia attributing the details of these doctrines to Zeno, see V. Arnim, *SVF*, I, 24-26 (*Frs.* 85-92). On the active principle as *pneuma, cf.* II, 145.1-3 (*Fr.* 440); 145.16-34 (*Fr.* 441); 154. 7-9 (*Fr.* 473); 310.24-25 (*Fr.* 1051); 311.11-15 (*Fr.* 1054). On the *ekpyrôsis* and *palingenesis,* see I, 27 (*Fr.* 98); 32 (*Fr.* 107); II,181-191 (*Frs.* 596-632).

Pleasure is but a by-product and an aftermath. In plants everything is regulated by nature without sensation. In animals, impulse (*hormê*) is added. In brute animals, nature's rule is to follow immediately the direction of the impulse. In rational beings, however, nature requires life according to reason. In them, impulse is to be directed by reason. For them, to live according to nature means to live according to reason (D.L., VII,85-87). This means living according to the common law, the law that is right reason and is identical with the Stoic Zeus. Such virtuous life is chosen for its own sake and not from any external motive like hope or fear. It is accordingly the supreme end of human endeavor.

On this basis the Stoics drew up their lists of the virtues, all of which contributed to making the individual's life conform with reason. The virtues involve one another reciprocally. He who has one virtue will therefore have all the others (D.L., VII,125). To act according to reason was called one's duty (*to kathêkon*). Zeno was said to have been the first to use the word as a technical term.[16] Passion and emotion were defined by him as irrational and so as an unnatural movement in the soul (VII,110). The wise man, the man who lives according to reason, is therefore passionless. All good men, accordingly, are austere, for they will have nothing to do with pleasure (VII,117). The Stoic will take part in politics, since by so doing he will promote virtue and restrain vice. Of the three types of life, the contemplative, the practical, and the rational, he will choose the rational, that is, the life that combines both contemplation and action, because by nature man is meant for both. In his own work *The Republic,* Zeno is said to have advocated like Plato community of wives and children among the wise. The Stoic wise man may find it reasonable to make his own departure from life if it is necessary for the sake of homeland or friends, or in case of extreme suffering or incurable disease (D.L., VII,130-131). The example of Socrates seems to have been in mind in this teaching.

Zeno was succeeded by Cleanthes of Assos, noted for his *Hymn to Zeus,* and then by Chrysippus of Soli in Cilicia, the great

---

[16] D.L., VII, 108. Actually, the term had been used in that sense by Plato, *Plt.*, 295B. The same meaning in military usage for the verb may be seen in Xenophon, *Anab.*, I,9,7.

systematizer of the Stoic teaching. Other outstanding names in the Stoic tradition were Panaetius of Lindus (active during second half of second century B.C.). and Posidonius of Apamea in Syria (active during first half of first century B.C.). In the Roman Empire Stoic philosophy obtained considerable vogue, was accepted by court figures like Seneca, and influenced the thinking of men like Cicero and Horace, and the emperor Marcus Aurelius. The imperturbability usually associated with the notion of Stoicism is found perhaps best expressed in the *Discourses* and *Encheiridion* of the slave-born philosopher Epictetus, who lived in the last half of the first and first quarter of the second centuries A.D. These works,[17] written down by his disciple Arrian, carry to its unnatural extreme the attitude of not letting external things or happenings affect one's disposition of mind; e.g.: "For only cease to admire your clothes, and you are not angry with him who steals them: cease to admire your wife's beauty, and you cease to be angry with the adulterer. Know that the thief and adulterer have no place among things that are your own, but only among things that are another's and beyond your power. . . . Who then is the man who is invincible? He whom nothing beyond his will can dismay." (*Discourses*, I,18, 11-21; tr. P. E. Matheson). The Stoic school died out in the third century A.D. It continued indirectly to exert its influence upon the gradual systematization of the Christian moral doctrine on the virtues, and its detailed divisions of virtues and passions played a notable role in the early development of mediaeval moral philosophy.

RETROSPECT

During this long period of philosophical discussion, from which so little remains, the different schools carried on their activities mostly in open hostility to one another, and yet with a quite free borrowing of technical notions and terms. The Stoics, for instance, took over the Epicurean doctrine of the preconceptions (*prolêpseis*), in the sense of common concepts.[18] In general, the efforts

[17] A convenient edition may be found in the *Loeb Classical Library*, by W. A. Oldfather, *Epictetus, With an English Translation*, 2 vols. (London & New York, 1925-1928). For bibliographical information, see Oldfather's *Bibliography of Epictetus* (Urbana, 1927 and 1952).

[18] SVF, II, 28 (*Frs.* 82-83); cf. Cicero, *De Nat. Deorum*, I,17,44.

of this period were directed towards the attaining of ataraxy or a life undisturbed by the inevitable troubles and adversities of earthly existence. The enthusiastic absorption in being and form and goodness that had characterized the youthful vigor of preceding Greek philosophy gave way to the more restrained ambitions and interests of a long middle age. The old ardor for pure contemplation, however, was to break forth once more in all its brilliance, as renewed interest in Platonic thought gradually prepared the way for the final phase of ancient pagan philosophy. This was the movement that since the last century has been known under the name of Neoplatonism.

SELECTED READINGS AND REFERENCES

EPICUREANS

Cyril Bailey, *Epicurus: The Extant Remains,* With Short Critical Apparatus, Translation and Notes (Oxford: Clarendon Press, 1926).

————, *The Greek Atomists and Epicurus* (Oxford: Clarendon Press, 1928).

————, *Titi Lucreti Cari De Rerum Natura,* Edited with Prolegomena, Critical Apparatus, Translation, and Commentary, 3 vols. (Oxford: Clarendon Press, 1947).

Johannes William, *Diogenis Oenoandensis Fragmenta* (Leipzig: Teubner, 1907).

F. Solmsen, "Epicurus and Cosmological Heresies," *AJP,* LXXII (1951), 1-23.

Gaetano Capone Braga, *Studi su Epicuro* (Milan: C. Marzorati, 1951).

R. Schottlaender, "Kynisiert Epikur?", *Hermes,* LXXXII (1954), 444-450.

Norman Wentworth DeWitt, *Epicurus and His Philosophy* (Minneapolis: University of Minnesota Press, 1954).

André Jean Festugière, *Epicurus and His Gods,* tr. C. W. Chilton (Cambridge, Mass.: Harvard University Press, 1956). Published in French, 1946.

STOICS

Hans von Arnim, *Stoicorum Veterum Fragmenta,* 4 vols. (Leipzig: Teubner, 1903-1924).

John Bonforte, *The Philosophy of Epictetus* (New York: Philosophical Library, 1955). English tr.

William Abbot Oldfather, *Contributions towards a Bibliography of*

Epictetus (Urbana: University of Illinois Press, 1927. Supplement, 1952).

Edwyn Bevan, *Stoics and Sceptics* (Oxford: Clarendon Press, 1913).

C. B. Armstrong, "The Chronology of Zeno of Citium, *"Hermathena,* XX (1930), 360-365.

Max Pohlenz, *Die Stoa,* 2 vols. (Göttingen: Vandenhoeck & Ruprecht, 1948-1949).

Benson Mates, *Stoic Logic* (Berkeley: University of California Press, 1953).

Margaret E. Reesor, "The Stoic Categories," *AJP,* LXXVIII (1957), 63-82.

E. Vernon Arnold, *Roman Stoicism* (New York: The Humanities Press, 1958).

B. Wiśniewski, "The Problem of Cognition of the External World in Stoic Philosophy," *Classica et Mediaevalia,* XIX (1958), 110-119.

P. G. Walsh, "Livy and Stoicism," *AJP,* LXXIX (1958), 355-375.

[CHAPTER 18]

Neoplatonism

THE LAST GREAT effort of ancient pagan philosophy is now called Neoplatonism. The term dates only from the nineteenth century. The movement itself was regarded by its exponents as the direct continuation of Platonic thought. To themselves and to their contemporaries these men appeared simply as Platonists. Attempts have been made to see some of the characteristic doctrines of Neoplatonism in preceding thinkers, but as a distinct and developed philosophy it is not found in any writings earlier than those of Plotinus. Plotinus, accordingly, may for all practical purposes be considered its founder.

PLOTINUS (204/205-270 A.D.)

Life. Practically all that is known about the life of Plotinus comes from the biography written by his disciple Porphyry. According to Porphyry, Plotinus would never say anything about his family or birthplace. He even seemed ashamed of having to lead a bodily life (*Life*, 1). His racial origin and his native city remained unknown for Porphyry, though around the end of the fourth century "Lyco" (Lycopolis ?), Egypt, was given by Eunapius (*Vitae Soph.*, III,1,1; ed. Giangrande) as the place of his birth. He was born, Porphyry relates, during the thirteenth year of the reign of Septimius Severus. As Porphyry seems to begin the years in Egyptian fashion at August 29 or 30, and to count incomplete years as well as complete ones, he would be placing the birth of Plotinus sometime within the year commencing with the end of August, 204 A.D. Similarly, in stating that Plotinus died at the age of sixty-six towards the end of the second year of the reign of Claudius, he would mean not long before the end of August, 270 A.D., in the sixty-sixth year of life.

395

At the age of twenty-seven Plotinus became intensely interested in philosophy. He was disappointed, however, with the most highly reputed teachers at Alexandria, until he heard a discourse by Ammonius Saccas. Ammonius, Porphyry wrote, had been brought up a Christian but had abandoned the Christian faith.[1] Under Ammonius, Plotinus continued the study of philosophy for the next eleven years. Then, in search of an opportunity to investigate Persian and Indian thought, at the age of thirty-nine he joined the expedition of the Emperor Gordian against Persia. However, he did not get any further than Mesopotamia, and there is no reliable evidence that he ever acquired a direct knowledge of Indian philosophy.

Escaping with great difficulty after the failure of Gordian's expedition, Plotinus came to Rome, settled there, and engaged in philosophical discussions for ten years. Only after that period, and so at the age of about fifty, did he begin to write (*Life*, 3). He became a close friend of the Emperor Gallienus and of others high in political life, but in his writings he shows no sign of political inclinations on his own part. Porphyry mentions, however, that Plotinus nearly persuaded Gallienus to rebuild a city for philosophers in Campania. It was to be called Platonopolis, and was to be governed according to Plato's laws (*Life*, 12). Porphyry further records that Plotinus was opposed to eating the flesh of animals, or using medicines containing any substance taken from animals (*Life*, 2).

Porphyry, himself thirty years old at the time, met Plotinus in the tenth year of Gallienus' reign, when Plotinus was about fifty-nine (*Life*, 4). He relates that four times during the period that he knew him, and so during the next seven or eight years, Plotinus attained a state of ineffable union with "the god above all things."[2] The achievement of this ecstatic union was, according to Porphyry, the one goal of Plotinus' life. Porphyry himself reached this state of union once, in his sixty-eighth year (*Life*, 23).

Writings.   The treatises of Plotinus, written from about the age of fifty on, all belong to the last seventeen years or so of his life. They do not allow much time for doctrinal development, at least in any radical

---

[1] Eusebius (*Eccl.Hist.*, VI,19,10) denies the assertion that Ammonius gave up the Christian teaching, perhaps confusing this Ammonius with another of the same name.

On the chronology of Plotinus, see Hans Oppermann, *Plotins Leben* (Heidelberg, 1929), pp. 29-57.

[2] *Life of Plotinus*, 23.16. The texts of Plotinus and of his *Life* by Porphyry are cited in this chapter according to the lineation of E. Bréhier's *Ennéades* (Paris, 1924-1938). The translation of the passages from the first five *Enneads* follows the text established by Paul Henry and Hans-Rudolf Schwyzer, *Plotini Opera*, Vols. I and II (Paris and Brussels, 1951-1959).

sense. Therefore, in spite of some minor differences that may be found in them, they may all be taken to represent his mature thought. According to Porphyry, they were never arranged systematically or given titles by their author. In fact, they were not even read over by him, partly on account of his poor eyesight. They were arranged by Porphyry according to their subject matter, starting with the ethical discourses, into six groups of nine treatises each. This was the origin of the name *Enneads*, or groups of nine. Porphyry, who had been entrusted by Plotinus with the revision, faithfully respected the text itself, at least as far as can be ascertained. He changed only the arrangement, using titles that had become accepted, and recording the succession in which Plotinus himself had written the different groups of treatises (*Life*, 4-8; 24).

PHILOSOPHICAL TEACHINGS

Ascent of the Soul. The exhortation of Plotinus to his hearers was to follow the path that leads to union with the supreme principle of all, the union that was the single purpose of Plotinus' own strivings. In the treatise *On Beauty*, listed first in the earliest group of his writings, the upward journey of the soul is made dependent upon a godlike and seemly disposition. The journey is then described in the manner of the ascending dialectic in Plato's *Symposium* (210A-211B). It reaches the order of intelligence, in which the Ideas function both as offspring and as entity of intelligence itself. Beyond the whole world of the Ideas, however, is their source, the good, which Plato's *Republic* (VI,509B) had described as the origin of being to the Ideas and of all knowledge of them. It is represented as screened off from the intellectual gaze. Plotinus urges: "Let everyone, then, first become godlike and everyone beautiful, if he is to behold god and anything beautiful. For ascending he will come first to the intelligence; and *there* he will know that all the Forms are beautiful; and he will say that beauty consists in this, the Ideas. For through these, the children and entity (*ousia*) of intelligence, are all things beautiful. That which is beyond this we call the nature of the good, having the beautiful raised shieldlike before it" (*En.*, I,6,9.32-39). The region above the sensible world is regularly referred to by Plotinus as *there*, and the visible universe as *here*.

Platonic Background. As emerges clearly enough from the

above way of speaking, the movement of Plotinus' philosophy is an intuitional dialectic, starting with the cognition of sensible things and rising from their participated beauty to the vision of the Ideas, with the aim of penetrating somehow still further to an absolutely primal source beyond the Ideas (V.9,1-2). It is dependent on one's own affective disposition for its start and its progress. It was thought out by Plotinus himself in profoundly logical sequence, yet, as Porphyry remarks, "to no one do the cogently reasoned links involved in his discourse readily come to light" (*Life,* 18.7-8). The upward way, as presented in the *Enneads,* is the dialectic that "having left aside the region of deception, nourishes the soul on what is called the 'plain of truth,' using Plato's method of division for the distinguishing of Forms, using it also for the establishing of essence, using it likewise in so far as the primary genera are concerned and weaving by way of intellection the genera that proceed from these, until it has gone through all the intelligible order; and in opposite fashion it unravels them until it reaches the first principle" (I,3,4.10-16). Only when one has seen the whole intelligible world in all its multiple and intricate complexity is one in a position to analyze it in a way sufficient to disengage its supreme principle of unity and somehow rise to that principle. So dialectic, in Platonic fashion, is the highest part of philosophy, and not merely an instrument in the form of rules and propositions (I,3,5), as it would appear from the Peripatetic viewpoint. As is evident enough from the passages already cited, Plotinus is retaining the sharp Platonic division of things into sensible and intelligible: ". . . there is, on the one hand, that which is always in motion and which admits of all kinds of change and is distributed throughout all place, which accordingly should be named 'becoming,' but not 'being' (*ousia*); on the other hand, there is that which always *is,* which is not distributed, which is identically the same in nature, neither becoming nor perishing nor having any space or place or any abode, neither emerging from anywhere nor passing in turn into anything, but abiding in itself, . . ." (VI,5.2.9-16).

The soul, moreover, is not as it was for Aristotle a corporeal form (IV,2,1). In Platonic fashion it is something complete in itself. It "makes use of the body as of an instrument" (I,1,3.3). Even though it may be spoken of as the form of the body, it still leaves the body outside the notion of man proper. The soul, when regarded as the other principle concerned in man, "is most dominant and is the man himself. If this is the case, it stands in relation as to matter (the body) in so far as it is the form, or as to instrument in so far as it is the user; and in each of the two ways the soul is himself" (IV,7,1.22-25). Plotinus puts his finger very deftly on the weak point of the Aristotelian doctrine that the human soul is a corporeal form and yet a principle of supersensible cognition. In order to explain intellection, he notes, the Peripatetics have to introduce what he would like to call a further type of soul, over and above the soul that is a corporeal form: "Therefore even they themselves bring in another soul or intellect, which they posit as immortal" (IV,7,8⁵.15-16). For properly intellectual cognition and for immortality the Aristotelian doctrine required the further principle called intellect (nous), which Plotinus is trying to view as another soul. Though maintaining that for the soul "the body is an imprisonment and a tomb, and the cosmos is for it a cavern and a den" (IV,8,3.3-5), Plotinus keeps in mind the additional Platonic doctrine that soul becomes joined to body in the course of natural necessity.[3] He finds no contradiction in this double explanation (IV,8,5).

Aristotelian Influence. The general background of Plotinus' philosophy is therefore unmistakeably Platonic. But an equally unquestionable Aristotelian cast is given the Ideas in relation to intelligence, vitally affecting the intimate nature of the very first object of the Plotinian intellect. This difference radically changes the whole procedure, and makes the thought of Plotinus a new and different philosophy. Porphyry had observed: "In his writings . . . even Aristotle's treatise *The Metaphysics* has been compressed" (*Life,* 14.4-7). Through intellection, as Aristotle had maintained, the knowing subject and the object known are one: "To the extent in which it knows does the knowing subject—for now earnest attention must be given this point—come into unity with the thing known" (III,8,6.15-17). This principle is understood as identifying the object of intellectual knowledge with the intelligence knowing it: "If this is the case, the act of contemplation has

---

[3] For a discussion of this question, see A. H. Armstrong, *The Architecture of the Intelligible Universe in the Philosophy of Plotinus* (Cambridge, Eng., 1940), pp. 83-90.

to be identical with the thing contemplated, and the intelligence
has to be identical with the object of intellection" (V,3,5.21-23).
The object of intelligence, however, is being. Being is therefore
located in intelligence in a way that identifies it with intelligence.
To it Parmenides' dictum, understood now to mean identity of
being and thinking, is applied: "In intelligence, it is now clear
that subject and object are one, not by making the object its own,
as is the case in even the best of souls, but by very entity (*ousia*),
in that its 'being and thinking are the same' " (III,8,8.6-8). The
Ideas or intelligibles, accordingly, are found *within* the Plotinian
intelligence—somewhat as for Philo they were placed within the
mind of God—and not outside it.

Other Influences. Plotinus draws not only upon Plato and
Aristotle, but on other leading Greek philosophers like Heraclitus, Parmenides, Empedocles, and Anaxagoras, as well as upon
the Pythagorean tradition. Stoic influence is frequently apparent,
for instance in his use of the doctrine of seminal reasons: "For
the universe is intricate in the highest degree, and in it are all
(*seminal*) reasons, and powers unlimited (*in number*) and of
many varieties" (IV,4,36.1-2). However, though he dealt considerably with Stoic philosophy, he does not seem to have been at
all profoundly affected by it. He takes an extremely restricted
view on "reasonable" suicide (I,9). He speaks of seminal reasons
and the *logos* in general, understanding by these terms powers of
the soul concerned with ordering matter in accord with intelligence. Although he may speak of the seminal reasons as to some
extent identical with souls,[4] he usually describes them as psychic
forces that exist in souls but are not the same as souls. As specifically Stoic principles the seminal reasons are not a very operative
feature in the development of his thought. Still less is there any
evidence of real Oriental influence. Plotinus was acquainted with
and deeply interested in Oriental philosophies, as his Egyptian
background and his journey to Mesopotamia would indicate. Yet
there seems to be nothing in his entire thought that cannot be
explained as a regular development of his Greek sources, even
though he may have had Oriental philosophies in mind as he
worked out his own conclusions.

The Intelligibles. Although human cognition is aroused

[4] See E. Bréhier, *La Philosophie de Plotin* (Paris, 1928), p. 53.

through sensation, the starting point of philosophy proper is found rather in the objects of intellectual cognition.[5] These intelligibles exist within the intelligence, after the fashion of strict Aristotelian union between the knower and the object. The fifth book of the fifth *Ennead*, as its title indicates, undertakes to show "That the intelligibles are not outside the intelligence" (V,5). The treatise seeks to establish this doctrine through the difference between sensation and intellection. Sensation consists in attaining things outside the cognitive subject, through representation, in accordance with the derivation of the word *doxa* from the Greek verb "to receive." Truth, therefore, is not concerned with something that is received from without and that is other than the intelligence. It bears rather upon an object already identified with the intelligence in spite of the duality to which they give rise. If this were not the case, intellection would not differ from sensation (V,5,1). "One should not then either seek the intelligibles outside it, or say that they are impressions of being upon the intelligence, or in depriving it of truth render the intelligibles unknown and non-existent, and even do away with the intelligence itself" (V,5,2.1-4).

The reasoning of Plotinus, accordingly, is based upon the teaching that there has to be truth, not just opinion (*doxa*). That was the fundamental Platonic position on human knowledge, and could easily be taken for granted in the environment in which he was discoursing. However, in order to safeguard truth in its status above sensation and opinion, and to render secure the whole order of being, Plotinus teaches that the objects of intelligence have to be located within the intelligence itself, and not at all outside it: "Rather, if both knowledge and truth are to be admitted, and beings and the knowledge of each thing's essence upheld, . . . all things have to be placed in the veritable intelligence. For in this way it will both know, and know veritably, and will neither forget nor go about seeking; and the truth will be in it and it will be the abode for beings, and will be living and will be exercising intellection" (V,5,2.4-12).

Identity and Plurality. In that union all beings are identified with the intelligence: "We have, then, this one nature, intelli-

[5] *En.*, I,3,4. On this topic, see W. R. Inge, *The Philosophy of Plotinus* (reprint, 3rd ed., London, etc., 1948), II, 39-64.

gence, all beings, the truth. If so, it is a great god, or rather, these may claim to be not *a* god but deity entire" (V,5,3.1-2). In spite of the identity, however, the intelligibles remain distinct from one another and from the intelligence: "Let intelligence, accordingly, be the beings, and let it contain them all within itself, not as in place, but as containing its own self and being one with them. 'All are together' *there* and none the less they are differentiated. For even soul, in having many sciences at once in itself, does not have anything fused together; and each science does its own work when required, without drawing in the others along with it; and from among the thoughts that keep lying inside, each individual thought comes into actuality clear of any admixture. In this way, and much more so, is the intelligence all things together and yet not together, because each thing is an individual power; and the whole intelligence encompasses them all as a genus its species or as a whole its parts" (V,9,6.1-10). The union of intelligence and intelligibles is accordingly illustrated by the union of a genus with its species. The genus comprehends all its species, yet can be distinguished from them; and similarly every species can be distinguished from the others, in spite of its union with them in the genus. The comparison helps to explain the way in which Plotinus can speak almost indifferently of intelligence and intelligences, or of soul and souls, or of being and beings.

Priority of Being.   The union of intelligence and beings is not left open to an Idealistic interpretation,[6] in the sense that being would result from thinking. Plotinus repeatedly asserts the primacy of being over intelligence, even though the two belong on the same level of reality: "First, then, one should understand what holds in all cases for the being (*ousia*) of the Forms, that they do not exist because the thinking subject thought of each of them, and then by that very thinking endowed them with existence. For not because it began thinking what justice is did justice come into being; nor because it began thinking what motion is did motion attain existence" (VI,6,6.5-10). From this

[6] P. V. Pistorius, *Plotinus and Neoplatonism* (Cambridge, Eng., 1952), p. 1, presents the philosophy of Plotinus as an Idealism, though in the meaning that the world of concepts has more reality than the world of sense. However, the three principal hypostases become merely different "aspects of the same Being" (p. 59).

viewpoint intelligence is only second in order: "Since being is
first, one has to place being first in the order of understanding;
then, intelligence; . . . and intelligence is second, for it is being's
(*ousia*) actuality" (VI,6,8.17-20). In order to be known, things
have to be prior to the knowing: "For the object of intellection
must be prior to this intellection. Otherwise, how would it reach
knowledge of it?" (V,9,7.16-17). The very nature of knowledge,
then, prevents the Ideas or intelligibles from having the role
merely of thoughts produced by thinking.

Individuality. For Plotinus, nevertheless, being and intelligence are co-ordinate. The order of being is the order of intelligence. True beings are all intelligibles, and are all found in the
intelligence, in a living identity that allows them to remain distinct from one another as well as from intelligence. In this living
identity is realized the doctrine of Parmenides (*Fr.* 8.25) that
being closes in on being and that the all forms a compact whole
(*En.*,VI,4,4). On account of this identity *all* the intelligibles
are many in one and one in many (VI,5,6). Each one is identified
in the intelligence with all the others in such a way that a sufficiently keen vision would perceive everything whatsoever in any
one of the intelligibles: "Besides, every one of them has them all
within itself, and moreover sees all in any other, so that all are
everywhere and every one of them is every one and each is every
one, and unlimited is their splendor. . . . *Here*, of course, one
part does not emerge from another part, and each can be only a
part; but *there* each always emerges from the whole, and is
simultaneously individual and whole—it shows itself indeed as
part, but to the beholder with penetrating sight it is visible as
whole" (V,8,4.6-24).

In the same way, every intelligence is identical with and yet
distinct from the one intelligence. This variety in unity allows the
intelligible world as well as the sensible universe to be regarded
as a cosmos: "We consider it, accordingly, an intelligible cosmos,
since there are also the individual intellectual powers and intelligences included in it—for it is not one alone, but one and
many" (IV,8,3.8-10). In that way there is an individual intelligence for each individual soul, yet all such intelligences form
one supreme intelligence (IV,3,5). Absorption in the intelligible

world, however, excludes all memory of earthly things and of individual personality (IV,4,1-2).

The One.   Being and intelligence, therefore, constitute an order that is multiple. Such an order cannot be absolutely primary, since unity precedes multiplicity. This consideration prompts inquiry about a cause prior to both being and intelligence: "Who is he, then, who engendered this intelligible cosmos? It is he who is single-natured, and who is prior to such a multiplicity, who is cause both of its being and of its being multiple, the producer of plurality. For plurality does not come first; since even before duality there is the one, and duality comes second" (V,1,5.3-7). That primal cause is identified with the good that Plato's *Republic* had placed above being: ". . . . know that it is the good—for, as it is a power, it is cause of wise and intellectual life, with life and intelligence proceeding from it; that it is cause of entity (*ousia*) and being; that it is one—for it is single-natured and primary; that it is first principle—for from it come all things" (V,5,10.11-14). It is unlimited in the sense that it will never fail as the source of all other things: "But neither is it limited. For by what could it be given bounds? Nor on the other hand is it unlimited as though it were a magnitude. For where would it have to keep extending? Or why might anything accrue to it when it is in want of nothing. But its *power* has the nature of the unlimited; for it is never any different nor will it ever fail, as even indefectible things have their permanence through it" (V,5,10.18-23).

Being, consequently, is not unity. It can only *participate* unity: "But if the being of an individual is a multiplicity, and it is impossible for the one to be a multiplicity, being and the one will differ from each other. . . . The more so, accordingly, will entire being, containing all beings in itself, be multiple and other than the one. But in having unity by participation, it will also be partaking of the one" (VI,9,2.17-24).

Negative Predication.   Since the one is beyond the order of being, it is not able to receive the predication of any of the categories of being. It is not even a substance or a "this." Only negative predication can properly be made of it (VI,9,3-4). Since it is above the order of intellection, it cannot be attained by any intellective act, but by a superior and indescribable act

of presence and union, that may be called vision only in contrast
to discursive reasoning (VI,9,4). Intellection can merely show
that there has to be a one prior to being; it cannot attain the
one through any act in its own order. Even when the one is called
the good, it is denominated not from anything in itself but from
what it causes in others: "In it, then, there is no willing of anything; but it is above good, and it is good not for its own self
but for other things, if they are at all able to partake of it"
(VI,9,6.40-42). Nor does it know itself, any more than it could
will itself. Intellection is essentially a movement towards the
good, and so cannot be found in it (V,6,5). But that does not
mean that the one is ignorant of itself. It is negative even in regard to ignorance. Rather, it is of its very nature one with itself
and so requires no intellection to unite it with itself: "The *alone*,
however, neither knows, nor has anything that it does not know;
but being one, being united with itself, it does not need intellection of itself. In fact, 'being united with itself' should not be
added, in order that you may keep intact the 'one'" (VI,9,6.48-
51). Even the term "one," when applied to it, is not to be taken
in any positive sense, but merely as a negation, in so far as it
does away with multiplicity: "But perhaps even this name the
'one' has a negative meaning, in reference to plurality by doing
away with it. . . . If the one—both the name and what is signified
—were positive in meaning, it would become less clear than if
no name were mentioned for it. Perhaps indeed this name was
mentioned in order that the inquirer begin with that which most
of all is expressive of singleness, and then end in a negation even
of that. It was asserted as the best adapted to what was under
discussion; yet not even it is suitable for the manifestation of
that nature" (V,5,6.26-35). Only in this restricted sense may Plotinus speak of the first principle as loving itself, seeking itself, and
producing itself (VI,8,13-15).

In accordance with the Greek metaphysical tradition that goes
back to Parmenides, being is kept strictly equated with form and
finitude. It is what can be defined. But its source is beyond the
whole order of finitude. That source "is necessarily formless. And
since it is formless, it is not being (*ousia*). Being has to be a 'this,'
and a 'this' is limited. . . . It is therefore 'beyond being.'" (V,5,6.4-
11).

Emanation. The first principle of all things is, as Plato (*Ti.*, 29E) had stated, without jealousy. It therefore tends necessarily to realize all the possible effects of its unlimited power. Goodness, accordingly, appears as the reason for the production of other things: "How then would the most perfect and the primary good stay within itself, as though begrudging of itself or lacking the power—it the power of all? And how would it still be first principle? Accordingly, there must also be generation of something from it, if there is indeed to be any of the other things too, things that of course derive their existence from it; for in it must they have their origin" (V,4,1.34-39). This reason for the emanation requires that all possible effects be realized, and so makes the real coextensive with the possible: "It was not befitting to stay this power as though enclosing it in jealousy; but it should always keep going onwards, until all things reach the limits of their possibility down to the ultimate detail" (IV,8,6.12-14). The procession of being and intelligence from the first principle is of course eternal. It involves no motion, and so does not occur in time: "Let us, however, put aside temporal generation in treating of the eternal beings; but in verbally attributing generation to them, we will be assigning them causes, causes of order in their procession too. We have to say, then, that what is engendered *there* is engendered without any motion having taken place in its source" (V,1,6.19-23). This necessity is understood as excluding free choice from the process of emanation. All possible good has to be realized. The notion of universal providence arises only from the viewpoint of a lower order of things: "Providence, then, either over anything animate or over this universe in general, did not proceed from a reasoning process; for *there* there is no reasoning out at all. But it is called reasoning, to indicate that all things are as a wise man would have arranged from reasoning in the matters of a subsequent order; and it is called foresight, because they take place as a wise man would have provided in affairs on the subsequent level" (VI,7,1.28-32).

The Hypostases. The emanation proceeds from the one through intelligence (being) and soul to the material order. What proceeds from the one is stabilized by turning towards the one and thereby acquiring the character of *being;* while its own self-knowledge, so stablized, makes it intelligence: "For, being perfect by reason of neither seeking anything nor possessing nor needing anything, the one as it were overflowed; and its over-fullness has produced something else. And what was engendered turned round to it and was satisfied to the full and became set in its gaze upon itself; and this is intelligence. And on the one hand its stabilization upon the one caused the being, and on the other hand its looking upon itself caused the intelligence. Since it was stabilized upon the one, then, in order that it might behold, it is rendered simultaneously intelligence and being" (V,2,1.7-13). In a corresponding way, soul proceeds from intelligence and being: "As the intelligence is like the one, then, it produces in like manner, . . . And this actuality issuing from being (*ousia*) is the actuality of soul, . . ." (V,2,1.14-17). Soul in its turn gives rise to the visible world of nature, though now through a process of motion: "Without any change on the part of the intelligence was soul born its likeness; for also without any change on the part of its own prior source did the intelligence come into being. Soul, however, does not produce without change, but in motion it engendered an image. . . . an image of itself, sense and nature, the nature found in the vegetal order" (V,2,1.17-21). The whole process of emanation, however, remains one continuous life: "There is, then, as it were a life far extended in length. Each part is different from those that follow; yet it is a whole continuous with itself" (V,2,2.27-29). The one, intelligence (being), and soul were known as the three principal hypostases, considered as set and definite stages in the process.

Soul. The order of being and intelligence was seen to be both one and many, after the manner of the unity and multiplicity found in genus and species. Similarly, the order of soul is both multiple and unitary: "Correspondingly, souls too had to be many and one, and the many differing souls had to come from the one soul; just as from one race (genus) comes types (species) some better, some worse, some more intellectual, others less actually so" (IV,8,3.10-13). In this fashion the differing capacities of the various individual souls are explained. The highest grade is left to the universal soul: "If a city, for example were endowed with soul, containing other living things within its bounds, the soul of the city would be more perfect and more powerful; yet nothing would prevent the other souls too from being of the same nature" (IV,8,3.16-19).

Besides the function of thinking, soul has also the role of ordering matter. In this way it differs from intelligence, even though, in the Platonic contrast of sensible and intelligible, soul belongs to the higher sphere: "The functioning of the more rational soul is indeed intellection, but not just intellection. For how then would it differ at all from intelligence? Yes, in receiving over and above the intellectual nature something else, it did not remain essentially intelligence. . . . But on the one hand in facing towards what is prior to itself it engages in intellection; on the other hand, in looking to itself it looks to what comes after it, which it sets in order and manages, and rules over it" (IV,-8,3.21-28).

In soul, accordingly, is found the transition from the order of being to the order of change: "For life *here* is in a process of motion; but *there* it is immobile" (III,2,4.12-13). The soul itself lives in both orders: "Having turned back towards intellection the soul is freed from its bonds and journeys upward, when from recollection (*anamnesis*) it takes its starting point to 'behold beings.' For in spite of everything it always possesses something superior. Souls, then, come to lead as it were both kinds of life, obliged to live in part the life *there* and in part the life *here*. Those who are able to be more united with the intelligence, live in a greater degree the life *there;* while those who either through nature or through conditions of fortune have been disposed the opposite way, live in a greater degree the life *here*" (IV,8,4.28-35).

Souls proceed downward through the heavenly bodies to the more crass and earthly, in accordance with the Platonic traditions of transmigration.[7] The immortality of the soul is proven from its incorporeal nature, and by other Platonic arguments, for instance that it is essentially a vital principle and that it knows the Forms: "That the soul has its kindred to the eternal and more divine nature, is also made clear by the proof that it is not a body. Moreover, it has neither figure nor color, nor can it be touched. Besides, it can be shown too from the considerations that follow"

[7] *En.,* III,4,2; IV,3,15; 17; VI,4,16. On the extent of the Plotinian notion of soul, see Pistorius, p. 76.

(IV,7,10.1-4). All souls, without exception, are therefore immortal: "Regarding the soul in other living things—any souls that have fallen so far as to reach the level of bodies of wild beasts—these also are necessarily immortal. And if there is any other type of soul, this too has to come from no other source than *the* living nature, since *it* indeed is the cause of life to living things; and the same holds for the soul in plants" (IV,7,14-1-6).

Nature. The necessary process of emanation requires that soul produce corporeal nature: "If it is to go forth, it will engender for itself place, so also body" (IV,3,9.22-23). It is by contemplation alone that the soul produces the entire sensible world: "The production therefore reveals itself to us clearly as a contemplation. For it is a result of a contemplation that remains contemplation without having done anything else, but it produced by being contemplation" (III,8,3.20-22). Nature itself is represented as explaining how this happens: "And what contemplates in me produces what is contemplated, just as geometricians during their contemplation draw what they contemplate. But I do not do any drawing. I contemplate, and the figures of bodies come into existence as though falling out of my contemplation" (III,8,4.7-10). Production and action, accordingly, are but a weakened form of contemplation: "Everywhere then will we find production and action either a falling off of contemplation or a by-product of it. . . . The duller types of children also bear witness to this. As their disposition renders them incapable of studies and contemplation, they are relegated to the crafts and trades" (III,8,4.39-47). The visible cosmos has always existed and will exist forever (II,1,1; III,2,1). The entire dependence of the sensible universe on contemplation makes manifest the doctrine that body is in soul, not soul in body. Body is contained as well as conserved by soul: "For it lies in the soul that sustains it, and in it is nothing that does not share in that soul" (IV,3,9.36-38).

All things, as has been seen, form one vital process. This allows the individual soul to retain and make operative its union with everything else: "For the soul is both many things and all things and the things above and the things below, on to life in its entirety; and we are each of us an intelligible cosmos, joined by the things below to this world, but by the things above, and those of a cosmos, to the intelligible world" (III,4,3.21-25). By its thinking, then, the soul can journey in reality back to the unity of the intelligible world: "For both what is ours is brought back to the order of being and we ourselves; and we return to it as from it we first came. And we know the things there without having images of them or impressions. But if we know them without such aid, we know them because we are those things. If then we partake of veritable knowledge, we are the things there not by receiving them in ourselves, but by ourselves being in them. And as not only we but also the rest of things are they, we all are they. In being together with all things, therefore, we are they. We are therefore all things as one" (VI,5,7.1-8). Shrines and statues are meant to reflect the omnipresence of soul, and so indicate that the nature of the all is everywhere (IV,3,11).

Evil and Matter.   With the soul, the process of emanation is still in the order of the divine (V,1,7). The continued emanation, however, is a descent from the good. It involves increasing devolution and deterioration. The necessity implicit in such a process requires that it continue till it reaches the opposite of the good, evil: "Since, then, the good is not the only thing that exists, it was necessary in the emanation outside it—or, if anyone should wish to say so, in the perpetual descent and recession from it—that the ultimate, yes, that after which there was nothing more to be engendered, should come. Evil, it can be understood, is this" (I,8,7.-17-20). Evil is accordingly a lack of goodness. It is likewise not-being. To call it not-being does not at all imply that it does not exist, but asserts that it is opposed in character to the Greek philosophical notion of being: "And 'not-being' does not at all mean what is in every respect not-being, but only what is other than being; yet not in the sense in which motion and the stability concerned with being are other than being, but as an image of being, or even as not-being in a still more pronounced sense" (I,8,3.6-9). Evil, then, consists either in sensible things or in something still more remote from being than the sensible. This latter kind may be described only through lack of form and lack of finitude: "For one would come to a notion of it in considering that it is as lack of measure in comparison with measure, and unlimited in comparison with limit, and formless in comparison with something form-giving, and always needing in comparison with self-sufficient, always indeterminate, in no respect stable, entirely passive, unsated, absolute destitution; and that these features are not accidental to it, but they are as it were its very entity; . . . and that whatever other things partake of it and become like to it do indeed become evil, but are not of their very essence evil. . . . And if besides it there is anything of evil character, it either has evil mixed with it, or through facing towards evil is of evil nature or is a productive cause of what is evil" (I,8,3.12-34).

Absolute evil, then, is described by Plotinus in the terms that Plato used for the receptacle of generation and those applied by Aristotle to the absolutely primary matter. Evil, accordingly, is necessarily present in the material world: "The nature of bodies, in so far as it shares in matter, will be evil, though not the primary evil" (I,8,4.1-2).

Lapse, Return of Souls. Individual souls become evil through forgetfulness of their divine origin. This is caused by their rash decision to be self-sufficient in the world of change and otherness: "The source, indeed, of their evil plight is recklessness and becoming and the primary otherness and the will to belong to themselves. Glad to all appearance at their independent status, they became steeped in the movement proceeding from their own selves; running the course opposite their true destiny, they brought themselves to a state of extreme recession from it. In consequence, they came to be without knowledge even of their own origin *there*" (V,1,1.3-8). Individual freedom and responsibility are upheld by Plotinus in this sphere of moral action: "But each thing has to be an individual, and there have to be our own actions and thoughts, and the good and bad actions of each have to proceed from the individual himself. No, the causing at any rate of evil things is not to be ascribed to the all" (III,1,4.24-28).

The soul, though, never lapses entirely into the not-being that is nothing. It can always turn again to the intelligible order and rise through the intelligibles to the one: "For the nature of the soul will not reach the point of complete not-being. In going downwards it will sink to the level of evil, and in this sense to not-being; yet not to what is in every respect not-being. But in running the opposite course it will come, not to something else, but to its own self; and in this way, since it is not in anything else, it will be in nothing at all except in its own very self. But the location in itself *alone* and not in being is location in that beyond;

for even one's self becomes, not being, but 'beyond being,' by this *self alone* with which one consorts" (VI,9,11.35-42). If, in the solitude of consorting with his soul's self alone, a man is conscious that he has penetrated beyond the order of being, he has already constituted himself a likeness of the one; and if from himself as image he passes over to the one as prototype, he has reached the terminus of his journeying. A man will indeed fall back from this sublime height, but he will arouse once more his virtue and proceed again through intelligence to the one. "And this life of gods and of divine and fortunate men is a release from the alien things of this world, a life rid of pleasure in things here, a retiring of an *alone* unto an *alone*" (VI,9,11.48-51).

The philosophy of Plotinus is a life in which a man strives to rise above the sensible world to live first in the intelligible realm, and then through it to mount to the order that is above the intelligible. This is an order that cannot be expressed by any positive predicates. It is an order above being, above intelligence, above anything that can be conceived or expressed by men. Yet it is the goal of all human striving, and philosophy is the means by which it is attained. In such philosophical journeyings of Plotinus many problems are discussed, problems regarding the nature of sensation, of memory, of light, of sound, and other such topics. Through what is found participated in the sensible phenomena the soul is prompted and guided in the direction of their ultimate source. In these philosophical discussions the upward journey of the soul to its homeland and natural destiny remains the dominant motif. The goal of the journey never ceases to be represented as indescribable and incommunicable by way of any intellectual process. The intellect in its reasoning can only demonstrate that the goal must be such. The rest has to be left to the ecstatic act of union and presence to which an intense and prolonged philosophical life of the soul within itself is said to lead. The philosophy of Plotinus became in this manner the uttermost Greek development of the traditional Delphic precept to know one's self (IV,3,1). It provided an intellectual weapon that his successors used to combat the Christian teaching and to explain and justify rationally the cult of the pagan divinities.

PROCLUS (410/412-485 A.D.)

The Neoplatonic way of thinking was continued and systematized by the immediate successors of Plotinus, Porphyry (233-201 + A.D.) and Iamblichus (died ca. 330 A.D.). It reached its fullest systematization and extension in Proclus, who was known as the Successor on account of his position as head of the Platonic Academy, which had already become Neoplatonic in its teaching. The principal source for the life of Proclus is the biography written by his own successor and disciple, Marinus. It relates that he was born of Lycian parents in Byzantium (410 or 412 A.D.). He received his early education at Xanthus in Lycia and later at Alexandria. When not yet twenty years old, he went to Athens to pursue philosophical studies at the Academy. Finally he became head of the Academy and continued in that position till his death, April 17, 485 A.D. His most important philosophical works are *The Elements of Theology,* presenting his philosophy in a systematic format modeled on Euclid's *Elements; The Platonic Theology,* helpful for the details of his teachings; and *Commentaries* on the *Timaeus, Parmenides, Republic,* and *First Alcibiades.*

Proclus made use of a triadic method to systematize the Neoplatonic doctrine: "Socrates therefore says that everything divine is beautiful, wise, and good, and he indicates that this triad pervades to all the progressions of the Gods" (*Theology of Plato,* I,21; tr. Taylor). The Platonic good is explained in the same way: "But in the Philebus, Plato delivers to us the three most principal elements of *the good,* viz. the desirable, the sufficient and the perfect" (I,22; tr. Taylor). The intelligible order is similarly described: "Such therefore, is the first triad of intelligibles, according to Socrates in the Philebus, viz. bound, infinite, and that which is mixed from these" (III,12; tr. Taylor). In this strongly triadic fashion the different key Platonic concepts are presented. In such systematization Proclus remains within the general framework of Plotinus' teachings. The one, the first principle of all things, "exempt from the whole of beings, is God, defined according to the ineffable itself, the unical alone, and superessential" (III,3; tr. Taylor). It is identified with the good. From it proceed intellect, soul, and bodies.

Proclus was the last important pagan Greek philosopher. Forty-four years after his death, in the year 529 A.D., the schools of philosophy were closed by Justinian, and thereby the history of ancient pagan philosophy may be said to have come officially to an end. The philosophical tradition was continued by commentators down into the Middle Ages. In the meantime, from the early era of Patristic writing, a new type of philosophical thinking was being developed within the framework of Christian faith. On account of this setting, however, so radically different from that of the pagan world, it constitutes a long phase of European thought that is more conveniently treated[8] as part of a history other than that of ancient Western philosophy.

RETROSPECT

In Neoplatonism many of the leading aspects of Greek philosophical tradition found their most harmonious synthesis. The notion of the whole cosmos as a living being, present from the start in Greek thought and modified considerably in the Platonic doctrine of the world soul and the Aristotelian teaching on the animated heavens, was more completely rationalized in the Plotinian development of the progression of life and soul. The Parmenidean contrast between the world of being and the world of the *doxa,* in the light of which Plato and Aristotle had thought out their metaphysical tenets, was explained and absorbed in the process of gradual devolution from the supreme and ineffable perfection of the first principle. The Greeks, Parmenides not excepted, had all frankly admitted the evident plurality and motion of the things in the visible cosmos. The problem was to reconcile them with the immutable being, of which they somehow bore the imprint. Plotinus, in locating unity itself outside and above the order of being, and making being a stage in the process of devolution, provided the most consistent escape in ancient times from the tyranny of the all-embracing Parmenidean concept. The presence of evil and the irrational, admitted regularly throughout the course of Greek thought, found a justification in his doctrine of the successively deteriorating phases of the emanation process and its necessity. As with his predecessors, an over-all necessity reigned supreme in the universe. As with them, free choice was recognized for ethical purposes, but it was kept on a lower level and seemingly did not call for any profound philosophical explanation. A

[8] E.g., as in Étienne Gilson, *History of Christian Philosophy in the Middle Ages* (New York, 1955).

different setting from that of Greek philosophy would be required to see it in the highest level of being. In this respect as well as in the other features of his thought, Plotinus remained within the tradition of his philosophical forbears, and from the viewpoints of both time and internal consistency he brought their way of thinking to its culmination. Contemplation, now raised above the hindrances of intellectual duality, remained the supreme goal of human living, while production received a coherent explanation as a much weaker and lower type of contemplative activity.

SELECTED READINGS AND REFERENCES

Thomas Whittaker, *The Neo-Platonists*, 2nd ed. (Cambridge, Eng.: University Press, 1918). First published 1901.

E. R. Dodds, "The *Parmenides* of Plato and the Origin of the Neo-platonic One," *CQ*, XXII (1928), 129-142.

Philip Merlan, *From Platonism 'to Neoplatonism* (The Hague: M. Nijhoff, 1953).

Plotinus

Plotin, Ennéades, 7 vols. in 6, ed. E. Bréhier (Paris: Les Belles Lettres, 1924-1938). A new critical edition of the Greek text is being prepared by Paul Henry and Hans-Rudolph Schwyzer, *Plotini Opera*, of which the first two volumes (Brussels and Paris: Desclée de Brouwer, 1951-1959), containing the first five *Enneads*, have already appeared. There are English translations of the *Enneads* by K. S. Guthrie, *Plotinos, Complete Works*, 4 vols. (Alpine, N.J.: Platonist Press, 1918), and Stephen MacKenna, *Plotinus, The Enneads*, 5 vols. (Boston and London, The Medici Society, 1917-1930; 2nd ed., rev. B. S. Page, London, Faber 1956). Recent and more literal translations of selections may be found in J. Katz, *The Philosophy of Plotinus* (New York: Appleton-Century-Crofts, 1950) and A. H. Armstrong, *Plotinus* (London: G. Allen & Unwin, 1953).

Bert Mariën, *Bibilografia Critica degli Studi Plotiniani* (Bari: Laterza, 1949).

William Ralph Inge, *The Philosophy of Plotinus*, 2 vols., 3rd ed. (London, etc.: Longmans, Green, 1929). First Published 1918.

René Arnou, *Le Désir de Dieu dans la Philosophie de Plotin* (Paris: Alcan, [1921]). Émile Bréhier, *La Philosophie de Plotin* (Paris: Boivin, 1928). English tr. Joseph Thomas, *The Philosophy of Plotinus* (Chicago: University of Chicago Press, 1958).

Arthur Hilary Armstrong, *The Architecture of the Intelligible Universe in the Philosophy of Plotinus* (Cambridge, Eng.: University Press, 1940).

Joseph Katz, *Plotinus' Search for the Good* (New York: King's Crown Press, 1950).

Philippus Villiers Pistorius, *Plotinus and Neoplatonism* (Cambridge, Eng.: Bowes & Bowes, 1952).

Jean Trouillard, *La Procession Plotinienne* (Paris: Presses Universitaires, 1955).

————, *La Purification Plotinienne* (Paris: Presses Universitaires, 1955).

Hugo Fischer, *Die Aktualität Plotins* (Munich: C. H. Beck, 1956).

PROCLUS

Proclus, The Elements of Theology, with Translation, Introduction, and Commentary by E. R. Dodds (Oxford: Clarendon Press, 1933). There are Teubner texts of the commentaries: on the *Republic*, *Procli Diadochi In Platonis Rem Publicam Commentarii*, 2 vols., ed. W. Kroll (Leipzig, 1899-1901); on the *Timaeus, Procli Diadochi In Platonis Timaeum Commentaria*, 3 vols., ed. E. Diehl (Leipzig, 1903-1906); and on the *Cratylus, Procli Diadochi In Platonis Cratylum Commentaria*, ed. G. Pasquali (Leipzig, 1908). There is also a recent text of the *Alcibiades* commentary: *Proclus Diadochus, Commentary on the First Alcibiades of Plato*, ed. L. G. Westerink (Amsterdam: North-Holland Publishing Co., 1954). For the *Parmenides* commentary, there is Victor Cousin's revised edition, *Opera Inedita* (Paris, 1864), 617-1244.

————, *The Six Books of Proclus the Platonic Successor, On the Theology of Plato*, tr. Thomas Taylor (London: A. J. Valpy, 1816).

————, *La Teologia Platonica*, tr. E. Turolla (Bari: Laterza, 1957).

Laurence Jay Rosán, *The Philosophy of Proclus, The Final Phase of Ancient Thought* (New York: "Cosmos," 1949).

[APPENDIX]

The Chronology of Empedocles

THE CORRECT dating of Empedocles is of notable importance for understanding the history of Greek philosophy during the fifth century B.C. The activities of Anaxagoras, Democritus, Gorgias, and others have to be kept in close chronological relation with the work of Empedocles. A late dating for Empedocles, which for the most part has been accepted by historians, renders much of the evidence about movements of philosophical thought in the fifth century difficult to understand. A brief survey of the chronological indications regarding the dates of his life is therefore necessary at least to remove any prejudice that may arise from a fixed opinion on this score and so predetermine the datings of other philosophers in the century.

The oldest source for the chronology is the reported testimony of Glaucus of Rhegium, a contemporary of Democritus. Of all the authorities he is the closest to Empedocles in point of time. He was quoted by Apollodorus as stating that Empedocles came to Thurii, a city on the gulf of Tarentum, shortly after its foundation (D.L., VIII,52; DK, 31A 1). Thurii was founded in 444/443 B.C. No details are given by which this report might be checked. Apparently on its strength Apollodorus (cf. D.L., VIII,74) placed the *floruit* of Empedocles in the eighty-fourth Olympiad (444-441 B.C.). The most trustworthy account of Empedocles' age seems to be the one taken from Aristotle by Diogenes (VIII,52; 74), according to which Empedocles was sixty when he died. On this basis the dates for Empedocles' life would be from about 484 to about 424 B.C., or up to a decade earlier.

According to the manuscript text of Diogenes Laertius (VIII,67; DK, 31A 1), however, the Sicilian historian Timaeus, writing over a century later than Glaucus, seems to have recorded that when Acragas was being "settled" the descendants of Empedocles' enemies prevented his return to the city. At any rate, Timaeus stated that Empedocles left Sicily and never returned, the manner of his death remaining unknown

417

(VIII,71). This "settling" of Acragas cannot mean the founding of the city around 582 B.C. If it refers to the complete reorganization of the city-state that took place in 461 B.C.,[1] it would indicate that Empedocles disappeared from history in that year. Timaeus, who had carefully investigated the stories about Empedocles, wrote as though unaware of any account of the Thurii visit.

Finally, Apollodorus transmitted the narrative of some historians that Empedocles went to Syracuse and fought against the Athenians (415-413 B.C.). Apollodorus himself considered that this report was completely mistaken, as Empedocles at that time would have been either dead or in extreme old age (D.L., VIII,52).

Besides the age of sixty taken from Aristotle, the ages of seventy-seven and one hundred and nine were given to Empedocles by other Greek historians (D.L., VIII,73-74). If these three ages are compared with the three different dates of Empedocles' last recorded appearance in history, a rather curious phenomenon ensues. There is, it is true, no definite testimony as to which goes with which; but if the dates of his last appearance in chronological order are ranged with the age spans in order of length (461+60, 444+77, 413+109), the year of his birth in all three cases would be the same—522/521 B.C. It would look as though the originators of all three traditions had definite information about the time of Empedocles' birth, and adapted to it the other data that they accepted.

Tentative as such a computation may be, it makes intelligible two statements of Aristotle about Empedocles. The Stagirite is reported (D.L., VIII,57) to have written that Empedocles was the founder of rhetoric, as Zeno was of dialectic. Rhetoric was flourishing in Sicily as a cultivated art around 470 B.C. This should mean that Empedocles' reputation as a rhetorician had been established before that date. The year 481 B.C. as his *floruit* would permit this statement of Aristotle to be understood without difficulty. Secondly, Aristotle records that Anaxagoras was "earlier in age, later in works"[2] than Empedocles. But in Socrates' youth, and so by the middle of the fifth century, Anaxagoras

---

[1] So G.F. Unger, "Die Zeitverhältnisse des Anaxagoras und Empedokles," *Philol.*, Supplbd. IV (1884), 513-514. Zeller, *Philos. d. Griechen*, 6th ed., (1920), I (2),942, n. 1, claimed that it was "linguistically impossible" for the Greek verb to denote the return of the exiles in 461 B.C. In Unger's explanation the verb referred rather to the new civic organization that followed their return.

[2] *Metaph.*, A 3,984a11-13; DK, 31A 6. "Later" means quite evidently subsequent in time, and not "inferior." See Otto Jöhrens, *Die Fragmente des Anaxagoras* (Bochum-Langendreer, 1939), pp. 93-94. The contrast with "earlier" in the meaning of age, and the none too high opinion that Aristotle had of Empedocles as a philosopher, indicate this sense.

was no longer a living voice in Athens, but only a "book." This would indicate that the treatise of Anaxagoras was written prior to 460 B.C. Empedocles' main literary work, accordingly, must have been completed well before that year, if Aristotle's remark is to have its proper bearing. The fragments of Empedocles, moreover, show ample evidence of the influence of Parmenides, but they are unruffled by any concern with Zeno's dialectic. This fact seems to confirm their chronological priority to the treatise of Anaxagoras, in which a background corresponding to that of Zeno is discernible.

The year 521 B.C. would therefore be about the correct date for Empedocles' birth. If sixty is accepted as his life span, according to Aristotle's reported statement, the date of his disappearance from history and presumably of his death will be 461 B.C. In this case Apollodorus' uncontrollable excerpt from Glaucus about the Thurii visit will have to be regarded as mistaken, in view of the comparatively easy way in which names and persons could become confused in Greek biographical tradition; or, if the Thurii visit has to stand, the less likely age of seventy-seven years is required.

A horse race in the seventy-first Olympiad (496 B.C.) is also brought into the chronological considerations. In that year an Empedocles was reported as the Olympic victor. The victory was accredited by some authorities to the grandfather of the philosopher, by another to the philosopher himself (D.L., VIII,51-53). In any case, there would be nothing extraordinary about a septuagenarian Greek aristocrat keeping horses and winning the race. The story, consequently, whichever way it may be taken, can hardly have any decisive bearing on the chronology.

Index of Persons and Subject-Matter

Boldface figures indicate principal reference

Aalders, G. J. D., 144 n.
Academy, **191-192**, 193 n., 221, 258, 277 n., 284-285, 291, 378, 386, 413; Old, 226, 371; Middle, New, etc., 371-374
Accident, **298-299**, 309, 329, 380, *et al.*; fallacy of, 305
Achilles (Byzantine), 9 n.; (Homeric), 85, 88, 155
Acroamatic writings, 287
Act, actuality, 88, 312, 313, 319, 320, **326-331**, *et al.*
Adam, J., 271 n.
Adiaphoria, 369 n.
Aenesidemus, 368, **375**
Aeschines, 166 n., 175
Aeschylus, 133 n.
Aëtius, 14 n., 32 n., 60 n.
Aidoneus, 104, 105 n.
Agnosticism, 370
Agrippa, 375
Aidos, 144, 271 n.
Air, **19-20**, 105, 108, 115-117, 120-122, 128, 129, 144, 151, 310
Aither, 21, 318; *see* Ether
Alcidamus, 116 n.
Alcmaeon, 33
Alexander of Aphrodisias, 287 n., **365**
Alexander the Great, 179-180, 281, 284, 285, 292, 369, 378

Allan, D. J., 289 n.
Alone, the, 405, 411-412
Alteration, 16, 47, 313, 317, 318
Ameinias, 57
Ammonius Saccas, 396
Amyntas, 283
Analogy, 331, 340
Analytics, 295
Anamnesis, **205-206**, 228, 408; *see* Recollection
Anaxagoras, 16, 20, 21, 27, 64 n., 103 n., **112-127**, 128, 129, 136, 137, 149, 152, 155, 400, 417-419
Anaxarchus, 369
Anaximander, 4, 11 n., **12-18**, 19, 20, 26, 60
Anaximenes, 14, **18-20**, 21, 26 n., 27, 30, 43, 112, 113, 120, 121, 128, 129, 230
Anderson, F. H., 220 n.
Andronicus of Rhodes, 287 n., **293-294**, 364
Anepikrita, 370
Animation, of the heavens, 333; of the cosmos, *see* Vitalism
Anthropocentric, 117, 125
Anthropomorphism, 23
Antiochus of Ascalon, 374
Antiphon the Sophist, 164
Antisthenes, 176-177

Wehrli, F., 364 n.
Well-being, 140
Wholeness, 63-66
Wickedness, 352
Wiersma, W., 37 n.
Wild, J., 213 n., 215 n.
Wilson, J. Cook, 225 n.
Wimmer, F., 364 n.
Wisdom, 4, 7, 32, 45-47, 50-53, 139-141, 150-151, 172, 262, 264, 276, 349, 359, *et al.*
Wish, 346
Wiśniewski, B., 13 n.
Wolff, H. M., 224 n., 275 nn., 372 n.
Wonder, 4-5
Woodbury, L., 61 n., 65 n.
Work, 141
Workers, 263
World, 60; *see* Cosmos; -egg, 153

Xenarchus, 174
Xenocrates, 191, 226, 285, 386
Xenophanes, **22-26**, 30, 31, 41, 46, 57, 79, 109, 114 n.
Xenophon, 155 n., 166-173, 176 n., 291, 391 n.
Xerxes, 113, 114, 137

Zafiropulo, J., 59 n., 67 n., 104 n., 115 n.
Zeller, E., 37 n., 42 n., 77 n., 113 n., 189 n., 271 n., 418 n.
Zeno of Citium, 372 n., **385-391**
Zeno of Elea, 25, 57, 73, **79-90**, 91, 100, 116, 117 n., 119 n., 120, 132, 159, 288, 313, 418-419
Zeus, 23-24, 47, 104, 105 n., 144, 390-391
Zürcher, J., 193 n., 288 n.